Indians and Emigrants

Indians and Emigrants

Encounters on the Overland Trails

Michael L. Tate

UNIVERSITY OF OKLAHOMA PRESS : NORMAN

Also by Michael L. Tate

The Frontier Army in the Settlement of the West (Norman, 1999)
(ed.) *Crossing the Plains to Oregon in 1853: The Oregon Diaries of Maria Parsons Belshaw and George Belshaw* (Fairfield, Wash., 2000)

Library of Congress Cataloging-in-Publication Data

Tate, Michael L.
    Indians and emigrants : encounters on the overland trails / Michael L. Tate.
      p.   cm.
    Includes bibliographical references and index.
    ISBN 0-8061-3710-X (alk. paper)
      1. Indians of North America—West (U.S.)—First contact with Europeans. 2. Indian trails—West (U.S.)—History. 3. Whites—West (U.S.)—Relations with Indians. 4. Frontier and pioneer life—West (U.S.)—History. 5. Indians, Treatment of—West (U.S.)—History. 6. Overland Trails—History—Sources. 7. Overland journeys to the Pacific—History—Sources. I. Title.

E78.W5T38 2006
978'.02—dc22

2005043934

The paper in this book meets the guidelines for permanence and durability of the Committee on Production Guidelines for Book Longevity of the Council on Library Resources, Inc. ∞

1 2 3 4 5 6 7 8 9 10

Contents

Illustrations

FIGURES

MAPS

Preface

B eginning with publication of various dime novel series during the latter half of the nineteenth century, a standard literary device emerged that would be imitated by successive generations of writers. The anticipated Indian attack upon the western-bound wagon train became such a familiar formula in art and literature that audiences had little reason to question the legitimacy of the image.[1] Hollywood furthered the popular stereotype with movies such as James Cruze's *The Covered Wagon* (1923) and John Ford's *The Wagon Master* (1950) that celebrated the "civilized community's" ultimate triumph over "savage" Indian raiders and lawless white men, both of whom represented societal instability at its worst.[2] Later, big-budget films such as *How the West Was Won* (1962) and *The Way West* (1967) affirmed the long-cherished notions with respective wide-screen versions of a Cheyenne attack upon a group of peaceful overlanders and a menacing Sioux war party seeking revenge for the death of a Sioux child. In the latter case, the make-believe "Hollywooden Indian" actors dressed inappropriately, performed Sioux rituals incorrectly, and spoke a form of improvised and incoherent Lakota language.[3]

No reasonable person can deny that novelists, artists, and movie-makers have a right to employ a creative license that speaks more to aesthetics and passion than to strict historical reality. Likewise, no one can doubt that Indian attacks did occur on wagon trains during the heyday of the transcontinental migration of the mid-nineteenth century.

Rather, what is questioned here is the formulistic way in which the subject has been treated in popular culture and the frequency of the attacks that did occur. Furthermore, an accurate assessment of these documented conflicts can be achieved only by examining the cultural misunderstandings that led to them. Anxieties, ambiguities, and distrust clearly produced more problems between American Indians and whites than did acts of innate barbarism or premeditated malice.

In a pathbreaking 1979 study of the trails to Oregon, California, and the Salt Lake Valley, historian John D. Unruh, Jr., moved beyond literary and anecdotal accounts to provide a statistical analysis of two decades of Indian-white relations along these trails. He found that for the entire 1840–60 period, only 362 emigrants were killed by Indians. This represents a mere eighteen mortalities per year during a two-decade cycle that witnessed perhaps 500,000 travelers using these routes. By contrast, Unruh found that during this same period, 426 Indians were killed by whites. Most died in small skirmishes associated with livestock raids or because of misperceptions about the Indians' true intentions. Their deaths were not the result of major wars or even organized plans of aggression.[4]

Glenda Riley's subsequent investigation of 150 women's trail diaries, journals, memoirs, and letters from all sections of the West revealed that 113 recorded no trouble with Indians, 22 noted minor problems, and only 15 reported significant conflicts.[5] Another statistical examination of women's trail diaries led historian Lillian Schlissel to conclude that in only 7 percent of the surviving accounts were significant Indian threats recorded, and some of those were only hearsay.[6] Similarly, in a more focused eleven-year study (1845–55) along the Platte and Sweetwater sections of the trails, Robert Munkres uncovered only nine eyewitness accounts and four secondhand reports of substantial Indian attacks.[7]

The numerical record thus repudiates a treasured image of the corralled wagon train under relentless assault by feather-bedecked warriors. Additional studies have conclusively proven that emigrants had far more to fear from accidents, epidemics, and lack of sustenance than they ever had to fear from American Indians. Patterns of cooperation, mutually beneficial trade, and acts of personal kindness clearly outnumbered the cases of contentiousness and bloodshed in the two decades before the Civil War. That relatively tranquil pattern would not begin to change until the late 1850s, when many of the tribes found their resources under duress from the massive migration and their sovereignty challenged by new treaty obligations demanded by the federal government. Indian relations with the overlanders worsened with each passing year after 1856, but even in the bleakest of years, incidents of cooperation far outnumbered cases of conflict.[8]

No specific contemporary account can convey all the experiences of overlanders during the thirty-year cycle of trail use, but a single letter helps later generations understand the prevailing depth of fear about American Indians. Written in 1854 by J. D. Willoughby, a Pennsylvania friend of the John Stewart family, it shed considerable light on public reactions to the so-called Lost Wagon Train episode of the previous year. Willoughby wrote from the comfort of his eastern home to John Stewart's teenaged daughter Agnes, expressing his great relief that the family had safely reached its Oregon destination. Rumors had circulated throughout late 1853 that the entire party had been massacred by Indians, a rumor strengthened by the fact that no Pennsylvania neighbors or family members had received a letter from the group since it passed beyond the Sweetwater River. One eastern friend, without verification of any kind, had reported that John Stewart and his wife had died while crossing the Great Plains and that the others had been murdered by Shoshones in the Snake River country. A Pittsburgh newspaper had even gone so far as to print the Stewarts' obituaries.

Willoughby explained to Agnes the level of grief that the presumed deaths had created. In a fit of unrestrained imagination, he recalled his anguish:

> I saw or fancied I saw the savage foe approach you with the scalping knife and deadly tomahock [*sic*]. I saw them rush upon you with fiendish rage and terrific shouts. I saw your men fight they fought long and hard they fought bravely they fought for wives, for children for friends for life but they fell being over powered by numbers. I saw the Indians rush upon the defenceless women and children. I saw you (Agnes) throw up your arms in defence, and cast an imploring look but youth and beauty receive no favour from the savage foe. Your heaving bosom received a wound from which the tide of life soon flowed and left you a lifeless corpse with naught but hoarse winds to sign your funeral requiem. I saw them butcher the women and children, then sack the wagons, drive off your cattle and leave your mangled bodies to putrify [*sic*] in the sun or to be eaten by the hungry wolf or ravenous vulture.[9]

In a fusion of early-nineteenth-century romanticism and the darker imagery used in later dime novels, Willoughby thus conjured up a portrayal of conflict between American Indians and whites that embraced the worst imaginable stereotypes of Indian behavior. Furthermore, his fears echoed the apprehensions of many other Americans and Europeans who dared contemplate a trip to the West or who had friends and relatives living there. No amount of statistics rendered to the contrary could have erased the powerful images from the minds of nineteenth-century whites, and the perceptions remained well ensconced even among twentieth-century audiences.

A larger reality that has remained relatively unexplored is that American Indians had more to fear from overlanders than the reverse. Surviving Indian oral traditions about the trail experience are not abundant, but those that do exist closely parallel the ones examined by Joseph Marshall III. This modern Lakota author found that his tribal ancestors regarded the emigrants as a strange lot who valued the wrong concerns in life, were totally unpredictable in their actions, and were seemingly without remorse about the widespread destruction that they brought throughout Indian Country. For all their efforts to make whites into friends and allies, the Sioux and other western tribes discovered that the great majority of these *wasichu* ("one that takes the fat" or "greedy") remained strangers at best and enemies at worst.

Marshall repeated stories of the Old Ones who measured the collective trail experience by its long-term consequences. Rather than viewing it as a heroic enterprise undertaken by intrepid and resourceful pioneers triumphing over all forms of adversity, they saw it by the end of the nineteenth century as the opening salvo against tribal sovereignty and cultural traditions. By way of contrast, the generation of American Indians who lived through the prime years of the Oregon, California, and Mormon trails had little opportunity to gain a long-term perspective on these events, and thus their views were shaped by a mixture of positive and negative feelings. Only the passage of time could fully reveal the destructive impact of this white migration into the West, but even in the best of circumstances, these emigrants remained inscrutable to the American Indians who dealt with them.

Marshall related two stories that he had heard repeatedly from Lakota elders during his childhood. In the first, a small group of warriors came across a lone wagon near the North Platte River. A woman and her children were beneath the wagon "cowering in wide-eyed fear." Although the Sioux men did not speak English, they tried to relate their good intentions through sign language and a calming tone in their voices. Noting the nearby fresh grave of what they deemed to be the husband and father of these wayfarers, the Indians started a fire, made tea, and fed these orphans of the prairie. They remained with the beleaguered family for at least two more days, during which time they brought in fresh meat and helped tend the livestock. These Lakota Good Samaritans then escorted the woman and her children to link up with a wagon train that was passing through the area. They acted purely out of compassion, and at no time did they demand or expect compensation for their aid.[10]

In the second story, another party of Sioux hunters found a small white boy crouched in some bushes and crying uncontrollably. They calmed him, fed him from their rations, and protected him during the night. Although communications were difficult, the hunters concluded that the child had probably wandered away from his wagon train and had become lost during the night. Fearing that they might be misperceived as the boy's abductors if they took him directly to a nearby train, they wisely took him to a point just beyond a westward-moving caravan. From a short but safe distance away, they waited to make sure that the boy was discovered and reunited with his people.[11]

Marshall noted that when twentieth-century Lakota elders told these and similar stories about the events of over 150 years earlier, they would sometimes discuss the efficacy of their ancestors having aided the most vulnerable of emigrants. In virtually all cases, the elders agreed that their grandparents had acted correctly by helping people in distress regardless of the ultimate consequences of the larger westward migration. The morality of these past actions was clear to them, and yet they found it difficult to understand why whites had paid so little attention to the seemingly limitless acts of Indian kindness during that era of earliest contact. Furthermore, the elders could not fathom why whites had so routinely rejected these and other stories of compassion, while simultaneously creating an entirely unjustified version of savagery and barbarism.[12]

What American Indians did not fully comprehend was that many emigrants found the trail experience to be harsh and ambiguous, frequently leading to a greater sense of paranoia. Their trying ordeals often combined with preexisting eastern stereotypes about Indians to create a higher level of stress. As troubles mounted along the way, the affected overlanders felt more vulnerable to the ever-changing environment around them. When California miner James Evans wrote a letter to his brother, Ellis, in October 1850, he laid out a long list of things that could and did go wrong on his westward journey. Among other things, disease, starvation, exhaustion, fetid water, loss of livestock, incessantly bad weather, and Indians—always Indians—had made the trip into a virtual nightmare. To his brother, and all others who needed to hear his sad tale, Evans drafted a strong warning: "Be it known throughout the world, to remotest nations, from the shivering Laplanders to the rude Hottentots, that if any man hereafter should take a notion to come to California—not to cross the plains for the Lord sake!!!! Come by water—or stay home. . . . $25000000000000000000000000000 and no sense would not induce me to cross the plains again."[13]

While many travelers would have considered Evans's words to be pure hyperbole, all could relate a litany of difficulties they had experienced along the trail. Some took the hardships in stride, while others allowed the fears and frustrations to multiply in their imaginations. As new rumors passed up and down the perpetual line of wagon trains, the most inflammatory stories were about Indian threats. The majority proved untrue, but rumors always persisted even beyond their exposure by facts. Along the trails that radiated from the Missouri River and headed along the Platte River valley, the Real West and the Imagined West came together in the minds of mid-nineteenth-century argonauts. Too often, the Imagined West—or, more precisely, the collective fear of American Indians—outweighed the reality of Indian assistance, barter, and friendship.

It is little wonder that as the relatively tranquil decade of the 1840s gave way to the later years of the 1850s, tensions increased and ultimately led to greater conflict. In the immediate post–Civil War era, these conflicts escalated to the brink of organized martial resistance among some western tribes and in some cases to open warfare. Yet even during the bleakest days of the American Civil War and the five years that followed, cross-cultural relations never deteriorated to the point that patterns of friendly exchange and mutual benefits ever entirely disappeared. Fittingly, two army wives most accurately assessed the deteriorating relations of 1866, especially the victimization of Sioux and Cheyenne peoples in the lands north of Fort Laramie. Frances Carrington and Elizabeth Burt, the respective spouses of Col. Henry Carrington and Capt. Andrew Burt, wrote that the Indians were far less at fault for the troubles than were the unrealistic government policy-makers and the inconsiderate wayfarers who crossed through their territories. Both women saw the Indians as justified in resisting the worst forms of oppression and for trying to maintain their resources against the invasion. Even though both women's husbands fought against these very tribes between 1866 and 1868, their fair-minded judgments never wavered.[14] Had all emigrants of the mid-nineteenth century harbored similar feelings while facing frontier adversities, perhaps the important story of Indian-white relations would have been a more amicable one in the coming decades.

Any interpretative history so wide in scope as the saga of Indian-white relations on the overland trails presents special problems for the researcher and the reader. To what particular time period should the study be limited? Should all trails leading toward the Pacific coast be included in the analysis? What are the unique concerns associated with the reliability of trail diaries and letters, as well as later-written memoirs and reminiscences? How plentiful are surviving Indian accounts of these mid-nineteenth-century events, and what can oral traditions reveal to persons who are not part of the cultural framework in which they were created? What is the proper terminology for the various groups that encountered each other along the trails, and how did the impreciseness of defining them within primary source materials affect earlier interpretations? These questions must be answered to help explain the nature of this book and its inherent limitations.

The initial issue of selecting beginning and ending dates for the study of the overland trail experience has posed problems for historians. John Unruh, Jr., tackled a host of topics about the trail experience, and he limited his coverage to the period from 1840 to 1860 for reasons that lie outside the singular matter of Indian-white relations. Likewise, Robert Munkres terminated his study at the same year because he considered the Civil War to be more connected to the later Indian war period than to the peak years of overland trails history. Even narrower in coverage was Christopher Clark's article, which examined only the early contacts between 1849 and 1853. Historians Glenda Riley and

Lillian Schlissel began their chronologies at approximately the same dates as Unruh and Munkres, but both drew examples from throughout the entire decade of the 1860s.

In short, there is no universally agreed-upon set of dates to mark the absolute beginning and ending of the trail experience along the central route. I have, therefore, elected to use the larger extent of time from 1840 to 1870 as the framework for this book. This allows for a full examination of events from the earliest attempts to settle larger numbers of people in the Willamette Valley of Oregon to the gradual decline in friendly relations during the 1850s. Extension of the dates through the full decade of the 1860s completes the cycle of relationships that were graphically upset by federal neglect of the western tribes during the Civil War and that worsened during the bloody wars of the late 1860s. The uniting of the Union Pacific and Central Pacific railroads at Promontory Summit, Utah, in 1869 adds further justification for terminating the study at that general date. Even though wagon trains continued to travel along the Platte River after completion of the transcontinental railroad, the heyday of the main trail arteries to the West had passed.

Deciding which western trails should be investigated in a book of this type also creates possibilities and complications. Like Unruh and the other aforementioned historians, I have focused on the central route, which included all primary extensions and bypasses of the Oregon, California, and Mormon trails. Other trails followed a variety of southern longitudes, crossing Indian Territory and Texas before traversing the desert Southwest and terminating in California. But these routes had an entirely different history than did those that followed the Platte River. Primarily connected to the California goldfields, they were of little importance until after the 1849 gold rush had begun.

Furthermore, the older Santa Fe Trail that had linked Missouri with New Mexico since 1821 was primarily a merchant's trail. Its history evolved in a way that contrasted with the family-oriented migrations along the Oregon and Mormon trails. The Indian tribes associated with the various southern routes also were not the same tribes located along the central route. To relate the diverse histories of all these trails and their inhabitants would necessitate constructing a complicated maze of cultural information that would obscure larger themes of relationships between whites and Indians. Each tribe had its unique lifeways and means for dealing with travelers who passed through its lands between 1840 and 1870. The historian who attempts to develop a similar synthesis for the southern trails will probably discover that the pattern of Indian-white relations was more troubled from an earlier time in that section of the West. Such comparisons need to be made, but not before exhaustive studies have been written for each of the two regions during the same expansive eras.

In researching the experiences of emigrants who traveled the central route, one is struck by the vast array of source materials that have survived. Merrill Mattes's massive bibliography, *Platte River Road Narratives*, identified 2,082 primary accounts, and these do not include the many valuable interviews found in the three multivolume series edited by Kate B. Carter, *Our Pioneer Heritage*, *Treasures of Pioneer History*, and *Heart Throbs of the West*. Yet the sheer amount of material somewhat disguises an inherent problem with much of it. Diaries, journals, and letters written at the time of the actual events constitute the most important sources of emigrant perceptions about the journey, but often the descriptions of particular events are inaccurate. Frequently, the entries were based on secondhand accounts that were themselves drawn from rumors. Therefore, the author must take special care to double-check controversial assertions with other primary accounts of the same event. The detailed annotations in Mattes's *Platte River Road Narratives* again provide some guidance to the most questionable portions of each source.

An even sharper critical eye must be directed at the memoirs and reminiscences written decades after the actual events. Pioneers who later wrote accounts for possible publication or to please inquiring family members or local historical societies frequently embellished their tales. Others simply suffered from bad memories over time as they confused events, misidentified individuals, and even misappropriated tales from other published sources. A healthy skepticism about some descriptions and a diligent search for corroborating evidence can partially correct this deficiency, but not always.

A similar caveat must be considered for sources generated by American Indians. In comparison with the vast amount of documents produced by whites, there are few remaining Indian accounts of this era, written or oral. The greatest disappointment came in my investigation of the massive guide entitled *Oyate Iyechinka Woglakapi*, which describes the contents of several hundred interviews conducted with Indian peoples of the northern plains and Pacific Northwest during the late 1960s and early 1970s.[15] A check of the index and each individual interview annotation uncovered few oral traditions devoted to the overland trail years among the tribes that were most affected by the events. Reading the transcripts that did contain information proved to be even more frustrating, because they contained material that was generic at best. My own interviews with Omaha and Lakota peoples reveal the same problem when it comes to remembrances of the overland trails period.

How, then, does the researcher find and use indigenous sources for this type of study? Indian "autobiographies" such as John Stands In Timber's *Cheyenne Memories,* George Hyde's *Life of George Bent,* Susan Bordeaux Bettelyoun's *With My Own Eyes,* Sarah Winnemucca Hopkins's *Life Among the Piutes,* and Annie Lowry's *Karnee: A Paiute Narrative* offer important insights into American Indian recollections of mid-nineteenth-century events, but all were organized within a white storytelling framework and were heavily influenced by their white editors.[16] Subtle nuances of language and meanings were often lost as the stories passed from Indian chronicler to editors from a different culture. The accuracy of some of these accounts can also be questioned by contradictory evidence and the fact that the Indian chroniclers generally were relating events they had only heard about rather than experienced.

Sadly, the Indian record is not as complete as the white record, but modern approaches to cultural studies can partially offset this deficiency. By using ethnohistorical methodologies that place the reader within Indian frameworks of thinking, a fairer reading of sources can be made. For instance, rather than uncritically repeating ubiquitous white assertions that Indians were natural thieves, one can examine American Indian concepts of reciprocity. This produces a more balanced understanding of why Indians did not necessarily consider their actions to be stealing but rather the forced completion of the gift-giving cycle. By no means, however, is this book a sophisticated ethnohistorical treatment of Indian-white relations. Because it covers so many diverse tribes over a long time period, it cannot present the amount of cultural detail that ethnohistorians expect when they write about a single tribe or a subtribal community. Still, I attempt in this larger synthesis to present Indian viewpoints fairly from within the diverse cultural nexus of the mid-nineteenth century. No study can achieve perfection in this regard, but the ethnohistorical approach opens significant doors for reinterpreting trail history.

A final issue that had to be addressed concerned the selection of proper terminology for identifying the principal players. Throughout the book, I use the word "white" (and, less frequently, "American" and "European") to identify the people who most often traveled the Oregon, California, and Mormon trails via the central route. To be sure, African Americans and Indians from the eastern parts of the United States also accompanied these same wagon trains but in far fewer numbers. Oregon was legally closed to black emigration during the key years of emigration, and the Mormon faithful included no blacks during that era. Most African Americans who went to the California goldfields in the 1850s did so along the southern trails across Indian Territory, Texas, and the Southwest. Using the word "white" to describe the great majority of people who traveled the central route is imprecise, but, for want of better terminology, it is not too misleading.

The issue of defining the other side of the racial divide is even more complex. Throughout the study, I use the terms "American Indian" and "Indian" interchangeably. Where identity of a particular tribe or even subtribal group was accurately given in the primary records, I use the specific tribal or subtribal designation. Because most overlanders were unsure or confused about specific identities of the peoples they met along the way, they frequently made no distinction and merely used the word "Indian" in the most generic of ways. In those cases where the original records are unclear, I elected to use the general words rather than hazard a guess as to the exact tribal or band designation. In matters relating to one particularly large and important group of people, I use the terms "Sioux" and "Lakota" synonymously. Where the more particularized identity is known—such as Oglala or Brulé—I have chosen these terms. Shoshone, Paiute, and Ute groups are especially difficult to distinguish in early white accounts because overlanders rarely understood the differences between the numerous bands.

No matter how careful one is in addressing the above-mentioned concerns, a book devoted to analyzing the full range of Indian-white relations on the Oregon, California, and Mormon trails between 1840 and 1870 cannot explain every unique case or eliminate every misleading generalization. My hope is that the book deals honestly with the complex subject and that it offers a view of intercultural relations that supplants popular images of savage Indians perpetually attacking intrepid pioneers and greedy whites brutalizing noble Indians.

Acknowledgments

Mass migrations of people are among the great events that shape history, and the relocation of over 550,000 men, women, and children to Oregon, California, and the Salt Lake Valley between 1840 and 1870 was certainly no exception. Even though many argonauts who went in search of quick mining wealth ultimately returned to their eastern homes, the great majority of emigrants remained as permanent residents of the vast domain between the Missouri River and the Pacific Ocean. In ways both noble and scandalous, they changed American history forever.

Precisely because this story of westward migration was so compelling and consequential, it captured the imaginations of each new generation of Americans and spurred interest worldwide. Since the 1950s, publication of books and articles has increased dramatically, both for scholarly and popular audiences. Some modern writers have focused on identifying and marking precise sections of the original trails. Others have dealt with the human emotions embodied in personal triumphs and tragedies along the way. During the 1990s, a new wave of popularity surfaced with several documentary films that artfully linked eyewitness descriptions with paintings, photographs, and music of the era. In the same decade, an engaging computer game, "The Oregon Trail," brought the story to younger children in an interactive format that allowed them to make decisions along the imaginary route without suffering the dire consequences of unfortunate choices. In short, public and scholarly interest in this story has remained undiminished over time, and the broad range of subject matter invites new analysis and interpretation in the twenty-first century.

As with the broader range of subject matter, books are never the product of the author alone. Their gestation and birth require the efforts of many people at each juncture, and all are deserving of recognition. At the apex of my list is John D. Unruh, Jr., a young scholar who died in 1976, before his academic career could achieve its full potential. His prize-winning *The Plains Across: The Overland Emigrants and the Trans-Mississippi West, 1840–60* (1979) remains a classic interpretation of the western trails, and it has encouraged other researchers to continue the investigative work that is still necessary. My own book clearly has been shaped by Unruh's chapter on Indian-emigrant relations and especially by his statistical information on the frequency of violence and homicides. I have extended Unruh's coverage by a full decade, have devoted ten chapters to a subject that he covered in one chapter, and have looked at Indian cultural views in greater depth than he attempted. Despite these differences in our final products, I feel a great kinship with this intellectual pathfinder.

Also essential to the completion of this book were the detailed comments and corrections made by two gifted historians who served as outside readers for the University of Oklahoma Press. Will Bagley, an acknowledged expert on the Oregon, California, and Mormon trails, provided not only some different conceptualizations but also alerted me to a number of factual errors and to some additional sources that proved crucial. Likewise, Robert Wooster gently questioned some of my assumptions and made excellent suggestions for reorganizing material and for rephrasing ideas that might have confused readers. I appreciate both of these scholars, who put considerable time and thought into their editorial remarks.

Securing archival and printed materials also necessitated help from other individuals. John Schneiderman and staff members of the Interlibrary Loan Service at the University of Nebraska at Omaha secured a wide variety of necessary items from distant institutions. Government document specialist Jim Shaw directed me to critical federal records. Archivists at the National Frontier Trails Center in Independence, Missouri; Nebraska State Historical Society; Kansas State Historical Society; Bancroft Library at the University of California at Berkeley; and Lane County Pioneer-Historical Society in Eugene, Oregon, were especially helpful in guiding me through manuscript collections during personal visits and by photocopying documents.

The Oregon-California Trails Association (OCTA), headquartered in Independence, Missouri, represents the largest official group of trail historians in the nation. Their annual meetings and quarterly publication, *Overland Journal*, offer excellent forums for exchanging information and identifying vital new sources. As a member of the organization and a beneficiary of its efforts, I thank the presiding officers for inviting me to present a paper at the eighteenth annual meeting. I am also indebted to the publications committee for printing an extended version of that earlier paper in the Winter 2000–2001 issue of *Overland Journal* as "From Cooperation to Conflict: Sioux Relations with the Overland Emigrants, 1845–1865." These twin forums allowed me to test some of the ideas that eventually found their way into this book. Comments and suggestions from audience members and readers helped sharpen my interpretations and expand my array of sources. One of OCTA's original founders deserves special appreciation for making available numerous copies of rare trail diaries, journals, and letters that he had assembled over a lifetime. Charles Martin, Sr., a resident of Omaha, extended many kindnesses prior to his untimely death, and all who knew him will testify to his extraordinary generosity and depth of knowledge about the trails.

Although the procurement of rights and permissions for this book proved frustrating at times, a host of individuals demonstrated remarkable skill and patience by helping me secure the legal rights to art work, photographs, and maps that eventually found their way into the book. Especially noteworthy in this regard are Robert Clark, president of Arthur H. Clark Company and editor of *Overland Journal*; Terri Raburn, assistant curator of library/archives at the Nebraska State Historical Society; Jim Potter, associate editor of *Nebraska History*; Superintendent Ralph Moore, Chief Ranger Deb Qualey, and Ranger Kelly Mansfield at Scotts Bluff National Monument; Larry Mensching at the Joslyn Art Museum in Omaha; Virgil Dean and Nancy Sherbert at the Kansas State Historical Society; Lee Brumbaugh, curator of photographs at the Nevada Historical Society; Anne Salsich at the Western Reserve Historical Society; Doug Misner at the Utah State Historical Society; and Daisy Yoku at the Smithsonian Institution, National Anthropological Archives. I also would like to recognize the help of Marshall Shore of Spokane, Washington, who provided the photographs and biographical materials on two of his Oregon Trail ancestors—George Belshaw and Maria Parsons Belshaw.

Among the greatest of all my debts of gratitude are those extended to the staff at the University of Oklahoma Press. Editor-in-chief Chuck Rankin ably guided this project through all of its many phases, and he has always been a source of sage advice on organizational and interpretive matters. Editorial Assistant Bobbie Canfield kept me on schedule with the delivery of manuscript pages, revisions, and photographs. Especially valued was the assistance of Steven Baker, associate editor at the University of Oklahoma Press, and Robert Burchfield, copyeditor, who helped improve the flow of the manuscript and who made corrections of stylistic miscues.

Finally, I would like to thank my wife, Carol, who not only prepared the final draft of the manuscript but who also corrected numerous errors of my own making.

Indians and Emigrants

1

Preparing the Way

A Cacophony of Confusion, Misinformation, and Alarm

Even before people set out from Europe and the areas east of the Mississippi River to make their way into the West in the mid-nineteenth century, most already possessed strong preconceptions about the problems they would encounter there. Some fretted about leaving friends and family members forever; others worried about reestablishing their lives in a distant and alien land. Many also voiced a fear that dangers along the trail were so overwhelming that they or their loved ones might not survive the perilous journey. A small proportion of these, including Benjamin Franklin Bonney, received not an encouraging farewell from their friends and neighbors but rather a crescendo of warnings that they would certainly perish in the suicidal venture.[1] In keeping with that fatalistic spirit, the men of Sarah Sutton's 1854 wagon train prepared special boards and laid them across the floor of one wagon so that they could be used for constructing a coffin in the likely event that a member of the party should die while on the trail.[2] Even more pessimistic was the mother of nine-year-old Barnet Simpson, who grew so distraught from the frightful Indian tales that, prior to undertaking an 1849 Oregon trip, she wove burial shrouds for each member of her family.[3]

Death from disease, heat, starvation, poisonous plants, and accidents punctuated a long list of potential terrors raised about overland travel, but no danger loomed larger in the minds of emigrants than the fear of torture or death at the hands of murderous Indians. Hardly a journal, diary, or set of letters survives that does not offer some evidence of the writer's initial fear that this possibility would come true. Yet the great majority of people who voiced so much alarm about American Indians had never experienced any direct contact with them. Thus overlanders' preconceived notions clearly came not from firsthand knowledge but rather from a long tradition of literature, art, journalism, and family stories that stretched back to the early colonial days along the Atlantic coast.

Soon after the founding of Massachusetts Bay Colony in 1630, captivity narratives began to be published in Puritan New England as a way of metaphorically explaining God's role in testing the perseverance of the new chosen people. American Indians emerged from the narratives in a stereotypical fashion that highlighted their barbaric customs and fiendish tortures inflicted upon stalwart pioneer families. Especially threatened were the piety and purity of English women who fell into the clutches of evil "savages," a fate overcome only by an abiding faith in God's divine intervention. The highly embellished stories gradually moved beyond serving as religious tracts that demonstrated the power of faith, to providing dubious justifications for taking Indian lands. Puritan writers merged religious doctrines with temporal needs to justify the bloody military actions undertaken during the Pequot War of 1637 and King Philip's War of 1675–76, which liquidated most Indian land claims in New England by the end of the seventeenth century.[4]

The impact of these books reached well beyond the time and place for which they were written. Many were republished in their entirety, or large sections were pirated and used by a new generation of authors who wanted to tap into an expanded marketplace. Literary historian Frank Luther Mott notes that four of these captivity narratives were among the best-sellers of the American literary tradition—books by Mary Rowlandson, John Williams, Jonathan Dickinson, and Mary Jemison. Published in 1682, Rowlandson's *The Soveraignty of Goodness of God* quickly became second only to the Bible in popularity and ultimately appeared in thirty editions. An equally appreciative audience for the book quickly developed in England, where this narrative of capture by Wampanoags was viewed as an exotic and even risqué tale. Also compelling was John Williams's *The Redeemed Captive Returning to Zion* (1707), which sold approximately 1,000 copies in its first week of publication—a rare feat in the early eighteenth century. By the time of its last reprinting in 1918, it had sold over 100,000 copies.[5]

This literary genre continued to command public attention well into the early nineteenth century. *The Remarkable Adventures of Jackson Johonnet* (1791) was published in fifteen languages during the following three decades and was widely printed and excerpted by newspapers and almanacs. Even as late as the Second Seminole War of 1835–41, a popular pamphlet entitled "Captivity and Sufferings of Mrs. Mason" drew upon the earlier themes of captivity narratives to create support for a punitive campaign against the "barbaric Indians" of Florida. Although the tale was apparently fictitious, it typified a two-hundred-year tradition of vilifying American Indians through literary treatments.[6]

The captivity narratives created an early predisposition to view American Indians harshly, but they were not the only literary tradition that affected popular viewpoints. As the spirit of romanticism spread its influence into music, art, and fiction at the beginning of the nineteenth century, a more positive symbolism for American Indians found its way into literature. British poet Thomas Cooper published the long poem *Gertrude of Wyoming* in 1809, stressing the delicate sensibilities, lofty virtues, and courageous actions of the fictional Oneida chief Outalissi. More important, in 1801 the French writer François-René de Chateaubriand published *Atala*, a tale of unrequited love between a young man and woman of rival tribes. Set amid a picturesque landscape and a range of human emotions, this popular book helped present American Indians in a positive light that soon was widely imitated by other French, British, and German authors.[7]

Out of this emerging age of romanticism sprang a new dichotomous view of American Indians—a contrast between the "savage" and "nature's nobleman." Despite his admitted lack of contact with and knowledge about Indian peoples, American novelist James Fenimore Cooper became the sublime articulator of this dualistic image.[8] Drawing upon a tradition already hinted at by earlier authors, his novel *The Last of the Mohicans* (1826) contrasted the nobility of Mohican elder Chingachgook and his doomed son, Uncas, with the thoroughly malevolent spirit of Huron warrior Magua. Although people such as former secretary of war Lewis Cass criticized Cooper for overly romanticizing and stereotyping Indians and some novelists made the same observation, many of the latter utilized his dualistic characterizations in their own books.[9]

In truth, Cooper wrestled with the same divided sentiments about Indians that most eastern-seaboard Americans felt during the first half of the nineteenth century. They tended to see Indians as inferior to whites in the attainment of civilized culture, but many also saw a kind of primitive nobility that emerged from close contact with nature. Clearly, American and European romantic infatuation with these "sons and daughters of the forest" emerged strongest in regions mostly devoid of Indians. Amid the western sections of the American nation, where Indian wars were a recent memory or Indian residency was still well established, frontiersmen were less likely to reflect on this nobility theme than were easterners. Furthermore, those who did subscribe to the more positive image generally agreed with the romantic poets, playwrights, and novelists that the "Noble Red Man" lived only in the past and was not part of the contemporary "Indian problem."[10]

Gradually, James Fenimore Cooper's dualistic interpretation of Indian identity replaced the earlier Chateaubriand version of the "salon-Indian," who had been universally portrayed in an overly sentimental and one-dimensional way. European audiences were thrilled in multilanguage editions by the novels of Friedrich Gerstäcker, Friedrich Arman Strubberg, Baldwin Möllhausen, and Karl Postl, the last of whom, while writing under the pseudonym Charles Sealsfield, became known as the "German Cooper."[11] In their works, as well as those of Cooper, "bad" Indians served to test the fortitude and skills of white heroes and to provide the sadistic tortures that readers expected from this type of publication. "Good" Indians, on the other hand, served as faithful companions to white heroes and as masterful brothers and sisters of nature's environment. "Bad" Indians were present in all these writings, but as the nineteenth century wore on, novels increasingly blamed villainous whites for causing Indians to become brutal avengers.[12]

Early-nineteenth-century romantic art imitated literature in capturing the essence of the dualistic image. George Catlin was inspired directly by the writings of James Fenimore Cooper to create a massive traveling exhibit of his sketches and paintings that would convey the spirit of wild America and its Native inhabitants before both disappeared under the inevitable march of progress. Catlin and other artists such as Karl Bodmer, Charles Bird King, Seth Eastman, and Alfred Jacob Miller played upon the additional theme of the vanishing Indian to emphasize the fleeting nobility of Indians and their growing decadence in the face of war, disease, and alcohol.[13]

In this vein, noted historian Ray Allen Billington later concluded that mid-nineteenth-century Americans thus encountered a third dimension of alleged Indian identity. Native people could no longer be viewed only through Cooper's dualistic prism of "good" Indian and "bad" Indian, but to this must also be added the "ignoble savage." This image referred to the notion of a "decayed race, steeped in vice and indolence, unable and unwilling to adjust to the modern world, and hence doomed to rapid and justifiable extinction."[14] Emphasis was now placed upon Indians' filth, revolting dietary habits, physical repugnance, sexual promiscuity, and tendency toward drunkenness.[15] Such stereotypes, unfortunately, could only worsen common preconceptions about American Indians and their predisposition to slovenly behavior.

Novelists and artists exercised considerable influence on public perceptions about American Indians during the romantic era, but travel narratives published during the first half of the nineteenth century also shaped popular attitudes. As with works of fiction, these books presented the conventional triad of images—good Indian, bad Indian, and ignoble savage—but they did so with greater authority than fictional tales because they were supposedly accurate representations written by eyewitnesses.

Most of these travel narratives discussed individual acts of Indian bravery, nobility, honesty, and sociability, but all contained highly descriptive examples of Indian tendencies toward violence and untrustworthiness. British adventurer George Frederick Ruxton detailed a bloody Ute scalp dance performed on Arapaho scalps.[16] A similar scenario was related even more graphically by Santa Fe Trail sojourner Josiah Gregg, who concluded that Indians "employ every wile and stratagem [sic], and faithless subterfuge, to deceive their enemies, and in battle are relentless and cruel in the extreme."[17] Gregg further promoted the image of Indian "blood-thirsty propensities" by repeating unconfirmed tales about how, in earlier times, some had devoured the hearts of their victims in a cannibalistic rage. Scalping stories punctuated Washington Irving's 1835 book, *A Tour on the Prairies*, replete with images of "mouldering skulls and skeletons, bleaching in some dark ravine," and in his widely read *The Adventures of Captain Bonneville*, which was printed two years later.[18] Scottish naturalist John Bradbury updated the savage image by swearing that he had seen Arikaras on the Missouri River who possessed the body marks of having drunk the blood of a slain enemy.[19]

These types of stories that filled the publications of fur traders, military explorers, and early travelers in the West both titillated and frightened their American and European audiences, who took much of the information as gospel. Especially troubling were the direct warnings that Indian behavior was unfathomable and, in most cases, downright deceitful. Scottish fur trader Alexander Ross stressed the trickery of Pacific Northwest tribes whose main stratagem was to lure unsuspecting travelers into ambuscades from which escape was impossible.[20] Even "civilized" Indians were not above reproach. Isaac Cooper recalled that while traveling in John C. Frémont's expedition of 1845, his party met members of the seemingly peaceful Kaw, or Kansas, tribe in northeastern Kansas. Despite their offers of friendship and aid, Cooper presumptuously concluded that they would have happily robbed individuals in his party had they been given the chance.[21] Even more alarming was the advice given to readers by Francis Parkman following his 1846 excursion along the Platte River to Fort Laramie. He admonished future travelers to show only the strongest resolve toward all Indians, and under no circumstances should the white men demonstrate weakness, indecision, or compassion, for, as he warned, "you convert them from that moment into insidious and dangerous enemies."[22]

No one today can achieve a precise accounting of how many Americans and Europeans read from the aforementioned books or viewed the sketches and paintings in exhibits and portfolios. Even less reliable are any statistical conclusions about how many persons who traversed the Oregon, California, and Mormon trails actually read these books beforehand or viewed these works of art. Yet it seems likely that these were the general conceptions that most overlanders shared about American Indians during the mid-nineteenth century, and the contrasting stereotypes of good, bad, and ignoble Indians certainly created confusion within the popular imagination. Precisely because of this ambiguity, wayfarers tended to be curious about American Indians, but they also prepared themselves for the worst kinds of deceit and mayhem. Out of this ill-defined meeting between Indian and white worlds emerged a level of mistrust and cultural misunderstanding that made each contact point a potential tragedy for both sides. In essence, white travelers hoped to encounter wise and friendly

Indians who might aid them, but they felt that the more likely meetings would be with decadent or even hostile tribes.

Because most expectant sojourners had no direct experience with the lands west of the Missouri River, they came to rely upon the highly touted "trail guidebooks." These inexpensive publications supposedly contained the kind of practical information that could ameliorate the worst problems of a grueling wagon trip. They were especially valued for their advice on the supplies that should be packed, the types of livestock and wagon that could best serve the owner, the strategies necessary for crossing dangerous rivers, and the varieties of flora and fauna that should be avoided. Most important, they contained precise information about trail grades, distances between reliable sources of water and grass, and the natural landmarks that dotted the trail. Although these guidebooks led readers to believe that they had been carefully prepared by men who had been on the trails, had experienced the unique environmental problems, and had written knowledgeably about exact conditions, readers often found the information to be unreliable.

Two types of guidebooks became readily available for use on the trails—commercial guidebooks and personal narratives. Lansford W. Hastings's *The Emigrants Guide to Oregon and California* (1845) well represented the first category and proved to be one of the most enduring of all self-help sources. Despite its controversial nature and connection to the ill-fated Donner Party, Hastings's guide was used by tens of thousands of emigrants and went through five reprintings. Unfortunately, no effort was ever made to correct the misleading and patently false descriptions that it contained. Especially troubling is the fact that Joseph E. Ware and other compilers of later guidebooks excerpted liberally from Hastings's original work without questioning some of its dubious assertions.[23]

Two features that all the commercial guidebooks shared were their limited coverage of Indians and their shortsighted advice on how to relate to the Native inhabitants of the plains and mountains. Joseph Ware's admonition in his *The Emigrants' Guide to California* (1849) was for travelers to be alert to the universal Indian tendency toward theft. He especially directed this charge at the Pawnees of Nebraska and the Shoshonean groups of the Great Basin. Warning that their begging was often a prelude to thievery, he cautioned readers to "never allow an Indian to come within your lines under any pretext—they seldom have a good object in view."[24] This closely mirrored Lansford Hastings's earlier sentiment that "a more villainous and treacherous race of thieves, can scarcely be found."[25]

Every guidebook followed the lead of Hastings and Ware in downplaying the image of Indians as inveterate murderers but playing up the theme of Indian pilfering. In their 1846 publication, *Route Across the Rocky Mountains*, Overton Johnson and William H. Winter wrote that most problems with Indians could be averted simply by maintaining a constant vigil, traveling in large groups, avoiding direct contact, and never placating Indian supplications or demands in any fashion.[26] In their *Hand Book to the Gold Fields of Nebraska and Kansas*, published in 1859 to hasten miners' frenzied travel to the newly open goldfields around Denver, William N. Byers and John H. Kellom alerted readers to another danger that was on all western travelers' minds. They provided information on how to protect livestock from being driven off by Indian raiders. Should the raiders be successful in mounting a stampede, a skill they all seemed to master, an overland party could become marooned and vulnerable to disaster amid the harsh environment.[27]

Such dire images even found their way into John B. Hall's satirizing of the commercial guidebooks. Writing as a Boston printer who had never been west but who asserted his firsthand knowledge of the trail experience in his title, Hall overdramatized the Indian menace in his fanciful *Delights of an Overland Journey to California by One Who Has Experienced Them*. In stereotypical fashion, he warned that "Western Indians always appear just at sundown or sunrise, or a little before," and that every man of the party must be armed and ready because "he will be sure to be taken, scalped, and murdered, if he shows running or cowardice."[28]

While one or more commercial guidebooks found their way into the wagons or saddlebags of virtually everyone who traversed the western trails after 1846, the second type of guidebook probably had more impact on their perceptions about American Indians. These personal narratives were lengthier, provided far more detail, and often were written by men whose very names symbolized honesty and integrity. Though it was not published until 1859, relatively late in the pioneering process of the overland trails, Capt. Randolph B. Marcy's *The Prairie Traveler* became a widely cited and pirated source partly because of the author's well-known accomplishments as an explorer. This career military officer, who had conducted several important reconnaissances on the southern plains, was in a good position to provide sound advice to fellow western argonauts. Ironically, most of his firsthand knowledge was derived from lands far to the south of the Oregon, California, and Mormon trails. Likewise, his descriptions of Indian customs and life-styles fitted plains tribes not usually contacted by people traversing the Platte River route. Yet in the mid-nineteenth century, when easterners and Europeans tended to homogenize multiple tribes into the singular concept of "American Indian," the distinction made little difference. Thus Marcy's book became the virtual Bible of information and advice for many of the later overlanders, no matter what their origin point, destination, or choice of trail.

Even though Marcy achieved some notable friendships with individual Indians during his lifetime and relied heavily upon the services of Delaware guides John Bushman and Black Beaver during his explorations of the West, his book sowed additional seeds of doubt about American Indian behavior. In discussing the thievery issue, he especially emphasized that bartering with American Indians should be kept to a bare minimum because any gesture that Indians might perceive as an insult could quickly lead to violence. In warning about extending and receiving presents as goodwill gestures, he was even more emphatic. Marcy falsely asserted that American Indians possess little sense of benevolence or charity and that "when they make a present, it is with a view of getting more than its equivalent in return."[29] He further charged that plains tribes would routinely intimidate whites as a way of receiving more gifts, so members of a wagon train must demonstrate a unified resolve against this misbehavior. To do otherwise, he concluded, would only invite more trouble.[30]

Unlike the briefer commercial guidebooks, Marcy's *The Prairie Traveler* included twenty pages of advice on how to handle specific circumstances regarding Indians. For instance, any man separated from his companions and alone on the prairie must keep Indian warriors at bay no matter what insult he might give them. He must face them directly, steadfastly point his gun at their leader, and be prepared to fire, but only as a last resort. In cases where small parties of warriors demonstrated friendship toward white men and asked to camp with them at night, their seemingly benign request must be emphatically rejected. Otherwise, according to the captain, they will spy out a party's weakness and exploit it during the night's darkness. Furthermore, Marcy instructed his readers on how to properly pursue Indians who had made a successful raid upon a wagon train's livestock.[31] Anyone who read such an account of Indian treachery in the mid-nineteenth century and then undertook an overland trip across the continent would certainly be conditioned to fear the worst about any American Indian inhabitants encountered along the trail.

While most of these guides warned about the probable negative effects of extending gifts to Indians, a few happily reported that trade with them not only was a normal part of the overland experience but could also ease the difficulties of passage. In 1846, J. M. Shively published a brief commercial guidebook based upon his trip from Oregon to Missouri during the previous year. Except for his remarks about recent troubles with tribes located between Fort Hall and the Dalles of the Columbia River, Shively played down Indian threats. He instructed overlanders to seek out peaceful Indians and to trade with them for the types of goods that would otherwise be unavailable or in short supply on the trail. Barter would be especially important for food items and for western horses, which he considered to be far superior to those raised in the East. Shively also advised his readers to hire Indians as guides and as boat pilots on the Columbia River. Furthermore, he, like Joseph Ware, strongly recommended that overlanders take along a large supply of notions and trinkets to trade with Native peoples encountered along the way.[32]

Despite differences of opinion about whether to seek trading relationships with American Indians, most commercial guidebooks and personal narratives confirmed preexisting stereotypes about the inscrutable nature of Indian behavior. Washington-bound Winfield Scott Ebey later recalled that his preconceptions about Indians were drawn from Washington Irving's *Crayon Miscellany*, which had characterized the Pawnees as "warlike savages" and "sons of Ishmale [*sic*] who often went on predatory expeditions." Ebey's preconceptions had been augmented by his reading of an unidentified guidebook that portrayed Indians in an unsavory light. Thus, when Ebey reached the jumping-off town of Council Bluffs on the Missouri River, he purposely avoided all Indians there because he regarded them as "lazy, untrustworthy savages."[33]

By the mid-nineteenth century, the jumping-off towns of Council Bluffs, Iowa; Omaha, Nebraska; St. Joseph, Missouri; and the several communities now embraced by the greater Kansas City, Missouri, metropolitan area were also contributing to the anti-Indian climate. These rumor mills drew their sometimes hysterical stories from transient frontiersmen, and the tales were often printed in local newspapers without substantiation. Typical of this journalistic fare were the many trail-related articles printed in the *Frontier Guardian* at Council Bluffs. Echoing a theme contained in commercial guidebooks, the May 2, 1849, issue warned travelers to maintain extra vigilance at night because "this is the very snare that the shrewd and cunning fellows will seek to catch you in." Two weeks later, another article rebuffed advocates of a turn-the-other-cheek policy toward Indians. It argued that moderation and kindness could be extended only to a certain point, but persons who allowed themselves to become too trusting of Indians and who permitted them into their camps were courting disaster.[34]

Even the relatively fair-minded *Daily Missouri Republican*, printed at St. Louis, could not refrain from reporting some of the most outlandish stories. A September 9, 1847, issue told of the fictitious massacre of approximately one hundred travelers on the Applegate extension of the Oregon Trail. The writer, however, cautioned that the tale might not be true since some of the people who were supposedly massacred had already arrived at their destinations. Three years later, an article in the same newspaper overdramatized the level of bloody intertribal warfare in eastern Kansas and Nebraska and provided vicarious thrills by relating supposed firsthand accounts of Indians carrying many freshly taken scalps.[35]

Eastern newspapers often excerpted entire articles from newspapers published in the jumping-off towns along the Missouri River. Many of the reprinted stories were embellished with patently false information to enliven the events, and similar tales were manufactured from letters allegedly sent back to family members in the East. One such account in a summer 1849 issue of the *Louisville (Ky.) Examiner* identified the mysterious author as a "French gentleman" who had formerly resided in the city. Supposedly writing from Fort Laramie, the correspondent described in grandiose detail how he had participated in a major battle with Iowa Indians, had directed the women and children of his wagon train to safety at the fort, and had bravely returned on the following day to repel the ferocious attack. Alleging that his party had killed some one hundred Indians, many in hand-to-hand combat, the author had fabricated a tale involving the wrong tribe in the wrong geographical area. The number of readers who might not have discerned the tale's exaggerations and instead interpreted it as further evidence of "bloodthirsty Indians" can merely be surmised, but it is clear that these types of hoaxes frequently found their way into eastern newspapers, where they were read by an even larger audience.[36]

In a recent study of American journalism's reporting of news about American Indians between 1820 and 1890, John M. Coward found that this trend toward anti-Indian sensationalism was driven more by economics than by poor investigation. The midcentury newspaper circulation wars are best represented in the efforts of James Gordon Bennett, the flamboyant editor of the *New York Herald* who raised his paper's daily sales to 20,000 copies within the first year of its founding. Likewise, Horace Greeley's *New York Tribune*, first printed in 1841, achieved similar sales results within seven weeks and by 1860 had 40,000 paid readers.[37] The editors recognized that sensationalized stories of Indian mayhem attracted subscribers, and these publications turned out a steady stream of Indian news. To be sure, Coward acknowledges, articles about noble Indians did appear within these pages, but most of the stories graphically described the savage Indian at war with the United States or the despoiled Indian living an uncivilized life. He concludes that "a harsh and paternalistic Indian identity dominated American newspapers for decades," and with the aid of exchange programs beginning in the 1820s, these negative articles were widely circulated even to small-town newspapers, where they were frequently reprinted.[38] Similarly, historian George Hyde blames eastern newspapers for so tainting people's perceptions about the Pawnees that the tribe could get no fair hearing in either public or governmental arenas during the mid-nineteenth century. In regard to the use of the Platte River Trail by emigrants, argues Hyde, the journalistic stereotypes produced a shoot-first-and-ask-questions-later philosophy among many overlanders.[39]

Another form of literature came to have an impact on adult perceptions about American Indians. Dime novels, which had their origins in the 1830s and reached their peak at the end of the century, became even more graphic in their portrayals of the barbaric Indians and their bloodlust. The earliest of these pulp publications were crude imitations of frontier novels. Typical was *A Narrative of the Horrid Massacre by the Indians, of the Wife and Children of the Christian Hermit* (1840), which tried to outdo the earlier novels it used as models. It increased the frequency and detail of fictitious atrocities and concluded with a message about the folly of trying to Christianize and civilize savages.[40]

The lowbrow and derivative dime novel, printed on cheap paper and sold at low cost, was aimed at readers who relished action, adventure, and lurid scenes developed around moralizing accounts of good triumphing over evil.[41]

One such Indian-hating "yellowback" appeared in 1865 as part of the Beadle's Dime Novel series under the title of *Quindaro; or, the Heroine of Fort Laramie*. The simplistic storyline presented the impassioned feelings of hero Quindaro, who viewed the frontier as a pristine Garden of Eden, marred only by the presence of savage Indians. In a plot sharply reminiscent of seventeenth-century Puritan sermons and captivity narratives, Quindaro prophesies the redemption of humankind and the purification of the wilderness through the extermination of Satan and Satan's Indian minions.

A more important dime novel that appeared three years earlier was Ann S. Stephens's *Esther: A Story of the Oregon Trail*, also a volume in the Beadle's Dime Novel series. By merging themes of James Fenimore Cooper's "Leatherstocking Tales" with real and imagined aspects of Daniel Boone's life, the author created a new protagonist in the personage of Kirk Waltermyer. This fictional hero repeatedly demonstrated his courage and daring by accomplishing incredible feats against raw nature and by rescuing beautiful heroines from Indian clutches.

Sales records of dime novels from the House of Beadle and Adams testify to the success of these inexpensively produced books. The first of the series, Ann S. Stephens's *Malaeska: The Indian Wife of the White Hunter* (1860), sold 65,000 copies within a few months, and its profitability encouraged the publishing company to issue a new book every month.[42] Not all of these volumes focused on American Indians, but at least through the 1860s Indian villains were most often the source of contention for the featured hero. Under Erastus Beadle's steady hand, the frontier series sold almost five million copies between 1860 and 1865. Soon, other New York publishers began to produce their own serials, many of which explored the same frontier themes and offered Indians as convenient villains.[43]

Such was the widespread impact of these dime novels that respected essayist William Everett wrote a mildly condemnatory article in an 1864 issue of the *North American Review*. In evasive words, he complained that these formulistic and base writings had "undoubtedly obtained greater popularity than any other series of works of fiction published in America," and yet he encouraged the House of Beadle and Adams to continue its outpouring, but only with the most literate of its authors.[44] When sales took a slight downturn because of competition from other pulp series, Beadle's editor, Orville J. Victor, ordered his stable of writers to "kill a few more Indians" as a method of restoring the book-buying audience.[45]

Although the various forms of literature available in the midnine-teenth century were geared mainly toward adults, children were not entirely immune to the impact of racial stereotyping. Children's text-books reflected much of the dualistic spirit of good and bad Indians that had been formulated in James Fenimore Cooper's novels. Specific Indians such as Squanto, John Sassamon, and Pocahontas were singled out for praise because of their important aid to the early Puritans and Virginia settlers. Occasionally, textbooks even heralded the noble attempts of Indian leaders such as Metacomet (King Philip), Pontiac, Joseph Brant, and Tecumseh to defend their lands against avaricious whites.[46]

Despite these periodic nods of recognition to some long-dead Indian leaders, the textbooks generally reflected an anti–American Indian tone. Ruth Miller Elson's exhaustive 1964 examination of scores of schoolbooks from this era reveals that Indians were mainly treated in a generic way. Tales of their atrocities during the colonial and Revolutionary eras filled the books, and numerous drawings of scalpings, tortures, burnings, and babies being ripped from mothers' arms reinforced the stereotypes. In keeping with the horrific images, virtually none of these texts questioned the alleged inherent right of white Americans to seize Indians' land and put it to a "more efficient use." It is little wonder, then, that children shared with their parents a jaundiced, or at least confused, view about American Indians. Young-sters who traveled the overland trails would take the preconceptions with them, and the biases would shape their responses when real Indians were finally encountered.[47]

Captivity narratives, novels, romantic art, travel accounts, commercial guidebooks, personal narratives, newspapers, dime novels, and children's textbooks all helped define common impressions about American Indians among whites who had no intimate knowledge about them and their diverse cultures. Yet one other form of communication also promoted misinformation and a sense of alarm—rumors spread orally from one individual to another. Many of these came through family stories that had been told for generations within the context of an earlier frontier environment east of the Mississippi River.

Luzena Stanley Wilson, who made the trip to California in 1849, was fairly typical in her preconceptions. She had set out with her husband and two toddlers, filled with apprehension about Indians derived from chilling family tales and having read novels about their "massacre of harmless white men, torturing helpless women, [and] carrying away captive innocent babes." When it later turned out that her party experienced no problems when they first encountered Indians, she felt somewhat guilty at the prejudgment, but she held her children close throughout the night "and felt imaginary arrows pierce my flesh a hundred times during the night."[48]

Similarly, twelve-year-old Virginia Reed Murphy recalled her grandmother's frequent tales of earlier Indian attacks on her ancestors and the horrible suffering of an aunt who had been held captive by Indians for five years. Her fears reached a near crisis point when the wagon train encountered its first American Indians—a group of Kaws who maintained a ferry on the Kansas River. As they transported the wagons across the river on their flatboat, she watched closely, feeling certain that they would intentionally sink the ferry and its treasured contents. Her foreboding gave way to feelings of relief amid the help of these friendly Indians, and she wrote that she "was very thankful when I found they were not like grandma's Indians."[49]

Paralleling Murphy's experiences were those of John Berry Hill, who confessed his fears about undertaking a journey across the plains in 1850. After all, as a child his head had been filled with his mother's bloodcurdling stories about earlier Indian raids upon their farmstead near Louisville, Kentucky, and the captivity of two relatives. His first nights spent on the open prairie west of St. Joseph proved unnerving, as he remained awake in expectation of the certain Indian attacks to follow. Hill remarked that even the innocent howl of a wolf or any unfamiliar sound brought forth on a gentle night's wind caused his hair to stand on end and him to prepare to flee in the opposite direction. His self-imposed "cowardice" soon gave way to new-found courage after a few more days on the trail, and, as he said, from then on he "feared neither man nor the devil."[50]

Other travelers, whether imbued with anti-Indian family stories or not, soon found that wagon trains bred their own rumors about impending dangers around the next bend. Cyrus Hurd, Jr., wrote to family members while on the way to the California goldfields in 1850 that such terrifying stories told in the East had never affected him. Yet similar tales spoken around the campfires by members of his wagon train were not so pleasant to hear once they had crossed the Missouri River into Indian Country.[51] Martha Ann Wooten feared leaving her Johnson County, Missouri, farmstead in 1857 because of the Indian threat and other problems that would be encountered on the overland journey. She also doubted that her father would follow through on his plans to take the family to California, especially since the Kansas City area was filled with rumors of frequent Indian attacks all along the Platte River.[52]

As wagons assembled at various locations waiting for transit across the Missouri River, travelers were subject to a barrage of unsettling stories. Margaret Frink, while camped at St. Joseph during the spring of 1850, heard incessant tales of Indian depredations on the plains. She remarked that some faint-of-heart members began to discuss a return home, but their leaders breathed a new spirit of resolve into their efforts. As they continued westward for several days, however, they received a new alarmist message from several circulars. These hastily printed newspaper sheets painted an alarming picture of lurking Indians ready to attack any wagon train that traversed their territories. With foreboding, the Frink family continued on, scanning the horizon with a telescope and worried that their one rifle and one Colt revolver would not be adequate to make much of a defense. During the first few nights on the prairie, Frink remained awake most of the time, refusing even to change into bedclothes or remove her shoes because she wanted to be prepared for the anticipated attack.[53]

Similar stories presented themselves to William Keil while his party was camped near the Missouri River in 1855. Rumors circulated that 8,000 Indians had assembled between Forts Kearny and Laramie and were robbing emigrants with impunity. Other gossip alleged that all the soldiers at Fort Laramie had been massacred. Adding to the seeming credibility of these tales was the information directly related by the stage station manager on the Big Blue River that Indians were carrying freshly taken white scalps in what was generally considered to be a safe region.[54]

Fears manifested themselves in a myriad of ways. One party, camped on the eastern banks of the Missouri River at Council Bluffs, faced a near mutiny in 1854. Many of the women—some sick and others homesick—

refused "to go over the river among the Indians to be scalped," and instead of continuing the journey, they wanted to take up farms in western Iowa. After extended discussions, however, the group did continue on to California.[55] In another case, young Allene Dunham recalled that she feared having her feet extend out of the back of the wagon while sleeping because she was sure that Indians would sneak into the camp and cut them off.[56] Teenager John Minto traveled by steamboat from his home in Pittsburgh to St. Louis, and, while in the latter city, he spent virtually all of his money on weapons to outfit himself for the perilous trip across the plains. He bought a brand new rifle, five pounds of powder, twenty-five pounds of lead to make bullets, a dozen boxes of percussion caps, five pounds of shot, two sheath knives, and a hatchet to serve as a tomahawk. This one-man army was now ready to meet the Indian foe.[57]

And so it was, this cacophony of confusion, misinformation, and alarm that filled the minds of overlanders even before they crossed the Missouri River and entered Indian Country. Two centuries of literature, art, trail guidebooks, newspapers, and family stories played on the overactive imaginations of people who were responding to mythical Indians long before they ever met any real ones. At best, the stereotypes created confusion about good, bad, and ignoble Indians whose behavior seemed so mysterious that no white person could ever dare trust them. At worst, the two centuries of anti-Indian hysteria that had periodically gripped the nation's attention now set the stage for a possibly contentious relationship with the tribes along the western trails. Further frightened by rumors circulating through jumping-off towns about impending Indian depredations, the overlanders turned their sights westward, expecting violence and often precipitating it by their own cultural ignorance.

2

Across the Wide Missouri

First Impressions of Indian Country

Throughout the spring and early summer months of 1841 to 1854, as thousands of wagons assembled along the eastern banks of the Missouri River to await their conveyance by ferries, migrants had a last chance to reflect on their future undertaking. They could look across the wide river valley and see a vast frontier area stretching to the horizon. No large settlements existed beyond that line, only a few buildings to serve the ferries and a few Indian missions. In the minds of most European and American overlanders, the expansive and seemingly empty landscape conformed to their preconceptions of an untamed wilderness. By statute, the federal government had defined all lands encompassing the present-day plains states as "Indian Country," and this legal status remained until Kansas and Nebraska were organized into formal territories in 1854.

In the years prior to the Kansas-Nebraska Act of 1854, American citizens were severely restricted in their movements beyond the Missouri River. A confusing web of federal laws and dozens of treaties with indigenous groups and other tribes recently removed from the trans-Appalachian states guaranteed Indians the use of these lands. This concept of separating "Indian Country" from the "states" had its origins in a loosely connected set of statutes collectively known as the Trade and Intercourse Acts, which had been in effect throughout the period from 1790 to 1834. The generation of the nation's founders had recognized the vital need to restrict white entry into Indian lands because, in the past, easy access had produced cultural misunderstandings, despoliation of resources, and expensive wars. By licensing the trading system, outlawing the flow of alcohol, and arresting white trespassers on tribal lands, the U.S. government hoped to minimize violence and achieve an orderly pattern of western settlement.

This system, which had generally failed in the East, still had a residual effect in the areas beyond the Missouri River after the demise of the Trade and Intercourse Acts in 1834. Throughout the 1830s and 1840s, fur traders, missionaries, and Santa Fe–bound entrepreneurs had to solicit government approval to operate in Indian Country. To be sure, these "passes" were issued more generously than in earlier decades, and officials in Washington, D.C., hesitated to interfere with the profits of fur trade companies and Santa Fe traders. Yet restrictions still remained on the numbers of whites who legally could travel in treaty lands and on the kinds of trade goods that they could carry with them.[1]

The advent of overland emigration in the 1840s occurred precisely at the time the federal government was relaxing restrictions on western access. Politicians and other advocates of easier passage to Oregon, California, and the Salt Lake Valley also argued that these wagon trains would merely be passing through Indian Country, and therefore their impact on the tribes would be minimal. This assertion was a dubious one at best because these overlanders would indeed leave a mighty track on the landscape, and some areas of the Pacific coast and Great Basin would soon feel the ponderous weight of their overwhelming numbers. Dubious or not, this philosophy of temporary consequences was used to justify the opening of the Platte River Trail and its extensions beyond the Rocky Mountains. Henceforth, government treaty relationships with the tribes would remain in force, but many of the guarantees and protections would stand second in rank to the exigencies of America's great migration and its immediate demands.

Overlanders who were preparing for a ferry crossing of the Missouri River between 1841 and 1854 saw little on the western horizon except for small Indian camps. By contrast, those who turned their eyes westward from those same vantage points between 1854 and 1869 encountered an entirely different landscape. Towns and farmsteads now dotted the western bank of the river, and physical improvements seemed to spring up monthly. The legal designation of "Indian Country" was slowly disappearing, but in people's active imaginations, the "Indian

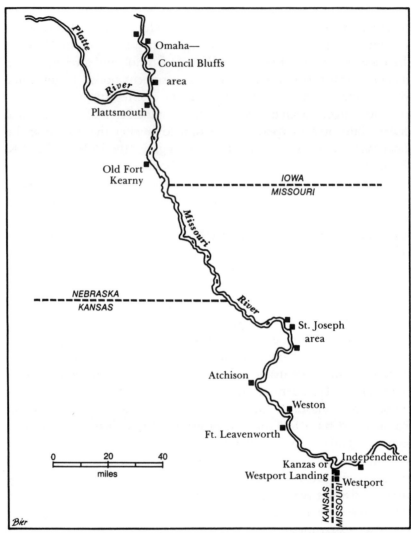

The Missouri River frontier. Reproduced, with permission, from John D. Unruh, Jr., *The Plains Across: The Overland Emigrants and the Trans-Mississippi West, 1840–60* (Urbana: University of Illinois Press, 1979).

threat" was still very much a reality. Both groups of travelers—whether in the early period or in the later stages—had to face the possibility that in a matter of days, even hours, they would meet the first real Indians in their lives, and their preconceptions would be sorely tested.

For many pioneers, crossing the Missouri River was a profound event, almost comparable to a voyage across the Atlantic Ocean. The distances involved in the two endeavors were, of course, totally different, but many of the participants experienced the sense of leaving one world and entering a radically different place. Pierson Barton Reading cheerfully recorded in his journal entry of May 21, 1843, "We have now bid farewell to the home of the Pale faces."[2] On a more somber note nine years later, Mary Ann Boatman contrasted the town of Council Bluffs, burgeoning amid its thriving businesses and neatly constructed homes, with the yet-to-be-built community of Omaha. She imagined that the hills and bluffs surrounding Council Bluffs could tell much of the human joy and sorrow that had already occurred at this place, which was to be "our last camping in civilization." "From now on," she lamented, "we got to face the savage."[3]

To J. M. Harrison, crossing the Missouri River into Indian Country was merely the beginning of the perilous adventure, for his party was already beyond the protection and comforts of civilization. In the coming months, the dangers would only become magnified with each new mile traveled into the plains and desert environments that were, according to Harrison, "inhabited by numerous tribes of Savages."[4] In the estimation of Clarence Bagley, the threat was even more immediate, for at this "westerly limit of civilization," he could see a village of Omahas, whose population he grossly overestimated to be in the thousands.[5] Twenty miles beyond that point, the California-bound party of Cephas Arms met its first Indians, a small group of Pawnees whose mere presence gave enough alarm that Arms and his compatriots increased their night guard and prepared for trouble. Yet even amid the heightened foreboding and extra precautions, Arms wrote in his journal during that spring night of 1849 that the Pawnees were amiable and helpful to their guests.[6]

Persons who crossed the Missouri River at Council Bluffs invariably headed in a slightly northwestern direction as they skirted the hills of the river valley and turned toward their next formidable obstacle, the Elkhorn River, whose danger was not its width but rather its steep banks. Somewhere in that first twenty miles of their excursion, many overlanders encountered a frequently told story that was even more frightening than those rumored back east or in the jumping-off towns. So many variations on this Rawhide Creek story were conveyed that its exact origins and initial version are impossible to establish, but each retelling seemed to uncover a more grizzly detail of Indian barbarism.

The small and nondescript Rawhide Creek, which flowed into the Elkhorn River near present-day Fremont, Nebraska, was the location of a supposed atrocity brought on by the alleged Indian tendency toward a cycle of bloody vengeance. As early as 1853, Oregon-bound Calvin B. West was so impressed with the story that he recounted it in a letter to his children in Defiance, Ohio. Perhaps to assure more believability for the tale, he transferred the location of the atrocity from Nebraska to an area of northeastern Kansas near Fort Leavenworth, the exact region through which he was traveling. West wrote that a young man bound from Ohio to the California goldfields had boasted that he had armed himself with an ample supply of knives and guns so that he could kill many Indians. His first encounter chanced to be with an inoffensive Indian woman, whom he shot without any display of remorse. A large group of Indian men tracked the murderer back to his wagon train and demanded that he be turned over to them. Rather than face the wrath of the massed warriors, and sensing the severity of the young man's deed, his compatriots turned him over to the Indians, "who took his knives and began to peel and tear off his skin while he was alive. After they got him skinned, they cut him up in pieces."[7]

Although West's version took liberties with the earlier Rawhide Creek stories, it was no more graphic than its predecessors nor more extreme than the tales to come. Sometimes the story attributed a specific name to the young man who had been skinned alive, such as the 1853 account that identified him as Mr. Tormey.[8] Another variation affirmed that the young man had been turned over to Indian women for the skinning and that when they finished their gruesome business, he jumped in the air, ran about fifty yards, and fell dead along the creek whose name forever bore reference to the tragedy.[9] Helen Clark, traveling the Elkhorn River route in 1860, reported the event in her diary not as a trail story but as if she had actually witnessed the bloody episode.[10]

Despite the longevity of the Rawhide Creek legend, trail historian Merrill Mattes could find no reliable eyewitness evidence that the event actually occurred in a Nebraska, Kansas, or Wyoming setting. It seemed to be an early fabrication that grew in importance with each new trail season, and its repeated retelling made it seem all the more credible to each subsequent wave of emigrants.[11] Perhaps its persistence rested upon the fact that it closely conformed to the preconceptions held dear by so many people.[12]

Old fears seemed to rekindle at that point where East met West and where "civilization" gave way to the wilderness. Elisha Brooks was only eleven years old when he first confronted Indians near the banks of the Missouri River in 1852, but his reactions mirrored those of many of his elders. As members of his party yelled "Indians, Indians," he looked up to see "a band of blanketed, feathered, beaded, fringed, wild looking" warriors blocking the way of the wagons. For days, he had been planning how he would be prepared with his pistol to resist the first dangerous Indians, but now he panicked and left his weapon behind as he fled. Instead, he later wrote, "I slunk under the wagon in abject terror, peering through the wheels to watch the proceedings and take my last look at the landscape." To his relief, they were a band of friendly Pawnees, yet he was prepared at that moment to give them all the wagon's contents for the sake of having them go away.[13]

Unlike young Brooks, most travelers did not experience a meeting with American Indians during their first day after crossing the Missouri River, but they encountered no shortage of disconcerting rumors about what lay immediately ahead. The party of James Enos heard so many alarming tales about Indians along the line of march that they began special military drills for resisting attacks and so that they could organize their two hundred members into a virtual army.[14] Helen Marnie Stewart recalled that at this early juncture of the trip, rumors were so abundant that she could not easily sleep.[15] Another traveler who experienced recurrent nightly dreams about Indian attacks was Carl West, who, while camped at the Elkhorn River crossing, "ran screaming from his wagon." Catherine Margaret Haun observed that "he was bear [*sic*] footed and half clad but he ran so fast that it was all that two of his companions could do to overtake him."[16]

Even as late as 1865, when virtually no American Indians still resided in the immediate vicinity of the Missouri River crossings, the rumors had not entirely dissipated. Sarah Raymond wrote in her diary that only one woman within her party had publicly voiced a desire to turn back because of the Indian threat and other privations, but she believed that others would follow suit if stronger spirits did not prevail. Raymond remained adamant that these were exaggerated fears and that those who contemplated a return home should be rebuked by their peers.[17]

Some of the warnings that were sounded in eastern Kansas and Nebraska carried more weight than others, because they came from people who occupied positions of authority, had direct connections with various tribes, or had resided in the territory for a number of years. For instance, Nancy Osborne Jacobs noted in 1845 that Joseph Robidoux, resident trader for the Kickapoos, Iowas, and Sacs and Foxes, promised to keep his Indian charges near the agency for a few extra days until several wagon trains could pass through their country. He feared that while on their way west for a bison hunt, the Indians might attempt to drive off some of the overlanders' livestock. Robidoux would delay the departure by taking extra time in grinding the corn that was owed to the Indians as part of their federal annuities. Unfortunately, his tactic did not work, because two Indians did stampede some of the livestock during a hailstorm, and they killed one of the Jacobs's cows.[18]

A more unlikely source of warning about troublesome American Indians came from several Kaws who greeted the 1841 party of Joseph Williams at the Kansas River crossing. In addition to helping the overlanders find their way along the trail, these Kaws advised them to be on the alert for menacing Pawnees, who were supposedly pillaging in the area of northeastern Kansas. The advice apparently played on Williams's overactive imagination. While riding through a grove of trees a short time later, Williams thought that he saw a Pawnee warrior waiting to spring a trap. He instinctively galloped in the opposite direction at such a furious pace that he temporarily became separated from his friends, a maneuver that, ironically, placed his life in even greater peril.[19]

Nine years later and 120 miles to the north, Upton Swingley became so upset from his first encounter with Omahas and the persistent rumors of their murderous nature that he could not rid his mind of fear. He especially dreaded having to assume night guard duty, but he dared not risk the condemnation of the others in his party if he shirked the duty required of all. He spent the night marching back and forth, "thinking every minute that Indians would attack us." Relieved to have survived the crisis, he greeted his friends with enthusiasm before they countered with their own questions about what he might have done in response to a night attack. Proudly, Swingley informed them that he would have shot the threatening Indians, but his pride turned to embarrassment when his friends reminded him that his gun had not even been loaded during the excruciating ordeal.[20]

At approximately the same time just west of the Elkhorn River crossing, Byron McKinstry related how rumors had triggered repeated false alarms ever since his party had left the Missouri River. He especially blamed Charles Potts for raising these unnecessary alarms, which were feeding a level of paranoia that had existed among the group even before they had departed the States. He recorded his personal exasperation with the fainthearted by poking fun at their overreactions: "We had a hard rain last night—and an alarm of Indians!!! Blood and murder, what shall we do. We shall surely all be slain!! Why did we not make our wills and have our lives insured before we adventured among these horrible savages." Continuing in his sarcastic tone, McKinstry blasted Potts for a second false alarm, during which everyone ran around aimlessly in a hard rain, making valiant speeches but accomplishing nothing. He concluded the diary entry with acerbic words for the women of the party, whose panicked outcries were so loud that they surely would have scared away any threatening Indians.[21]

Whether a party of travelers traversed the Missouri River into Kansas or into Nebraska, their first encounter with Indians was usually at the subsequent river and creek crossings where extra help was frequently needed and generally welcomed. As overlanders poured out of the various jumping-off towns in and around modern-day Kansas City, Missouri, they often encountered Kaws along the trail. Rather than concentrating their attention on rendering services at the smaller waterways, men of this tribe offered help across the more formidable Kansas River, whose dangers closely paralleled those of the Missouri River. Several crossings existed in the area of present-day Topeka, Kansas, but none could be forded by wagons alone, so ferry services were established to transport passengers and wagons. Although Kaws apparently did not own these means of transportation, they played key roles in popularizing the various sites, directing emigrants to the proper landings, and operating the flatboats at those sites.[22]

When Jesse Applegate made the river transit in 1843, he praised the Kaws for helping the overlanders' cattle and horses swim across in return for a small fee. He noted that the work was very dangerous due

to the swift currents and unpredictable whims of the frightened livestock, but the Kaws swam among the bobbing animals as if they had
considerable experience with the undertaking. Seven-year-old Applegate was favorably impressed not only with the hard work of these men
but also with the fact that several of them stood at least six feet tall,
demonstrated a pride in their look, and were accommodating in every
way to the needs of their white clients. The fact that they lived in cabins
and successfully grew corn, beans, and pumpkins likewise struck him as
an oddity, considering his earlier notions about "wild" Indians.[23]

When David Jackson Staples made the same crossing six years
later, he noted that the flatboat was owned by two mixed-bloods—
Joseph and Louis Pappan—and most of the labor was provided by four
unidentified Indians. On that particular day, rains and high waters prevented a crossing, but on the following morning the Indians poled the
loaded boat across the river without incident.[24] While traveling alone
in 1841, Joseph Williams not only received help from the Kaws at the
Kansas River crossing, but the leader among the Indians also directed
him on how to find the trail, where to camp, and how to catch up with
members of his party who had proceeded on ahead of him.[25] The
Donner Party, upon crossing the Kansas River in 1846, received an
even more generous offer from a Kaw elder. In return for strings of
glass beads, tobacco, cotton fabric, salt pork, and flour, he agreed to
lead them through Kaw territory. Together with several other warriors,
he kept his promise by escorting their train, helping drive the livestock,
and protecting the members from pilfering by other Indians.[26]

A different type of aid was available at the smaller creeks and rivers
of northeastern Kansas. For instance, the Wakarusa River was neither
wide nor especially deep, but its precipitous banks posed special problems
for heavy wagons. By 1849, a small Shawnee settlement had been
established on the river by enterprising tribal members who farmed
and attended to the overland trains. When William Johnston's party
became hopelessly mired in the mud of the steep riverbank, they felt
fortunate to have the Shawnees free their wagons with the use of a pair
of oxen and sturdy ropes. Johnston went on to report that several
members of the same tribe worked for competing ferry owners, and
each tried to lure Johnston's group to his favored spot at the upper
or lower crossing on the Kansas River, probably in return for direct
remuneration from the respective owners. In Johnston's mind, the

choice between available services mattered little since both operations were competently managed.[27]

Three years earlier, Edwin Bryant had crossed near the same spot on the Wakarusa River, and although he mentioned no Shawnees, he favorably remarked on a handsome Potawatomi man who was selling moccasins. Business was brisk that day, and the entrepreneur soon sold all of his wares, but he rejected repeated entreaties to sell his spirited pony, which was the object of much attention from members of Bryant's party.[28]

Twenty-five miles to the north, at St. Mary's Mission, Potawatomies provided similar support to passing wagon trains. When James Pritchard reached the nearby Indian village in May 1849, he found a productive community operating a sawmill, tending crops, and maintaining a toll bridge on Cross Creek that could be traversed for a fee of twenty-five cents per wagon.[29] The following spring Madison Moorman found several hundred wagons, which had been slowed by several days of rain, preparing to traverse Cross Creek. By this time the overlanders could choose between two bridges, with the toll across one being five cents per wagon and the second, ten cents. The two Potawatomi toll collectors competed for customers that morning, as one heralded his cheaper price and the other argued that his bridge was sturdier and safer. The Moorman party paid the higher price, elected what seemed to be the safer bridge, and departed with some bemusement about the fierce economic rivalry between the two Potawatomi attendants.[30]

Other overlanders who followed an even more northwestwardly course out of the Kansas City area and those who crossed the Missouri River at St. Joseph found a similar set of conditions among other tribes that occupied reservations near the Kansas and Nebraska border—Iowas, Kickapoos, and Sacs and Foxes. On reaching the Iowa mission in 1854, William H. Woodhams encountered two regularly operating toll bridges to serve the overland traffic. Most impressive was the Indian toll operator at one of the bridges, whom Woodhams described as a "magnificently handsome a man—tall, straight, well-proportioned, with glossy curling hair, hanging in curls to his shoulders, rich olive complexion and features, statuesque in beauty; he was absolutely perfect so far as person was concerned." Even more surprising was the man's command of the English language and his knowledge of things recognizable only by "one educated in the most refined society." Woodhams was completely bedazzled by this chance meeting, which contradicted all of his expectations, and he concluded his diary entry with the unanswered question, "What can he be doing here?"[31]

While crossing at the same spot only four years earlier during his trek to California, David Wooster encountered a member of the Iowa tribe. Although he mentioned nothing about the man's physical appearance, Wooster was struck by his honesty. The friendly Iowa man, indicating that he wanted to sell a pair of moccasins, removed a fifty-cent piece and drew his finger across its diameter. Wooster initially interpreted this to mean that the man would take twenty-five cents for the item, but he became confused by words spoken in the tribal language, one of which sounded like "charity." Rather than insult the man, Wooster offered payment above the value of the moccasins, but the owner refused to accept the higher amount. It soon became evident that the honest businessman was merely indicating by the gesture that if the moccasins were too long, he would make them shorter by use of a drawstring.[32]

Many overlanders were very impressed with the religious missions and the partially acculturated Indian villages that were located in northeastern Kansas. Niles Searls especially singled out a neatly fenced "plantation," supposedly owned by a Shawnee family.[33] Thomas Evershed praised the Potawatomies who had settled near St. Mary's Mission and had by 1849 plowed a sizable amount of prairie land in preparation for spring plantings of diverse crops. They shirked from none of the hard work and were living in good quality log houses built by their own labors.[34] Two years later, Father Pierre-Jean De Smet was lavish in his praise for the progress of this Catholic mission and for the economic progress of its Indian neophytes.[35]

The Sac and Fox mission, with its enclosed fields of waving wheat, sparked the interest of James Mason Hutchings, not because these productive farmlands lay beyond the commonly accepted area of intensive agriculture but because the crops were raised solely by Indians.[36] Likewise, Julius Merrill lauded Kickapoo families for tending various grain crops that exceeded their own consumption needs and translated into healthy sales to passing emigrants. Especially noteworthy was the Kickapoo woman who worked alongside her husband by hauling rails to erect a fence. In Merrill's estimation, she was as "good a man as himself."[37] Joseph Waring Berrien further noted that Kickapoo agricultural success occurred in an area where hay, corn, and oats were hard to come by because so many emigrants were passing through in 1849. Yet the Indians seemed to have produced enough crops that even by mid-April, they still had ready surpluses of corn to sell at $1.00 per bushel and a half.[38]

Not everyone who passed through northeastern Kansas during the twenty-five-year period made positive assessments about these resettled tribes or about their "progress." Peter Decker remarked that the Presbyterian Mission on Wolf Creek, home to ten or twelve white people in 1849, was "the prettiest place I have seen," with its church, school, several houses, and fields of wheat. This stood in sharp contrast to the "thatched huts" and "filthy looking natives" that he saw. Like so many overlanders, Decker failed to realize that even the most acculturated of Indians often preferred Native-style dwellings and clothing to the framed houses and machine-made clothing that were expensive to produce and difficult to maintain.[39]

Such misdirected value judgments abounded in the diaries and letters of overlanders whose ethnocentrism was deep-seated. William Kelly dismissed the level of Christianization among these "border tribes" and belittled their facility with the English language. But he was especially harsh in condemning their alleged lack of industriousness and their propensity to get by merely on the produce of an occasional hunt or a small garden. Even though some did hire themselves out for odd jobs of repairing the emigrants' bridles, stirrups, spurs, guns, and powder flasks, Kelly noted, they had been reduced to dependency on government annuities and alcohol.[40] John Hawkins Clark echoed this sentiment when he groused that the Indian toll collector at Wolf Creek was gouging his customers and would certainly use the money only to drink himself into oblivion with the readily available supply of "rotten whiskey."[41]

While many observers added to these negative stereotypes, a significant number of overlanders blamed whites for the partial despoliation of these "removed tribes." An overly righteous Adam Mercer Brown observed in 1850 that the Indians of the Iowa mission were a "dissipated and debased people" who had "acquired all of the vices and none of the virtues of whites."[42] A few months later, Subagent William P. Richardson confirmed that the Iowas had produced only an average crop of corn, pumpkins, squashes, and grains for the season. He attributed their temporary reduction in output to the turmoil of having so many overlanders passing through their lands, too many interruptions in daily tasks, and the corrosive effect of ubiquitous supplies of alcohol. Only the Sacs and Foxes had done well with their agricultural activities, reported Richardson, because many of their people had remained somewhat isolated from the flow of trail traffic and its numerous temptations.[43]

Lodisa Frizzell was especially eloquent in expressing her sympathy for an elderly American Indian man whose retiring demeanor seemed to serve as a metaphor for the passing of a primal Indian nobility. Describing the shy individual as having "an air of greatness about him, his tall and erect figure, and noble features," she went on to surmise that "he had doubtless sat arround [sic] the council fires of his tribe when they were many, before the white man had reduced their numbers to a mere handful." This allusion to a natural nobility being trampled by an aggressive and uncaring nation fitted perfectly into the emerging literary archetype of the vanishing Indian.[44] In more direct terms, William Kelly assailed the local white traders for cheating the Indians with shoddy products, easy credit, and cheap liquor, which assured the perpetuation of the vile system.[45] James Pratt also noted the corrosive effect of white vices on these "peaceable, inoffensive people," and he called upon missionaries and government representatives to protect the Indians more stringently, while simultaneously working toward their gradual assimilation into white society.[46]

Persons who crossed the Missouri River into Nebraska usually did so at the point where Council Bluffs and Omaha are now located. Those who made this particular passage between 1840 and 1854 had a good chance of meeting Indians within the first day or two of their transit because Omaha villages dotted the landscape at several locations, and other tribes, such as the Potawatomies, still drew annuities from the nearby Council Bluffs subagency at Bellevue, on the Nebraska side of the river. When Jacob Hammer's party crossed the Missouri River in May 1844, they received hospitality from a prominent Potawatomi chief, who provided a small boat for the occasion. The men stayed several days at Bellevue, observed tribal dances, and watched with great interest the exchange of presents between government represen- tatives and the headmen of several tribes. The Potawatomi elder— whom Hammer identified as Pa-reesh—gave his new friends a sack of salt and helped rescue their cattle from a muddy riverbank.[47] Adelia Almira Hatton, upon reaching Bellevue nine years later, was struck by the friendly and helpful manner of these same Potawatomies. She was especially happy to note that these were the first Indians her children had ever seen and that it was a positive and reassuring experience.[48]

Members of the Omaha tribe provided even more extensive contact with overlanders, and their range of services often proved more valuable but also more contentious on occasion. Because the initial ten miles of trail beyond the Missouri River was bisected by three fingers of Papillion Creek, Omahas recognized that establishing toll bridges at multiple points could provide badly needed income. Fittingly, they erected crude bridges, especially on the Big Papillion, which represented the largest impediment to heavy wagons. Most people routinely paid the dime toll over what was little more than cottonwood poles lashed together and covered by brush. Charlotte Stearns Pengra was surprised by the obvious intelligence and resourcefulness of the Omaha toll collector, who told her in remarkably good English about his previous trip to Washington, D.C.[49] Another toll collector proudly showed a picture of President Millard Fillmore to passersby, in an apparent attempt to demonstrate his importance and his friendship for Americans.[50]

Other emigrants, however, were not impressed, and they viewed the charge as virtual highway robbery, especially since the Big Papillion Creek was estimated to be no more than ten feet wide and eight feet deep.[51] Furthermore, the cost of the toll seemed to be ever changing, and its fluctuations angered travelers beyond belief. When George Belshaw agreed to pay the toll of ten cents per wagon, only to find that it had been raised to a quarter, he bargained the price down to nine cents per wagon. His argument that the bridge was totally unsafe for wagon travel seemed to strike a responsive chord among the Omahas, and they accepted his offer.[52] Not so amused was the party of Mary Burrell, whose men showed their pistols rather than coins when forced to pay a toll on Little Papillion Creek. The Indians relented, but Mary's mother, perhaps out of a guilty conscience or out of a desire to assuage the angry Omaha, gave one of the Indian women a small piece of silk, which seemed to please her very much.[53] Another emigrant group traveling through the area in 1853 paid $1.00 per wagon to cross the bridge on the Big Papillion Creek and subsequently encountered a second group of Indians demanding a similar payment. Enraged, they knocked the Indians down and continued on their way, admittedly with some sense of relief when they were not followed by the aggrieved warriors.[54]

By 1855, the Omahas no longer resided in the area of the Papillion Creek toll bridges. During the preceding year, they had been forced to sign a treaty with the U.S. government in which they relinquished virtually all that remained of their lands. In return, they were promised annuities, agricultural equipment, military protection from Yankton Sioux raids, and a much smaller reservation sixty-five miles up the Missouri River.[55] Ironically, public pressure to remove the Omahas and other small tribes of eastern Nebraska emanated from the desire to clear Indian land titles along a narrow corridor that roughly followed the Platte River to Fort Kearny. Not by accident, the lands cleared of Omaha, Ponca, Potawatomi, and Oto-Missouri tribal peoples approximated the primary route of overlanders through the eastern sections of the future state.

Four years prior to that removal, John Roger James could not possibly have known the prophetic nature of his observation when he saw his first Indian on the Big Papillion Creek. Though no words were exchanged between the two, they watched each other with great curiosity for quite some time from opposite hillsides. James later noted that the man "sat there looking at us, like some of the scenes we see of an Indian watching the white people coming in to possess his hunting grounds."[56] The sentiment paralleled the earlier words of Omaha chief Big Elk following his visit to Washington, D.C. During his extensive tour of the eastern half of the United States, Big Elk had seen the power and seemingly limitless population of the Americans. He therefore warned his people that "there is a coming flood which will soon reach us, and I advise you to prepare for it. Soon the animals which Wakonda has given us for sustenance will disappear beneath this flood to return no more, and it will be very hard for you." Then the elderly chief gently advised his people to "speak kindly to one another; do what you can to help each other, even in the troubles with the coming tide."[57] Unfortunately for the Omahas, the flood came even more quickly than he had assumed.

As increasing numbers of American and European emigrants crossed the Missouri River and entered the vast prairie lands during the 1840s and early 1850s, they came with preconceptions about the Indians who resided there. At best, their earliest contacts with the removed and indigenous tribes that inhabited the Missouri River valley left them conflicted. Many still held tightly to their lifelong stereotypes of murderous savages who would plunder their wagons and kill their relatives. Others who met their first Indians in those immediate days of travel into Indian Country began to question their negative preconceptions. Surprising to many of them, the Indians that they initially encountered seemed to be friendly, helpful, industrious, and somewhat acculturated into white lifestyles and technologies.

For the majority of overlanders, their westward migration experience was only beginning, and it was still too early to have firm judgments about what future trail contacts with the western tribes would bring. Most travelers probably still clung to their harsh stereotypical notions about American Indians, but at least for some, their eyes had been opened to the possibility that real Indians might share some of the noble characteristics found in the romantic literature of the day. Those who had changed enough to expect more positive possibilities of cultural exchange welcomed the chance to learn more about these indigenous peoples as their epic journey continued.

For now, the conflicted feelings of fear, awe, and curiosity remained interconnected in the psyche of travelers who were just beginning the second leg of their sojourn. They were beyond the Missouri River and would soon be on the Great Plains. Here they would find a more difficult environment for wagon travel, and they would meet tribes that would little resemble those they had met in the Missouri River valley. To the Plains Indians, these migrants would also be great sources of curiosity. But more important, these argonauts would bring goods that were of great value in the long-established intertribal trade network of the West. For both populations, the meetings of radically different cultures simultaneously promised potential benefits and conflicts. How they handled those interchanges would determine the future utility of the Oregon, California, and Mormon trails and the futures of these Indian nations.

3

A Mutual Bargain
Trade on the Overland Trail

Shortly after European ships first reached the Grand Banks during the late 1400s to exploit the rich harvests of codfish, Europeans unintentionally encountered a second source of economic reward—trade with the indigenous peoples of the New England coastline. Captains steered their ships to the many islands that dotted the exposed shores from Newfoundland southward to Chesapeake Bay, where they established temporary camps to salt and dry their catch. In making these most transitory of visits to the North American continent, Europeans quickly learned that various Indian communities desired to establish casual trading relationships. Even the smallest of items such as needles and mirrors caught the attention of American Indians, who in turn exchanged furs and food for these and other manufactured products. Within a century of these earliest contacts, a complex and extensive series of trade networks existed not only along the coastal belt of the thirteen English colonies but also in the French-controlled areas of the continental interior, via the St. Lawrence River, and in the Spanish lands extending from Florida to California. At every juncture on the North American continent, from the colonial period through the mid-nineteenth century, trade between Indians and whites represented a major factor in defining regional, national, and international economies.[1]

During the first half of the nineteenth century, the vast area of the trans-Mississippi West was host to a heightened version of the earlier trade networks. American, British, Spanish, and Russian fur companies competed with each other for expansion of their markets and for influence among the diverse tribes that inhabited the immense landscape. The stories of imperial fur trade rivalries have been related many times, but less attention has been directed to the reality that the extensive barter system was a two-way street. Virtually all Indians welcomed trade, and many came to see it as necessary for improving their futures. Western tribes prized whatever was in short supply—knives, hatchets, guns, flints, powder, lead, tools, pipes, awls, metal pots, ornamental beads, woolen blankets, tobacco—and they wittingly paid premium prices for those scarce items. Some of these goods became important to performance of rituals; others merely added pleasure to life; but the majority of prized goods were sought as labor-saving devices that could improve day-to-day existence. In addition to revolutionizing Indian ways of life, control of the flow of white goods was crucial to many tribes that established themselves as "middlemen" in the exchange system. By situating themselves as the go-betweens, they could dominate more remote tribes that were outside the normal trade nexus, and they could create lucrative economic situations for themselves by controlling the supply and flow of furs and manufactured products.[2]

By the 1840s, as wagon trains began to push westward toward Oregon, California, and Salt Lake City, travelers encountered this well-established bartering system and soon found themselves to be a part of the process. Both Indians and whites welcomed the opportunity to exchange items, and in many cases they did so without alarm or recrimination. In other cases, however, cultural misunderstandings and racial biases obscured the mutual benefits, thus leading to harsher relationships and occasional acts of violence between the two sides. Because overlanders were in a constant state of movement toward their ever-distant destinations, they had little time to remain in an area and to become familiar with any of the American Indian populations they met along the way. Therefore, the two groups always remained strangers, having established only a generic understanding of each other's ways. Subtle nuances remained unexplained for the most part, as both populations continued to evaluate the appropriateness of actions only within the context of their own cultural norms.

When members of one group violated the other's sense of etiquette, either by design or out of misunderstanding, umbrage was often taken. Rather than both sides being able to ameliorate their differences quickly, a residue of mistrust and fear was left behind to complicate relations with other overland groups that would pass through the same region in the future. Despite American Indian resilience to a host of cultural offenses that were directed toward them, their patience could extend only so far. Likewise, emigrants entered into Indian Country with preconceived notions of American Indian duplicity, and thus many were quick to assume the worst about any overtures toward trade. Each initial attempt at an exchange of goods with the Great Plains tribes was therefore crucial, because it went a long way toward either opening minds to greater acceptance of Indian people or toward hardening the pejorative stereotypes that travelers had brought with them from the East.

As overlanders moved beyond the hilly areas of the Missouri River valley onto the transitional prairie lands that soon gave way to the Great Plains near the ninety-eighth meridian, they encountered Indians who were different from those they had met earlier on their journey. Some, such as the Pawnees, lived in fixed villages of earth lodges, while others, such as the Lakotas and Cheyennes, frequently moved their villages of tipis from place to place, depending on seasonal migration patterns and the need to relocate closer to natural resources. These were truly Plains Indians, the exact people whom westward-bound pioneers had been warned about in much of the pulp fiction, newspapers, and rumor mills before they departed "civilization."

Migrants who traveled through the Kansas City, St. Joseph, Nebraska City, and Council Bluffs–Omaha areas most likely encountered Pawnees early in the trip, if they met any Indians at all. Unknown to many of these travelers was the fact that the Pawnees were already facing a crisis situation by the late 1840s. When Lt. James Henry Carleton visited their villages on the Loup and Platte rivers in 1844, he was favorably impressed by the men's physical attributes and resourcefulness, which he contrasted with the less inspiring tribes of the East.[3] Carleton's superior, Maj. Clifton Wharton, held a council with these Pawnees, and both officers were fascinated with the forthrightness of their leaders and their collective martial power. Wharton addressed them directly about the important matter of emigrants using the various trails through their domain, and he requested that the chiefs "afford them every relief, and by their kindness to lighten their hearts on their long and comfortless route." The headmen responded positively to this request, in return for further government promises to punish their Sioux enemies, deliver annuities in a timely manner, and provide tribal members with agricultural equipment.[4]

Carleton's flattering assessments of the Pawnees obscured a demographic disaster that had been facing the tribe for more than four decades. By the beginning of the nineteenth century, most of the southern bands of Pawnees had been forced northward into Nebraska by epidemics and aggressive Indian enemies. A virulent smallpox epidemic in 1832 had killed more than 3,000 of their number, and five years later a return of the dreaded killer had carried off another 2,000 persons.[5] These rapid population declines came at the same time that intertribal warfare put additional pressure on Pawnee hunting lands and forced them into a smaller area of the Loup and Platte River valleys, where Carleton and Wharton visited them. They still continued to hunt bison throughout the western regions of Nebraska, but always at greater risk from Lakota attacks.

Within three years of this meeting between soldiers and Pawnees, the latter were preoccupied with a bleak present, and their relationships with the overlanders certainly would shape their future. Trade prospects promised new hope, but the accelerated rate of white entry into Pawnee lands signaled additional pressure on their resources and increased the possibility of a new round of epidemics. Meanwhile, by 1847 their Loup River mission had been closed and removed eastward to Bellevue, their harvest had failed, government annuities had been delayed, and the Sioux had destroyed their primary village on Cedar Creek.[6]

To secure trade goods and cash with which to purchase other supplies, some Pawnees took advantage of a crucial wagon crossing on the Elkhorn River over which virtually all outbound wagons from Council Bluffs–Omaha had to pass. Here, they sold their services rather than relying on the transfer of goods. Arriving there in the spring of 1849, the Edwin Hillyer party found no bridge on which to cross the swiftly flowing river, which extended about forty yards across. Members of the wagon train constructed a crude raft from dry cottonwood poles and then hired a Pawnee man to swim across the river and lash a cord to a large tree. Despite the dangerous current, the strong swimmer carried out his task, and the travelers were able to pull their raft along the anchored line. All wagons were safely moved

across the watery impediment in this manner, and the grateful beneficiaries paid an unspecified sum to their short-term associate.[7]

Three years later, Clarence Bagley noted that Pawnees were operating a pontoon bridge at the same crossing, although it remained
unclear as to whether tribal members had constructed the conveyance
or whether it had been built by a passing group of pioneers as a temporary solution to their transit problems and had then been abandoned.
Despite its unsteady look, the bridge could support the weight of a
fully loaded wagon and a team of animals. Bagley's compatriots were
happy to make the river crossing so easily, but they balked at the
Pawnee toll of $5.00 per wagon. Instead, they offered $1.00 per
wagon, which the Indians refused. Harsh words were spoken by both
sides, and the frustrated whites got out their rifles to reinforce their
rebuke of the toll keepers. Further trouble was averted when the
lower price was agreed upon, but the overlanders went away feeling
that no Indian was to be trusted.[8]

Similar opportunities existed for other Pawnees situated immediately to the west at separate points where Shell Creek and the Loup
River flowed into the Platte. In the former case, however, the crossing
provided nothing but a source of contentiousness because a white
party had built the bridge and abandoned it, only to have it reoccupied
by Pawnee toll keepers.[9] Typical were the experiences of unrelated
groups of travelers that included L. A. Norton, Nathaniel Myer,
Martha Read, and Enoch Conyers during the 1852 and 1853 trail seasons.
In each case, the emigrants refused to pay even the smallest of fees
because they considered the bridge to be available for free use. Instead,
they challenged the Pawnees' alleged "extortion" by drawing their
weapons and moving across the bridge without further incident.[10]
Martha Read was especially relieved that her group numbered approximately fifty wagons and that the outnumbered Indians would not dare
block so large a group.[11]

What many whites labeled as an act of extortion, the Pawnees
saw in a very different light. When the leader of William K. Sloan's
wagon train refused to pay in foodstuffs for passage, the Pawnee
headmen explained that their people were starving because the Sioux
had blocked their access to the western bison ranges. Furthermore,
they told the emigrants that the food toll was not being levied
merely for the passage across a crude bridge but also to compensate
the Pawnees for all the grass, wood, and small game that the whites

were consuming free of charge from tribal treaty lands. This time the Indians prevailed, but on account of their superior numbers, not on the strength of their moralistic argument. Sloan's group gave them a virtual king's ransom in return for safe passage—1,400 pounds of flour, 100 pounds of sugar, 100 pounds of coffee, and an unmeasured quantity of lead and powder.[12]

On several occasions, the Pawnees utilized a different tactic to secure badly needed revenues. They removed part of the Shell Creek bridge so that no wagons could cross until the toll was paid. When Phoebe Hogebroom Terwilliger's party reached the crossing in the late spring of 1854, they drove the Pawnees away and fixed the bridge themselves.[13] By contrast, when another wagon train had tried to cross there two years earlier, after its members had repaired the bridge themselves, the Indians resisted, and a brief gunfight apparently resulted in nine Pawnees being killed and several others being wounded.[14]

Pawnees established better relations with overlanders at the Loup River precisely because there was no bridge at that crossing to spur a debate about ownership or tolls. Here, the Pawnees performed much of the physical labor rather than merely posing as passive "gatekeepers" to collect a fee for nonexistent services. California-bound Charles Ferguson noted how the Pawnees marked the best crossing spot, instructed whites on how to use the sandbars while making their transit, and then led their clients across with an effective zigzag motion that avoided the worst effects of the swift current. For this important service, the Pawnees happily accepted only the supply of sugar that was offered to them. Whether they intended it for personal use or to treat it as a valuable commodity for further trade remained unclear to Ferguson.[15]

An even greater adventure awaited several young girls from an 1857 Mormon handcart party who were carried across the Loup River while mounted behind Indian men on horseback and while hanging on for dear life.[16] In another case, Pawnee women rushed to the aid of a white woman whose wagon became mired in quicksand. As she panicked with the plaintive outcry of "we are lost, we are lost," the five or six Pawnee women took hold of the wagon and lifted it beyond the precarious spot.[17] No standard fees were set for the performance of these and other services at the Loup River crossing, but virtually no one complained about the small compensation of goods that seemed to satisfy the Pawnees. Typical was the payment of several needles and a spool of thread to a Pawnee man who had taken a family's wagon across the river and then had returned to carry the children across one by one on his pony.[18]

Indians tended to make no distinction between charging a toll for crossing a bridge and levying a fee for physically helping overlanders move their wagons, livestock, and people across an unbridged river. Whites, on the other hand, made a sharp distinction between what they considered passive labor in the first case and active labor in the second. Yet in both instances, whites and Indians agreed that this was only a prelude to a more important form of commerce—the direct exchange or sale of physical items, rather than the performance of services as was available at the river crossings. Likewise, in this pursuit, both sides had to resort to sharp trading practices because they lacked sufficient quantities of preferred items to sustain their bartering throughout an entire trail season. Neither group could afford to be too generous in making its deals, and yet cultural misunderstandings about prices, the quality of goods, and the terms of the exchange sometimes led to greater mistrust and, in some cases, to violence.

Plains tribes generally had sufficient quantities of three types of goods that they could readily trade to the passing emigrant trains—moccasins, bison robes, and food. In the case of footwear, overlanders quickly discovered that their hard-soled and ill-fitting shoes were inadequate to the demands of the trail. Since adults and children alike did considerable walking during the course of a day, their shoes deteriorated, and their feet routinely developed blisters and other lesions. Word quickly spread that Indian moccasins were well designed for the rigors of travel and that they could be secured for modest prices from virtually any Sioux village along the Platte River Trail.

In their diaries and journals, travelers routinely mentioned purchasing at least one pair of moccasins at some juncture in the trip. While most people remarked about the moccasins' comfort and durability, a significant number also praised the aesthetic qualities of the tightly sewn and beautifully beaded works of art.[19] When cash was paid for a pair of moccasins, prices ranged between $0.50 and $2.00, but bargaining always seemed to precede the completion of a deal.

Because Indian women routinely made the moccasins, the women often conducted the marketing by themselves. At a well-established trading village at Ash Hollow, William Watson observed a virtual factory of Lakota women working on footwear that was intended purely for sale to passing white families. He happily purchased a pair for fifty cents.[20] On at least two other occasions, however, when the supply of tradable footwear had dwindled, Indian men remained intent on closing the deal, regardless of the depleted stocks. One Pawnee man took the pair off his own feet and traded them for a small amount of tobacco.[21] In the second case, a Sioux man not only interfered in his wife's sale of her moccasins, but he also took most of the coins from her hands and kept them for himself.[22]

Although the sale or barter of moccasins represented the most basic of financial transactions, problems could sometimes develop when one or both parties felt aggrieved by the quality of the exchange items. On one such occasion just west of Fort Laramie during the summer of 1853, Amelia Knight traded with some Sioux women for moccasins. The women wanted to exchange their crafts for bread, but Knight had only a few biscuits and hard crackers. Negotiations seemed amicable, but after Knight's train had traveled a short distance, a visibly agitated Sioux man caught up with the caravan. He forcefully indicated that the crackers were no good, and he wanted the moccasins returned, even though his family had already eaten some of the crackers. Knight's husband doubted that a misunderstanding about the quality of the crackers was behind the demand. Instead, he remained convinced that the Sioux man and his friends were trying to stir up trouble so that they could intimidate the whites for the payment of additional goods or that they wanted to use the manufactured conflict as a way to steal supplies from the wagon train. To avoid further trouble, Knight's husband returned the moccasins and continued on with the journey as quickly as possible.[23]

The trade of bison robes for either cash or in barter created an equally brisk market on the trail. A few overlanders purchased these as mementos of the trip, but the majority who acquired them did so because of their utilitarian value in protecting an exposed body on a chilly evening or during a rainstorm. Prices for the robes averaged $3.50 to $5.00 each, although more decorative ones, featuring fringe borders and artful beadwork, could garner higher amounts.[24] George Keller praised the Sioux women's artistry and originality of beaded patterns as well as their thoroughness of work, which left the hide "almost as soft as buff cassimere [*sic*]."[25] Likewise, a soldier marching down the trail during the 1857–58 Mormon War noted that "I have seen some beaded buffalo robes, that had work upon them that would astonish the most active civilized worker in embroidery."[26] Not everyone, however, had such a pleasant experience. When Ira Butterfield, Jr., traded a red woolen blanket for a heavier bison robe from some Sioux who were camped near Fort Laramie, he thought that he had won the better part of the bargain. Unfortunately, the prized robe was infested with lice, and Butterfield and his friends had to boil all their clothing and bedding for an extended time to get rid of the tenacious little vermin.[27] William Kelly escaped the same fate by noting the presence of lice in a bison robe before he had traded with a Pawnee for what would otherwise have seemed to be a valuable item.[28]

White acquisition of moccasins and bison robes eased the hardships of trail life, but trade for food often proved essential for improving the otherwise poor diet of overlanders. Nathaniel Myer was happy to exchange bread for dried bison jerky at one of the Sioux camps near Fort Laramie.[29] Ada Millington's father was likewise quick to barter two pints of flour and some bread for the forequarter of a freshly killed antelope.[30] In a Mormon party of 1856, which included Peter Howard McBride, members were instructed not to kill bison or other game animals because it might antagonize the Indians. Instead, the party would rely on "hiring" Indians to do the hunting, and the meat would be acquired directly from them. McBride later recalled that the system worked well for both sides and that his group moved through the area unmolested.[31]

As each season progressed, however, more indigenous animals were slaughtered by white passersby, white-owned livestock devoured their forage, and they modified their migratory habits to move away from the heavily traveled trails. These changes had a profound impact on the Pawnees, Sioux, and Cheyennes who had established trading relationships with overlanders. When William Barlow made the continental crossing in 1845, he could happily report that the Sioux and Cheyenne villages near Fort Laramie were well stocked with jerked bison meat. He estimated that this supply amounted to several tons and that the Indians welcomed trade with white trappers and travelers throughout the year.[32] Charles W. Smith, traveling through the same region five years later, reported that some of the Sioux camps had already exhausted their limited stores of bison meat and that they had no extra supplies with which to barter.[33] The anecdotal case that Smith noted in 1850 was only a small measure of what would become a much bigger problem for these plains tribes by the end of the decade.

For the Pawnees, the exhaustion of food stocks came even earlier than it did for tribes farther out on the Great Plains. Yet even while facing this grim reality, many Pawnees continued to exchange their limited food supplies because they desired the goods that overlanders brought. They were trapped within a vicious circle of consumption, hoping that these forms of wealth could better position them to face the new realities of the future. Helen Carpenter recorded that as late as 1857 Pawnees were selling dried bison meat at Fort Kearny, the product of one successful hunt that probably could not be repeated in the face of increasing Sioux pressures. Emigrants quickly bought up the meat, and by the following year the Pawnees were again dependent on government annuities, limited trade with and altruism from overlanders, and the theft of livestock from passing wagon trains.[34]

Because the plains tribes they encountered along the Platte River Road were not primarily agriculturalists, emigrants rarely purchased vegetables and other foodstuffs from them. Tribes of the Great Basin and the Pacific Northwest, however, specialized in trading a greater variety of foods beyond the usual bison, deer, and antelope meat. Even in the seemingly desolate Humboldt River area of Nevada, John Bidwell's 1841 party was able to trade for great quantities of honey, which the Indians pressed into balls about the size of a fist. Members of the group consumed the protein-rich concoction with great glee, until they realized that it was the product of a revolting-looking insect whose body parts were liberally included in the food balls. At that point, Bidwell remarked, "we lost our appetites and bought no more of it."[35]

More fortunate was the 1857 California-bound party that included Helen Carpenter. In the arid landscape near the alkaline Humboldt River, she and her compatriots were able to buy wild ducks and fish from the local Paiutes.[36] A few years earlier and to the northeast, along the Utah-Idaho border, a group of forty-niners encountered friendly Shoshones who were interested in trade. For the exchange of a bar of lead, the whites received a large share of meat taken from three mountain goats. Diarist Elisha Douglass Perkins fondly recorded the succulent taste and how welcome it was to their palates since they had not tasted fresh meat in quite some time.[37]

The trade in foods was even more prolific in the Pacific Northwest, especially in areas that provided abundant wildlife and fertile soil for Indian agriculture. Most evident was the ubiquitous sale of trout and salmon at various camps along the banks of the Snake and Columbia rivers.[38] So ample were the fish at Salmon Falls that Abigail Scott found the Indians willing to take just about any kind of item in exchange for them.[39] Harriet Talcott Buckingham was even more surprised to see that the exchange of one metal fishhook could bring forth enough fish to feed a large family.[40] Henry Gilfry contrasted the delicious meals of fresh salmon with the monotonous diet of salt bacon that he and his friends had been consuming almost daily for several weeks.[41]

Migrants heading for Oregon generally found Indians willing to trade wild plants and domesticated crops in the areas west of Fort Hall. Martha Read encountered unidentified Indians who were selling a type of huckleberry near the fort in 1852, but sales opportunities were bleak because the berries were so plentiful and near the trailhead that overlanders could pick their own.[42] During that same year, Parthenia Blank praised the productivity of the Cayuses who were camped in the Umatilla Valley. She bought a few potatoes from them and remarked that they were selling fresh beef for fifteen to twenty cents per pound.[43] At virtually the same spot two years earlier, David Maynard noted that his party purchased both peas and potatoes from representatives of the Cayuse and Walla Walla tribes.[44] Jesuit priest Father Pierre-Jean De Smet was equally impressed with the constant activity at the Dalles on the Columbia River, where whites and Indians engaged in a virtual trade fair throughout each busy trail season.[45] Peter Burnett was even more exuberant in his praise for the Indians who traded corn, peas, and potatoes to his party in 1853. He later recalled, "I have never tasted a greater luxury than the potatoes we ate on this occasion. We had been so long without fresh vegetables that we were almost famished, and consequently we feasted this day excessively."[46]

Yet even the relatively prosperous tribes of the Pacific Northwest faced limitations on what they could produce for the trail marketplace. Mary Ellen Todd was only nine years old when she passed through the Umatilla Valley in 1852, but she later vividly recalled that the Indians were very industrious and successful with their domesticated crops. When her father tried to buy some vegetables, however, the Indians shook their heads and indicated that they only had enough to meet their own fall and winter needs. Todd remembered how hungry her family had been at that juncture of their trip, but she surmised that the Indians had faced so much pressure from emigrants for the sale of their crops that the experience "had hardened their hearts" against genuine cases of suffering by passersby.[47]

When Overton Johnson and William Winter published their trail guide in 1846, they painted an entirely negative picture of the Indian traders who operated in the vicinity of Salmon Falls. In addition to unfairly calling them "the filthiest, most depraved and degraded creatures," the authors further blamed the Indians for creating their own suffering by following a feast-or-famine cycle of trade. Johnson and Winter's judgments were based on no direct experience with these Shoshones, and the two men failed to take into account the problems associated with food storage in the fall and winter months.[48]

Virtually all western tribes desired to be involved in the trade to one degree or another, but some bands consciously positioned themselves to participate more fully than others. They located their camps precisely along the trail, and some remained in those locations year-round. They, among all others, virtually institutionalized the exchange system and even took on the outward trappings of "success." In addition to wearing items of white clothing, conversing partially in the English language, and forever professing their loyalty to the United States, they adopted a banner that came to symbolize a welcoming of all persons into the trade nexus—a white flag. James Bennett, traveling in the valley of the Big Blue River of Nebraska in 1850, interpreted the white banner carried by Pawnees to be not only a sign of friendship but also an open call for bartering.[49] Luella Dickenson encountered a similar gesture when the leader of an unidentified group of Plains Indians came forward under a white flag to initiate the exchange of bison hides for beads and tobacco. The fact that this small party of warriors was accompanied by women convinced the whites that trade truly was the motivation and that deceit for purposes of robbery was not part of the plan.[50]

A slightly different variation of this theme was present at Bull Tail's village near Fort Laramie in 1845 when Col. Stephen Watts Kearny arrived to negotiate with the Sioux. This otherwise tranquil trading village had swelled to perhaps 1,200 Sioux men, women, and children by the time the diplomatic exchanges began. Observer Capt. Philip St. George Cooke was struck by the relative prosperity of this camp, which had merged its traditional business connections to the fort's fur traders with the increasing number of overlanders who were traveling along the Platte River. Though no white flags flew at the Lakota village, two American flags did. Standing alongside the pair was a flag made by the Sioux that incorporated their own iconography. Cooke described its field as "crossed diagonally by two bands, said to represent the winds; beneath were clasped hands; above, disposed in a regular curve, were nine stars."[51] Such a vision must have presented a welcome sight to trail pioneers who wished to trade with these Indians, and maybe that was part of Bull Tail's thinking all along.

Because commerce was a two-way relationship, initiated and shaped by both parties, overlanders needed some sense of which goods would be accepted and which would be rejected. They sometimes gleaned advice on this subject from trail guidebooks or from eastern newspapers that published the letters of local residents who had undertaken the trek. One letter of 1845 from James M. Maxey advised future travelers to "take Blue Calico and Beeds [*sic*] in little narrow Red Blue and Green Ribbon," because many Indians desired these items for personal adornment.[52] A similar bit of wisdom came from Elizabeth Dixon Smith Geer while camped at the crossing on the Deschutes River in 1847. She noted that the friendly Indians were willing to barter for many manufactured items, but she recommended that anyone who was preparing to come into this wild country should bring an ample supply of calico shirts because Indians prized these above all things.[53]

Perhaps many whites interpreted such seemingly trivial items to reflect a level of unsophistication by the Native inhabitants. But the Indians had a different vantage point from which to measure the value of trade goods, and their judgments were generally based upon the rarity and utility of the item. In these relatively remote areas of the West, where machine-made products were always in short supply, their perceived worth rested upon their ready availability, not upon their intrinsic commercial price established at the point of their manufacture. This principle had determined pricing and bartering systems ever since the earliest fur trade days in the trans-Mississippi West, and it continued to apply even in these less formal arrangements. Furthermore, Indians who traded for these products along the trail could then take them into more remote areas and barter them with other tribes for items more closely identified with traditional American Indian life, such as herbal medicines, ceremonial materials, dietary items, and horses.

Items of manufactured clothing remained highly sought objects among American Indians throughout the three decades of primary trail use. P. V. Crawford was amazed at the number of trading encounters in which various tribes stipulated that they mainly desired shirts.[54] On the Boise River, other travelers found that Indians were intent upon requesting pieces of clothing as the accepted charge for helping wagon trains to raft across the river.[55] J. W. Broadwell found out how important a particular item of clothing could be to a Pawnee man who noticed Broadwell's red flannel underwear beneath his outer shirt. The man adamantly demanded that Broadwell give him his "extra" shirt. When Broadwell responded that he only had one, the agitated Pawnee pointed to the red flannel underwear that he coveted and pronounced in English, "Dam [sic] lie! You got two."[56]

Although cotton and woolen shirts had a remarkable appeal among Indians, they possessed at least one major liability in that they could easily tear or separate at the seams. When a Shoshone man traded a large supply of salmon for several old shirts, he expressed delight with the deal. Upon closer inspection, however, he noticed that one of the shirts was ripped. He immediately took the item to a woman of the train, pointed to the flaw, and made gestures of using a needle and thread. The woman gave him the necessary repair tools, and he walked away much pleased.[57] California-bound Margaret Frink later recalled her own good fortune when she packed a large supply of needles and thread, which Sioux women coveted. Along with a few small mirrors, gilt frames, and other trinkets, these sewing items proved to be essential to the Frink family being able to trade for fresh bison, deer, and antelope meat throughout Sioux country.[58]

Male and female Indians alike were frequently attracted to other paraphernalia that served as attention-getting adornments. Elias J. Baldwin heeded important advice before undertaking his 1853 journey by including a small supply of inexpensive jewelry that he could trade with tribes along the way.[59] A year earlier, eighteen-year-old Esther Belle McMillan chose to give away, rather than sell, several finger rings to Sioux west of Fort Kearny. They were much pleased with the gesture and went out of their way to be friendly with the emigrant party.[60] Even more exotic was a Shoshone man's proud acquisition of an umbrella from members of a wagon train camped along the Green River. Observer James Bennett noted that the man must have wanted to use the umbrella as an eye-catching decoration to parade through his village, because when rain began to fall, he tucked it safely under his blanket.[61]

Also notable was a Lakota village leader's repeated efforts to swap three fine ponies for a large opera glass. The pricey deal, however, apparently was not consummated.[62] Equally unsuccessful was a Cheyenne woman who badly wanted to trade for a decorative fan and parasol. When rebuffed, she and at least one elderly man tried to take the items. They also repeatedly grabbed at the fancy dress that one young white woman was wearing and demanded the item in return for all the beads they had to offer.[63]

One misperception that many overlanders shared, especially early in their journey, was that the presence of so many articles of manufactured clothing among Indians was ample proof that the western tribes were thieves and frequent murderers of white people. While theft and homicides certainly did occur, this exaggerated assumption failed to comprehend that Indians acquired most items of white apparel by bartering or by picking up items that were frequently discarded from overloaded wagons. Although many emigrants penned accounts about their own trading of clothing items to Indians, Robert Chalmers was one of the few to record the second method of acquisition. This California-bound gold miner noted how Paiutes gathered in droves along the trail to trade for clothing and weapons. He also observed that many of the decorative items they wore were simply picked up from the vast cargoes of trunks and other containers that were removed from badly overloaded wagons and left behind.[64]

The two contrasting vantage points on how Indians acquired whites' goods were evident in the opposite reactions of two overlanders who were traveling the trail in 1864 in separate wagon trains. Albert Jerome Dickson humorously described the many Sioux women near Fort Laramie who covered themselves in gaudily colored silk handkerchiefs and especially one woman who was draped in a red-checkered tablecloth. When he saw an equally ornate Sioux man carrying a cavalry saber in a scabbard, he automatically concluded that the owner had received the weapon as a government gift or as part of the cast-off military equipment.[65] Mary Ringo, traveling in the same general area, saw a similar sight and concluded that the saber probably had been acquired by an act of theft or aggression. When she asked the Sioux warrior how he came by the prized weapon, he unabashedly informed her that he had killed a soldier and taken it.[66] Perhaps both observers were accurate in their conclusions about separate encounters, especially since Sioux conflict with the army had risen to an all-time high in the Civil War era. Whether correct or incorrect, the contrasting opinions reflect how prejudgments colored different people's views of similar events.

Besides items of apparel, American Indians placed a high priority on obtaining processed food items, which wagon trains carried in significant quantities. Chief among these were flour, sugar, and coffee, supplies that could not be adequately stocked by the western fur-trading posts or delivered on a consistent basis by Kansas City traders or government annuities contractors. Charles W. Smith observed in 1850 that many Sioux had accumulated sizable bankrolls by selling their handicrafts and jerked meat to overlanders and that they intended to use this cash specifically to purchase these coveted food items from wagon trains. Flour commanded a price of from $1.00 to $3.00 per pint when sold to Indians, and the other commodities often sold for even greater sums.[67]

When in 1852 Matthew Small's party met a group of Pawnees demanding payment for crossing their land and using their resources, members of the wagon train pooled portions of their foodstuffs. They brought forth a collection of items as diverse as flour, sugar, corn-meal, rice, coffee, salt, and pepper. The leader of the Pawnees laid out a bison robe, ordered all the piles of gifts placed there, and then folded the edges of the robe across each other to make a bundle for easy transport. Small later wondered what the Indians would have called such a hastily improvised concoction after all of these contents became mixed together and indistinguishable from each other. He also wondered what this "funny mess" would have tasted like among the hungry warriors who were eager for a good meal.[68]

Tobacco was also a highly prized trade item among American Indians, not merely for recreational smoking but also because it occupied a central place in many spiritual traditions and ceremonies.[69] Andrew Chambers recalled many years after his transcontinental trek a scene that occurred just west of Fort Laramie in 1845. In order to establish friendship with an apparent leader of the Sioux encampment, Chambers's father presented a gift of tobacco to the man. His father was descended upon by other members of the camp who repeatedly indicated that they, too, were "chiefs" and hence deserving of the gifts of smoking tobacco.[70]

A similar motivation of friendship compelled another overland party in 1850 to exchange fishhooks and tobacco for some trout that Paiutes had caught. In this case, the tobacco was of the chewing variety, and the whites cut off an unusually large piece to complete the transaction. They then marveled to see one of the Paiutes swallow the entire plug in a matter of seconds. Fortunately, the dietary misunderstanding did not lead to any immediate health consequences for the Indian or any delayed hostility toward the whites who might have been unfairly viewed as would-be poisoners.[71]

With notable exceptions, western Indians seemed most interested in exchanging abundant goods for scarcer ones, and in their endeavors to acquire these tangible items, they generally expressed little desire for money in place of goods. A. C. Sponsler, Margaret Frink, and George Belshaw were surprised at how determined Sioux and other plains tribes were in their refusal of money. In each of these three cases of the early 1850s, bread, sugar, and trinkets were much more desirable to the Indians.[72] Alonzo Delano was even more emphatic when he stated that Shoshones camped at American Falls would not accept any form of cash for fish and that they considered currency to be "worthless."[73] When the John Zeiber party reached Fort Boise in 1851, they discovered the first Indians on the entire length of the Oregon Trail who were willing to accept money for salmon. Yet even in this case, the Indians made it clear that they would give many more fish in exchange for shirts than they would for coins.[74]

Currency and coins that were available in remote areas of the West clearly lacked the purchasing power that they possessed in the eastern settlements. Among Indians, they could only be used as ornamentation or to buy other goods from overland travelers or at trading posts. Such forms of wealth had little use in the extensive intertribal trade networks, and even white fur trappers preferred to barter with Indians for goods, not for cash. The eastern values assigned to various forms of money remained a mystery to western Indians who encountered three national currencies—Mexican, Canadian, and American. For instance, when an unidentified Indian tried to sell a pony to an overlander near Tooele City, Utah, in 1862, the white man gave him $20.00 in gold and $5.00 in silver. The Indian refused the deal because he did not like the "red money" (gold) and wanted all of his payment in "white money" (silver). In short, he did not trust the value of the unfamiliar money, which had no broader utility for carrying out daily activities.[75]

At the apex of the trade network along the Oregon, California, and Mormon trails stood the mutual exchange of horses and mules. By this era, plains and northern plateau tribes had already assembled vast herds of horses, but they always clamored for more because such a form of wealth was considered laudable. Those who were quick to denounce a man for hoarding and shamelessly displaying other forms of wealth amid less affluent tribal members rarely condemned him for acquiring more ponies. Furthermore, horses and mules provided the mobility that made possible the distinctive plains and plateau cultures of the mid-nineteenth century. Bison hunts, seasonal migrations, success in raids and intertribal warfare, and freedom of choice rested upon ready access to horses and mules. In contrast, the Paiute, Goshute, and Western Shoshone bands that occupied the more arid regions of the Great Basin often lacked a sufficient supply of horses and mules as well as the unique goods to trade with other tribes in return for their surplus livestock. However, "rich" and "poor" tribes alike came to view the wagon trains as another vital source of horses and mules for the betterment of their own lives.[76]

Overlanders also came to recognize that western Indians held the exact commodity that could make the difference between success and disaster in the transcontinental crossing. Because white-owned livestock frequently became ill, injured, lame, or even died during the rigorous trek, it had to be replaced immediately, or a family would have to desert its wagon or some of its load to accommodate the lack of a full team. Most people started their trip with several yoke of oxen or sometimes more expensive mules, but they rarely had enough extras to replace all those that died or were injured along the way. While some owners purchased replacements from other trains or at trading posts, others came to depend on Indian livestock. The trade flourished almost exclusively in horses and mules because the Indians rarely kept oxen for the purposes of barter or sale. Yet no matter what the specifics of each case, the trade in horses and mules paralleled the barter and sale of other objects in that all exchanges were based upon a two-way relationship.

Typical were the deals arranged by Joseph Waring Berrien, partners Vincent Geiger and Wakeman Bryarly, and Appleton Milo Harmon during the 1848 and 1849 trail seasons. In the first example, the owner of several broken down horses traded them for four or five mules. In the second, the exchange items were reversed when the Indians gave six healthy ponies for a similar number of mules. In Harmon's case, he simply recorded that he traded his horse for a stronger Indian pony. All three of these exchanges occurred in Sioux camps located between Ash Hollow and a point just west of Fort Laramie.[77] Virtually every white observer who recorded similar scenes in this region and beyond indicated that the Sioux possessed the largest herds of horses and mules among all western tribes situated along the trail, and they were the most likely to initiate trade negotiations.

Not all overtures were blessed with positive results, however, and the outcomes could be devastating, especially among whites who faced the prospect of being stranded on the open prairie. California-bound Benjamin Gatton had expected to find a ready availability of horses that could be exchanged along the trail during his 1849 trip, but he encountered few Indians and even fewer horses that were offered for sale. Similarly, Quincy Adams Brooks had anticipated numerous opportunities for procuring Indian horses, so much so that he loaned his ailing partner his own mount. Unfortunately, no replacement animals could be secured, and poor Brooks ended up walking a great distance before solving his problem.[78]

Sometimes the trade initiative hinged on the perceived value of a particular horse, especially if it was a white-owned animal fervently desired by Indian men who were renowned for their knowledge of good horseflesh. James Hamilton resisted repeated efforts by Lakota warriors to purchase his two fine racehorses. They started the initial bidding at an exchange ratio of six of their best ponies for one of the coveted mounts, and the price escalated considerably over the next several days as the Lakota men followed along with the wagon train. Hamilton even rejected the offer of "a whole herd of ponies," and the would-be buyers rode off in disgust.[79] A reversal of roles occurred when members of the Hastings-Lovejoy party crossed through Cayuse country in 1842 and noted the many beautiful horses the tribe possessed. Fur company employee Francis Xavier Matthieu concluded that some of these could be categorized as legitimate "racehorses," but their owners prized them so much that they would not even sell them at a premium price of $500 each. Likewise, an offer of $300 for an especially appealing Shoshone horse by members of Byron McKinstry's party produced a polite rebuff as the owner proudly rode the animal in front of them to demonstrate its many qualities.[80]

Personal perceptions and the specific goals of buyers and sellers are not always clarified in the historical record, but individual decision-making, rather than a rigid pattern of trade practices, seems to have predominated. William Carter was totally convinced that Indian ponies possessed a vital instinct totally lacking in horses bred by whites—for example, the ponies' innate ability to detect sources of grass that were hidden, such as under substantial amounts of snow. In his crossing of 1857, Carter remained intent on securing Indian horses for this purpose and also because he believed that mules were subservient to the will of Indian horses and would follow them anywhere.[81] Yet for all of the perceived superiority of Indian horses, Indians seemed eager for almost any type of horse bred by whites. A member of Eleazar Ingalls's party was delighted to exchange one of his worn-out mounts for an Indian horse near Bear River, that is, until he discovered that horse was "the wickedest little witch of a pony that I ever saw." The mare in question apparently had never been ridden except with a rope around her neck, and it took the better part of a day for the new owner and his friends to harness her.[82] The desire for consummating a "good deal" seemed to be the only consistent motivation in the two-way trade, and the definition of a "successful trade" seemed to lie purely in the eye of the beholder.[83]

Many emigrants attested to the fairness of American Indians in the bartering relationship, but even the most satisfied of overlanders remained convinced that Indians were sharp traders who generally got what they wanted from a sale or swap.[84] Catherine Margaret Haun echoed the sentiments of other travelers when she wrote, "The Indian is a financier of no mean ability and invariably comes out A1 in a bargain. Though you may, for some time, congratulate yourself upon your own sagacity, you'll be apt to realize a little later on that you were not equal to the shrewd redman—had got the 'short end of the deal.'"[85] Haun's appraisal was not made in homage to Indian behavior. On the contrary, she went on to complain that western Indians, and especially those of the Great Basin, were so brazen as to steal livestock from one wagon train and sell it to the very next group that traversed the area.

W. S. McBride lodged a similar complaint in his 1850 journal when he told the sad tale of an acquaintance who had sold a good rifle to a Paiute man for what he thought were eight $5.00 gold pieces. The coins, however, turned out to be merchant's tokens from a Cincinnati hardware store, barely worth their weight and certainly of no use in the western desert lands. By the time this discovery was made, McBride conjectured that the Indian had long departed for the mountains on a fast horse.[86] This may indeed have been true, but given the general Indian misconception about coinage values, the alleged thief may well have viewed this as an honest exchange, not as a deceitful act.

No western tribe escaped at least some condemnation for its bartering practices during the era of the fur trade and the overland trails. Alexander Ross, Scottish fur trader and former employee of both British and American companies, noted in his 1849 classic, *Adventures of the First Settlers on the Oregon or Columbia River*, that the Chinooks were "crafty and intriguing, and have probably learned the arts of cheating, flattery, and dissimilation in the course of their traffic with the coasting traders."[87] More self-pitying was the brief remark of James Payne, who, after trading horses with some Sioux near Fort Laramie, recorded in his diary that he "got badly cheated."[88] Even famed entrepreneur Nathaniel Wyeth observed one of his men receive a vicious slap in the face by a Shoshone warrior who apparently took personal offense when the white man offered a less than acceptable price for some fish. Even worse, the Shoshone drove away the man's mule with a swift kick, and the surprised individual had to walk back to camp with his fish.[89] Apparently, not only did the "success" of an exchange lie in the eye of the beholder, but so, too, did the accepted etiquette of the arrangement.

Other than alcohol, the trade items most likely to cause trouble were firearms, powder, and lead. Ever since the first arrival of Spanish, French, and English traders in the West during the colonial era, guns had remained prized items among Indian warriors. Even though these weapons were difficult to repair, ammunition hard to procure, and traditional bows and arrows superior to muzzle loaders, American Indians viewed guns as status symbols. Cheyenne elder John Stands In Timber recalled oral traditions among his people about the earliest arrival of guns and how the Cheyennes associated the power of sky and thunder with these miraculous objects.[90]

In 1846, California-bound Heinrich Lienhard described a similar display of reverence when he witnessed a small group of Western Shoshone hunters carrying a pistol that they recently had found. While they carelessly twirled and played with it, the loaded revolver discharged and slightly injured one of the startled participants. Lienhard described the Indians as totally in awe of the object and fully convinced that it was a product of the Creator, who would punish them for mishandling it. After a short discussion among themselves, they gingerly grasped the mysterious cylinder and gave it to the white men with whom they had camped for the evening. The recipients played along with what they judged to be "an Indian superstition" and gained a valuable revolver without expending any effort.[91]

Despite frequent Indian overtures to exchange virtually everything they had for guns and ammunition, most travelers were disinclined to enter into such negotiations.[92] Some reluctance was voiced because the trade in firearms had produced inadvertent deaths, such as the time a Shoshone girl was accidentally killed by her own brother, who was unfamiliar with a recently purchased gun.[93] On another occasion, a supposedly unloaded dragoon pistol discharged during a demonstration for a Sioux customer. Negligent handler E. D. Pierce thoughtfully conjectured in his reminiscences, "what would have been the result had I fired in the crowd and killed two or three Indians and wounded many more. It would have been impossible to explain to them that it was an accident, right there and then we would have had trouble, we did not propose any more trading fire arms to Indians in the Plains."[94]

The possibility of accidental violence incurred by weapons trade was not, however, the primary concern of most overlanders. More frequently voiced was the belief that any firearms traded to Indians would almost certainly wind up as weapons of choice to be used against later wagon trains. Margaret Hecox recorded in her memoirs that each passing year on the trails invited greater Indian depredations simply because too many thoughtless emigrants traded weapons and ammunition to Indians, who quickly became more skilled in their use.[95] Dr. Israel Lord warned whites to resist the urge to trade an old rifle, "not worth three dollars in the States," for an Indian pony of far greater value, because this weapon would surely be used for future mischief.[96] M. G. Kellogg took special pride in his own resoluteness at refusing to barter ammunition to Pawnees, even though they had promised that they would use it only against their Lakota enemies.[97] Most direct in his commentary was Calvin Taylor, who flippantly remarked about the Utes, "they teased us for powder balls and caps which we very unceremoniously refused giving them, thinking it bad policy to lend a club to break our own heads."[98]

Other travelers warned future trail emigrants to destroy weapons rather than merely disposing of them along the way to lighten overloaded wagons. When Henrietta Reynolds's family lost three horses to alkali water, they lightened their load by leaving behind many personal items, including a gun, which they broke up so that Indians could not use it. On the pile of quilts, cooking utensils, a keg of syrup, and a feather bed, they hung a handmade sign inscribed with the words "help yourself," in hopes that the next train might find the items of use.[99] During his crossing of 1850, Finley McDiarmid saw many firearms that had been jettisoned from wagons on the western reaches of the Sweetwater River, but he was quick to praise their owners for having broken the stocks and bending the barrels to prevent Indian scavenging.[100] A feeling of guilt hung over George Forman after he traded away his Ballard rifle for an Indian pony. He subsequently became convinced that the weapon had been used against an innocent white family, even though no evidence of such a crime ever presented itself.[101] George Keller witnessed a different kind of mistake when he saw overlanders throw away many of their guns near Ash Hollow in order to lighten their loads. Later, in the area of Lassen Cutoff, they ran into an Indian scare, and the entire company could muster only a single rifle and a few pistols. Luckily, the scare proved to be another exaggeration based on rumor rather than fact.[102]

While intertribal trade was a well-established and important component of American Indian life even before the arrival of Europeans, it constantly reshaped itself to embrace the new wave of exchange items that were made available since the colonial era. Indians of the Great Plains, Rocky Mountain Plateau, and Pacific Northwest eagerly entered into sophisticated commerce with British, Spanish, Russian, and American fur companies during the first half of the nineteenth century to acquire horses, firearms, and manufactured goods that could improve their lives and increase their power relative to other tribes and to the white entrepreneurs themselves. Fittingly, by the 1840s many of these same tribes recognized the utility of exchanging commodities with the hundreds of thousands of emigrants who would traverse the Oregon, California, and Mormon trails during the following two and a half decades.

Successful patterns of barter offered mutual benefits to both groups, as American Indians secured relatively scarce labor-saving devices such as metal pots and steel-edged knives, decorative items such as machine-made clothing, and ceremonial mainstays such as tobacco. At the same time, white overlanders traded for food, livestock, and Indian accoutrements, while also hiring Indians to assist with river crossings and for the performance of other services. For overlanders, these exchanges often made the difference between either continuing the westward trek or being forced to turn back.

Even though the time of contact was brief between individual Indians and whites along the trail routes, American Indian willingness to trade symbolized more than a mere economic relationship. In effect, Indian leaders and their peoples were assigning these transitory sojourners a status that had been formerly reserved only for other tribes and for employees of established fur companies. They viewed these travelers as "allies," and the desire to trade and interact with them fitted into the ancient Native traditions of making peace and alliances with "friends." Certainly these amiable relationships, which were based upon respect and mutual benefit, were fragile at best. Bad behavior among members of a specific wagon train was sufficient to sever good relations with that party. Yet at least until the mid-1850s, most tribes along the trails demonstrated remarkable tolerance toward bad behavior because they wanted the "alliance relationship" to continue. Only after wholesale assaults began on Indian resources and sovereignty did the collective friendship mechanism begin to collapse.

Nineteenth-century American Indians were not unsophisticated children, easily victimized by every larcenous white person who crossed the western landscape. In truth, Indians were shrewd traders who usually acquired the prized items they sought. In pursuit of these scarce commodities, they also evidenced a healthy curiosity about these white travelers and were quick to aid them in their difficult endeavor. Motivated sometimes by profit and other times by human compassion, tribal peoples helped facilitate the greatest mass migration in American history. At that time, none possessed the requisite crystal ball that could predict the full tragedy and reversal of fortunes that occurred by century's end. For now, many western tribes stood as allies of these "friends" from the East, and they would perform many valuable services for them.

4

Seeing the Elephant
Indian Assistance to Beleaguered Overlanders

T he great westward migration of the mid-nineteenth century has long been celebrated in popular imagination as a splendid triumph of the human spirit. Indeed, people who embarked on the perilous journey did have to overcome incredible obstacles to reach their destinations and to establish new beginnings. Yet this theme of personal triumph obscures the equally important reality that multitudes of sojourners did not succeed, nor did they remain in the West to make new lives for themselves. This was especially true for many of the expectant gold miners who reached California during the 1850s and found conditions impossible for accumulating even the smallest of grubstakes. These discouraged dreamers eventually returned home somewhat the wiser from their ordeal, or they dispersed into other areas of the country.

Even more neglected by historians are the overlanders who gave up the venture before they reached their western destinations. These people rarely included Mormons, since their religious fervor, communalistic cohesion, and well-ordered migrations obviated some of the worst trail problems. For other migrants, however, especially those who traveled as individuals or in small family units, the rigors of the experience were too great to continue beyond even the Platte River section of the migratory route. Some were overwhelmed by high death rates associated with cholera, frequent accidents, persistent illnesses, and the agony of having to bury their friends and relatives in unmarked graves at unnamed locations in the harsh western landscape. Others were not prepared physically or emotionally even for beginning the trek. They purchased the wrong types of wagons and livestock, overloaded their cargoes, tried to move their trains too quickly, or simply became victims of bad luck.

The exact numbers of people who made the quick return will never be known, but trail records provide an enticing glimpse at the magnitude of the problem. As early as May 1850, the second full year of the California gold rush, the *St. Joseph Gazette* reported on several hundred emigrants who recently had departed from the Missouri town and had reached a point somewhere beyond the Grand Island on the Platte River. Members of these discouraged companies allegedly "saw the 'Elephant,'—head, tail, and all—large enough to satisfy them. Tomorrow their teams will be sold at auction [and they will return home]."[1] The newspaper reference to "seeing the elephant" was appropriate for this large group of returnees because the phrase was widely used at that time to denote people who had reached the limits of endurance and had given up on their migratory dream.[2]

A year earlier, Capt. Howard Stansbury's military exploration party, outbound for a reconnaissance of the Great Basin, had encountered dispirited overlanders in northeastern Kansas. These forty-niners had progressed as far west as Fort Kearny before losing heart, selling off their flour and bacon at one cent per pound, and heading for their eastern homes. Members of this party informed Stansbury that "many more were in the same melancholy case" and were debating a similar retreat from the Great Plains. A second returning group that was intercepted three days later affirmed the grim reality, and they described how "turnbacks" were selling their wagons for as little as $10.00 or $15.00 each and were practically giving away the remainder of their supplies. Capt. Stansbury attributed the large number of failures to their own folly. He blithely wrote, "So much for arduous enterprises rashly undertaken, and prosecuted without previous knowledge or suitable preparations."[3]

Other overlanders showed more sympathy for these downhearted souls, but they echoed Stansbury's conclusions about the naïveté of many of those who had undertaken the difficult trek without much thought. Charlotte Stearns Pengra felt compassion for a small group of wayfarers who barely had made it beyond the Elkhorn River of eastern

Nebraska before having to give up because of injuries to three of their oxen. For another sick man she encountered at about the same juncture, Pengra provided shelter and food so that he could revive himself before returning east.[4] George Gibbs, a civilian accompanying Maj. Osborne Cross's 1849 Mounted Riflemen expedition along the Oregon Trail, also noted the plight of a sizable emigrant company that had broken up after sixty head of their livestock had stampeded and left the owners virtually stranded in southeastern Nebraska.[5] At about the same time and location, Giles Isham grew so weary of one compatriot's constant warnings that the party could not get over the distant Rocky Mountains, he advised the man to return east, which the man immediately did.[6]

In another party traveling between the Big Blue River and Fort Kearny a month later, an overlander identified only as "Horace" noted that hardly a day had gone by that his party had not encountered at least some returnees. He further recorded: "They have seen the tail of the elephant, and can't bear to look any further. Poor forsaken looking beings they are, I assure you. Some are on foot, and some on horseback, and we see now and then one with wagon and oxen."[7] Even more poignant was the tale penned a year later by Eleazar Ingalls, who had observed the grave of a man at Devil's Gate. According to the story told to Ingalls, the unidentified traveler, reduced to the last of his provisions and depressed by the entire trail experience, had taken out a jackknife and had slit his own throat.[8]

While many people undertook the westward migration without proper planning or patient dedication, a few were simply hard-luck cases beyond any hope of redemption. A reporter known only as "Pawnee" contributed a May 1849 story to the *Missouri Republican* about a mysterious loner who was sponging his way across the West. The California-bound gold hunter insisted that he had walked all the way from Maine, accompanied by his savage-looking bulldog and carrying only a long rifle and a small bundle of his personal effects. He had no other provisions with him but rather lived off the "Christian charity" of fellow travelers who took pity on him.[9]

Another reporter, identified as "Cheyenne," encountered a similar character during the following summer and also reported it to the *Missouri Republican*. He dubbed the stranger, James Gordon Brookmire, as the "wheelbarrow man," because ever since leaving St. Joseph twenty-five days earlier, the odd individual had been pushing along all of his possessions in a light wheelbarrow. He seemed oblivious to the hardships that lay ahead and was concerned only with becoming the first man to reach the diggings during the current trail season.[10] A week later, "Observer," another reporter for the *Missouri Republican*, also encountered the solitary foot traveler who was still refusing to join any other company because they might slow down his pace. Brookmire possessed a level of skill and luck that would have surprised even his sharpest of critics, for he did reach the California goldfields pretty much on his original schedule. As it turned out, Brookmire had a falling out with his companions and departed from their company probably at Fort Kearny. Despite losing his wheelbarrow and equipment in a ferry-boat accident on the Weber River near Salt Lake City, he continued across the Sierra Nevadas and allegedly took out $15,000 worth of gold dust before returning to a comfortable life on his Pennsylvania farm.[11]

Given the large numbers that migrated along the trails between 1840 and 1869, the ever-present difficulties that faced them, and the high level of unpreparedness that dogged their every step, it is little wonder that so many of the travelers encountered major hardships along the way. Except for help that they occasionally received from soldiers, fur traders, and fellow overlanders, these travelers could turn to only one other source for aid—American Indians. Today's observer can only surmise what the number of "turnbacks" would have totaled had Indian people not routinely extended trade items, gifts, and information that made possible the continuation of the sojourners' trips. In many of these cases, American Indians profited from the enfeebled positions of the immigrants, as the Indians were able to market goods and services at very dear prices, but in so many other cases remuneration was not demanded. In those instances, token gifts, extended in the time-honored way among friends, were all that Indians sought or required.

Ever since the advent of international fur trade operations between the Missouri River and the Pacific Northwest during the mid-eighteenth century, Indians had routinely provided crucial information about the vast western landscape to the white traders who visited there. They described the existing Indian trails, identified the locations of rich flora and fauna, and even guided their new "allies" along these well-traveled routes. Historian J. Roderic Korns would later summarize the importance of this relationship by observing that "no wagon, it is safe to assume, was ever taken anywhere in the Great Salt Lake country save upon paths already beaten out by the red man. The journals of James Clyman and Edwin Bryant bespeak this indebtedness to the Indians, both for the trails themselves and for aid and advice received."[12] What Korns described for the singular region of the Great Basin could be equally applied to all parts of North America. Overland emigrants of the mid-nineteenth century were, therefore, perfectly situated to become beneficiaries of these ancient trails and the collective Indian knowledge of the surrounding landscape.

Most overlanders were genuinely surprised at American Indian offers to provide directional information and even to guide parties for short distances. In the former case, where Indians provided only advice about which trail to follow or information about local camping conditions, the Indians rarely expected any payment. Typical was the experience of Phoebe Judson, who praised the friendliness of Nez Percé chief Red Wolf for precisely instructing her company on where to ascend the Blue Mountains and where to find the best grass and fine springs. His directions proved accurate, and the Judson party found a "virtual eden of green grass and fir trees" for their first camp-site.[13] A Blackfeet hunting party, members of a tribe dreaded by most Americans at that time, not only proved to be amiable but also explained in great detail to Reuben Cole Shaw the trail conditions all the way to the intersection point with the Columbia River.[14] Likewise, a traveling group of Paiutes visited the camp of Isaac Jones Wistar and described the physical realities of a particularly harsh stretch of trail just west of the Humboldt Desert. Wistar was especially pleased that they related the location of some boiling springs, whose cooled waters might be potable.[15]

Even when American Indians charged for their guide services, few people complained about paying a fee, so long as the duty was per-formed well. Joseph Goldsborough Bruff happily gave a horse to an elderly Bannock man who escorted his party from Fort Hall to nearby Cantonment Loring.[16] Pierson Barton Reading expressed similar satis-faction that his group was able to easily secure several Indian guides to accompany them through the difficult area immediately west of Fort Boise.[17] Even more relieved was Edwin Bryant, who, for the exchange of a few shirts and pants, was able to find badly needed water at Lone Rock Spring through the aid of a Paiute man. Bryant's only disappoint-ment was that he could not convince the man to become a paid guide for his party while traversing the full extent of the dangerous Humboldt route through western Nevada.[18]

Especially unique in providing assistance were the "Christianized" Indians of eastern Oregon, who frequently hired out their escort services to wagon trains in the area between the Grande Ronde Valley and the Columbia River. Most of these were Cayuse who had settled near Marcus and Narcissa Whitman's Waiilatpu mission, which had been established in 1836 near the present-day city of Walla Walla, Washington. Although they remained firmly entrenched within their own cultural world and rejected aspects of "civilization" and Christianity that they considered repugnant or unfathomable, many Cayuses eagerly entered into a lucrative relationship with the overlanders.

James Nesmith's 1843 excursion through the Blue Mountains was made easy by the scouting of respected Cayuse leader Stickus (Istukus), who accompanied the party for several days.[19] Even more recognizable to the reading public was Poor Crane, a middle-aged Cayuse man who befriended Thomas Farnham and guided him to the Whitman Mission three years after its founding. In his later travel book, Farnham described Poor Crane as "a very kind man" and told of his many virtues, including his loaning Farnham his best saddle horse for the journey. Furthermore, Farnham portrayed Poor Crane as a perfect father thoroughly devoted to his two small sons who accompanied him on the trip.[20]

Marcus and Narcissa Whitman came to depend so heavily on their religious neophytes that Marcus entrusted the welfare of an 1843 wagon train that he was traveling with to the care of a Cayuse man. Peter Burnett, a member of the train and future governor of California, later recalled that the Indian guide "proved to be both faithful and competent" in leading the train to the Waiilatpu mission.[21] Narcissa bestowed equal praise upon the two Nez Percé boys, Richard and John, who accompanied her 1836 party from the Missouri River to Oregon. In all manner of ways they helped the group and proved indispensable in driving the extra livestock along the trail. At the same time, fellow missionary Eliza Spalding wrote about the help that the Nez Percé gave to the migrating party and how they supported her husband, Henry, in establishing a new mission at Lapwai, Idaho.[22] Even though only a minority of Cayuses and Nez Percés formally converted to Christianity and settled near the two missions, the great majority continued their friendly relations with white migrating parties, at least until the Cayuse attack of 1847 on the Waiilatpu mission that cost Marcus and Narcissa Whitman their lives. This reprisal, undertaken by a small group of Cayuses, was in response to a measles outbreak that had been brought back from Sutter's Fort by a trading party.[23]

Despite the widespread aid provided by many Indian guides during the heyday of overland travel, relatively few gained any lasting fame in the historical record. One notable exception was the Northern Paiute headman known as Truckee, a name immortalized by Capt. John C. Frémont during the 1843–44 exploration through the Great Basin. Truckee's positive reputation among white overlanders began in 1844, when he informed members of the Stephens-Townsend-Murphy wagon train about an alternative route beyond the dreaded Humboldt Sink and personally led them there. This trail followed the Truckee River into California and became the preferred route of many people until eclipsed by the Carson route five years later.[24]

Truckee's important role did not end with that singular act, because he continued to help other troubled parties as they searched for the best approach to the Sierra Nevadas. When Margaret Hecox's party passed through the same region two years later, they were elated that Truckee led them from Big Meadows to the eastern foothills of the Sierra Nevadas.[25] Even when the chief was unavailable for escorting wagon trains, he frequently provided scouts who proved entirely reliable. Edmund Booth recalled that this band comprised the "most civilized Indians I ever met," and he praised the five who accompanied his party toward the juncture of the Truckee River.[26]

When they were unable to secure Indian assistance, overlanders in a few cases resorted to strong-arm tactics that had near-fatal consequences. Two separate parties, both traveling to California in 1849, captured Indian men and forced them to become unwilling guides. In the second case, Louis Nusbaumer demonstrated no regret about the hostile act, and when his group later became lost and almost starved in the California high country, he blamed his friends for having freed the two Indian captives prematurely.[27]

The most sordid case of ill-treatment of Indian guides occurred during the winter of 1846–47 as the unfortunate Donner Party remained stranded in the High Sierras. With food stocks exhausted and little chance of securing supplies from the western California settlements, many members of the beleaguered party turned to cannibalism of the dead in order that the living could survive. Two young Indian men, Luis and Salvadore, repeatedly risked their lives for members of the group as they tried to extricate the white families from the mountain snows and reach the warmer valleys near Sutter's Fort. Rumors circulated that the two were marked for death so that their bodies could serve as food for the living. W. H. Eddy warned the young men about their impending fate and advised them to flee immediately. They made it barely two miles beyond the camp before they were murdered. Their flesh was then cut from the bone and dried to provide several meals for some of the most unrepentant members of the party.[28]

Examples abounded of Indian informal advice about following correct trails, locating good campsites, and avoiding the worst perils of travel, and they well supplemented the more direct aid rendered by American Indian guides. But an attendant form of directional help was also made available by Indians—the preparation of maps. In contrast to modern cartographic techniques, which employ detailed topographical information and precise measurements of distances, these nineteenth-century maps were crude at best. Yet Indian mapmaking was a tradition that stretched back far beyond the arrival of Europeans on the North American continent.[29] Rather than attempting to provide literal representations of all landmarks and distances within a region, maps produced by Indians conveyed only a minimal amount of information and often in imprecise ways. Rivers and streams, distinctive mountain peaks, a military post or trader's house, a grove of trees—these were the types of references typically painted onto an animal hide as a permanent record or drawn into the dirt as an impermanent record. Oral traditions, spoken by people who had visited the sites, then provided elaboration on distances, travel conditions, and other pertinent information. Thus the visual and oral representations came together into a body of knowledge that could be employed by travelers proceeding into an unfamiliar area.[30]

White overlanders benefited from these maps, but only to the extent that local Indians expounded orally upon the visual information to provide further details. Ansel James McCall marveled at the information related in 1849 by an Indian man who drew a map in the sand to designate the best route across the Sierra Nevadas.[31] During that same summer, the party of Vincent Geiger and Wakeman Bryarly invited into their camp an Indian man who had made several trips into California. In return for their hospitality, he drew the different routes across the Sierra Nevadas onto a piece of paper. He then explained the pros and cons of each trail and urged the party to take the "left hand road" for the most direct route to Sutter's Fort. However, since they were headed to Pleasant Valley instead, they followed other advice and continued along the "right hand road."[32]

Sometimes the problems associated with language differences and imprecise maps combined to create confusion and delay for overlanders. In 1853, while camped at Well Spring, James Longmire and his compatriots became disoriented about the proper line of march. They sought the advice of some Indians who had been traveling with them on how best to reach Fort Steilacoom at the southern end of Puget Sound. Several Indians dutifully drew a map in the sand indicating two possible roads, each with a succession of dots representing one day's travel. Longmire elected to take the shorter route, but after a day's march it became clear that the party was moving northeast rather than northwest. They had to retrace their line of march back to Well Spring and begin anew. Only later did it become clear to Longmire that the Indians were leading his party to an entirely different post, the Hudson's Bay Company's trading center at Fort Colville.[33]

Although Indian trails dotted the entire landscape of the Great Basin, Rocky Mountain Plateau, and Pacific Northwest, most ultimately carried white men's names, as if these men had been the first to explore them. Especially notable was the Barlow Road, which provided a difficult overland route around towering Mount Hood. Most people elected to continue float trips westward on the Columbia River, all the way to Oregon City, but the mountainside alternative allowed parties to drive their livestock rather than transport them by flatboats. By no one's estimation did the Barlow Road provide a pleasurable excursion, but for the price of a toll and considerable hard work of moving along the stump-filled trail, it became a popular choice for overlanders. Although Samuel Barlow received full credit for initiating this shortcut and becoming its first toll collector, local Indians had actually pioneered it as another way for linking the Columbia River with the agriculturally rich Willamette River valley.[34]

While Indian guides, mapmakers, and trailblazers provided considerable help to overlanders who traversed the dusty western paths, they also proved crucial to the river traffic that developed along the Snake and Columbia rivers of the Northwest. Along these massive waterways, constructing crude bridges and developing shallow ford crossings could not solve the transit problem as such conveyances had for the smaller and shallower rivers of the plains. The Snake River crossings at

Salmon Falls and Fort Boise were made viable during the 1850s by white-owned ferries that could move wagons and passengers with a fair degree of reliability. The equally important task of transporting live-stock across the swiftly flowing river, however, was mostly left to Indians, who charged regular fees for their services. Henry Allyn, who crossed his livestock above Salmon Falls in 1853, noted that this was a particularly dangerous spot because the current could quickly carry panicked animals over the two rapids. Though his own mules made it safely across, he witnessed fifteen animals being washed over the summit and drowned.[35] During the previous year, Mary Ann Boatman watched an equally horrifying accident, as three men and a boy tried to cross by turning their corked wagon box into a boat. The improvised con-veyance broke loose from its anchoring ropes and went over the falls as if it were a toy. The three adults miraculously survived the ordeal, but the boy did not.[36]

The Columbia River posed even greater problems for overlanders, not only because it was the largest waterway in the Pacific Northwest but also because several wide rivers flowed into it from the south. Unfortunately for emigrants, these had to be crossed at particularly dangerous spots. The 150-yard-wide Deschutes River warranted special concern, and like the Snake River, its crossing was adequately served during the 1850s by a ferry whose white owner charged a transit fee of from $5.00 to $15.00 per wagon. Indians from several tribes likewise hired out their labor for moving livestock across the waterway. Twin sisters Cecelia Adams and Parthenia Blank noted in 1852 that the friendly Indians who performed this service were members of the Walla Walla tribe. Nine years earlier, James Nesmith had identified sim-ilar services rendered by members of the Chinook tribe at the same spot.[37] In keeping with the multitribal nature of the business, Charles Crawford's 1851 party hired a Cayuse man whose horse had made the crossing so many times that it instinctively knew the proper course, and the other horses simply followed it through the current to the opposite bank.[38]

Most unique of all the Pacific Northwest experiences was transit on the Columbia River between the Dalles and present-day Portland, Oregon. Employees of the Hudson's Bay Company had long utilized the labor of Indians to canoe passengers, pelts, and supplies between these two points. Capt. John C. Frémont hired several of the local tribesmen to take him and three of his men from the Dalles to Fort

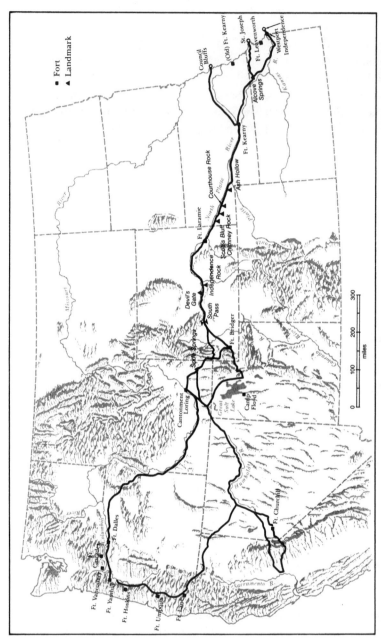

Principal army forts and landmarks along the Oregon-California Trail. Reproduced, with permission, from John D. Unruh, Jr., *The Plains Across: The Overland Emigrants and the Trans-Mississippi West, 1840–60* (Urbana: University of Illinois Press, 1979).

Vancouver in 1844. Five years later, Maj. Osborne Cross sought the aid of local American Indians, who made the trip to the Hudson's Bay Company post in ever grander style, complete with five mackinaws, one barge, and a whaleboat.[39]

Because the Columbia River flowed westward along a relatively straight course before emptying into the Pacific Ocean, it served as a virtual highway for the movement of people, wagons, and supplies to the northern end of the Willamette Valley, especially since overland travel along the south bank of the river was made exceedingly difficult by the heavily forested lands and the steep ascents along the northern edges of Mount Hood. Overlanders learned that they could, with hardship, drive their livestock overland along the Barlow Road, but moving their families and other possessions could better be accomplished by taking the watery highway. Eventually, steamboats would become available for facilitating some of this traffic at the westernmost stretch of the river, but many people still depended on Indian canoes and rafts for expediting their movements.

Furthermore, the Cascades of the Columbia, approximately midway between the Dalles and Fort Vancouver, provided a formidable enough barrier that larger boats could not move across the falls. Indian workers, therefore, congregated at the juncture to sell their essential services. Trail guide authors Overton Johnson and William H. Winter praised the expert techniques these Indian "engineers" used as they maneuvered the wagon-laden flatboats over the rapids. The two authors commented that "it requires the most dexterous management, which these wild navigators are masters of, to pass the dreadful chasm in safety. A single stroke amiss, would be inevitable destruction."[40] Nancy Osborne Jacobs described the portage operation at Cascade Falls even more matter-of-factly by detailing how her husband "hired some Indians to take it [the raft] out and turn it loose in midstream above the falls. Other Indians caught it when it came to the eddy below the rapids. Here we loaded and resumed our journey to Oregon City."[41] John Braly's father relied totally on the Indians' skills. Instead of unpacking his supplies, he lashed them securely to the raft and allowed the Indians to gingerly move the entire load across the barrier. Although the raft temporarily submerged in the frothy water, it popped right back up into the waiting arms of the trusted laborers.[42]

Indian boat pilots could be found all along the Columbia River, paddling canoes and rafts filled with overlanders and their personal effects on the last leg of the transcontinental adventure. Jacob Hammer's experience of 1844 was fairly typical of the events that occurred during the middle decades of the century. Hammer hired a Chinook boat pilot and two thirty-five-foot cedar canoes to transport his family and approximately 1,500 pounds of goods down the river.[43] John Roger James recalled how impressed he had been as an eleven-year-old with the pilots all along the length of the Columbia River. He later wrote: "Here is where the Indian is seen at his best, pulling and paddling a boat up the swift current of a forceful stream. With steady stroke and keen eye for hazards, he missed nothing."[44] Faith in Indian boating skills and their personal honor convinced William Colvig that he could entrust his wife and children to the care of two Indian pilots, while he took his wagon along the Barlow Road. The two pilots delivered his family safely to a point near Oregon City.[45]

Because the Columbia was such a wide and deep river, susceptible to rapidly changing weather and tricky currents, it presented considerable danger even to experienced boatmen. The family of Andrew Jackson Masters lost all of their possessions when their canoe capsized near the Cascades and the Indian pilots were unable to salvage anything from the deep water.[46] More fortunate was William Newby and his party of seven families, who had hired Indian pilots and were descending the Columbia in a regular flotilla of canoes. The vessel containing Newby, his wife, and another young man crashed into a submerged boulder, which they desperately grabbed hold of since it was the only anchored object in the swiftly moving current. Several Indians of the company rescued them and were able to save most of the property that had spilled into the channel.[47] In a separate incident, white and Indian paddlers joined in a common effort to protect their canoes and personal property when an unexpected wind roared down the valley and threatened to capsize all the conveyances. Only after a long interval and with total physical exertion among all the rowers did they safely reach the shore.[48]

Ironically, while the Columbia River valley was rich in timber, often to the point of impeding the movement of large emigrant parties, other segments of the western trails suffered acute shortages of firewood. Even in the well-watered river valleys of eastern Kansas and Nebraska, overlanders found that they sometimes had to purchase the vital resource from Indians.[49] Farther out on the Great Plains, the relative absence of wood became more noticeable since even the cottonwood trees that grew wild along the banks of the Platte River were not plentiful enough to answer the increased demand for each new trail season. Some migrants quickly learned from Indians and other whites the value of dried bison chips, which served as a relatively smokeless fuel. But to the uninitiated and the overly fastidious, the desire for proper firewood remained a high priority.

Although American Indians created no extensive market for this scarce item, those who settled directly on the trail routes did administer a lively trade when the resource was available to them. John Zeiber was shocked by an elderly Pawnee man who brought an armload of dry willow branches into camp just west of the Elkhorn River and, without any fanfare, started a cooking fire for the white family to share. Zeiber's wife praised the Indian's kindness and resourcefulness, but her husband remained convinced that the seemingly cordial act was nothing more than a ploy for begging food from the caravan. Zeiber failed to recognize the reciprocal nature of the act in which hospitality was freely extended but was also expected in return.[50]

Even in the regions of the Humboldt River, where only creosote bush and other prickly vegetation dotted a landscape that was mostly devoid of trees, Paiutes occasionally brought dried wood and brush from higher elevations to trade with overlanders. Bernard Reid was surprised to see Paiutes run two or three miles to collect fuel and bring it back to the wagon trains in return for food.[51] But in the desert and plateau lands, the physical exhaustion of limited sources of wood eventually created undue hardship for the local tribes. Historian Brigham Madsen conservatively estimates that 240,000 emigrants passed through Northern Shoshone lands during the heyday of the overland traffic. They, and their approximately 1.5 million head of livestock that foraged the area, utterly devastated the sources of firewood and grass along the Fort Hall stretch of the Oregon Trail. Not only did the Indians lose control of the valuable resources, they also received comparatively little compensation in the process.[52]

The abuse of grazing lands proved to be even more threatening than the exhaustion of firewood, especially since many of the affected tribes owned large numbers of horses that were dependent on the verdant grasses. This became a painful reality for the Sioux encampments situated along the Platte River Trail between Chimney Rock and Fort Laramie. During the 1840s, the Sioux had routinely shared the grasses with overlanders, but by the following decade the endless wagon trains had become a burden on the limited resources.[53]

When Laura Brewster Boquist camped near Fort Laramie in 1862, her party found a beautiful grove of trees and an extensive valley of nutritious grass for their livestock. They wondered why no other emigrants had discovered the spot, but their question was soon answered. A group of Lakota warriors rode up and, in no uncertain terms, ordered them to leave since this pastureland was reserved exclusively for Sioux ponies. The men of the wagon train extended gifts of tobacco, and some of the women made presents of sugar and salt as they pleaded their case that they were only a small group with few cattle and thus they would not damage the resources. After a friendly social gathering between the two parties and the further exchange of gifts, the Sioux allowed the small number of wagons to camp at the site. The impact of personal diplomacy and the proper etiquette of exchanging reciprocal "gifts" out of respect assured mutual benefits for both sides. This experience contrasted sharply with that of another train that had arrived with eighty wagons on the previous day and had tried to camp in the same Edenic grove. When the Indians warned them to leave, the overlanders resisted the demand, at least until the Indians returned with several hundred warriors and compelled them to move from the spot.[54]

Because grasslands were even more rare along the trail routes through Nevada, overlanders especially sought out Indians who made available any amount of forage for their animals. Melyer Casler was particularly relieved that his party was able to secure good quality hay from unidentified Indians before they began the most difficult part of their desert trip.[55] Equally pleased was Joseph Hackney, who much dreaded the passage along the alkaline and fetid Humboldt River but was able to secure freshly cut grass from Paiutes, who demanded only biscuits and an old shirt for their labor.[56] The men of William Kilgore's train joined with their Northern Paiute hosts to cut hay in the area east of the Humboldt Sink.[57] In these three cases and for many others who experienced the same good fortune, having access to grasses before crossing the formidable desert between the Humboldt Sink and the foothills of the Sierra Nevadas may well have been the difference between success and failure. Parties that had available neither water nor hay during this "dry march" watched their animals weaken and die within a matter of days. Only livestock in good health and fortified with adequate amounts of water and food could hope to complete the desert journey.[58]

An entirely different service rendered by Indians within all regions of the West was their willingness to carry letters for overlanders. Even though this assistance did not prove so critically important as some of their other roles, the help was nonetheless significant to people who felt the need to maintain contact with eastern friends and relatives. Many emigrants wrote letters within the first few days after crossing the Missouri River into either Kansas or Nebraska, but no facilities were available along the trail for posting these letters until the wagon trains reached Fort Kearny. Some emigrants therefore learned to improvise by entrusting the epistles to local Indians who promised to deliver them to established post offices on the east side of the Missouri River for a small reward.

This method constituted a long shot at best, since the letter carriers were in no way legally obligated to transport the mail. Yet William Wells was a beneficiary of this system in 1849 when he hired an Indian, whom he met on the banks of the Kansas River, to take a number of his party's letters back to the regular post office at Independence, Missouri.[59] In a comparable case of successful delivery, George McKinstry employed two Shawnees at Alcove Spring to take an assortment of letters back to the post office at Westport, Missouri. Despite the fact that they were returning from a bison hunt on the Platte River, the two hunters accepted the deal and faithfully delivered the items to Westport.[60] A similar opportunity presented itself to Edwin Bryant's party as it camped on the Big Blue River in 1846. There they met four Shawnees, also en route home from a bison hunt, and two of them agreed to transport private mail back to a post office in the Kansas City area. For the payment of some bacon, sugar, coffee, and flour, they carried out their mission without delay. This honorable act contrasted sharply with Bryant's own lack of success when he agreed to write a letter for a Shawnee man named John Wolf. Bryant penned the four-line note, folded, sealed, and addressed it, but he never could find the great Shawnee chief farther to the west for whom it was intended. He simply disposed of the message at a later time.[61]

In regard to mail service, no story of Indian loyalty to their word appeared more evident than in a promise made during June 1849. An overland party that camped southeast of Fort Kearny negotiated a deal with several Lakota men to deliver a packet of mail to Council Bluffs. Although Council Bluffs was well beyond the eastern realm of the Lakotas, and in fact was situated in dangerous Pawnee territory, the men agreed to the plan. They drove a hard bargain and received clothing, tobacco, jewelry, and small trade items as compensation. Reuben Cole Shaw happily reported that these letters made it to Council Bluffs and eventually to their intended destination of Boston. He also praised the Lakota men for faithfully carrying out this difficult mission since they could have easily discarded the packet at any time.[62]

The ultimate contribution of American Indians to the history of the overland trails came in the form of saving lives. No image flies more in the face of literary popularizations and Hollywood stereotypes than does the notion of Indians inconveniencing and endangering their own existences for the sake of extricating white emigrants from disaster. Some of the rescuers were motivated by the lure of economic reward, but others carried out their acts of kindness and bravery because of an innate sense of doing what was morally correct.

Overland diaries, journals, and letters abound with stories of individuals separated from their traveling companions who, by their own admission, would not have survived the ordeal had it not been for Indian assistance. Elias Jackson Baldwin experienced just this sort of near calamity when, in 1853, he traveled out of sight of his wagon train while hunting west of Fort Laramie. Unable to find this or any other wagon camp during the night's darkness, he stumbled aimlessly around the open prairie for three days. Finally, he spotted the fires of a small Indian encampment and, after some reflection on how dangerous it might be to enter unannounced, proceeded toward it with the conviction that he was going to die anyway because of a lack of food and water. The inhabitants greeted him warmly, fed him, and offered their hospitality. After considerable problems related to language differences, Baldwin made his hosts understand that if they would lend him a horse and guide him to his wagon train, he would compensate them for their efforts. They did so on the following day, and he richly rewarded them with gifts of knives, beads, pots, cotton ribbons, biscuits, tobacco, tea, and sugar. In this case, proper etiquette and compassion were extended by each party, to the benefit of both.[63]

An almost identical sequence of events endangered one of the young men in D. A. Shaw's California-bound train while it was traversing the Platte River Trail toward Fort Laramie during the summer of 1850. After being lost for a full day, the man walked into a Sioux village and asked for help. The apparent leader of the village immediately demanded the man's rifle, discharged it, and returned it to the wayfarer. The inhabitants then took care of his needs and provided him with a restful evening. The next day, "he was permitted to go, grateful for favors received."[64] Three years later, Sioux warriors rescued S. H. Taylor who had become lost in the Black Hills directly west of Fort Laramie. They not only extended every kindness during his four-day stay, but they also fed him, gave him the best-quality bison robe available, and bestowed on him the most honored sleeping spot in a tipi.[65]

Much farther to the west, similar favors were bestowed upon lost overlanders by members of other tribes. Stephen Staats recalled that his wagon train had listened to seductive tales about a shortcut that left the main trail beyond Fort Boise and headed northwestward toward the Burnt River. After a few days of following this new route, the party became hopelessly disoriented and suffered great privation. Staats bluntly stated that had it not been for the determination of some of the company and the expert guidance of an Indian who was hired on the spot, "many would have perished and suffered a most torturing death." The Indian man led them all the way to the Dalles, and from there the party made its own way, via the Columbia River, to Oregon City.[66]

Indian expert understanding of the landscape contrasted sharply with the inexact knowledge possessed by overlanders who only had their guidebooks and maps for reference. When William Lee Scroggs and one of his companions became separated from their wagon train, they wandered without food for several days. Upon encountering a party of Indians who were driving some horses along the south bank of the Columbia River, they received food and protection. More important, when Scroggs offered them two guns for their aid in reaching the Dalles, the Indians struck a bargain. The guides set out on a trail unknown to whites, and despite its rugged meanderings over a series of mountain slopes, the previously unnoted trail led them directly to the Dalles. Two days later, the rest of Scroggs's train reached the same spot, and everyone was happily reunited.[67]

The experience of fourteen-year-old Octavius Pringle demonstrated how difficult it was to shatter stereotypical notions of American Indian behavior even when Indians proved vital to the rescue process. Despite his young age and relative unfamiliarity with the wilderness, Pringle joined two young men to make the 125-mile journey to the

Willamette Valley to secure badly needed supplies for his stranded family. The other two travelers deserted him on the return trip, and he was unable to continue his journey. Taking a bold gamble, he approached an Indian camp and asked for aid. The Indian women, who were from Daniel Lee's Methodist mission, treated him as "though I had been a brother," and "when the men returned they treated me as royally as I had been a prince." Pringle stayed with them overnight and accepted their instructions for completing the remainder of his trek. Ironically, when he safely returned to his family, his mother expressed remorse that she "had sent him off into the wilds to be murdered by wild savages."[68] No two images of Indian behavior could ever be at greater variance— one grounded in reality and the other in rigid preconceptions.

Sometimes the threat to overlanders came not only from being lost in an unfamiliar landscape but also from worsening weather conditions. During the winter of 1856, a group of freighters employed by Russell, Majors, and Waddell became trapped in a ferocious blizzard near Ash Hollow. They survived for two full days in temperatures hovering around thirty degrees below zero and with wind-driven snow piling up so quickly that they could not travel in any direction. On the third day they were visited by some friendly Lakotas, who dropped off fresh bison meat and then invited the freezing bullwhackers to their camp a few miles away. They graciously accepted the hospitality, ate to their hearts' content, and restored their strength with plenty of rest. After regaining their vitality, the freighters tried to continue their trip, but again they almost froze to death because of the incredible cold and the deep snow. Instead of risking further injury, they returned to the Lakota village and stayed a full five weeks longer, until the harsh winter conditions had passed.[69]

On another occasion, Washakie, a respected headman among the eastern band of the Shoshones, saved the lives of some Mormon freighters who had become stranded in heavy snows and were on the verge of starvation. Suffering pitifully when discovered by Indian hunters, the men were taken to Washakie's village, where they were lodged in his wickiup and were shown every possible courtesy. In relating this story, Jeannette Young Easton, daughter of Brigham Young, added that the conventional wisdom among Mormons was that in times of danger, "if we can only make Washakie's camp we are safe."[70]

T. L. Jones averted a similar tragedy—not once, but twice—when he was saved by American Indian compassion and quick thinking. In the first case, Jones almost lost a foot to frostbite, but he was nursed back to health by unidentified Indians. They fed him and his snow-bound party, provided them with bison hide moccasins, and even rescued one of the exhausted men who had been left behind along the trail. On the second occasion, Cayuse warriors saved Jones's life by directing him out of a mazelike canyon and back toward the main trail, where he received food and water for his revival.[71]

Many eyewitness accounts have survived to document Indian aid to starving, lost, and injured overlanders, but some of the most dramatic tales concern the last-minute arrival of water to save dying people and livestock. While traveling through the Humboldt Desert in 1850 on their way to the expected riches of the California goldfields, James Evans and his friends suffered a total breakdown of animals and equip-ment after they ran out of water. One man refused to go any farther and simply laid down in the sand to await death. At that most desperate of moments, an Indian walked into the camp with a bucket full of water. He shared it with the nearly delirious men and then showed them the source of reliable water not more than four miles from where they stood. Beyond this act of humanity, the Good Samaritan then gave his pony for the use of the weakest man and escorted the entire party all the way to the Truckee River. Evans admitted that without the timely aid, no one in his group would have survived the ordeal. He also made no mention of compensation being paid to this unnamed savior.[72]

On other occasions, the presence of too much water, rather than too little of it, created life-threatening conditions. Upon crossing the Kansas River in 1843, one party was tempted to use its wagon boxes for floating across the wide and deep waterway. Despite warnings from other members, a man named Jackry overloaded his makeshift con-veyance and put two of his daughters atop the unstable load. At a point in midstream, well out of reach of both banks, the contraption capsized, and the two daughters were left flailing away in the dangerous current. Without concern for their own safety, two Indians dived into the water and rescued the girls. Although no compensation was expected for the brave act, the Indians did demand pay for repeatedly diving into the water to salvage the submerged supplies.[73]

At the western end of the Oregon Trail seven years later, William Kilgore witnessed a man trying to swim his horse across the Big Sandy. For unknown reasons, the horse sank beneath the surface far from the shoreline. Kilgore fervently concluded that if an Indian man had not jumped into the water and grabbed hold of the emigrant, the traveler most certainly would have perished.[74] Less fortunate was Celinda Hines's father, who was driving his cattle across the Snake River near Fort Boise when he was caught by the swift current and knocked from his mount. Not even his relatives would enter the dangerous waters to rescue him, but several Indian men paddled a canoe toward the place of Hines's disappearance. So rapid was the water's flow that the body was not located even after extensive searches of the area.[75]

Amid the many successful and attempted Indian rescues of whites, perhaps the most ironic of all occurred in the Sierra Nevadas during the winter of 1846–47. Members of the very same Donner Party that had killed and eaten the two loyal Indian guides were saved by other California Indians who joined the relief party from Johnson's Ranch. On the morning of January 10, twenty-five days after leaving the main group of snow-bound emigrants at Donner's Lake, seven desperate men and women miraculously scaled the summit of the High Sierras and stumbled into an Indian village on the west side of the mountains. To the inhabitants, these figures resembled apparitions more than they looked like human beings. Still, the Indians wasted no time in welcoming the suffering wayfarers, feeding them, and providing for their other needs. The village leader and several of his men subsequently escorted the strangers to M. D. Ritchie's house, about thirty-five miles from Sutter's Fort, where the survivors related the facts of their "ordeal by hunger." The same Indians then joined with white Californians to lead the final relief expedition to Donner's Lake.[76]

While case studies such as these are anecdotal at best, they do convey a pattern of Indian compassion and generosity that conflicts with the hoary stereotype of bestial savages. To be sure, not all white travelers experienced Indian acts of kindness, but those who did were eternally grateful for the aid that made their trek easier or, in some cases, made the difference between a successful crossing and one that ended in tragedy. Among the numerous accounts of direct assistance rendered by American Indians—both paid and uncompensated—the one ingredient missing from most of the stories was the establishment of a close relationship between benefactors and recipients. In a majority of cases, even the ones involving the saving of lives, the wagon trains continued their journeys within a matter of hours or days after the dramatic rescues. The principal players would never again see each other and, at best, would carry with them only good memories about the moments of crisis that had temporarily brought them together. Both parties often departed with greater empathy and admiration for each other, but both lacked a true level of understanding about each other's worlds. In contrast to the many overlanders who benefited from Indian acts of kindness, only a few would successfully transcend the cultural veil and begin to appreciate Indian cultures from an entirely different vantage point.

5

Humanizing the Experience
Getting to Know Strangers as Friends

When Meriwether Lewis and William Clark began their ascent of the Missouri River in 1804, they carried with them a list of specific instructions from President Thomas Jefferson. In addition to searching for an all-water route to the Pacific coast, assessing future economic potential along the line of march, and assiduously collecting and describing scientific data, they were to judge the extent of Indian power within the various regions. They particularly were to evaluate the levels of British and Spanish influence among the American Indians, as well as the relations between individual tribes. The two captains learned much about the indigenous peoples during their exploration and especially about the complexity of intertribal relations. They discovered that some patterns of cooperation and warfare between tribes were already well established and others were still evolving. Understanding and manipulating these intertribal alliances and conflicts would prove critical to America's expectations in the West, just as doing so would also decide the futures of various Indian nations.[1]

European and American fur trade companies raised the level of understanding to an even more refined state during the early nineteenth century, because their commercial goals rested upon establishing reliable trade with favored tribes. Likewise, their ability to survive and prosper in what was a competitive and sometimes hostile environment rested upon their success in connecting their interests with those of powerful Indian nations. In this pursuit of economic advantage, they made friends with some indigenous peoples and, by default, became enemies of rival tribes.

Fur trappers and traders married Indians out of necessity, because matrimonial relationships assured a broader array of kinsmen and women upon which whites could rely. They could call upon their new network of relatives for supplies, protection, and physical labor in their search for an even larger cache of furs. In return, their Indian kinsmen and - women received martial alliances, a more privileged position within the trade networks, easier access to trading posts, and a more secure flow of manufactured goods from the white-owned companies. These individual marriage bonds, when multiplied among the many trappers and traders, evolved into strong underpinnings for larger village, band, and even tribal alliances with the American and European entrepreneurs.[2] While economic concerns may have been important components of these arrangements, alliances based upon marriage and personal diplomacy were far more extensive and resilient than those based purely on profit motivations. Furthermore, the complex reciprocal obligations that were established through marriage bonds virtually guaranteed advantages to both whites and Indians and thus brought them closer together.

American Indians' perpetual search for friends and allies carried beyond the heyday of the western fur trade and into the peak era of the overland trails between 1840 and 1870. While Indians did not establish the same kinds of lasting and formal kinship ties with the highly mobile sojourners as they had with the mountain men who lived among them, they did adhere to similar cultural norms to create and maintain mutually beneficial relationships. Indian traditional respect for balance governed these associations, even when it was not understood or properly responded to by whites. The two populations possessed such radically different sets of values and worldviews, however, that even when sympathetic to each other, neither could fully appreciate the other's vantage point. Trappers, traders, and others who lived for extended periods with indigenous peoples had the best opportunity to cross the cultural chasm, but only rarely did they make the total crossing. For overlanders, fully bridging the cultural divide was even more unlikely because their transient nature allowed them very little time to get to know individual Indians. Ironically, for all the effort expended to cement good relations along the trails, the two peoples remained strangers who were unable to fully complete the circle of friendships and alliances that Indians desired.

One particular cultural difference especially separated American Indians and whites and fomented problems along the western trails. Generosity, a cardinal virtue among all tribes of North America, bonded together Indian communities because it emphasized a mutual obligation of sharing wealth within the broader kinship group. Those with an excess of food, horses, trade goods, or other forms of material wealth willingly gave these items to other members of their family, village, or band who did not possess adequate amounts. Prestige came to the giver, and the sharing produced a social leveling effect that usually prevented an accumulation of wealth by the few. This intrinsic mechanism helped promote harmony within the community and provided a constructive means for attaining individual status while aiding the group. For persons who refused to abide by this all-important tradition, banishment from the population was the ultimate punishment. With this form of social ostracism, the personal status, kinship connections, and safety network that protected one's well-being would all be severed.[3]

Implicit within the culture of generosity and the ritualistic give-away of presents was a strong notion of reciprocity that governed the exchange of goods and services. Historian Wilcomb Washburn has best defined the notion of "Indian giving" by observing that "the 'gift' is freely extended, but an equivalent return is anticipated and, if received, evaluated in terms of the original gift. If seen as a psychological equivalent, whatever its monetary worth, the exchange is satisfactory. Satisfaction encompasses not only an economic return (perhaps the least significant) but, more important, a diplomatic and human response."[4]

Within the context of intratribal and intertribal relations, the act of reciprocity, undertaken in response to an earlier gift or act of kindness, carried no precise time limit. The reciprocal action could be bestowed at any time, and, as Washburn notes, the second gift did not have to possess the same or greater economic value as the first. Some reciprocal gifts were mere tokens, but as long as they were graciously accepted, the circular pattern of gift giving was maintained. Both givers and receivers were honored by the act.[5]

Sadly, very few of the white migrants who crossed the western trails had any clear knowledge of this universal American Indian cultural trait. Influenced by eastern literature, art, and rumor mills, many of them also anticipated the worst features in Indian behavior. The linkage of cultural misunderstanding with a natural bias against Indians led many overlanders to misinterpret Native acts of kindness. At best, they came to view generosity as the subterfuge of an Indian giver and, at worst, as the immoral act of an Indian thief.

The notorious stereotype of the "Indian giver" originated in the colonial era and continued to gain credence with each new generation of Americans. In his 1833 book, disgruntled fur trader John B. Wyeth chided western Indians for acting like black slaves in the South by pretending to be friends with whites while simultaneously plotting acts of larceny and murder. He further remarked, "As to their presents, an Indian gift is proverbial. They never give without expecting double in return."[6] The fact that Wyeth spent only one trading season in the Far West and never got to know Indians intimately partially explains his ignorance of the custom. The fact that he came to despise American Indians even beyond his original biased precepts further explains his negative and misleading remark.

John Wyeth was certainly not alone in his judgments, and his sentiments were repeated by one group of emigrants after another. For instance, upon reaching the difficult crossing at Oregon's Deschutes River in 1845, Joel Palmer was quite relieved to find Indians who were willing to help ferry his party's disassembled wagons and goods. No price was discussed for the service, and the transit proceeded smoothly. Palmer and his compatriots were extremely happy with the aid until they found that the Indians had "stolen" some powder and shot, two shirts, and a pair of pants. What the Americans judged to be common theft, the Indians probably viewed as merely the fulfillment of reciprocal expectations. In their minds, they had rendered a valuable service, and they were deserving of the goods in return. Knowing full well that they would never see this wagon train again, the Indians probably recognized that the usual open-ended time frame for meeting reciprocal obligations could not apply in this case or others like it. Within his group, only Palmer seemed to have some appreciation for this explanation of Indian behavior.[7]

In a more alarmist way, Appleton Milo Harmon discovered four years later how the carefully orchestrated notion of reciprocal acts had given way to coercive tactics that bore only slight resemblance to the original cultural concept. He observed that as his wagon train pulled away from its campsite, M. D. Hambleton continued to trade with the friendly Crows. After the wagons had moved approximately four hundred yards and over a slight rise, one Indian grabbed the reins of Hambleton's horse, while the others pulled the owner from the saddle. As they prepared to ride away with the prized animal, they tossed a quiver, bow, and three arrows to the startled man, exclaiming in broken English, "Swap, swap."[8]

The nuanced distinction between "theft" and "swapping" produced an especially unlikely outcome in 1849 when a soldier from Fort Laramie stole the commanding officer's most valuable horse. When the Charles Ferguson wagon train encountered the deserter on the prairie, he was not only without the expensive horse but also minus every stitch of clothing except for an old bison robe to cover his body. It seems that a Crow hunting party had relieved him of horse, saddle, bridle, and clothing in return for a poor quality pony, some jerked meat, and the bison robe. With tongue in cheek, Ferguson later described the ethic of the moment by comparing the self-serving Indian action to "a modern Wall Street operation." He further added, with irony, "the Crows call it swapping. They say the Sioux are mean and will steal—but Crows, 'they good Indian, they swap.'"[9] Fur trader Rufus Sage noted the same ethic at work among the Crows: "they may take his robe, horse, or gun; but . . . they will return another robe, horse, or gun; acting upon the principle that 'exchange is not robbery,' even though it be compulsory."[10]

During the same year that Ferguson met the hapless deserter, the Regiment of Mounted Riflemen came across a Sioux warrior who was riding a horse clearly carrying a "U.S." brand. A different army deserter apparently had sold the horse to the Sioux man, who could see no reason for returning it to the regiment. Soldiers seized the animal but gave the aggrieved warrior and his friends some small presents to placate them. Unfortunately, the forced seizure of the horse had not only severed the reciprocal expectations of the original exchange, but the lack of good faith had also alienated the Sioux, and, as Maj. Osborne Cross noted, they were "too much offended to carry off the provisions that had been given them." Cross pondered the dangers of the events and concluded that the agitated Sioux man should be allowed to keep the horse, because the man and his friends would certainly use the cover of darkness to take what they considered to be rightfully theirs. On reconsideration, the horse was returned to the Sioux man with an apology, and the warriors fulfilled the proper etiquette by also riding back to the soldiers' camp and accepting the presents that had been offered to them. In seeking a balance of positive gestures, these Sioux from Bull Tail's village protected the property of the Mounted Riflemen and extended the full spectrum of hospitality.[11]

While Cross seemed to possess at least some understanding of the indigenous concept of reciprocity, other overlanders encountered the practice without comprehending its ritualistic origins. John Hawkins Clark routinely recorded in his 1852 journal the facts of how he took pity on some destitute Indian women and children on the Weber River and gave them considerable food and clothing. Although he was not seeking any compensation for the humanitarian act, Clark was heartened to see the Indian response. Later that day, three of their men rode into camp and supplied his party with freshly killed mountain sheep and venison.[12] Similarly, while Lucena Parsons waited for ferry service at Council Bluffs in 1850, she mustered enough courage to speak to an Oto headman and learn about his ways. As an offering, she took along a loaf of bread, and he responded with heartfelt thanks. Two days later, he called upon her, and they shared dinner. In return for her kindness, and much to her surprise, he gave her a knife, an item of great value among western Indians.[13]

While traveling to Oregon in 1855, William Keil encountered seven Indians at Ham's Fork. He prepared a full meal for the dignified father and his six adult sons and sent along even more food and several presents to other relatives at a nearby village. The grateful Indians returned the following morning—this time twenty-five strong—and Keil graciously shared his food again. In honor of their newfound friend, the Indians bestowed upon him a healthy ox that they had discovered in the surrounding hills. Describing these Indians in a letter to eastern relatives, Keil remarked "they were united with us in a common bond."[14]

Another Oregon-bound traveler of 1853 drew a harsher lesson from the apparent charity shown by members of some wagon trains. Andrew McClure warned that whether one gave presents to American Indians out of respect for them or out of fear of their retribution, caution must be maintained in both cases. Otherwise, the profligate givers would soon exhaust their bounty of goods as more Indians came seeking their largesse, and they "would soon be out of both provisions and money and placed in a more suffering condition than the savage whom [they] would try to accommodate."[15] Echoing that sentiment was William Carter, whose party had experienced the problem firsthand by the time they reached Ash Hollow. Upon meeting some Sioux at that point, Carter and his friends had to turn down the simple request for some sugar and tobacco because they had already given away their entire surplus to other Indians.[16]

Part of the reason that many whites failed to fully comprehend the importance of reciprocity and gift giving among American Indians was that if they did discern the practice at work, they tended to define the exchange relationship in a very limited way. In other words, they could understand the simple notion that a present given should be honored with a present extended in return, but they failed to comprehend that, for Indian people, the act of allowing whites to cross through their lands and to utilize their resources was in itself a gift bestowed.

British adventurer George Frederick Ruxton recorded during the mid-1840s the mocking words of Yankton Sioux leader Mah-to-ga-shane, who "invited" some American trappers to turn over the goods that they were trying to conceal from his party. In a taunting voice, the chief suggested that surely the white men wanted to make gifts of all the items for burning the Yanktons' wood, drinking their water, and killing their game. This indirect reference to desired compensation was conveyed fully within the cultural context of reciprocal expectations. Unfortunately, in this particular case the trappers chose not to honor the bilateral obligations. They insulted the Yanktons, a fight erupted, and one trapper and three Indians were needlessly killed.[17]

While all western tribes regarded the compensatory process as a natural part of the reciprocal cycle, they also saw it as essential to their futures. To allow the overlanders unrestrained use of natural resources would surely lead to long-term disaster, and all the tribes knew it. Thus they attempted three strategies to protect their own interests: to limit the use of these resources by wagon trains; to receive direct compensation and additional trade from the overlanders; and to seek larger guarantees of protection and compensation from the federal government. Most emigrants, of course, resented such an ill-defined system that brought a new set of compensatory demands from a different group of Indians almost weekly and sometimes even daily. Individual migrants could not afford to meet all of these demands, nor did they feel especially guilty about removing resources from the land that they considered to be "owned" by the American people. Relatively few diaries, journals, or letters made more than passing reference to the growing difficulties associated with American Indian resource management. Most people who recorded their feelings were more concerned about their own daily problems than they were about the futures of specific tribes or individual Indians.

Hugo Hoppe recalled long after his 1851 trip across the Great Plains and Far West: "'It was years and years later,' my great uncle used to say, 'that I learned that the early Indian regarded the land as belonging to him and emigrants going over it should pay him for the grass their cattle ate. They were right, but like all minorities, what they thought did not matter.'"[18]

In citing his great uncle's matter-of-fact observation, Hoppe captured the essence of why the reciprocal connection between Indians and whites ultimately failed along the overland trails. With relatively rare exceptions, only the former were attempting to abide by the rules of the relationship, while the latter were preoccupied with radically different matters.

Advocates for prior "aboriginal rights" to the land rarely came from the ranks of overlanders, who depended on its bounty for their successful journey. Military officers and Indian agents did a much better job of articulating the dilemma facing Indian nations and in calling for direct government aid to the aggrieved tribes. In a final report summarizing his exploration of the central plains during the mid-1850s, Lt. Gouverneur K. Warren offered an honest judgment about the Sioux perspective on reciprocity—a perspective that he could have equally applied to other tribes along the trails. After praising the Sioux for being reasonable and honest people, Warren went on to state that "what they yield to the whites they expect to be paid for, and I never have heard a prominent man of their nation express an opinion in regard to what was due them in which I do not concur."[19] Unlike so many other casual observers of the age who were quick to dub Indians as beggars and thieves, Warren came closer to capturing the essence of an Indian viewpoint operating from within the framework of their cultural values.

As early as 1850 Agent John E. Barrow, of the Council Bluffs Agency, informed Superintendent D. D. Mitchell that the resources for the agency's Omaha, Oto, and Pawnee charges had been so badly depleted by emigrants that only congressional compensation in the form of money and supplies could save the Indians from impoverishment.[20] At about the same time, former mountain man and current Indian agent Thomas Fitzpatrick affirmed that the plains tribes were similarly troubled by increased pressures on their resources. Fitzpatrick sided with the Indians, pointing out that they had legitimate concerns about their future access to game, timber, and grass, and he also blamed overlanders for giving tribal leaders too many false hopes in this regard. Apparently, people traversing the trails during the early years of the migrations learned that by unjustifiably making promises about forthcoming government financial aid, they could better manipulate their relationships with the various tribes. After all, Indians who anticipated compensation based on their good relations, helpful deeds, and promises of protection for overlanders would not endanger the promises by misdeeds or acts of noncooperation.[21]

Commissioner of Indian Affairs Orlando Brown noted the increased importance of this issue along the Oregon, California, and Mormon trails when, in his 1849 annual report, he urged that Congress recompense the affected tribes. Like Fitzpatrick, he expressed sympathy for the Indian complaints, but he also took a more practical approach toward assuring congressional action. Commissioner Brown turned the issue around by focusing upon white, rather than Indian, concerns. He argued that wagon trains would gain even greater help from American Indians if Indians were paid fairly. Indian theft of livestock would likewise moderate, and even divisive problems associated with intertribal warfare would be somewhat ameliorated.[22]

Dangerous times lay ahead, but through at least the first half of the 1850s a spirit of cooperation and friendship still prevailed along the overland trails. Both Indians and whites had much to gain from earlier associations that had been established upon the barter of foods and services. Indian warnings about white misuse of resources were being voiced, to be sure, but the problem had not yet reached the critical stage to warrant martial resistance.

Successful interpersonal relationships between American Indians and whites represented the high-water mark for trying to bridge the racial and cultural divide. Although surviving Indian testimony about this issue is scarce and fragmented, the writings of overlanders abound with uplifting examples of how the two groups came to associate with each other on a basis of friendship. Their mutual contacts may have been of short duration, and their understanding of each other's ways may have been superficial at best, but people on both sides of the divide found common denominators on which to build short-term associations. In so many small ways, some of these Indians and whites came to better appreciate each other for their differences as well as their similarities. By instituting these voluntary associations on the most human of all levels, they sought neither compensation nor advantage over each other. They merely sought the fellowship of others, and for the moment at least, they related to each other as friends.

Curiosity governed the most primordial feelings between these two groups of strangers, and it formed the cornerstone for initial contacts. Laura Brewster Boquist was much impressed when she and her party first encountered American Indians. These Pawnee men were "fine stalwart-looking specimens," and their wives and children perfectly suited the image of domesticity, exclaimed Boquist.[23] Eleven-year-old Lucy Ann Henderson expressed the same amazement at watching the Indian dances at Fort Laramie and marveling at the beauty of one particular Lakota woman who was dressed in the most stunning costume. Young Lucy wanted to get to know these Indians more intimately, but family warnings and an innate sense of caution won out, so she maintained her distance from them.[24] Richard Hickman was also interested in Indian ways, especially their use of dogs to haul heavy loads on the small travois. The fact that these dogs closely resembled wolves that he had seen in the East made their domestication seem even more incredible. But the most improbable scene of all was that of Indian babies being lashed to the back of these dogs, who "appeared to be harmless and gentle as a lamb." Furthermore, the massive canines followed every command of their Indian masters.[25]

"Curiosity" was a word commonly chosen by overlanders to describe their initial feelings about American Indians, but many also described the curiosity that Indians seemed to reserve for whites. Some characterized Indians as almost childlike in their inquisitive style of asking questions in languages that whites could not comprehend and their gesturing to get the emigrants to show them unfamiliar items and explain how they worked. In their perceptions of Indians' juvenile behavior, these white observers failed to perceive that their own innocent inquiries about Indian ways and accouterments might well have seemed infantile to the Indians.

When Jesse Applegate accompanied his brothers to Oregon in 1843, he began the trip with a wonderment about Indians, a spirit that he maintained throughout the journey. His brief encounter with a group of Shoshones mirrored the experiences of those on many other wagon trains. These Shoshones were especially intent upon lifting the sides of the wagon covers so that they could examine the diverse contents. Rather than fearing this invasion of privacy, Applegate and other members of his party accepted the inconvenience because the Shoshones seemed like pleasant enough people who were legitimately curious about the unfamiliar items. Applegate further remarked that they were especially interested in visiting with the white women and children of the train because they allegedly had never seen any prior to this occasion.[26]

Seven years earlier, while traveling to the Oregon Country to begin missionary life among the Indians, Narcissa Whitman found virtually the same pattern of curiosity among the tribes of eastern Nebraska. She praised the "noble Pawnees" and marveled at their exuberance in greeting white women, whom they had only rarely viewed at the Bellevue trading post on the Missouri River. Rather than being frightened by their behavior, Whitman welcomed their attention and wrote: "we ladies were such a curiosity to them, they would come and stand around our tent—peep in and grin their astonishment to see such looking objects."[27]

Another missionary woman trekking through the same region of eastern Nebraska two years later found the Pawnees delightful but also slightly larcenous if given the opportunity. Sarah White Smith discovered that she was the primary object of interest, probably because she coyly kept her identity hidden beneath a parasol. She noticed that the Pawnee men would look at her, laugh, and talk light-heartedly among themselves. When one of them approached to look under the parasol, she raised it slightly, smiled, and said, "ha, ha." In response, she noted, "he was pleased with the attention and quickly said 'ha, ha,' shook hands with me and passed off."[28]

Curiosity alone was not sufficiently strong to create meaningful relationships between whites and American Indians, but it did often help initiate a cycle of events that brought the two groups of people together, even if only for the briefest of moments. More often than not, Indians initiated these contacts by visiting the wagon trains and asking permission to camp overnight or even to accompany the wagons for several days. This ancient custom was born out of a sense of hospitality whereby members of allied tribes often joined each other's groups during migrations and bison hunts. Moreover, the custom eventually had grown to encompass Indians and fur trappers who made common cause while traveling with each other. Tribes of the Great Plains and the northwestern plateaus that had long been associated with British and American fur-trading companies would have seen Indians' accompaniment of wagon trains as a logical extension of this time-honored tradition.

Typical of the many descriptions of this pattern of hospitality was the 1849 journal entry of Edwin Hillyer. Upon meeting a group of Lakota families, smoking a pipe of friendship with their leaders, and providing gifts of food to them, Hillyer and his partners tried to communicate with the men on weightier topics. Language problems did not dissuade their efforts, and the "chief" made it clear that he would escort his new friends through the unfamiliar country and prevent any trouble for them. Although the association lasted only a couple of days, Hillyer felt comfortable about the good intentions of his benefactor.[29] During the same year, Hugh Brown Heiskell's California-bound party encountered a lone Paiute man who wanted to travel with them. In camp the next morning, he made himself particularly useful by preparing the cooking fire and fetching water. Instead of joining the train, however, he graciously took his leave to return home. He also took a saddle blanket that the white men had loaned him for sleeping purposes.[30]

Anna Maria Goddell's party encountered no such problems when they gladly accepted the company of a small number of Nez Percés who wanted to travel with them from Fort Boise to their village north of the Grande Ronde. The leader indicated that his people did not want to travel alone through the lands of their Indian enemies, and thus the two groups joined together out of common need.[31]

On other occasions when Indians remained with the wagon trains, they conducted as much social interaction as language differences would allow. David Wooster affectionately described an Iowa man who spent an entire evening with his party in northeastern Kansas. He dined with the expectant gold miners and entertained them for almost two hours with a descriptive lexicon of tribal words.[32] Similarly, Medorem Crawford and his companions listened to the tales of a Cheyenne warrior about recent raids on Shoshones and Paiutes.[33] In a more unconventional display of communication skills, another party of gold miners told their stories and listened to others related by Sioux who were camped just west of Fort Laramie. John Hawkins Clark fondly recalled this 1852 soiree, in which several of his young friends jockeyed for position to sit beside an especially beautiful young Sioux woman throughout the festivities. In due time, the white men passed photographs of their wives and sweethearts around the circle. Sioux men regarded the images with great interest, "but the lady Indian passed them by with supreme indifference," noted Clark.[34]

While American Indians frequently found themselves as the honored guests of emigrants, they were just as likely to be the hosts of social gatherings. Lorenzo Stephens's party was treated royally by a Shoshone or Bannock headman who directed them to his camp, gave them a grand tour, and invited them on a bison hunt. The visitors remained in the camp for a full day but declined the offer of an extended stay because they needed to continue on their way and because some of the older men of the party feared possible duplicity from the Indians. Although Stephens thought that the display of Indian hospitality was genuine and he enjoyed conversing with the headman's English-speaking wife, he departed with his friends nonetheless.[35]

Other acts of kindness captured the attention of overlanders as they camped or traveled with American Indians. Moses Schallenberger was especially moved by the well-disposed gesture of Shoshones who helped some of his party drive their cattle quite a distance back to the Green River.[36] David Longmire forever remembered the kindness of a Walla Walla "chief" who accompanied his wagon train and provided a substantial amount of its food.[37] Likewise, Anna Maria Goddell appreciated the sensitivity of four Pawnees who camped with her train just west of the Elkhorn River. Not only were they amiable and helpful, they also handed their weapons to the white leader so as to reduce any apprehensions their hosts might have about their intentions.[38] Forty-niner Washington Chick was notably pleased when his small group was able to join a larger band of Wyandot men as they departed Westport, Missouri, for California. The desire for greater numbers to assure protection out on the plains surpassed any fears that they might have harbored about traveling with Indians—especially those who were acculturated.[39]

These acts of hospitality were representative of the deeply honored virtue among American Indians, and they carried no demand for a specific reciprocal act or compensation. Naturalist John Bradbury was a recipient of several such gestures as he visited with different tribes during his excursion up the Missouri River in 1811. Bradbury described the widespread ritualistic practice in his subsequent book, and he concluded that "no people on earth discharge the duties of hospitality with more cordial good-will than the Indians."[40] Things had not changed by 1850, when frontier dragoon Percival Lowe warmly described the reception he received while visiting a Lakota village near Fort Laramie. Men, women, and children rushed to greet him, shake his hand, and provide him with food. Even though Lowe was not a man of prominence or wealth, they treated him like a relative who was deserving of their complete attention. When he tried to present the village leader with a brightly colored silk handkerchief as a symbol of his gratitude, the man and his wife indicated that it was not necessary. Apparently, the day's revelry and spirit of brotherhood sufficed as the soldier's reciprocal gift, whether he realized it or not.[41]

Wherever Indians and whites came together in peace, even for the briefest of moments, chances increased for each side to better appreciate the other. Mountain men, military officers, and government agents spent more time than did overlanders learning about American Indians firsthand, but even highly mobile emigrants had ample opportunities to observe Indian ways, if they cared to trust the situation and make the effort. Simultaneously, many Indians had a compelling desire to learn about these strangers who passed through their lands. Those who were able to sit down and interact with each other on the basis of equality and open-mindedness often came away with a new appreciation for their counterparts. That lowest level of friendship also paid tangible dividends for both sides as they helped each other attain their goals.

Social interaction took a variety of forms. For instance, Plains Indians seemed especially to delight in providing music and dances for emigrants whom they had found to be friendly and receptive to Indian ways. In only a few cases involving tribes living along the Missouri River was there any expectation of monetary reward.[42] For the western tribes, these events were conducted not for the purpose of passive entertainment, which carried a price tag, but rather to serve as a bridge between the Indians and their guests. Often they were held in the evening after a successful day of bartering or following a feast.

Joseph Aram's party hosted a dinner for a large group of Sioux who were camped near Fort Laramie in 1846, and amid the celebratory atmosphere, the Sioux performed a series of dances and songs. Conversation, fellowship, and music coalesced into a "degree of refinement" that Aram had not expected to find among Indians.[43] A year later Jesse Crosby's train received a similar reception from the Sioux at Ash Hollow during two days of successful trade. In honor of the happy occasion, the emigrants hosted a feast, and the Sioux honored the Americans' generosity with a series of dances and music. On the following evening, the

Sioux invited some of the white men to dine amid their lodges, and the two groups passed the time pleasurably.[44]

Even during the more troubled days of the American Civil War, when relations between the Sioux and whites had reached a breaking point, some of the Lakotas who had remained near Fort Laramie continued to greet overlanders in the same friendly spirit that had marked the previous two decades. Pvt. Hervey Johnson, a soldier in the Eleventh Ohio Volunteer Cavalry, which had been sent west to guard the Platte River Trail, described in a letter to his sister the dances performed by seven Indian men and thirty or forty women. Although he was not particularly enamored with the unfamiliar style of dance and accompanying instrumentation, Johnson was pleased with the friendly gesture in what he otherwise judged to be a hostile land.[45]

Overlanders also entertained appreciative Indian audiences with music of their own. While camped near Fort Laramie in 1854, Mary Burrell played her melodeon for a small group of Sioux men and women, while her brother playfully resisted the women's efforts to dance with him.[46] At about the same time, William Woodhams shared his food with a few Paiutes, who soon became an appreciative audience for his accordion playing.[47] In return for Sioux performances of song and dance, the Mormons of George Benjamin Wallace's Emigrating Company reciprocated with a dance that was accompanied by violin, fife, and drums. To add further formality to the festive occasion, the Mormons fired a cannon in honor of their guests.[48]

Although some musical performances were intended merely to entertain audiences, both Indians and whites frequently took the opportunity to literally join hands in each other's activities. In 1847, Loren B. Hastings and some of his compatriots danced with the Indian women at Fort Bridger to the accompaniment of a well-played fiddle.[49] Two years later, at a Lakota village near Chimney Rock, William Johnston opened a large bag of toy musical instruments and distributed them among the adult inhabitants. This assortment of horns, harmonicas, and Jew's harps was an instant hit with the Indians, who played the instruments as loud as possible and "danced about in great glee." Such was the unharmonious cacophony of sounds that Johnston jokingly recorded in his diary that the scene "almost made me repent my folly." But Johnston was also correct to note the goodwill that was generated among both Indians and whites. Furthermore, many of the

Sioux began taking off their moccasins to trade for the prized musical instruments.[50]

Because feasting was such a traditional feature of American Indian generosity, it is little wonder that the sharing of food became the most visible symbol of interpersonal communications along the western trails. More often than not, this involved a two-way exchange of edible items, followed by representatives of both sides smoking the friendship pipe, exchanging gifts of honor, engaging in conversation, and possibly joining in recreational activities. Typical was the experience of Henry Allyn's party, which, while traversing the Snake River country in 1853, met a poor but proud band of Shoshones. Despite their apparent need for sustenance, they did not beg or demand anything but merely talked among themselves in their own language. Sensing no danger, the Americans decided to host a lunch for the Shoshones. Upon accepting the invitation to what turned out to be a successful social encounter, the Shoshones took some prized tubers from sacks and gave them to each of the emigrants. Allyn remarked favorably on this act of reciprocity, and he pronounced the taste of the tubers to be superior even to that of the sweet potato.[51]

Reuben Shaw's California-bound party happily accepted a small quantity of dried venison from some luckless Sioux hunters and, in return, offered a larger amount of food stocks from their own wagons.[52] In a reversal of the situation two years later, John L. Johnson's party was honored by several Sioux hunters who left a considerable portion of a freshly killed bison for their dining pleasure.[53] Celinda Hines's wagon train was equally blessed two summers hence when a successful Sioux hunting party provided them with ample supplies of meat. In the latter two cases, the benevolent gestures were made without any demand for payment or even any extended socializing.[54]

Sometimes Indians brought foods that seemed highly exotic and even occasionally revolting to the palates of a few wagon train members. Various emigrant diaries and reminiscences mentioned roots and wild vegetables, jams made of berries and grasshoppers, mixtures of seeds, pigeons, prairie dogs, screech owls, and, above all, dog stews, which were a commonly served delicacy.[55]

Helen Carpenter proved too fastidious in her views of dietary cleanliness, as she refused to buy or accept a gift of dried bison strips from a Pawnee hunter. Even though she and her family were desirous of procuring meat to improve their monotonous diet, the sight of food she declared to be "unclean" proved too overwhelming for her reconsideration.[56] The wife of Thomas Tootle also reported that the fresh antelope meat provided by some Sioux was "delicate and pleasantly flavored," but her husband could not stomach it because of the amount of dirt that had to be washed from the exterior.[57] No such culinary reluctance prevented John Hawkins Clark from joining in a Sioux feast and remarking that "but for the slight difference in our looks one would have sworn we were brothers of the same mould."[58] Clark's remark about a type of brotherhood being created at these social gatherings captured the essence of the relationships, even though they might be fleeting at best.

Besides the sharing of food and conversation, the festivities often led to other forms of recreation. Marksmanship demonstrations were common events, usually initiated by Indians and sometimes with a small wager in mind. Many overlanders first witnessed these impressive feats at or near the jumping-off towns along the Missouri River. At Council Bluffs and on the Wakarusa River in northeastern Kansas, people of various ages and from different tribes routinely utilized bows and arrows to shoot at tiny marks for nickel and dime prizes, which appreciative audiences willingly paid to the winners.[59] Even more spectacular was the demonstration provided by a Potawatomi man just east of the Little Vermillion River in Kansas. According to an eyewitness, he let fly an arrow about sixty yards "and then shot one after another til he had all 6 in a direct line about 6 feet apart all inclining the same way."[60]

On many occasions, displays of miraculous marksmanship gave way to even more riveting shooting matches, where pride in victory was the ultimate reward. Beneath the shadows of Scotts Bluff in 1859, the teenaged boys of Joel Barnett's wagon train got into a boisterous but good-natured contest with Sioux teenagers, both groups armed with bows and arrows. They placed pieces of bread at twenty-five to thirty yards and took turns firing arrows at these minute targets, with the victor receiving all the bread pieces that he could hit. While the Indian boys' vast experience assured their dominance in target shooting, every participant seemed to enjoy the competition.[61] Jane Gould took special pride in another episode three years later, when her husband outshot two Sioux men who challenged him to a shooting match with his own gun.[62]

Foot races and horse races also served as friendly outlets for the competitive spirit, especially between the various plains tribes and the overlanders.[63] Although these informal competitions were normally reserved for males, on at least one occasion in 1849 a "battle of the sexes" occurred when several Lakota women challenged William Johnston to a race across the prairie. Mounted on their fleet-footed ponies, they easily outdistanced Johnston's much slower mule. Even after they tired of the one-sided event, the winners remained gracious in their victory.[64]

Wrestling contests were less often mentioned in emigrant diaries and letters, but they sometimes were observed. One memorable case began with deadly seriousness but ended in an amiable fashion. A group of soldiers socializing in an Indian village witnessed four other soldiers beating up a Sioux man and then being pounced on by nearby warriors. The violence was halted by authorities from both sides, and a series of wrestling matches were arranged to settle the grievances. An enlisted man who observed the one-sided proceedings noted the Indian victories, and he pronounced "that night there were four as well trumped men in our camp as ever were met with a bruising match in the prize-ring." Instead of breeding further calls for revenge, the event actually signaled an increased level of social exchange between these Indians and soldiers.[65]

A more cordial demonstration of physical prowess was made at Fort Laramie by Christopher Jacobs. This Mormon teenager put on a display of acrobatic skills that impressed his Sioux and American audience to no end. According to his version of the events, his somersaults reached such heights that the Indians examined the nature of the ground and his muscular legs to determine how he was able to spring so forcefully from a fixed position. Their amazement produced further acts of trade and social intercourse between Jacobs's train and members of the village.[66]

One of the most extensive celebrations recorded in a trail diary was the July 4, 1852, gathering at Soda Springs described by Gilbert Cole. Shoshone guests joined with men and women of the California-bound expedition and spent an entire day in joyous homage to American independence. Shooting contests, foot races, horse races, and other games and sporting events filled the afternoon and evening. Cole described it as a raucous time in which Indians and whites both let down their guard and reveled in each other's company. It is doubtful that the Shoshones understood all of the ramifications of the holiday, but Cole wrote that "when we had finished we were prouder than ever to be Americans."[67]

Shared laughter and harmless practical jokes also had a way of relieving anxiety and increasing Indian and white sensitivity toward each other. J. Watt Gibson humorously recalled the eastbound trip that he and his brother, Isaac, had made from California in 1851. Isaac desperately wanted to trade an unruly mule for a gentler horse, and he made the offer to some Sioux. They inquired about the demeanor of the mule, and its owner assured them of its docile nature, but when he attempted to prove this to them, the mule began bucking unmercifully and threw Isaac off. Watt wrote: "I never saw anything give as much delight as this gave the Indians. They whooped and yelled and kept it up. Now and then it would subside and then break out again. We joined the Indians and laughed as they; everybody enjoyed it but brother Isaac."[68]

The Lakotas near Fort Laramie got the last laugh in another 1851 encounter, an event that ultimately created humor for everyone except the wagon boss. This six-foot-one, 210-pound man was regarded as the strongest person in the train, but he could not pull the string on a bow that was presented to him. Eyewitness Hugo Hoppe noted that one of the Indians "ran his hand down the full length of our boss almost to the ground and then held some imaginary article about his shoulders," much to the Indians' amusement. At Fort Laramie, Hoppe and his friends learned that the gesturing had described a woman's dress and blanket, implying that the wagon boss was a woman because he could not pull the bowstring.[69]

Whites of all ages also attempted their own tricks on American Indians. Twelve-year-old Virginia Reed Murphy surprised an inquisitive group of Lakotas who kept peeking in her wagon to see a mirror. Mischievous and unafraid, Virginia took the extension of a small telescope and placed it at the end of a stovepipe. The contraption resembled a moving eye, and the young girl delighted in her ability to make the Indian men run away.[70]

Lorenzo Stephens observed an even more improbable scene from a man who repeatedly removed his false teeth in the presence of Indians and contorted his face in such a way as to expose his gums with a massive grin. Stephens thought the Indians might have turned away in fright because they perceived the man to be an evil spirit, but on further reflection he doubted the simplicity of the explanation. He truly wondered "just what they did think," and, by doing so, accepted the Indians' actions on their own terms.[71]

Unfortunately, not all attempts at humor were so well received by some emigrants. When a group of Lakota men descended upon a Mormon handcart encampment in 1859, they took on the personalities of fierce warriors as they danced and sang and lassoed some of the carts. William Atkin recognized that they were "play acting" and were reveling in the apprehensions of the Mormons. Amid their ferocious outcries, the Lakotas simultaneously laughed and joked about the effect they were having from "their own fun."[72] Five years later near the same spot, J. W. Broadwell witnessed another group of three hundred to four hundred Sioux who surrounded his train and made threatening but comical gestures. He concluded that these warriors had planned the scare as a joke, but the emigrant party remained vigilant just in case.[73] How many similar events were conducted in jest but were misinterpreted as provocative acts can only be surmised.

The reciprocal exchanges of social interplay between American Indians and overlanders did not limit themselves to feasts, conversations, dances, and games. These interludes of demonstrable trust and friendship manifested themselves in more tangible ways that benefited both groups of people. One such altruistic act was performed by a Dr. Harris while on the way to the California goldfields in 1850. Amid his socializing with a small band probably of Paiutes or Goshutes near Humboldt Lake, he observed that they were not only malnourished but also sick with what he diagnosed as "congestive fever." The doctor provided them with four boxes of pills in exchange for two horses that his party badly needed. Apparently, the pills had the desired effect, because the Indians returned and asked for further aid. Harris and three of his friends accompanied the Indians downriver to the village, where they administered more examinations and pills in return for additional horses. Both groups departed with eternal pledges of friendship for each other.[74]

In a reversal of roles, American Indians also provided emigrants with occasional medical help. When Isaac Ball was thrown from a wagon and broke his leg, a Dr. Blackerby set the bone and joined with other members of the wagon train who voted to leave the man in the care of local Indians. The Indians were favorable to the arrangement, but Ball was reluctant to be left behind. On the following day he and a close friend who remained at his side rejoined the train.[75] More ironic was the fate of an unidentified man who had been inadvertently shot by members of a nearby wagon train while on guard duty. When challenged by their sentry in the night's darkness, he foolishly "gave an Indian yell," and they fired on him. Rather than delay their departure, his friends left him in the care of an Indian who was agreeable. The historical record remains silent on whether the injured man recovered or whether he died from the severity of the gunshot wound.[76]

A more moving expression of American Indian sympathy for whites occurred not in extending health care but in a demonstration of concern through a traditional Sioux mourning rite. Christian Lyngaa Christensen was only five years old when his Mormon immigrant parents undertook the overland trek to Salt Lake City in 1860. While traveling along the Platte River, his father was accidentally shot and killed by a fellow traveler. The funeral drew the attention of a number of Sioux men and women, who paid their respects in traditional ways and offered help to the sorrowful widow and her children. As an adult, Christensen later wrote: "It was so wonderful to see the sympathy and pity and weeping for Mother by large, husky women of the Great Sioux Nation, who had befriended us out in the wilderness on the Plains of Nebraska."[77]

The lamentations directed by a group of Sioux men and women toward this Mormon family in their hour of need epitomized the ultimate expression of human sensitivity. Efforts to comfort the grieving kin transcended matters of race, language, and culture and the fact that the persons involved were not close associates or relatives. None of the differences between these two groups mattered at that moment, when all persons could fully appreciate the need for emotional support. In the display of unity, strangers truly seemed to be like friends, and the moving event was doubtless remembered by participants on both sides for many years to come.

In so many grand and small ways, American Indians and whites came to better appreciate each other during the banner years of overland passage to Oregon, California, and the Salt Lake Valley. Of course, many people from both populations maintained their biases and suspicions throughout the thirty-year mass migration, making little effort to see each other as anything except a potential threat. But for those who opened their minds, lowered their guards, and extended their generosity, an entirely new range of potential experiences lay ahead. Overland emigrants may not have had much time to spend with any specific population of Indians and not much opportunity to traverse the cultural chasm to achieve a true understanding of tribal life. Yet even a partial crossing of the chasm could lead to important new relationships and a willingness to see American Indians as human beings rather than as the romanticized or villainous caricatures conveyed by eastern popular culture. Those whites who correctly perceived the cultural values of reciprocity, generosity, and hospitality at work, and responded to these in kind, profited from their relationship with Indians. Social exchanges involving feasting, conversation, fellowship, entertainment, and recreation would prepare the way for more substantial acts of friendship between Indians and whites. In contrast to earlier-mentioned examples of aid rendered by American Indians for purposes of increasing trade or for specific compensation, these more substantial actions were often granted without any demands or expectations of tangible reward. In both types of cases, the interpersonal relationships that were successfully established marked a humanizing of the trail experience for both American Indians and their eastern guests.

6

Accruing the Benefits
Friends as Advocates and Benefactors

S mall acts of interracial kindness were common along the western trails, frequent enough to sensitize both American Indians and emigrants to each group's basic humanity. As the 1840s gave way to the 1850s, and as the numbers of overlanders substantially increased, the opportunities for contact and communications multiplied. Although lasting personal friendships were impossible to maintain among the migrating populations, the amiable relations created by thousands of individuals blossomed into a climate of improved feelings all along the line of march.

Fortunately for both groups, these enhanced connections paid dividends that transcended mere curiosity and neighborliness. In many cases, the new level of understanding achieved in these personal linkages created a kind of advocacy role between both groups for each other. Fittingly, many American Indians protected and aided the progress of their white counterparts, even while other tribal members provoked problems for the passing wagon trains. Likewise, many white men, women, and children championed Indian causes in both actions and the recorded word. The best documentation of these trends is found in the diaries, journals, letters, and reminiscences that were written while the trail experience was at its peak by the very people who became genuinely sensitive to Indian viewpoints.

Overlanders disagreed not only about the reliability of American Indians for rendering aid but also about what propelled these people toward acts of kindness. For some observers, Indians remained such ambiguous figures that their motivations seemed either totally incomprehensible or intrinsically villainous. But American Indians did act out of both practical concerns and cultural traditions that were thoroughly honorable. Furthermore, these actions made perfectly good sense within the context of American Indian worldviews, even though they were not always correctly perceived by whites.

Four categories of behavior encompass most of the reasons that western Indians cooperated closely with emigrants. First, the desire for cordial relations was a type of defense mechanism to prevent trouble with the heavily armed wagon trains. Indians who lived near the trails could ill afford constant friction with these "strangers," especially of the type that could lead to bloodshed.

Second, these villages depended heavily upon the trail traffic to provide the continuous flow of livestock and trade goods around which their economies and daily lives were structured. Any long-term disruption in the exchange process would certainly endanger the existences of tribes that had chosen to affix themselves to the American migratory process. Furthermore, an interruption in the flow of goods would create a secondary impact on the distribution of trade items to the more remote areas of the West. As crucial middlemen in the extensive network of trade, these commercial intermediaries were increasingly essential to the expectations of distant American Indian populations as well.

A third motivation for good conduct concerned the Indians' desire to affect policy-making in Washington, D.C., and to win influence among the agents of the Indian Bureau and the military officers of the U.S. Army. By 1850, many of the headmen of the villages that dotted the trails had made one or more diplomatic trips to the nation's capital, or at least to St. Louis, to meet with government officials. Throughout the decade, their comprehension of negotiating tactics improved, and they were tireless in their efforts to point out their many acts of kindness in facilitating the cross-continental migration. William Kilgore was struck by the level of sophistication among a group of Sioux who had settled near Chimney Rock at the time of his visit in 1850. In addition to elaborating their long record of friendship for Americans, the chiefs urged the overlanders to sign a petition that they wanted to present before Congress. The document specifically called upon the government to make remuneration to the Indian nations because of their incalculable acts of generosity and because of the diminution of their resources.[1]

The fourth motivation was primarily a private one, and it was more deeply connected to patterns of traditional Indian behavior than were the other three pragmatic concerns. This virtue was recognized and practiced across all of Native North America, both intra- and intertribally, and it was soon directed toward white people who were deemed worthy of its graces. This virtue of "individual honor" was only as strong as the possessor was willing to make it, but American Indians of all social ranks took the ethical concept very seriously. While righteous conduct was the visible representation of this virtue, the heart of the concept rested upon remaining true to one's word in spirit and in deed. Repeatedly, Indian men and women who came to have even brief and casual relationships with individual overlanders demonstrated this time-honored etiquette. More often than not, their word proved dependable because dishonor followed any person who pledged his or her word and then broke it in the spirit of planned deceit.

Unlike the first three categories of Indian motivation that were often governed by some sense of expectant reward, the fourth category issued from the heart, and no repayment or reciprocal obligation was expected. But conversely, if a personal bond such as this was established across racial lines, whites were also obligated to be true to their word, whether they understood the principle or not. Should they break their word and their ties of friendship, swift punishment might follow.[2]

Whether motivated simply by practical matters or loftier notions of righteous behavior, American Indians and whites who came to empathize with each other were capable of unlocking a great reservoir of benevolent feelings and actions. Even more promising was the realization that both groups could accrue important benefits from each other without sacrificing any of their own cultural integrity.

One of the most frequently articulated themes of Indian assistance to overlanders was the return of missing or purloined livestock. Given their susceptibility to often-repeated negative stereotypes, it is not surprising that many whites were quick to blame Indians for the theft of horses, oxen, and mules any time they were missing. This charge was a common one because the animals had to be turned out for grazing in the evenings, often at a distance from the wagons. Even when placed under the watchful eyes of night herders, the livestock were prone to wander away in the darkness or to drift into herds belonging to nearby wagon trains. But as the trip progressed, overlanders learned that every "missing cow" was not necessarily a "stolen cow." Some discovered that when approached with respect, American Indians could provide the best hope for retrieval of these valuable animals.

Examples of this form of Indian cooperation appeared at every juncture of the overland trek. For instance, Mormons who utilized Winter Quarters as their jumping-off spot to the West between 1846 and 1852 experienced numerous cases of Omaha tribal members taking oxen to feed their hungry families. Brigham Young and other Mormon elders tolerated some of the "theft" as the necessary price of living on Omaha treaty lands and utilizing their resources. Yet when they considered the frequency of the act to be excessive, they took their complaints to tribal leaders and negotiators such as Big Elk, Young Elk, and Logan Fontenelle. Sometimes, at great personal expense to themselves, these and other Omaha spokesmen returned the livestock in question or made some other compensatory agreement.[3] Unfortunately, the tenuous relationship between Omahas and Mormons further deteriorated after Brigham Young departed with the Pioneer Band in 1847 for the Salt Lake Valley. Because the area surrounding Winter Quarters was inadequate to support both populations, mutual seizures of food supplies increased, and the two groups gradually became less tolerant of each other.[4]

The Sioux villages located along the Platte River between Ash Hollow and Fort Laramie were also the settings for parallel negotiations during the early years of contact. For one, Brulé leader Spotted Tail worked toward the restoration of harmonious relations after a missing ox was found butchered some distance from the military post. The Sioux indicated that a teenaged boy had committed the act and that no offense was intended by the broader population. Spotted Tail went to the aggrieved owner, a Mr. Leroy, and remunerated him with a bison robe and a pony. To make further amends, he gave a second white man, a Mr. Ferber, three ponies to make up for three of his oxen that had been missing since the previous evening. The fact that wagon train members then gave two sides of beef and half a sack of flour in return probably symbolized to the Indians a completion of the compensatory cycle in the best of ritualistic fashion.[5] Another Oglala Sioux chief named Whirlwind, best known for his six foot two height and ample girth approaching 250 pounds, was also frequently cited by overlanders during the early 1850s for his many generous acts. Several observers were quick to point out that Whirlwind routinely punished even his own people if they upset relations between the village and the emigrants.[6]

Farther to the west, similar actions were reported among the tribes of the plateau country and the Columbia River basin. When Washington Smith Gilliam's party reached the vicinity of present-day Pendleton, Oregon, in 1844, they solicited help from the Cayuse headman known as Stickus. They reported a missing horse to him and, in a respectful manner, indicated that they suspected it had been taken by one of the headman's relatives. Stickus indicated that the wagon train should continue its journey and that he personally would bring the horse to them. On the following day and true to his word, he returned the animal in question without hinting about any gift or present being necessary for the benevolent act.[7]

A personal guarantee of aid was also borne out at the Dalles during the following year when residents of a riverside village apparently stole two horses. Andrew Chambers and several men of his train called upon the leader of the village to explain their dilemma. The unidentified Indian promised to inquire about the charge, and within three hours he brought the horses to their relieved owners. Although the headman remained evasive about who had originally taken the animals—alleging only that they had been stolen by some "bad Indians"—he suggested that some payment was in order. The awarding of a single shirt for the two expensive horses seemed a fair exchange to Chambers and his friends.[8]

Christianized Indians from the Waiilatpu mission of Marcus and Narcissa Whitman received special praise from emigrants on several wagon trains because of their efforts to return missing livestock. Medorem Crawford's party not only received food and helpful directions from these Cayuses, but they also benefited from other unsolicited aid that required extensive efforts by the Cayuses. Rather than automatically assuming that Indians had stolen several of their horses, Crawford and his associates strongly suspected that the untethered animals had wandered away during the evening. Their suspicions proved correct, as the Cayuses promptly located and brought back the horses. Furthermore, several of them escorted the train to the Whitman Mission, ever vigilant to point out sources of good grass and water along their chosen route. On all of these counts, Crawford profusely thanked the tribal members and commended their "moral honesty" for not requesting or demanding compensation for their efforts.[9]

Sometimes the Indian searches for missing livestock did not appear so altruistic. Overlanders occasionally hired Indians to locate the animals, while simultaneously believing that these same men, or some of their friends, had stolen the animals in the first place. The white owners rationalized that payment of a few goods for the more valuable horses, oxen, and mules was the only way to restore the means to continue their western trip. Elizabeth Dixon Smith Geer noted in 1847 that her party rewarded several Sioux men with payment of $15.00 because they had been so honest in their diligent search for some cattle, even though it was the white owners who ultimately found the cattle.[10] On an equal scale of value, William Smedley's party was greatly relieved when an Indian man went in search of six valuable horses near the slopes of Mount Hood. Although they did not suspect him of any collusion in the disappearance of the animals, they dickered with his request for $6.00 compensation, and he lowered it to an unspecified amount.[11]

Less pleased were several emigrant parties that paid Indians for the return of livestock, even when evidence of theft was strong. Lucretia Lawson Epperson privately accused some Lakotas of stampeding horses and cattle from the night herd and then brazenly demanding $1.00 per head for each of the same. With no other options available, the owners "played the game" and ransomed their livestock at that price.[12] Even more agitated about this form of duplicity was Catherine Margaret Haun, who asserted in 1849 that this was a common practice among most tribes. She especially singled out the Paiute and Goshute bands for her ire, even though she possessed only thirdhand information to document her charges. Haun repeated an earlier rumor that a man had swapped his watch for a yoke of oxen from Indians who were camped near the Humboldt Sink. Several hours later, he learned that these oxen had been stolen from another party whose members could clearly identify the animals by their markings. Luckily, the two "owners" worked out a deal to share the services of the essential animals, but not without loudly cursing the Indians for their theft.[13]

In letters written to Missouri friends during 1855, William Keil revealed not only the strength of his religious and reformist spirit but also his newfound affection for American Indians. This messianic leader of a communal group heading to Oregon was tireless in his praise for virtually all the tribes he met along the way, and he included favorable mention of them in each of his letters. One such epistle, written at the end of the troubled journey, concluded with the words, "In short, my only happiness on the plains were the meetings with the Indians."[14] Keil offered insight into his feelings when he described how spiteful members of another wagon train tried to have him arrested at the Dalles because of his alleged anti-American statements spoken in the presence of Indians. The petty charges emanated from the fact that Keil was a recent immigrant from Germany and because of his numerous defenses of Indians. Maj. Granville Haller, the local military officer, listened to the charges and summarily dismissed them as groundless.[15]

Keil's infatuation with the Cayuse people transcended mere curiosity, and he remained in their Grande Ronde Valley village for several days. His efforts blossomed into a friendship with four chiefs, especially Camaspelo, who was much the diplomat and proper host. The chiefs invited Keil to remain among them and to settle into the farmer's life, but he felt responsible for the utopian group that he was leading and continued to his original destination in the Willapa Valley of western Oregon. Describing the Indians' offer in a subsequent letter, Keil plaintively wrote: "If I had done so, I would be better off than I am now, for no brother and sister could have loved me more than those people loved and respected me."[16]

William Keil was certainly one of the more outspoken defenders of Indians as trustworthy human beings, but he was not alone in articulating that viewpoint. Nancy Hunt, who journeyed the California Trail in 1854 with her consumptive husband, reduced the diplomatic equation to one of merely observing the Golden Rule on both sides of the racial divide. During the trip, she learned to dismiss the many rumors of Indians waiting in ambush, and instead she consistently offered food to any who requested it. In a simple, matter-of-fact style, she wrote: "We always treated the Indians well and with respect, and they never molested us at any time."[17] Teenager William Barlow took special pride in the open-mindedness of his father, Samuel, who never missed an opportunity to visit Indian camps, smoke with the men, and converse with anyone who was interested. Samuel transported a large supply of tobacco during his 1845 migration to Oregon because he had heard that western Indians highly prized the commodity for social and ceremonial uses. Rather than charging a price for the relatively expensive substance, he gave it away as a means for creating a respectful entry into the Indian encampments. In return, he was rewarded with the fellowship that he sought, rather than mere material gain.[18]

As with the experiences of countless other overlanders, Lavinia Porter had begun her 1860 cross-country trip filled with alarmist notions about Indians, but the farther she traveled, the more she came to appreciate their presence. Because she and her husband frequently split away from the larger wagon trains and proceeded alone or with small groups of emigrants, they had every reason to be fearful. Yet in her reminiscences she asserted that her fellow Americans were the far greater villains and instigators of mayhem, while the Indians were "chivalrous" and protective of her family.[19] Writing in 1858, a soldier traversing the trail to Salt Lake City extolled the virtues of the Lakota people. But he also warned that if government officials and migrating ruffians did not respect their rights, it "would cause the war cry to ring from the Platte River to the Canada lines."[20] His sympathies were clearly with the "peaceful" Lakotas, and his admonition about abuses of their rights proved prophetic within a few short years.

Other trail authors addressed even broader concepts to their audiences as they attacked the very stereotypes that dehumanized Indians in the public consciousness. William Chandless, author of a highly literate 1855 account of driving freight wagons along the Platte River to Salt Lake City, reached a large British audience when his book was published in London two years after the events. Although he was not completely free of his own prejudices, Chandless advised his readers not to measure Indians by white standards. Rather, it was important to judge them from within the context of their own societies and values.[21] Whether his message of cultural pluralism struck a responsive chord among the audience is not known, but the message was an appropriate one even for the mid-nineteenth century.

More important than mere philosophizing were the direct actions that overlanders undertook to benefit American Indians. Each of these examples, and many others like them, demonstrated respect for Indian people, and they were undertaken in a humanitarian spirit only after the whites got to know their Indian counterparts personally. The benevolent actions began in small ways, such as on the Malheur River in 1850, when William Frush brought a stray horse into camp and held it until local Indians arrived and identified it as theirs. Before returning the property, Frush participated in smoking the pipe of friendship and socializing with the Indians—all proper etiquette for the shared moment.[22] During the same summer, a group of Mormons apprehended one of their own at Bear River ferry and returned a horse to an elderly Shoshone man who had been victimized by the thief.[23]

The stakes were even higher in 1845, when Benjamin Franklin Bonney's mother and aunt nursed back to health a young Indian girl who had been found along the present Utah and Nevada border. Emaciated, nude, and covered with sores, the girl had subsisted on clover roots and grass for an extended period of time. Bonney's mother and aunt doctored the girl, provided her with clothing, and comforted her in every way. Having remained at the dry camp for several days, the party needed to push on, and they decided to leave the girl behind, with the hope that her people would soon find her. With no other options available to them short of kidnapping, Bonney's mother and aunt rejoined the train with tears running down their faces.[24]

On two occasions, the sublime and ridiculous natures of white behavior were demonstrated in the handling of "Indian problems." In the first instance, during the late summer of 1857, Helen Carpenter witnessed the formation of a lynch mob among the members of a nearby wagon train that had lost sixty head of cattle to Paiute raiders. They captured one of the alleged raiders and demanded that he take them to the Indian camp. Among the wikiups, they found the oxen, along with women, children, and elderly men. Having originally promised the captive his freedom, they now forced him to run across the rocky landscape, severely beat him with ramrods, and prepared to hang him. Fortunately, the father of Tom Rawls stood up to the lynch mob, waived his gun in their faces, and talked some sense into their vengeance-ridden souls. His bold act carried the day, as the Indian was released and fled the scene immediately.[25]

In the second case, Isaac Wistar and members of his California-bound party helped free some Indians captured by other white men who intended them harm. Although Wistar did not know these particular Indians as close friends or even as acquaintances, he was motivated to help them by an event that had occurred in the same vicinity almost three years earlier. Somewhat dubiously, he surmised that these were probably the same Indians who had helped members of the Donner Party prior to their final debacle in the Sierra Nevadas. As a kind of historical payback, Wistar distributed the last of his party's hardtack among these Indians, and they quickly dispersed into the wilderness.[26]

At times, a more extended relationship with American Indians occurred only after an overland family had settled permanently in the West. Many decades after completing the journey to Oregon, Amelia Hadley recalled how her family adopted a five-year-old Siskiyou boy. He grew up with equal status in the family, participated in all of its work and recreational activities, and excelled in the difficult task of breaking wild horses.[27] After years of cattle ranching in California, J. Watt Gibson moved to the mining region of western Nevada, where he developed a close association with one group of Indians. In his later recollections, Gibson described in great detail the joint hunts, feasts, social gatherings, and even the pasturing of horses and cattle on the same land. Gibson remarked that the level of friendship was so apparent that even his dogs sensed the right of the Indians to come and go at their will on the Gibson lands.[28] In both the Hadley and Gibson examples, their first sensitivities toward Indians emerged from the trail experiences and matured with the passage of time.

Advocacy of justice for Indians became even more pronounced among overlanders who bluntly defined white misbehavior as the primary cause of problems along the trails. In 1852, William Byers wrote in his journal that no "Indian problem" existed along the Oregon Trail, and even though considerable livestock had been stolen, it was mostly the work of renegade white men.[29] Nelson Miltmore testified that the alleged Indians who had attacked his train along the Humboldt River in April 1860 "spoke good English, wore long beards" and were unquestionably "whites in Indian disguise."[30] Susan Bordeaux Bettelyoun, a mixed-blood woman who grew up as an Oglala Lakota, observed the same type of deceit, especially during the chaotic years of the Civil War. She charged that white outlaws—whom the Lakotas called "Gray White Men"—were stealing the choicest livestock and other wealth from the territory, and the Sioux were being unfairly blamed.[31]

Sometimes the redemptive message about Indian actions and viewpoints reached a larger audience than did mere diary entries or letters sent to eastern relatives. In 1851, A. B. Chambers, editor of the widely circulated *Missouri Republican* out of St. Louis, penned an extended editorial explaining the changed behavior of the Cheyennes during the preceding half decade. He noted that they formerly had been looked upon "as the best Indians of the Plains," praised for their many virtues, their military power, and their friendship with whites.

But because of abuses directed against them by overlanders and traders, they had become "saucy and unscrupulous," and they viewed whites with contempt. Although Chambers did not excuse this haughty behavior among the Cheyennes, he did not see them as the cause of failed relations.[32] In truth, his judgment about their increasingly hostile intentions was premature at best, because most Cheyennes remained friendly toward the overlanders well into the late 1850s.

Government officials who were situated in the West also spoke in favor of Indian peoples who had been unfairly portrayed by whites. Agent Jacob Holeman was an especially strong advocate for the tribes of Utah Territory during the early 1850s, and he minced no words about certain types of white men being the instigators of trouble. He singled out the illegal liquor dealers—those who operated informally from the passing wagon trains and those who came year-round from the road ranches of California—as the primary disturbers of the peace. Because of inadequate law enforcement in these remote regions, these nefarious traffickers operated with virtual impunity. Even more threatening in Agent Holeman's mind were the frequent overtures made by these immoral ruffians to the Great Basin tribes to run off the livestock of wagon trains and sell them to the traders.[33] In an 1852 report to the commissioner of Indian Affairs, Holeman summarized his many conversations with emigrants who indicated that while tribes of the Great Basin generally had remained passive and even helpful, white outlaws were a constant threat to the wagon trains.[34]

At about the same time, Brigham Young reported that a small number of these same tribes had become hostile, but only because of injustices directed against them. He specifically cited an incident whereby members of a wagon train had killed at least two Shoshone women and had stolen horses from their relatives. This caused several Shoshones to seek revenge by running off the cattle of an entirely different, and uninvolved, train. Such cycles of vengeance were likely to recur, and innocents on both sides would suffer, according to Young.[35] Echoing that sentiment a decade later, Agent John Owen noted that the situation had only gotten worse, and the Great Basin tribes were increasingly reviled by people who could not possibly know their depth of suffering. Speaking of the injustice, Owen wrote, "Their present hostile attitude can in a great Measure be attributed to the treatment they have recd from unprincipled White Men passing through their Country. They have been robed [sic] Murdered their Women outraged etc. and in fact outrages have been committed by White Men that the heart would shudder to record."[36]

While white outlaws seemed to have been a widely reported phenomenon on the trails, other witnesses blamed the trigger-happy nature of some white men as the cause of major problems with Indians. Many overlanders attributed this phenomenon to a level of paranoia that emanated from the old adage of "shoot now and ask questions later." Helen Marnie Stewart told of an "old bachelor" traveling with her party who lived in constant fear of a massacre. He wanted to organize the armed men from several large companies, march to whatever Indian village was nearby, and kill all of the inhabitants, including the babies.[37] No such offensive was undertaken at the behest of this unstable character, but had the local Indians provided a provocative incident at that moment, some members of Stewart's train undoubtedly would have served in a campaign of vengeance.

Hugh Cosgrove witnessed another event at Salmon Falls that was innocent enough in its own context but which almost sparked a violent reaction from nervous American spectators. An Indian man came into camp dressed in an outlandish tall silk hat and vest, strutting around in a haughty manner. Some of the whites interpreted this as a threatening gesture, and they prepared to shoot him, regardless of the consequences from other Indians. Cosgrove perceived that the bold actions of the man were really to gain people's attention and to assure him a pivotal place in the day's barter. When he completed the transactions, he went away without fanfare and probably unaware of the danger he had created, according to Cosgrove.[38]

In an 1851 report to his superiors, Agent Jacob Holeman explained that because many emigrants were conditioned to think the worst about Indians, they were prone to accept the most outlandish of rumors. This led some of the nervous overlanders to lump all Indians in one menacing category and to shoot at them at the first opportunity. Even the most peaceful of Indians responded in kind, and countless cycles of retribution began on the Great Plains and in the Great Basin.[39]

While paranoia and trigger-happy tendencies sometimes led to needless acts of intimidation and violence, another phenomenon posed an even larger threat to peace—deep racial hatred and demonizing of American Indians. Many overlanders were quick to condemn these barbaric acts not only for their immorality but also because they often unleashed a wave of Indian reprisals. Perhaps the most frequently repeated trail story of such a shocking atrocity was one that appeared in several versions. By all accounts, mixed-blood trapper John Greenwood, who was traveling with the 1844 Stephens-Townsend-Murphy Party, had a strong hatred for Indians, despite the fact that his mother was of the Crow tribe and his father made his living in trade with many tribes. During the trip, Greenwood outraged his companions by blaming Indians for everything that went wrong and for his desire to kill them all. Moses Schallenberger disgustedly recorded that "it would require the utmost exercise of authority to prevent him from precipitating hostilities. It seemed as if he was more anxious to kill an Indian than to reach California."[40]

During the following year, Greenwood acted on his irrational obsession while serving as a guide for another wagon train on the way to California. Despite the friendliness of the Paiutes along the Humboldt River, Greenwood shot a defenseless Indian man who had come into the camp only to trade some skins. Witness William Swasey described it as a "wanton and dastardly murder," in marked contrast to the efforts of other members of the party to treat the mortally wounded man. They subsequently disarmed the murderer, held a "council of war" to decide his fate, found him guilty, and physically drove him from the train. Swasey disgustedly wrote: "We all felt that we would much rather take our chances of finding the trail than travel in company with such a vile murderer."[41]

Greenwood's shame may have been one of the most widely known tales of anti-Indian hostility, but it did not stand alone. Fortunately, other emigrants were prepared to rebuke the monstrous acts and even to take an unpopular stand if necessary. Benjamin Franklin Owen engaged in a heated debate with a Mr. Clark who wanted to mount up members of his company and kill several Indian men who had been following the wagons at a distance. Although Owen did not know the identities or intentions of the Indian trailers, he lambasted Clark for labeling them as "hostile" and possibly provoking them toward violent reprisal.[42]

Even more extreme were the rantings of an unidentified member of Cornelius Cole's 1849 western crossing. Cole, a future U.S. senator from California, recalled that the man had evidenced a pronounced anti-Indian bias ever since the wagon train had departed Missouri. The man fervently argued that one of his distant ancestors had suffered at the hands of Indians, and he now was going to administer his generational vengeance on the first Indian he encountered. Furthermore, he wanted to be able to boast about the act once he returned home from the goldfields. He stopped bragging and threatening only after other members of the party impressed upon him that if he killed any Indian, he would be next.[43]

Soldiers who traveled the western trails sometimes saw the same bravado among fellow dragoons. One participant in the 1857–58 Mormon War, who identified himself only by the pseudonym "Utah," told of the strong anti-Indian bias among his messmates. He further noted that this immaturity was not restricted only to the uneducated enlisted men but also permeated the officer corps at the highest ranks. To his newspaper audience, "Utah" wrote with irony as well as wisdom: "When you read of the dreadful doings of the red man, hereafter, remember that it is but the natural effect of the actions of civilized Christian men upon his 'untutored mind.'"[44] His words raised the question of which group really was the "civilized race."

Perhaps the kinds of Indian haters that "Utah" referred to were similar to the braggarts that Lavinia Porter singled out for scorn. After accompanying these people for over a week and listening to their endless invectives against American Indians, Porter and her family elected to leave the wagon train and travel alone. At no time during their trip were they bothered by any Indians, and in fact one Indian man briefly traveled with them as a guide and protector.[45]

An even stronger denunciation of this kind of malicious behavior came from Hugh Cosgrove, who was forced to listen to the racist rantings of two young men for several weeks. While out hunting, these two were surrounded by approximately forty Pawnee warriors and were forced to surrender their guns and clothing. The Indians jeered at and comically threatened the two panicked individuals before releasing them. Interestingly enough, the two rabble-rousers received no pity from members of the wagon train. Their fellow travelers, according to Cosgrove, deemed this an act of poetic justice, whereby the tables had been turned on these young men who had vowed they would kill at least one Indian apiece before reaching Oregon.[46]

Although overlanders were not likely to execute members of their company who were found guilty of abusing or killing Indians, more than one wagon train was quick to banish such culprits. Jesse Applegate remembered a dramatic confrontation that temporarily dampened the enthusiasm of his party while traveling through northeastern Kansas in 1843. A man whom Applegate contemptuously identified as a "Mexican" had apparently cut off the hand of an Indian and had placed it on a stake in the middle of camp. Public indignation reached a boiling point, which led to a meeting of the adults, who forced the man to leave their company.[47]

Two years later, members of Benjamin Franklin Bonney's wagon train faced a similar dilemma but acted with less dispatch than had Applegate's party. They feared the 225-pound "Southerner" who traveled with them, because he possessed a violent temper and a willingness to kill. This ferocious Texan, Jim Kinney, added to his sordid reputation when he captured a defenseless Indian man on the Humboldt River and literally made him into a slave. He bound the Indian's hands, tied a rope around his neck, fastened it to the rear of a wagon, and beat the defenseless man savagely with a bullwhip. After more than a week of ill treatment, the Indian made his escape and simultaneously managed to steal Kinney's prized Kentucky rifle. In this case, other members of the train could take no pride in having helped free the captive, but all apparently were elated that the feared bully had been foiled and belated justice had been served.[48]

Amid the great variety of responses between American Indians and whites, perhaps the only factor that remained constant in their relationships was their inability to totally trust each other. Differences in language, customs, value systems, and long-term goals separated the two peoples, a divide that many on both sides cared not to bridge. Furthermore, the faces of the strangers were always changing, as each wagon train left behind a group of Indians with which it had just traded and socialized, only to press on ever westward. Each new week brought the potential of meeting unfamiliar bands and tribes who might or might not share the inclinations of previously contacted groups. Relationships, therefore, had to be reinvented constantly, and this expenditure of energy and emotion proved taxing on both populations. Furthermore, even in the best of times, misbehavior, insults, and violence—whether accidental or intentional—occurred frequently enough that neither overlanders nor Indians could entirely lower their guards in the presence of strangers.

Yet for all the fundamental issues that separated American Indians and whites, enough people on both sides tried to understand and aid each other. Many of these helpful gestures came purely from practical concerns of maintaining peace and trade, but others truly emerged from the heart. In both cases, however, American Indians and whites profited from the improved relationships.

Simple acts of kindness prevailed on many occasions, such as Captain Howard Stansbury giving his goggles to an elderly Cheyenne man who was afflicted with chronically sore eyes.[49] Mormon faithful benefited when Indians periodically helped pull their heavy handcarts for some distance.[50] Dragoon Percival Lowe admired the hard work and humanity of Potawatomi families in northeastern Kansas, who freely gave pumpkins, cabbage, potatoes, and fresh pork to hungry soldiers without any compensation.[51] And mountain man Rufus Sage immortalized in words the grace of elderly Pawnee headman Red Eagle, who took the new moccasins off his own feet and gave them to Sage, whose footwear was old and beyond repair. The mountain man and trail traveler asked the rhetorical question of his reading audience: "What white man would have done the like? And this was done by the poor Indian, not from expectation of reward, but through the promptings of innate benevolence."[52]

The humanitarian acts that punctuated relationships between American Indians and emigrants helped collectively strengthen interracial harmony along the overland trails during the mid-nineteenth century. The mutually beneficial, and often reciprocal, actions were somewhat analogous to the situation found in what historian Richard White has labeled as the "middle ground" in his study of Great Lakes Indian-European relations during the colonial era. White argues that the two vastly different groups came together on the basis of rough equality, each able to supply to the other things that it did not possess. While the two cultures often misunderstood each other and even regarded each other as inferiors, they found "shared meanings and practices of the middle ground."[53] Curiosity, trade, protection, material assistance, and the need for friends—these were all proper motivations to make representatives of Native America and white America into friendly neighbors. Individual friendships were often fleeting, but the culture of generosity and empathy increased to encompass many more souls and to maximize the opportunities for further contact.

Unfortunately, the mutually advantageous exchanges were strongest only over the short run. As increased numbers of migrants set out from the East to follow the western trails, they also brought negative legacies of disease, alcohol, punitive government policies, and, above all, stress on western resources. By the mid-1850s, new tensions began to arise for the tribes that had settled along the well-trodden trails. To be sure, acts of friendship and mutual aid continued at a high level after that time, but alarming new factors would have to be reckoned with in the coming decade and a half.

7

Responding to the Alarm
Bison, Epidemics, Burials, and Fires

The great overland migration to the Oregon country began as a trickle in the early 1840s, gradually increased its surge throughout the rest of the decade as Mormons joined the exodus, and entered the 1850s like a torrent as California-bound gold rushers headed across the Great Plains and the Great Basin. American Indians, who had been so welcoming of emigrants during the first half of the migration cycle, gradually came to see the dangers of such an unimpeded migration, and some developed new strategies for dealing with the changes. To be sure, with the exception of the Mormons, very few of these overlanders were settling in locations along the trails. Most of their communities were initially confined to the Willamette Valley of Oregon and the mother lode country of California, where Indian populations were quickly decimated by their presence. But for the majority of tribes considered in this study, physical occupation of the land was less an immediate threat than was the pressure on natural resources and the disruption of long-established Indian ways of life by the encroachment of whites.

In reflecting back on these trends from today's vantage point, conflict between these two differing cultures seems to have been inevitable, but that was not necessarily the consensus among the generation who lived through the events. Even as late as 1856, when troubles accelerated between overlanders and some of the Great Plains and Great Basin tribes, peaceful commerce, mutual aid, and fellowship were still major components of the ongoing contact. Hope sprang eternal for continued good relations, and people on both sides of the racial divide worked toward that goal. Unfortunately, the sheer force of migrating numbers, not the evil engendered by a small percentage of participants, provided whatever element of inevitability for conflict that existed. The overlanders may have been merely "passing through" the lands of most tribes, but their passage left a mighty imprint on the landscape and threatened the very resources that made Indian societies possible.

Although precise migration figures remain elusive, military officers at Fort Kearny and Fort Laramie maintained unofficial registers for overlanders who visited the two posts and took the time to enter information about their families and traveling companions. These registers were by no means exact, and many people who camped in the area of these posts went unreported because they did not cross the Platte or Laramie River to visit the respective military settlements. Yet even the incomplete registers provide tangible evidence of how great the migratory flood became by the 1850s. Trail historian Merrill Mattes concluded that on the single day of May 24, 1849, a virtual tidal wave of traffic amounting to five hundred or six hundred wagons and 2,000 to 2,500 people passed Fort Kearny, and a steady stream of overlanders continued throughout the following four months.[1] Indeed, military records maintained by the fort commander documented approximately 22,500 emigrants passing the post on the south side of the Platte River and at least another 5,000 on the north bank of the river between May 8 and June 22, 1849.[2]

The magnitude of the migration was widely reported during the busiest seasons, especially by newspapers that solicited information from military officers, freighters, and even overlanders themselves. Periodic issues of the *Missouri Republican* printed various estimates, especially during the early years of the California gold rush. The June 14, 1849, issue carried a story by Capt. Stewart Van Vliet, who, under the byline "Pawnee," observed that even a conservative approximation would place at least 20,000 persons and 60,000 animals on the road between Forts Kearny and Hall at that moment. He further noted that this total would not even include the numerous freighters' trains and military columns that were operating in both directions along the trails.[3] In a subsequent report, Van Vliet offered additional numbers and exclaimed: "The prairie is dotted with them as far as the eye can reach;

not an instant for the last two weeks has there been, that emigrants and emigrant wagons have not been in sight from this post."[4]

Because the Missouri River jumping-off towns were in competition to lure prospective emigrants to spend money in their establishments, the towns' newspapers published numerous stories about the magnitude of the migration. Often the stories were exaggerated "boosterism," but the *Frontier Guardian*, published at Council Bluffs, provided some of the most trustworthy early statistics on the size of the exodus. Relying upon the carefully prepared counts undertaken by Calvin Sommerville, a clerk at Fort Laramie, the newspaper printed the impressive numbers for the 1850 trail season of those who had passed that military post up to June 10: 16,915 men, 235 women, 242 children, 4,672 wagons, 14,974 horses, 4,641 mules 7,475 oxen, and 1,653 cows.[5] The dominance of male adult travelers in these early months of the 1850 trail season revealed how quickly the California-bound gold miner traffic was eclipsing the earlier family-oriented migration to Oregon.[6]

American Indian perceptions of these migrations were uncertain and ever changing, but clearly, with the passage of each year, their apprehensions increased. According to Father Pierre-Jean De Smet, the Indians who traveled with him from the Pacific Northwest along the Wyoming section of the Platte River road in 1851 were awestruck by the width of the trail made possible by the passage of so many people. They called it the Great Medicine Road because it was allegedly mysterious and incomprehensible to them as a source of endless waves of white population. According to De Smet, they surmised that the lands to the east must by now be entirely uninhabited since so many persons had left them. They further marveled when he told them that the numbers that had already passed to the west were not even a noticeable portion of the American population that was still to come.[7] Washakie and his Shoshone relatives provided a more literal name to describe the trail—the White-top Wagon Road—a reference to the ubiquitous line of white wagon canvases on the horizon.[8]

Perhaps white observers overestimated Indian naïveté about the increasing numbers of migrants, but it is clear that few American Indians would have had an adequate reference point to even imagine the extent of the American population residing between the Atlantic Ocean and the eastern rim of the Great Plains. Some tribal representatives had traveled to Washington, D.C., and an even greater number had visited St. Louis, but aside from these occasional diplomatic trips, few would

have had any real understanding of eastern demographics. Furthermore, because American Indians of the West tended to live in relatively
small villages of a few hundred people each, they were culturally sensi-
tized to thinking in terms of village, band, and tribal populations being
quite limited.

As early as 1845, Lt. J. Henry Carleton heard from various white
traders that the Sioux were totally convinced that the emigrants whom
they had contacted must comprise virtually all the white people who
existed in the United States.[9] California-bound Israel Lord reported
that some Shoshones refused to believe that in St. Louis alone resided
a population of whites that exceeded the entire Shoshone population
of the northern plateaus.[10] In the same year of 1849, expectant gold
miner Elijah Farnham ruminated about how only a decade earlier the
Sioux had contact with relatively few white men, but now it was not
uncommon to daily witness the passing of a wagon train extending five
or six miles in length and requiring over two hours to pass a common
point. He concluded that the Sioux were awestruck by these sights,
which offered both opportunity and danger to tribal life.[11]

Even if American Indians did not have a clear knowledge of the
enormity of the American population or of the numbers that would
eventually undertake the westward journey, they were aware of the
negative effects of this migration even from the early years. Evidence
of this realization is best documented among the plains tribes that
had already witnessed major declines in animal populations due to
the fur and hide trade, as well as the increasing bison slaughters
along the earlier-established Santa Fe Trail. During the spring of
1843, Nathan Boone, son of Daniel Boone and well-known militia
officer and scout in his own right, estimated that 100,000 bison were
being killed each year on the Great Pains, especially in present-day
western Oklahoma and Kansas. This early foray into the hide trade
by amateur and professional hunters guaranteed increased hardships
for the plains tribes, reported Boone, and should the slaughter continue at that rate, he declared that in a few years, the bison "will only
be known as a rare species."[12]

Capt. John C. Frémont had already noted a similar pattern of bison
destruction during his several excursions through the plains region.
While visiting with a representative of the American Fur Company at
Fort Laramie in 1843, Frémont learned that, on average, 90,000 bison
hides were being marketed annually by Indian and white hunters on

the northern and central plains alone, and this pattern had existed throughout the previous decade. He further recorded that this massive destruction had created great alarm among the Sioux and that they were left with only two long-term options: rob the white settlements to the east and the overlanders who passed through their lands, or unite with the Cheyennes and Arapahos to attack the Crows and drive them from the best remaining bison-hunting country in present-day Montana.[13]

Frémont's unsettling reference to a bloody war of intertribal extermination was echoed by other observers who had a close knowledge of the situation. Edwin Thompson Denig, representative of the American Fur Company on the upper Missouri River, affirmed that the bison slaughter was the primary cause of increased friction among the northern plains tribes. He and others predicted a virtual Armageddon to be launched by the numerically superior Sioux and their allies against neighboring tribes. The probable location of this final conflict would be along the Yellowstone River and its tributaries, which drained northward toward the Missouri River.[14] Father Pierre-Jean De Smet also saw a virtual inevitability about this conflagration, which would assure the virtual extermination of the less-populous tribes.[15]

One of the most plaintive calls of the early period came from the Cheyenne chief Old Soldier, who in 1845 told Col. Stephen Watts Kearny that the slaughter of bison was so great that his people could not hope to continue their bison-hunting way of life much longer. He hoped to accompany Kearny's return expedition so that he could visit with the eastern tribes and learn how they had been able to adjust to the new realities of white domination. Lt. William B. Franklin, a member of the same military reconnaissance, was struck by Old Soldier's sincerity, and he wrote in his journal that had the Cheyenne representative been allowed to visit the eastern settlements and other tribes, "perhaps it would have done a great deal of good."[16]

Plains tribes rarely wasted an opportunity to make this same point to other military officers who were traversing their domain during the mid-nineteenth century. They did not issue these complaints simply as a release of pent-up emotions, but they truly expected that higher authorities would correct the abuses and compensate them for previous destruction of bison and other resources. Nor were the immediate authorities oblivious to their pleas. Thomas H. Harvey, superintendent of Indian Affairs at St. Louis, became an able advocate for these tribes as he filed numerous reports with his Washington, D.C., superiors about how serious the problem had become for the plains tribes. Repeatedly during his tenure of the mid-1840s, Harvey blamed the increasing numbers of overland emigrants for the massive destruction of wild game and their habitat along the Platte River. Even though the vast majority of bison, antelope, and other animals escaped the slaughter, to be sure, they were deserting the immediate trail environs and, ironically, making life precarious for the peaceful Indians who resided nearby and who were aiding the westward migration.[17]

Superintendent Harvey liberally quoted from the reports of his field agents to support his plea for greater government attention to the problem. Agent Thomas P. Moore affirmed in 1846 that Indians at the Upper Missouri Agency were complaining of overlanders' "wanton destruction of game, the firing of the prairie, and other injuries."[18] During the following years, Agent Thomas Fitzpatrick advised that the government needed to purchase the privately owned fur-trading post of Fort Laramie or build a new military installation nearby because of the inevitable conflict that would soon arise due to the rapid decline in game.[19] In a separate letter of the same year, Fitzpatrick indicated that some of the Lakotas, Cheyennes, and Arapahos were starving because of the contraction of the bison ranges along the Platte River and the Santa Fe Trail. He warned of Indian reprisals unless the government provided rations and found a way to guarantee traditional food supplies.[20]

Indian agents, military officers, and fur traders were not the only persons to document the impact of bison destruction on the Great Plains; emigrants were also quick to note the trend. Even as early as 1841, a full decade before the migration reached its peak, pioneer trailblazer John Bidwell observed that hide hunters had already done so much damage that if the bison "continue to decrease in the same ratio that they have for the past 15 or 20 years, they will ere long become totally extinct."[21] William Kelly, who made the cross-continent journey in 1849, also blamed the fur-trading companies for the lion's share of the slaughter, but in that same year Elijah Farnham accused overlanders of most of the damage to the bison herds.[22] "Old Boone," reporting to the *Missouri Statesman* at the same time, lamented the fact that not only were the bison fast disappearing from the trail as a food source but also that bison chips, a crucial fuel source, were becoming more difficult for overlanders to procure. Rather than conveying any sympathy for the Indians on the matter, however, this unidentified correspondent warned only that future wagon trains would face greater privations on the trail unless settlements could be built all along the line of march.[23]

Somewhat surprisingly, many emigrants identified their fellow travelers as the greatest source of this biological devastation. John Minto recalled the disgusting action undertaken by members of his train who slaughtered forty-five bison in a single day for no other reason than "sport." They failed to take any of the approximately 40,000 pounds of fresh meat and walked away from the bloody scene with no remorse. Minto added that other animals from the herd were injured and perhaps subsequently died or suffered unmercifully from the pain of their wounds.[24] Lorenzo Sawyer was also left wondering what motivated some men to kill fifty buffalo, so crucial to the Plains Indians' ways of life, and then depart in such a jovial mood.[25] During his 1859 trip across the plains, James Berry Brown recorded his disgust at seeing seventeen buffalo carcasses within a forty-acre square, all killed by emigrants, and Ira Butterfield noted two years later that the bison had virtually disappeared from the Platte River valley. He only observed skeletons and occasional petrified skins of animals that had been killed years earlier by thoughtless emigrants.[26]

While many people merely recorded their feelings about this wasteful slaughter, others took direct action against the perpetrators. William Barlow recalled how his father admonished members of the company for killing bison with no thought of harvesting their meat and leaving the Indians of the plains without their natural food supply.[27] Similarly, the captain of John Braly's 1847 train called a general council and ordered that his associates hunt only for sustenance and not for sport.[28] Brigham Young had been even more emphatic in warning members of his 1847 Pioneer Band not to kill any wild animals beyond the numbers necessary for feeding the column. Young had learned while camped among the villages of the Omaha tribe near Winter Quarters that profligate slaughter of declining game was the surest way to provoke troubles with Indians—especially hungry ones.[29]

Other travelers not only condemned the waste and irresponsibility but also contrasted American Indian treatment of game animals with the more shortsighted view evidenced by many whites. John Bidwell later recalled that members of his party initially killed only enough bison to fill their cooking kettles, yet they soon lapsed into a general slaughter for the sole purpose of taking tongues and marrow bones. This unpardonable behavior stood in dramatic opposition to the Cheyennes whom Bidwell met along the trail. He praised the Cheyennes for their conservationist instincts and remarked that most killed only what was necessary for their survival.[30] British military officer George Frederick Ruxton, who traveled extensively in the West during the mid-1840s, was more acerbic: "But, to their [Indians'] credit be it spoken, no more was killed than absolutely required—unlike the cruel slaughter made by most of the white travelers across the plains, who wantonly destroy these noble animals, not even for the excitement of sport, but in cold-blood and insane butchery."[31]

Nor was the wholesale slaughter limited only to bison. Antelope were a frequent target of hunters who enjoyed their meat, but many animals were killed in what Sarah Cummins referred to as a "cruel sport."[32] Even more reprehensible was the wanton killing of prairie dogs, whose towns spread out at intervals along the banks of the Platte River. The bodies of these unfortunate rodents offered neither sustenance nor noble sport to overlanders, and yet they seem to have been frequent targets of bored marksmen.[33]

Diaries and pioneer reminiscences were likewise filled with casual references about killing wolves, rabbits, birds, beavers, and other small animals.[34] While camped east of the Loup Fork in central Nebraska during 1850, Solomon Osterhoudt wrote rather matter-of-factly in his diary about the prairie dogs that were encountered that day—"killed one of them. They certainly are a curiosity."[35] Nearer Fort Kearny and at about the same time, William Kilgore recorded how he and his friends amused themselves for about two hours by invading a prairie dog town and shooting its inhabitants.[36] Two months later, just west of the Raft River in present-day Idaho, Joseph Rhodes penned the words "killed three hawks."[37] Farther west at Salmon Falls, Ralph Geer's party so successfully fished for salmon that they threw away two-thirds of the supply because it was far more than they could use.[38]

Such were the actions so widely condemned by western Indians, and the outcry grew loudest among the plains tribes. Many of these complaints also contrasted the behaviors of competing cultures—one characterized by a strong symbiotic relationship with nature, the other with an emphasis on manipulating and conquering nature. At an 1864 council with Gen. Robert B. Mitchell, Brulé Sioux orator Spotted Tail blasted the duplicity of white authorities who demanded the removal of his people from the Platte River valley, while simultaneously destroying the wildlife and vegetation of such a beautiful homeland.

Although Spotted Tail was generally regarded as a friend of whites in subsequent years, he minced no words about the bad conduct of these greedy wasichu who journeyed through Indian lands.[39]

Decades later, Crow medicine woman Pretty Shield revealed the same sentiments to author Frank Linderman when she recalled how the Crows had never believed that whites could kill all of the bison. Yet the extermination of the bison had spelled the gradual weakening of her people's traditions, which were so solidly based upon the tribe's relationships with the animals. Pretty Shield recalled that "the whole country there smelled of rotting meat. Even the flowers could not put down the bad smell. Our hearts were like stones."[40] On the southern plains, where the slaughter of animals was even more accelerated, the Kiowas made "antelope medicine" in 1848–49 to bring the pronghorns back to their old ranges. During the following four years, the Kiowa winter count calendars carried symbols representing few or no bison.[41]

Every American schoolchild has heard about how the Plains Indians utilized all parts of the slain bison to provide necessities for their day-to-day lives. These great shaggy beasts served as "walking commissaries" by yielding the primary meat of a vitamin-rich diet. Hides furnished the basic material for fashioning tipis, clothing, shields, boats, bedding, blankets, and storage containers. Sinew was used for bowstrings, thread, snowshoe webbing, and rope. Horns and bones were shaped into weapons, tools, and utensils; gall was made into paint; and hooves were turned into glue.[42] This description has been repeated so often that it has become a virtual stereotype. Yet the list of multiple uses is only a partial one for the many plains and plateau tribes who relied so completely on the bison for their livelihoods. The all-important spiritual life of these tribes also rested upon their fictive kinship attachments to the bison and other animals. The Lakotas especially evidenced this trait, which led mid-nineteenth-century traveler Francis Parkman to marvel about the literalness with which they claimed lineal descent from bears, wolves, deer, and other animals.[43]

But these notions of human and animal shared kinship transcended clan symbols and mythic protectors to include an ethic based upon reciprocal relationships between humans and the earth itself. Just as nature provided its bounty for use by people, these "two leggeds" owed an obligation to protect the earth and all of its life forms. Thus the Sioux and other tribes apologized for killing their animal relatives, but they also realized that Wakan Tanka (the Great Spirit or Great Mystery) intended that the kinship connection be based upon reciprocal sacrifice. Hunters begged animals' forgiveness before killing them and ritualistically thanked them for the sacrifice. In return, these same hunters swore themselves to the protection of their animal relatives and to guaranteeing their perpetuation through the future generations. Ethical taboos warned against killing bears during hibernation season, boasting about one's hunting prowess, making denigrating comments about nature's many forms, and, above all, abusing game by overkilling or destroying them only for personal gain.[44]

Animal spirits, which abounded in American Indian cosmology, were essential to healing ceremonies and subsistence activities. Shamanistic powers rested upon communication with animals, and nowhere was this in greater evidence than the bison culture of the Lakotas. Spiritual protector White Buffalo Calf Woman held an honored place among Sioux mythological figures because she brought from the *pte oyate kin* (the Buffalo People) a promise that they would sacrifice their bodies for the sake of the starving humans. Smoking the pipe between White Buffalo Calf Woman and the Sioux, and presenting the pipe to the four sacred directions, sealed the pact between the two. As long as the humans fulfilled their part of the reciprocal relationship by protecting and nourishing the bison, the pte oyate kin would make the blood sacrifice for their human relatives. A similar ethic pervaded Lakota linkages to other animals that were essential to the continuance of Indian life.[45] Thus the performance of various ceremonial rituals for the bison, Sitting Bull's participation in the 1876 Sun Dance as a supplication to the bison, and Agent James McLaughlin's tale of the Hunkpapa Lakotas' last major bison hunt reflect American Indian dependence on and kinship with the animals.[46]

Few mid-nineteenth-century emigrants would have truly understood or fully appreciated American Indian sacred connections to the animal spirits. Even fewer would have been able to reconcile evidence of mass bison slaughters by the Indians. In 1849, Agent William Hatton inspected the long stretch of the Missouri River from St. Louis to Fort Union, and he predicted that before long, the bison would be virtually extinct within the entire region. Hatton pointed to the horrendous impact that this was having on the diet and material cultures of many tribes, and yet he blamed Indians for most of this slaughter. In their haste to realize immediate profits from the larger commercial hide business, they were destroying their futures.[47] Two years prior to the filing of Hatton's official report, Mormon travelers witnessed direct evidence of this same trend along the Platte River. They found the carcasses of one hundred large bison, skinned and left to rot by Sioux hunters who were interested only in the hides and not the meat or other usable items. Furthermore, the Sioux had skinned many buffalo calves, an even greater affront to the animal spirits and their continued kinship with humans.[48]

As is the case of other peoples who tried to live in close association and harmony with nature, American Indians did not always live up to the vaunted ecological aspirations of their oral traditions. Many did break with their cultural values, slaughter their animal relatives for furs and hides, and accept the short-term profits of this slaughter. As individuals, American Indians may not have been perfect ecologists, and some may have contributed to the ruin of their own societies, but the ethic of coexistence with nature still dominated American Indian populations throughout the nineteenth century, just as it continues to do at the beginning of the twenty-first century.

Emigrants frequently blamed American Indians for despoliation of animal populations along the trails, but on closer inspection, some overlanders admitted that their initial impressions were based upon stories they had heard secondhand or upon stereotypes that they harbored even before undertaking the trip. Mrs. Thomas Tootle wrote in 1862 that the tribes along the Platte River were actually protective of the bison and apparently had driven them farther south so as to escape the butchery.[49] Laura Brewster Boquist, who also traveled the Platte River Trail in 1862, later affirmed the same theory, although she cited no specific evidence of it.[50] More to the point, Eleazar Stillman Ingalls observed a full decade earlier that his initial impression had been to blame Indians for the wasteful slaughter, but on seeing the frequency of white blood lust firsthand, he had come to believe that overlanders were the primary cause of the unjustified waste.[51]

The decline of wildlife along the trail was not the only concern of American Indians, because even more dramatic in its impact was the terrifying effect of the silent killers that struck with so little warning. Epidemics affected tribes that resided along the trails, but they in turn, through their own travels and trade networks, spread these virulent diseases even to the remotest areas of the West. No area was safe from the devastating effects that may have killed as many as half of the Kiowa population between 1849 and 1851 and produced a similar mortality rate for the Southern Cheyennes during the same era.[52] Although American Indians of the Great Plains, Rocky Mountain Plateau, and Pacific Northwest had experienced European-based epidemics far back into the eighteenth century and had been adversely affected throughout the fur trade era, the overland migration created a new conduit for spreading the diseases more rapidly and over broader areas.

The disease most identified with overland travel during the mid-nineteenth century was cholera, which was the bane of existence for Indians and whites alike. The jumping-off towns located along the Missouri River became breeding grounds for the disease, as emigrants camped in small areas for extended periods and without the advantage of adequate purified water. The microscopic bacillus of Asiatic cholera was transmitted through the excrement of infected carriers or through contaminated food and water. Contrary to popular notions of the day, it was not spread by direct contact between humans, but the presence of so many people camped closely together and utilizing the same resources certainly increased the chances for infection.[53]

Because cholera became so widespread beginning with the California gold rush of 1849, and because it hit without warning, the malady occupied everyone's attention. Alonzo Delano described the ferocity and capriciousness of the disease as it struck a Mr. Harris while he was camped at St. Joseph in 1849. Having no prior symptoms, Harris's groans awakened his friends at 4:00 in the morning, and his condition immediately worsened as he began writhing in agony. They administered laudanum and sent for a doctor. The patient suffered severely for the next three hours with intense pain, vomiting, cramps, and a clammy sweat. Later in the day, his health seemed to return to normal, he pronounced himself to be cured, and the improved state remained for approximately three hours. Then, without warning, he gasped for breath, and despite all efforts by his friends, he was dead within five minutes.[54]

Since the incubation period for cholera was a short one, most people who were affected by the disease were stricken somewhere between the Missouri River towns and Fort Laramie. Cases were certainly reported west of the latter point, but most of the deaths from the disease were statistically clustered along the Nebraska section of the Platte River Trail. While traversing this region in 1852, Richard Hickman was so overwhelmed by the frequency of cholera cases that he predicted that within ten years, "the road will be a complete grave-yard."[55] Maj. Osborne Cross dramatized the situation in even more human terms when he described a California-bound party of fourteen Cherokees who had departed Indian Territory in 1849 on their way to the goldfields. By the time he encountered this party west of Fort Kearny, six of the members were dead from cholera, one was in the last throes of life, and the remainder were too ill to even bury the dead. Of the fourteen individuals in question, only one was well enough to help the afflicted.[56]

First to be affected were the tribes that occupied the eastern regions of Kansas and Nebraska. Between 1849 and 1855, northeastern Kansas seemed to be a perfect breeding ground for cholera epidemics, as the wagon trains funneled along fairly narrow corridors and emigrants camped at many of the same forested groves and water sources. One unidentified observer noted in May 1849 that many of the Shawnees and Delawares were purposely eschewing the profits of the trail because they feared infection from travelers. Another member of the same party wrote that Indian families had deserted their prosperous farms at Bull Creek "to escape the tide of population and the dread scourge attending it." The author's rhetorical question—"How can the poor Indian escape it! Where can he go?"—might well have applied to all western Indians, not just those of northeastern Kansas.[57]

For the Pawnees, whose villages stretched along the Platte River between the Elkhorn and Loup Fork rivers, the results of continuous contact with ill overlanders were even more devastating. John E. Barrow, subagent at Council Bluffs, reported in October 1849 that during the preceding spring and fall, 250 Pawnee men and 900 women and children had fallen victim to cholera. An additional 84 Pawnees had died near the agency headquarters, raising the mortality rate to one-fourth of the entire tribe within the space of a mere six months.[58] During the following two years, many of the Pawnees abandoned their large village near present-day Fremont, Nebraska, and moved southward toward present-day Ashland, where they could escape the brunt of the overland migration. Unfortunately, the relocations did not bring relief, because the residents were unable to grow enough food at these new sites to feed themselves, and they were unable to protect their other village on the south bank of the Platte River, near present-day Grand Island, Nebraska, from Sioux attacks. Surviving Pawnees were thus compelled to beg and steal from overlanders, which resulted in a strong reprimand from the commander at Fort Kearny and a warning that he would chastise them if they bothered the emigrants in the future.[59]

Expansion of the cholera threat simultaneously affected the plains tribes residing along the Platte River Trail. A correspondent for the *Missouri Republican* predicted during the spring of 1850 that Indians would be scarce along the trail during the coming season because of their fear of the sickness. Many of the Cheyennes had moved south-westward toward the South Platte River, and many of the Lakotas had moved northward into the Nebraska sandhills and toward the White River.[60] Overlanders James Pratt, Henry Page, Calvin Taylor, and George Keller confirmed this trend during the 1849 and 1850 trail seasons, but they also took delight in the fact that fewer Indians presumably meant less likelihood for problems of theft or intimidation.[61]

Cholera not only affected the number of Indians who were willing to camp along the trail but also altered the behavior of those who did remain. F. A. Chenoweth reported that the Lakotas would not take items left beside the trail or in abandoned wagons because they so feared the epidemic.[62] They also would not let a grieving party of emigrants bury a man near their village at Ash Hollow because they suspected that he had died from the disease.[63] In a reversal of the situation, Capt. Howard Stansbury learned that one wagon after another had passed by a teenaged Sioux girl who had been left alone with the dead bodies of her relatives. No overlanders would help her because they had concluded that she, too, was stricken with cholera.[64]

Susan Bordeaux Bettleyoun, a mixed-blood woman who grew up as an Oglala Lakota, recalled the rising level of Sioux rage as their population was decimated by cholera and other diseases. Warrior White Round-head, who had recently lost several relatives to cholera and was himself suffering from its symptoms, was especially distraught. He stormed into Joseph Robidoux's trading post southeast of Scotts Bluff and swore that he would "kill every white man he sees." As he filled the air with his threats, sang his death chant, and menaced the employees, he was fired at and apparently killed. Bettelyoun also heard the story about her own uncle. Suffering from cholera, he dressed in his best clothes, painted his face for death, and killed himself with a single gunshot.[65]

Later in the nineteenth century, Cheyenne elder John Stands In Timber repeated the stories he had heard as a boy about his people's experiences with cholera. One tale concerned a warrior who came into the camp circle singing a war song and declaring, "I cannot see the enemy who is killing us. When I see an enemy I never stay back, but I cannot protect the people from this thing; they just fall and die." Within minutes, he was struck by the malady, and he dropped dead in front of his own tipi "as if he had been shot, dead."[66]

Although plains tribes often explained the advent of epidemics through spiritual concepts, they clearly equated white migrations with the spread of these maladies. Thus relocations away from the trails became a commonly accepted method for dealing with the problem. Southern Cheyenne mixed-blood observer George Bent recalled that his people moved away from the Platte River valley in 1849, but not before many of them had contracted cholera. Sharing of contaminated food and water supplies spread the disease quickly even among the bands that had not yet experienced the onslaught. Within a year, the Oktoguna Clan had been virtually destroyed, and the Masikota Clan was so greatly reduced that the survivors had to attach themselves to the Dog Soldier camp for protection.[67]

Not only did the dispersal strategy fail to protect Indian lives, it actually compounded the high death rates and spread them beyond the original zone of infection. Historians Ramon Powers and James Leiker have pointed out the final irony in this turn of events. Besides alienating many tribes and helping erode the earlier spirit of cooperation that pervaded the trails, cholera and other mid-nineteenth-century epidemics disproportionately killed the very Indian populations that had been most open to commerce and negotiations with whites. Amid the great demographic disasters that befell the plains tribal populations during the 1850s, the bands that remained far away from the points of continuous white and Indian contact most successfully weathered the storm. These were the populations most apt to choose armed resistance over diplomacy in the coming years. In effect, the mass epidemics undercut the authority of moderate elders, while strengthening the hand of the more assertive young men.[68]

Throughout the 1850s, the second most important biological threat to western Indian life was smallpox. Unlike cholera, which was transmitted through food, waste products, and contaminated water, this equally dreaded killer was conveyed through direct human contact. Furthermore, the affliction was often instantly recognizable because of the numerous scab-producing sores on the face and body. When Harriet Loughary reached the Pawnee camp on the Elkhorn River, she was clearly ill with the disease, and her appearance terrified the residents. All Pawnees who were visiting her wagon train immediately fled, and none returned to the spot until after the train had departed.[69] Mere rumor was enough to create a panic, such as that seen among a group of Lakotas as early as 1844. William Case witnessed an entire Sioux camp being evacuated within fifteen minutes when its inhabitants heard that Case's party contained smallpox-stricken members.[70]

One Mormon party of 1852 allegedly turned this situation to its advantage. Fearing the approach of a large group of Indians, its members placed flour on a boy's freckled face, put him in a bed between two sheets, and instructed him to appear deathly ill. Upon riding into the encampment, one of the Indian leaders asked what was wrong with the child. When told that the boy had smallpox and upon seeing the ashen face with the tell-tale spots, the Indian men bolted from the camp, and no others visited the wagon train during the subsequent two or three weeks.[71] A similarly conceived ruse worked to equal perfection in 1861, when an overland party engaged in loud wailing and informed a group of Indians that one of their loved ones had just died from cholera.[72]

Although smallpox and cholera posed their greatest threats in the broad expanse of territory between the Missouri River and Fort Laramie, their effects were not completely unheard of in areas farther to the west. In 1849, traders at South Pass told Joseph Waring Berrien that they had purposely circulated a rumor among tribes all the way to the Great Basin that many smallpox-stricken emigrants were on their way from the East. Because the virulence of this disease was well known from epidemics that had occurred during the heyday of the Rocky Mountain fur trade, many Indians reportedly began moving their villages away from the trails.[73] Shoshones of the Rocky Mountain Plateau country were second only to the Great Plains tribes in their susceptibility to cholera and smallpox.[74] Mary Ellen Todd remembered the fear of smallpox and how the Shoshones tried to treat it with sweat ceremonies and hot drinks made from indigenous plants. The procedures seemed to have had little positive effect upon the large number of ill Shoshones, and when she peeked inside a lodge, she saw a "stack of dead Indians" that frightened her and her youthful companions away.[75]

Even the Pacific Northwest tribes did not escape the onslaught. As early as 1852 Dr. Thomas White observed that in previous decades, the Chinooks had measured their population in the several thousands, and their villages had stretched over a broad area from the Umpqua River to Puget Sound. But within a relatively few years, their numbers had been reduced by more than 50 percent due to smallpox and measles.[76] Devastation had been so great for the tribes in and around the Willamette Valley of Oregon that some were on the verge of extinction even before the Oregon Trail brought significant numbers of farmers into the region. Smallpox, intermittent fever, whooping cough, venereal diseases, and measles transmitted by fur traders and coastal mariners had killed perhaps 90 percent of the indigenous coastal population between 1775 and 1840.[77] The spread of measles helped trigger the Cayuse attack on the Whitman Mission in 1847 that led to the deaths of Marcus and Narcissa Whitman as well as other mission employees.[78]

Precisely because so many American Indians died from epidemics during the heyday of the overland trails, it is little wonder that an attendant problem also incurred their wrath—the desecration of Indian burials. To be sure, some overlanders gained greater empathy for Indians by witnessing the spiritual dimensions of their mourning rites and devotion to the dead. Rather than displaying a stoic attitude or a superstitious nature, both of which were characteristic archetypes of nineteenth-century literature, American Indian mourners evoked a deeply human side that even outsiders could appreciate. White observers were often uncomfortable with the high-pitched sound of mass wailing, but they were more surprised to see the emotional side of a people whom they had been led to believe were uncaring savages.[79] William Woodhams was also struck by the superiority of Sioux platform burials near Fort Laramie. By placing bodies securely on platforms, elevating them to the highest branches of a tree, and placing important personal effects with each body, the Sioux had created a better burial than had overlanders, who left their relatives and friends in shallow graves dug along the trail. In the latter cases, noted Woodhams, the graves were quickly obliterated, and wild animals unceremoniously dug up and devoured the bodies.[80]

Among other overlanders, however, personal curiosity, tinged with a dose of disrespect for American Indians, led to horrible violations of burials. Upon observing the skulls of thirty recently deceased Pawnees on the Loup River, Harriet Young picked up one, took it to camp, "and showed it as a curiosity."[81] Similarly, Lodisa Frizzell and her friends retrieved a rusty knife and other items that had fallen from a

Lakota platform burial. On another occasion, Rachel Taylor and her friends removed sacred eagle feathers from another Lakota burial just west of Fort Laramie.[82] Emma Shepard Hill and her young friends likewise disturbed eagle feathers and other sacred funerary items, while a group of boys and girls joined Ada Millington in collecting beads from a burial and restringing them into necklaces.[83]

Although some transgressions were carried out by children and teenagers, adults were not guiltless. Some, such as Vincent Geiger, were merely curious and saw nothing wrong with tearing down a four-year-old scaffold burial of an Iowa "chief" merely to collect a single bead.[84] Others engaged in acts of desecration for the sake of science and personal profit. While camped at present-day Omaha in 1851, Harriett Buckingham watched as a physician and his wife scurried along the hillsides collecting numerous skulls and assorted bones for their personal study and perhaps to be sent to eastern academic institutions for further examination.[85] Israel Benjamin was an even more active "bone hunter," and his primary motivation was financial. He tried to rob several Sioux or Cheyenne burials so that the skulls and other funerary objects could be sent to a famous German sculptor who was paying good money for such discoveries. After being driven away from the burials by angry Indians, Benjamin tried to entice the local station keeper into a business arrangement whereby the latter would collect skulls, ship them directly to the sculptor's offices in Frankfort, and share the profits with Benjamin.[86] When another young medical student defended his grave robbing on the basis of advancing the science of craniology, Joseph Waring Berrien berated him for gross immorality. Berrien further argued that these were truly sacred sites warranting protection and that innocent people would certainly suffer from Indian retaliation.[87]

On rarer occasions revenge, not curiosity, set the stage for ghoulish grave robbery. During the Civil War, when tensions were highest between whites and Plains Indians, sojourner Mallie Stafford heard a story at Fort Cottonwood, Nebraska (later designated as Fort McPherson), about how soldiers had captured an Indian warrior, then killed, scalped, and buried him in a shallow grave. Subsequently, a different squad of soldiers arrived at the post and demanded proof of the execution. They dug up the body, scalped it a second time, and "bore away the ghastly trophies in exultation."[88]

As in the case of unjustified white slaughter of bison and other wildlife for sport, many overlanders were quick to condemn the grave robbing among their traveling companions. John Clark became upset when three members of his party climbed into the branches of a tree and cut down a platform burial. They then drove an ax into the body of the deceased Indian woman and collected many of the blue and white beads that popped forth from the clothing. Clark recorded how mortified he was about the degrading act, and when a fierce storm hit his camp later in the day, he regarded it as providential punishment.[89] J. A. Butler pronounced a similar desecration of a Sioux burial at Scotts Bluff to be "a cold unfeeling act—to disturb the dead to gratify an idle curiosity."[90] Laura Brewster Boquist later described the grizzly events of 1862, when children from her train went souvenir collecting among the tree burials just west of Fort Laramie. She condemned them for their insensitivity to Indian sacred rites and for stirring up interracial tensions that would be visited upon later wagon trains.[91]

Boquist's warnings about future Indian retaliation were echoed by many overlanders who were less moved by the immorality of the desecration than by the possible consequences of such acts. When one young man climbed into a tree to retrieve burial objects, Cutler Salmon, captain of the train, immediately ordered him down and lectured him in harsh language about how his actions could result in the massacre of the entire group.[92] Louisa Barnes Pratt observed the same concern among Mormon leaders of her train when some boys tore down the burial platform of a Lakota infant and appropriated the items that had been placed alongside the infant's body. Mormon elders quickly replaced the items with the body so as to avoid trouble, and they instructed their children to make no other such invasions of sacred sites.[93] Bullwhacker John Bratt did precipitate a significant act of violence in 1866 when he visited the burial site of Spotted Tail's daughter at Fort Laramie. Although intending no disrespect, he was assaulted by Lakota men when he began picking up stones from beneath the suspended platform. They chased Bratt for two miles, and had he not reached the safety of a wagon train, he was sure the warriors would have killed him.[94]

In the face of increased animal slaughter, epidemics, and disrespect for burials, American Indians living along the trails also complained about overlanders' misuse of fire and its destructive powers. Ironically, the deliberate setting of fires had long been a practice of tribes throughout North America. Indigenous peoples knew how to use controlled fires as a way of clearing areas for agricultural purposes, keeping forest trails open, and rejuvenating grasslands. They also employed fires to accompany some ceremonial activities, to produce ash as a crop fertilizer, and to control the migratory habits of animals to assure greater success for hunters. In the latter case, plains tribes burned off the forage in large areas so that the bison and other game animals would move toward the timbered river bottoms or to other prime grasslands where they could be hunted more efficiently. This became especially important in intertribal relations, as indigenous populations sometimes set fires to accomplish a scorched-earth effect that would keep animal herds from migrating out of their territory into the hunting territories controlled by enemy tribes. Whether set for ecological reasons or as a method for controlling economic resources, fires had long served as a vital tool for western Indians.[95]

Unfortunately, the advent of so many emigrants passing through these same areas between 1840 and 1870 caused additional problems with uncontrolled prairie fires. As each side blamed the other for the devastation, rumors drove a deeper wedge of misunderstanding between Indians and whites. When Adam Brown crossed through the farmlands of the "removed" tribes that had settled in northeastern Kansas, he was quick to conclude that they were responsible for the fiery confla-grations that had destroyed much of the vegetation. Although he possessed no evidence to prove this, Brown conjectured that Indians were more prone to this malicious behavior than were whites.[96] Joel Barnett evidenced a similar bias when he wrote about how members of his company refused to give matches to any Indians because they would certainly do damage with them.[97] With the same lack of proof, Mary Ackley alleged that Indians had burned bridges over the Carson River so as to impede the advance of miners into California.[98]

The few eyewitness accounts of western Indians starting fires with the sole purpose of harassing overland traffic were limited to efforts to create stampedes so that Indians could run off and capture emigrant livestock. While traveling just west of Fort Bridger with Col. Albert Sidney Johnston's column during the 1857–58 Mormon War, the soldier-journalist known only as "Utah" described how unidentified Indians started a blaze to panic the soldiers' horses and mules. The Indians rode in among the livestock but were driven off by concen-trated gunfire. The lone Indian casualty suffered nineteen wounds, and his body was buried by the same soldiers who had shot him.[99] Two years later, C. B. Wiley's wagon train experienced an equally terrifying event after seven unidentified Indians rode into camp at lunchtime and begged for food. After the train resumed its afternoon journey, it was confronted by a quickly spreading prairie fire. Amid the sudden confusion, the seven Indians returned on horseback, waived blankets with gusto, and tried unsuccessfully to stampede some of the livestock. A larger group of Indians returned the next day, but they found the wagons in a well-protected corral formation, and the warriors left without any further confrontation.[100]

Despite the infrequent and anecdotal nature of these attacks under the cover of fire, many overlanders persisted in their belief that such events were widespread. Members of Brigham Young's 1847 Pioneer Band were concerned about rumors that Indians had recently burned large areas on the north side of the Platte River and that grass would be in short supply for the initial Mormon migration. Young, however, remained adamant about keeping his people on the north bank of the Platte so as to avoid problems with non-Mormon emigrants who were departing from Missouri and who tended to stay on the river's south side during that period. The rumor turned out to be groundless, and the Pioneer Band progressed along its intended course without encountering major problems associated with prairie fires.[101]

Some emigrants changed their minds about the cherished stereotype of the "Indian firestarter," often because they repeatedly witnessed careless and malicious acts among their fellow travelers. William Johnston, bound for the California goldfields in 1849, recorded near the Little Vermillion Creek of northeastern Kansas that large caravans had apparently destroyed valuable grazing lands by leaving campfires unattended and not fully extinguished. What grass they had not blackened by their thoughtless acts, they had ruined by allowing their grazing livestock to crop too close to the ground.[102]

During the following April, J. M. Stewart witnessed the effects of a massive burn near the juncture of the Platte and Loup Fork rivers. His train encountered scorched earth during the next ten days of their journey, and Stewart blamed the parties traveling just ahead of his for repeatedly failing to douse their campfires and thus causing the prairie blazes. Not only were the livestock of his train deprived of necessary grazing, but the fires had taken a dreadful toll on the area's wildlife. Stewart saw bison whose hair had been burned completely off and who had been made permanently blind by the inferno. He and his friends shot eight or ten of the suffering animals to keep them from colliding with the ox teams and to put them out of their misery.[103] Traveling in a different caravan, Thomas Christy saw this same destruction, which continued on even beyond Fort Kearny. He blamed a particular company from Chicago, under the leadership of a Mr. Cook, for the spectacle. Christy described how ninety-three bison, deer, and antelope had burned to death within a three-acre plot, and another eleven had died in a sinkhole when they got hemmed in along the creek bed. Christy angrily wrote in his journal of the Cook party, "Hope they will reap their reward."[104]

While white observers commented frequently about dangerous abuses of fire by overlanders, surviving American Indian testimony on this topic remains slight for the primary years of the western trails. Susan Bordeaux Bettelyoun made only passing mention of the problem in her reminiscences, but she emphatically stated that white emigrants were the principal instigators of most of these destructive prairie fires.[105]

As the decade of the 1850s progressed, Indians came under greater duress because the level of white migration through their country was accelerating at a phenomenal rate. Naturally, villages located on or near the overland trails contained the hardest hit populations, but even people who lived many days' or weeks' journey beyond the trails were also adversely affected. Massive destruction of wildlife weakened the material cultures of tribes throughout the Far West, and it further undermined the ceremonial integrity of the spiritual bond that kept tribal members united. Yet the destruction of wildlife and other natural resources was only one ingredient in the new reality produced by the steady stream of eastern migrants. Epidemics assured more than a decade of demographic disaster as they destroyed anywhere from one-third to one-half of the American Indian populations living along the main corridors of the westward movement.

To meet these challenges, some Indians dispersed from the trails to seek new sources of wildlife and to put great distances between themselves and the raging epidemics. The majority, however, stayed in close proximity to those arteries so that they could enjoy the fruits of continued trade, technological exchange, alliance, and friendship that had been so universally established in the previous decade. Rather than trying to shut off the migration during the 1850s, tribal elders placed greater emphasis on demanding compensation for their losses. Unfortunately, more trouble lay ahead as the decade wore on, because neither the federal government nor overlanders were willing or able to provide the kinds of policies and compensations that western Indians demanded. This in turn led to increased incidents of Indian begging and theft, which were answered with a greater fear and loathing among many emigrants. To this explosive mixture was added a new level of rumors and innuendo that diminished the residual feelings of earlier friendship. Growing paranoia and misinformation on both sides of the racial divide would thus serve as catalysts for eventual violence on a large scale.

8

Massacred by Indians
An Exaggerated Tale

Because American Indian and European American cultures were based upon contrasting value systems and worldviews, misunderstandings about behavior and motivations were a common reality of trail life. Such misconceptions were inevitable, but they did not automatically trigger contentious feelings or violent reactions between the two groups so long as mutual benefits outweighed the negative costs of association. Although both Indians and whites harbored incorrect and even prejudiced notions about each other, whites certainly acted on these biases with a greater degree of alarm and predisposition toward hostile action. Expectations of Indians' savage conduct had been constantly reinforced in the American psyche by literature, art, newspapers, and rumor mills for a full two centuries before the advent of the Oregon, California, and Mormon trails. Now, in the midst of the nineteenth century, these stereotypes would further complicate relations between indigenous peoples and the migrating caravans of easterners. Amid this new round of myth making and delusion, it was often the trail experiences themselves that hardened the disparaging view about American Indians. In this ambiguous environment of incomplete and biased information, the perception of reality often eclipsed reality itself to worsen those relations. False rumors of constant Indian threats and periodic massacres of wagon trains abounded at midcentury, always obscuring the larger relationship that

was based upon mutually beneficial trade, cooperation, and friendship. In this increasingly hostile atmosphere, too many emigrants saw
an Indian lurking behind every tree and a scalp hanging in every tipi,
even when there was no evidence of either.

The experience of Frances Adams dramatizes in microcosm how
preconceived notions about Indian savagery could easily blend with
innocent events to produce a distorted and dangerous view. As mother
of four-year-old Inez and nine-month-old Helen, Adams faced a
daunting task in the overland migration, and she worried incessantly
about the safety of her husband and two small daughters. During transit
of Oregon's Cascade Range in 1848, while the men were meticulously
moving the wagons down a steep slope, she carried the youngest girl
to the bottom and placed her in an open area some distance off of the
trail. She then returned up the path to retrieve Inez and take her down
to the spot where the infant lay. To her horror, she saw a dozen Indians
appear as if by magic at the very spot, and at a distance, they appeared
to be trampling the baby to death with their horses. Adams raced
down the hill in utter terror, only to find that the Indian men were
protecting infant Helen while they awaited the mother's descent. Anti-
cipating only the worst from these "savages," the speechless mother
"motioned her thanks and they nodded, smiled and rode away."[1]
Adams certainly had reason to fear for the lives of her children in this
ambiguous situation, but the threat had been predicated on her false
expectations about Indian behavior.

If Adams could be so fundamentally wrong in her judgment, then
what was it about the trail experience that shaped the negative feelings
of so many people even beyond their preexisting eastern biases? Traveling in a strange land for six months, overcoming the rigors of daily
activities, and witnessing the deaths of friends and family members
from disease and accidents created a high stress level for most people
who undertook the journey. Any initial sense of security or comfort
proved fleeting in the early weeks of the ordeal, and many sojourners
came to expect the worst in the following weeks. They were prime can-
didates to be influenced by exaggerations that routinely circulated
from train to train. No matter that many of the tales were third- or
fourthhand, they often seemed believable among a population that felt
disoriented and vulnerable. Most prominent among the seemingly endless procession of troubling stories were the ubiquitous rumors about
recent atrocities and imminent attacks. Even stouthearted individuals

could be persuaded to this view if they heard the gossip often enough or if they saw what they thought was tangible proof of a threat.

One type of evidence that seemed to send companies into waves of alarm were the messages left along the trail by earlier wagon trains that had experienced problems with Indians. Because these were of recent vintage, specific to the dangers of the immediate area, and presumably written as firsthand accounts, they carried a measure of credibility that reached well beyond the usual spate of innuendo. In this regard, the 1849 experience of Reuben Shaw provided the kind of shock effect that overlanders hoped they would not encounter during the journey. Posted on a tree one day's march east of Fort Kearny was a note that had been left two weeks earlier by John Slade, captain of the Otter Creek Company. It informed future travelers to "look out for the red devils," allegedly Pawnees who had killed and scalped a member of their party after he had wandered away to hunt deer.[2] During the following years, Lucena Parsons declared that the area between the Missouri River and Fort Kearny contained numerous admonitions written on animal bones, most cautioning that the local tribes were busy stampeding livestock from inattentive trains. Buffalo skulls were also placed along the trails with words such as "look out for Indians" written prominently upon them.[3]

The Great Basin provided the setting for most of the warning messages that were recorded in trail journals. During August 1850, several parties reported trouble with Indians along the Humboldt River. The verbal cautions that they passed along were confirmed by a note left by an unidentified group: "Emigrants, be on your guard. Three families were robbed of their teams by the Snake [Shoshone] Indians. The Indians exhibited strong signs of hostilities." The warning proved prophetic, because four days later the Adam Brown party was surprised by Indian raiders who ran off fifteen head of their livestock. The nearly stranded overlanders were able to recover all of the animals, however, and resume their journey.[4]

Four years earlier, Jacob Wright Harlan and his friend Tom fought off a large group of Indians who were trying to stampede their mules on the Humboldt. Being heavily armed with rifles and pistols, they were able to drive away the raiders. On traveling a mile farther down the trail, the two young men found a board sticking out of the ground. It pronounced that dangerous Indians were in the vicinity and everyone should pay heed—a reality to which Brown and his companion could testify by direct experience.[5] Even as far west as Oregon's Rogue River, William Scroggs found a note attached to a tree by freighters who had been ambushed by "friendly" Indians whom they had allowed into camp. The message described the deaths of two of the packers, and it warned others not to be so trusting of Indian gestures of peace.[6]

Sometimes the frightening admonitions came not from messages written on papers, posts, or animals bones but rather emanated directly from experienced frontiersmen. While crossing Nebraska in 1865, Charles Stobie was especially struck by the warnings of teamsters returning from Fort Laramie. The alarm spread among various trains, and Stobie noted that the teamsters "never lost an opportunity of warning us to look out for our top-knots as the Indians were thicker than buffalo gnats ahead of us."[7]

Some of these alerts served their purpose by informing travelers of real dangers, but many others were nothing more than false alarms that only increased the level of paranoia and racial distrust. Diaries were filled with references to misidentified phenomena, especially wandering livestock whose silhouettes were cast against dim moonlight or whose meanderings created magnified rustling sounds in the buffalo grass. While on guard duty one night, Nathan Sutton heard a strange noise among the company's livestock. In a moment of panic, he fired at the supposed Indian who was trying to stampede the animals, and on first light of the morning, he and his heavily armed friends cautiously approached the area of combat. There they found the Martin brothers' $300 prized Kentucky mule dead from Sutton's bullet wounds. Although it was a serious matter and resulted in the loss of a considerable monetary investment, members of the party teased Sutton throughout the rest of the journey by repeatedly yelling, "Oh, Nate, when are you going to shoot another four-legged Indian?"[8]

Adam Brown recorded in a bemused tone how easily an instantaneous panic could be created among scores of people and how they all could share the same immediate thought: Indian attack! One of the night guards in his company fired twice into the darkness upon hearing noises. Both bullets struck their marks, wounding the man's own mule that had escaped from its tether. Upon the initial sound of gunfire, other men began firing indiscriminately to hold back the expected onslaught of Indians.[9] Wild animals also frequently set off a fusillade of gunfire. While camped on the Platte River several days march west of Fort Kearny, members of Vincent Geiger's and Wakeman Bryarly's

1849 party observed what they thought to be a group of Indian riders along the bluffs. The alarm was sounded, the men took their defensive positions, and they prepared all of their weapons for the certain attack. As the figures descended from the bluffs toward the riverbank, it became apparent that these were not menacing warriors but rather were six large elk in search of a drink of water.[10]

Because the vast western landscapes were unfamiliar to most easterners, overlanders had trouble correctly discerning distances and identities of faraway objects with the naked eye. They misidentified mirages as lakes, dust and low clouds as mountain peaks, and animals as human beings. Mary Rockwood Powers recalled how the desert areas of the Great Basin especially played tricks on people's perceptions. One day while passing along the Humboldt River, some members of her wagon train observed what they thought to be sixty or seventy mounted Indians at some distance ahead of them. The train stopped its advance, prepared for attack, and sent two scouts ahead to reconnoiter. Within the hour, the scouts returned, laughing "so loud they could hardly keep [in] the saddle," as they reported the source of alarm to be nothing more than a flock of buzzards.[11] Another party observed supposed Indian signal fires near Scotts Bluff, and one member was almost killed by a trigger-happy night guard because of the mounting apprehension. Although the fires appeared to be constantly moving—thus furthering the notion of stealthy Indians closing in on the train—subsequent investigations proved that these fires were merely stars changing their positions throughout the night sky.[12]

At other times, members of wagon trains concocted Indian scares to serve their own personal agendas. The captain of Catherine Margaret Haun's 1849 California-bound train tested the preparedness of his lackadaisical charges soon after they had crossed the Elkhorn River in eastern Nebraska. Without warning, he began yelling, "Indians, Indians!" and raced around to summon the people to defensive action. Just as he anticipated, the camp quickly degenerated into mass confusion, as people forgot his earlier instructions and panicked. Haun observed that some of the women fainted and others of both sexes were "nearly paralyzed with fear." Despite the embarrassing outcome of this event, Haun indicated that the warning drill had well served its purpose by alerting naive sojourners about Indian threats that might lie ahead.[13] Flora Bender suspected that the two captains of her train had entirely different motivations when they created an Indian scare. Both men came riding back to the column at breakneck speed, yelling that forty warriors were in pursuit. The wagons were quickly configured into a defensive formation to await an attack that never came. Bender and others concluded that the captains actually wanted to camp at this spot for the evening, and they had created this ruse as a way of expediting people's sluggish movements.[14]

Some overlanders fabricated Indian scares only as practical jokes to get attention or to poke fun at the less-than-heroic responses of other travelers. In the former case, two teenaged boys rushed into camp proclaiming that they had been frightened by Indians. On closer questioning, it became apparent that they were bored and merely wanted to stir up excitement. Unfortunately for them, the adults were not amused at the dangerous antic.[15] A more complicated ruse was resorted to by Moses Schallenberger and John Murphy, who took some of John Sullivan's cattle into the woods of northeastern Kansas and sounded the alarm of missing livestock. Sullivan, who was already very jumpy about the Indian threat in these early days of the overland journey, joined the two pranksters in the nighttime search. When they had reached a sufficient distance from the safety of the camp, Murphy fired his shotgun from concealment, and poor Sullivan ran headlong for the wagons screaming that he had been shot by an Indian. Throughout his subsequent travel with the 1844 Elisha Stevens party, the terrified man apparently never learned the truth of the event, because for months he retold the story of his narrow escape from the ferocious Otos.[16]

Sometimes the attempts at deception went awry and exposed the culprits. Ira Butterfield and several of his friends tried to scare the dictatorial leader of their group by posting a fictionalized note on the trail that warned of Indians in the immediate area. The leader of the group—a man named Blodgett—fell for the trick, but, by not allowing any campfires during the next several nights because of his fears of attack, he deprived the entire party of hot meals.[17] Another group of California-bound men went on a bison hunt, but not before proudly boasting to other members of their company that they would return with an ample supply of meat. They not only failed to find the bison, but in their enthusiasm for the hunt, they let their horses wander off with their guns and ammunition. To avoid embarrassment, they concocted a tale of having been ambushed by Indians. Their story proved

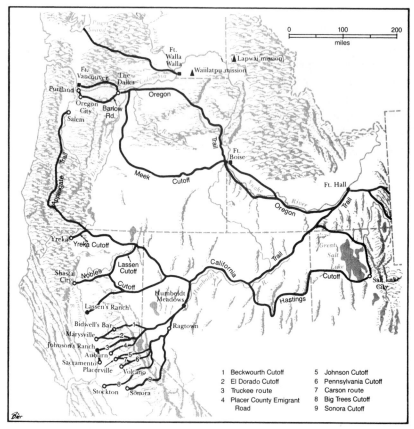

Route improvements undertaken by Oregon, California, and Washington. Reproduced, with permission, from John D. Unruh, Jr., *The Plains Across: The Overland Emigrants and the Trans-Mississippi West, 1840–60* (Urbana: University of Illinois Press, 1979).

so transparent, however, that they were forced to admit the truth and suffer the barbed comments of their compatriots.[18]

Not all the deception led merely to innocent fun and banter. When a teenaged boy placed a white blanket over himself and approached one of the night guards on the periphery of camp, the guard yelled for the shadow to identify itself. Upon receiving no response, the guard fired and severely wounded the boy.[19] Another practical joke led to similar results near Fort Hall, when a teenager concealed himself "Indian-fashion" in a red blanket and hid behind an obstruction. The boy intended to scare a camp guard who had a reputation for being especially frightened of Indians. As the guard approached the spot in night's darkness, the teenager walked out from behind his concealment, only to receive a full shotgun blast. Although the boy did not die, he had to lie in the back of a wagon for the rest of the trip to California, and he suffered considerable pain throughout the ordeal.[20]

These types of incidents—although innocent in intention—fanned the flames of human paranoia and led to further accidents along the trail. One young man shot and killed his father when the latter returned unexpectedly from night guard duty wrapped in a blanket to ward off the cold. Thinking he had targeted a lurking Indian, the young man initially took delight in having successfully defended the camp. But upon finding out the truth, "he nearly went crazy."[21] On several other occasions, overlanders accidentally shot themselves as they prepared for an Indian attack. In each case, the scare proved to be a false alarm. A Mr. Davis was so distressed about the presence of many Sioux near Scotts Bluff in 1864 that he left his rifle loaded and cocked while he slept. He inadvertently bumped against the rifle during the night; it discharged, and he died instantaneously.[22] During the same summer, Martin Ringo was killed by his own shotgun as he stepped up on the wagon box to get a better view of what was mistakenly thought to be some menacing Indians.[23] Twelve years earlier, Martin Gard had been severely wounded on the Humboldt River while trying to drive his light wagon and simultaneously load his pistol for an expected Indian attack that never materialized.[24]

Other cases of mistaken identity also came close to producing disaster. For instance, even with the aid of a telescope, Cephas Arms and several companions were unable to identify four rapidly approaching horsemen. When the four riders caught sight of Arms's party, they turned and fled. It was learned later that both groups were white men who had been hunting lost livestock and had assumed that the opposite party was composed of hostile Indians.[25]

Another example of near-confrontation occurred in 1845, when a guard sounded the alarm by firing into the night's darkness at what was deemed to be Indian thieves. This brought all of the men of the company to full alert, as they armed themselves and rushed to the direction of the rifle shot. Fortunately, the man's aim was off target, because out of the darkness came a badly shaken member of the party who had left the camp to free his mule from a mud hole along the Platte River.[26]

Similarly, when Finley McDiarmid went looking for some missing horses on the Sweetwater River in 1850, he and another overlander almost found themselves in each other's gun sights. Their mutual misidentification of each other as Sioux warriors was accentuated by McDiarmid having a wolf robe slung "Indian-style" across his horse.[27]

Two others cases of mistaken identity took ironic turns when overlanders corralled their wagons and prepared for a life-or-death struggle against large bodies of menacing Indians. Sarah Cummins's 1845 party flew into a general panic upon seeing a concentration of horsemen on the horizon. Women and children were crying, frightened men ran around without purpose, and even the leader of the train "looked frantic." To their relief, the war party turned out to be federal troops under the command of Stephen Watts Kearny, who provided escort service to the badly shaken wagon train for the following ten days.[28] Two years earlier, Sarah Hill's compatriots had become so alarmed by tales of Indian threats that they were sure they would be attacked as soon as they departed Fort Laramie. Sure enough, three days out, they spotted a cloud of dust in the distance, circled their wagons, and prepared to meet their fate. The expected angel of death proved to be a group of white trappers leading fur-laden pack mules toward the trading post.[29]

Overland diaries, journals, and letters are replete with similar cases of mistaken identity that raised levels of paranoia, but relatively few of these misperceptions produced injuries or deaths. American Indians sometimes contributed to the negative stereotyping by their own actions, and some of their efforts at humor furthered cultural misunderstanding. The group of Sioux men who descended upon a Mormon handcart encampment in 1859 appeared to be fierce warriors. But William Atkin recognized their dancing and singing and lassoing of some of the carts as "play acting." Between ferocious outcries, the Sioux laughed, enjoying the fear "their own fun" was evoking in the Mormons.[30] Five years later near the same spot, another group of allegedly several hundred Sioux surrounded the train of J. W. Broadwell and made threatening but comical gestures. Broadwell concluded that these warriors intended the scare as a prank, but his party remained vigilant just in case.[31]

Practical jokes of this type were a natural part of trail life, both for Indians and overlanders, but one can only surmise today about how many of these episodes were mistakenly interpreted as proof of the savage nature of American Indians. Modern historians of overland literature cannot easily sort out from the written record what was accurately recorded about American Indian motivations and what was misperceived. Nonetheless, it is clear from surviving accounts that relatively few overlanders interpreted the seemingly hostile actions of Indian men as "joke playing." Harry Roberts recalled years later how he and another boy had been surprised by three Indians while at some distance from their wagon encampment. The two youngsters fled in utter panic, yelling at the top of their lungs as they raced across the prairie to the relative safety of their train. Upon looking back for the expected pursuit, Roberts noted that the Indians "were bending double over their horses with their screams of laughter."[32] Hugh Cosgrove observed a similar event when approximately forty mounted Pawnees made a dash at some grazing livestock. Emigrants began firing at the fast-moving warriors, who were already beyond the range of their guns. Some among the defenders concluded that their quick action had scared away the marauders, but others, including Cosgrove, deduced that the Pawnees were merely "saucing" the emigrants because they could have driven off a substantial portion of the livestock with ease.[33]

The misreading of American Indian actions and motivations manifested itself in another macabre way that unfairly boosted images of Indian savagery. In a reversal of the usual situation where emigrants talked about their plundering of aboriginal burials, many overlanders alleged that Indians frequently dug up white graves. When Jared Fox first heard rumors of such heinous acts, he automatically concluded that the perpetrators were cannibals who devoured the dead bodies.[34] In a similar allegation of Indian barbarism, George Currey repeated an unsubstantiated tale about how Shoshones had killed a Mr. Booth at Salmon Falls on the Snake River. Not content with their dastardly deed, they had returned to the spot, dug up the man's body, stripped it of all clothing, and replanted it with the head shoved into the ground and legs sticking up in the air.[35] In another case, J. M. Harrison was inconsolable with the thought that Pawnees had probably dragged away the body of his dead friend so that they could further mutilate and dance around it back in their village.[36]

Although these observers had bizarre ways of perpetuating trail rumors and their own personal stereotypes about the western tribes, other overlanders ascribed the grave robbing to Indian efforts at stealing clothing and other burial objects. In none of the existing accounts, however, did people actually witness the sacrilege; they merely repeated rumors or deduced the conclusion from faulty evidence. The most frequently voiced misperception came from people who saw American Indians wearing items of white clothing. Rather than recognizing that Indians routinely bartered for these items of apparel or, in some cases, took them from abandoned wagons or chests discarded along the trail to lighten loads, they automatically assumed that the articles were pilfered from graves.[37] The daughter of Thomas Butterfield created an especially heartrending scene in her 1853 diary entry about how recent graves had been dug into by Indians, how bits of torn clothing and burial quilts had been scattered around, and how the grave robbers had probably been looking for guns.[38] In total reversal of the usual explanation, only one account offered a more positive view of Indian behavior, but even it was based on innuendo rather than eyewitness verification. Al Hawk recalled many decades later about how his family had found two recently dug graves on the banks of the Columbia River. He assumed them to contain the bodies of emigrants who had been buried by reverential Indians.[39]

Because most emigrants harbored preconceived notions about Indian barbarism and because they heard constant rumors to this effect, many failed to comprehend more rational explanations about the frequency of trailside grave disturbances. The simple fact is that natural erosion and desecration by wild animals accounted for virtually all of the exposed bodies, skeletal material, and torn clothing that were discovered by passing emigrants. The shallow graves that were dug along the banks of the Platte and Sweetwater rivers were especially prone to these natural phenomena, which occurred year-round. Furthermore, American Indians were unlikely to exhume such burials, which had often occurred in the wake of epidemics. Their fear of these rapidly spreading diseases may not have been based upon a precise scientific knowledge of the pathology of the maladies, but they well understood the cause-and-effect relationships between the dead bodies and the spread of epidemics among their own populations. Even the very concept of disturbing graves was anathema to the various tribes located along the overland trails. Their respect for and fear of dead men's and women's spirits precluded any tendencies toward grave robbing for the sake of acquiring clothing or other small objects. To engage in such illicit activity would certainly invite divine retribution and possible injury or death for the offending party.[40]

Cultural differences between whites and Indians further fed the flames of misunderstanding and sometimes pushed the two groups toward violent actions. Capt. Randolph B. Marcy, who had explored a significant portion of the southern plains during the mid-nineteenth century, well understood the apprehensions and misconceptions harbored by emigrants. In his 1859 book, *The Prairie Traveler: A Hand-Book for Overland Expeditions*, he warned readers not to overreact to every Indian gesture as if it were preparation for battle. He especially singled out the tendency of the men of plains tribes to rush forward on horseback when they first made contact with a new group of travelers. Rather than being a sign of their hostile intentions, this was a custom for greeting friends, and it ought not cause undue alarm. Marcy also cautioned that Indians frequently used sign language and hand signals to convey benign messages to each other. These should in no way be construed as threats or examples of Indian deceit, according to the army captain.[41]

The point of cultural confusion that Marcy alluded to bore itself out in the reaction of Helen Marnie Stewart while camped near Court House Rock in 1853. She and other members of her party became alarmed when a large group of Sioux came into the camp and "laid down their blankets." For some reason, the whites viewed this as a sign of hostility, when in fact, it was a universal plains gesture that the Indians were ready to commence the bartering process.[42] Similarly, when John Braly encountered some Kaw warriors in northeastern Kansas during the spring of 1847, he immediately concluded that they comprised a war party because they had small dabs of paint on their faces. He facetiously wrote in his autobiography: "I felt that the end had come, and my hair seemed to stand on end ready for the scalping-knife and tommyhawk." Only through a subsequent parley did it become evident that the ever-peaceful Kaws were beginning a bison hunt and that the face paint in no way insinuated an act of war.[43]

Cheyenne oral tradition has recorded one particularly vivid instance of cultural misunderstanding and how it led to violence for both groups. While hunting antelope along the Platte River in August 1856, three warriors watched as a mail wagon moved along the road between way stations. Two of the Cheyennes rode down to greet the driver and to request some tobacco, which was often the custom along the trail. Initially, the passengers prepared their weapons against a possible assault, but when the honorable intentions of the Indians became known, they responded with a gift of tobacco. When the two warriors rejoined their fellow hunter War Shirt, he indicated that he, too, would ride to the stage and seek a gift of tobacco. Despite his friends' warnings that the passengers seemed nervous and unpredictable, War Shirt tried to stop the coach and was cut down by several bullets. Some Cheyennes wanted to seek revenge for the killing, but Plum Man argued that they should report the incident to military authorities at Fort Kearny. Unfortunately, the "official story" was reported as an unprovoked Cheyenne attack upon the mail wagon, a serious violation of the 1851 Fort Laramie Treaty, and it prompted an army reprisal on a nearby Cheyenne camp. While white records referred to this as the "Tobacco Holdup," Cheyennes viewed it as a government violation of the 1851 treaty for not punishing the killers of War Shirt.[44]

When viewed from an Indian vantage point, the story of War Shirt and many others like it substantiate the fact that American Indians often had more to fear from traffic along the trails than overlanders had to fear from the indigenous tribes. Whether motivated by a fear of epidemics or a white propensity toward unprovoked violence, Indians frequently retreated from the trails to avoid trouble. Edward Lenox noted as early as 1843 that a large village of Shoshones gathered up many of their possessions and moved into the surrounding hills upon seeing a wagon train approach. Even the mediating efforts of mountain man Thomas "Pegleg" Smith, who was residing in the village at that time, failed to calm the inhabitants and prevent their flight.[45] William Keil observed a similar exodus among a Sioux camp at Ash Hollow, and Lester Hulin marveled at how the Indians on Rogue River "ran like wild animals from us."[46] Amos Steck was equally surprised when a Sioux man came forward on the South Fork of the Platte River to request that members of the train vouch for him among other trains so that he could pass back and forth among them without being shot by some trigger-happy fool.[47] In effect, the ambiguity worked both ways, as Indians and whites tried to size up the intentions of each new party they met along the trail. Each meeting was unique, and even if friendship and barter dominated the great majority of associations, a few bad encounters could poison the atmosphere, raise the level of hostile feelings, and precipitate violence.

American Indians sometimes voiced their fears about the precarious position that they found themselves in when trying to fathom the intentions of these strangers. Agent Garland Hurt wrote to Brigham Young in 1855 that on a recent inspection of the Thousand Spring Valley, he found only one Indian. The terrified man had explained that his people were so afraid of whites, especially the California miners who frequently invaded Nevada and indiscriminately killed Indians, that they had fled en masse to the remote corners of the desert. Hurt noted with irony that this reality stood in marked contrast to the numerous white reports that the Humboldt River valley was teeming with dangerous Indians.[48]

Even more heartrending were the childhood remembrances of the Northern Paiute woman Thocmetony, who became known in later years as Sarah Winnemucca. Although born into a relatively peaceful band that frequently aided overlanders, she was not immune to the buffeting forces of the migration that passed through her ancestral lands. By the time the young girl met her first gold miners on the Carson River, her head was already full of warnings about the unpredictability of these men. She and her brother began crying when they learned that their grandfather was going to camp his family among the miners and to use his letter of good behavior to solicit food from them. The children's lamentations grew so loud that the grandfather decided to relocate his family away from the miners' cabins even though it meant passing up a chance for gaining food.[49] Thocmetony had good reason for her apprehension, because at about the same time, other Paiutes and Shoshones were wantonly killed by overlanders in cases of mistaken identity, revenge, and outright acts of unprovoked homicide.[50]

One of the most underreported aspects of trail life was the white-on-white violence that was routinely blamed on Indians. Most of the surviving accounts point to the Great Basin as the main location of these depredations, and details indicate that a well-developed livestock trade in the California goldfields was the cause of this illicit business. C. B. Wiley noted that when the body of one dead rustler was examined, it turned out to be that of a white man who was dressed in Indian clothes and whose face and arms had been stained and painted.[51] Members of John Berry Hill's party also concluded that their attackers had been a white gang who had masqueraded as American Indians.[52] Even more encompassing was the judgment of the Oregon territorial legislature in 1851 when it complained to the U.S. Congress that the "lion's share" of livestock thefts on the Oregon Trail was due to gangs of white outlaws and their Indian associates. Congress demanded immediate military attention to this problem, despite the fact that army officers lacked clear legal authority to arrest and hold these men for prosecution.[53]

Even at the Missouri River jumping-off towns, Indians were unfairly blamed for white-initiated homicides. Traveling upriver together from St. Joseph, James Samuels and Waltenberg Mewett had seemingly become good friends, but while camped at Council Bluffs awaiting ferry passage across the river, Mewett killed his young friend with savage ax blows to the head and chest. Although no one had witnessed the crime, they found that the murderer's claim of an Indian attack did not coincide with the physical evidence. Following a unanimous guilty verdict by a jury of his peers, Mewett was hanged from a basswood tree on May 14, 1853.[54] Two years earlier at present-day Omaha, George Riddle concluded that the thieves who had stolen eight or ten head of cattle during the night were not Pawnees, as some people had assumed, but rather were white rustlers dressed as Indians.[55]

Because military posts attracted many people involved in the vice trades, they were also cited as dens of theft and murder. When Frank Root reached Dobytown in 1863, just beyond the military reservation surrounding Fort Kearny, he found a small but bustling community. The greater part of the population seemed to be primarily interested in robbing overlanders of their livestock and personal possessions.[56] A year later at the Durlock Ranch just west of Fort Laramie, a Mr. Ravel was shot not by Lakota warriors but probably by members of an out-law gang.[57] Many of the reports written during the 1850s and 1860s confirmed the allegations of a newspaper article that had appeared in the *Weekly Missouri Statesman* as early as 1850, which stated that "there is a tribe of white Indians upon these plains at this time that are more dangerous than the Pawnees. They carry on horse and mule stealing pretty extensively and even oxen do not escape their attention."[58]

For at least one widely publicized homicide, a large sum of money seemed to have provided the motive. While traveling west from Denver in 1862 with five men and $5,000 in gold, John Campbell was killed by what his associates said were sixteen unidentified Indians. Yet the more often the survivors described the details of this attack, the more they contradicted each other. Several parties of emigrants listened incredulously to the stories, but lacking physical proof of guilt, they refrained from any arrests or prosecutions. Still, the strong doubts remained, as overlanders conjectured about whether the five companions had committed the heinous act or whether it had been carried out by white freebooters who congregated around the ferry at Fort Hall and who probably knew much about Campbell's business dealings. Apparently, no one believed that Indians were the guilty parties, since $5,000 in gold would have done them little good except to draw undue attention if they attempted to trade any of it for durable goods or livestock.[59]

Other traders and guides profited not by overt violence but rather by creating false Indian alarms as a way of redirecting the travel plans of emigrant parties. When the Barlow wagon train reached Fort Hall in 1845, they were greeted warmly by mountain man Caleb Greenwood, who warned of serious Indian problems if they continued up the Snake River toward Oregon. The old trapper then offered to lead them to Mexican California, where there were no Indian threats, fewer steep mountain grades, and better trail conditions. Some members of the train, including the Jarvis Bonney family, accepted Greenwood at his word and accompanied him to California, while the majority continued to Oregon with Samuel Barlow. Greenwood's offer was not as magnanimous as it first appeared because he charged a fee and was bound for California anyway.[60]

More dangerous was the advice rendered in 1855 by an unidentified trader near Humboldt Lake to the party that included Lydia Milner Waters. Their original intent was to travel via the Truckee River route, but the trader convinced them to take an eight-mile detour to avoid Indian problems. The cutoff proved to be a disaster, as it wound along a stagnant slough that eventually dissipated into desert alkali. Waters suspected that this bad advice had been generated by the trader's unwillingness to share overland business with another competitor who was located along the Truckee route.[61] During the same summer, William Keil suspected that a trader at Fort Hall also had ulterior motives when he suggested an alternate route because Indians were threatening the wagon road near Salmon Falls. Keil deduced that the man was working with the ferry operator who could collect a toll for every wagon he transported to the opposite bank of the Snake River. The Keil party decided to avoid the toll, and they continued on their way without encountering any troublesome Indians.[62]

Despite much evidence to the contrary, rumors of Indian massacres abounded along the trails, and their frequency escalated during the latter 1850s. Although there were many believers, there were also many skeptics. By the time he reached the Humboldt River in September 1849, Dr. Israel Lord had experienced enough of reality that he could honestly write, "The rumors of Indian depredations, though thick as blackberries, are not much to be relied on."[63] In a more sarcastic tone, Charlotte Pengra recorded toward the end of her 1853 journal: "I have heard lots of bugbear stories about Indians. . . . I conclude the stories are about as true as they ever will be."[64] James Pratt found special humor in northeastern Kansas during the spring of 1849, as he gained an appreciation for how vivid and well traveled the massacre stories had become. Tales abounded of Pawnee depredations throughout the Platte River valley of Nebraska, and the number of casualties seemed to rise with each retelling of the bloody accounts. Pratt noted, however, that freighters and emigrants returning from the west denied witnessing any evidence of Indian problems.[65]

Ironically, soldiers who had been sent to protect the overland trails were sometimes the worst offenders in creating and perpetuating massacre stories. Julius Merrill recorded in his 1864 journal how two soldiers kept members of his party spellbound with outrageous tales of Indian atrocities and the massacre of an entire wagon train fifty miles west of Fort Laramie. He wrote: "Never did human beings tell more or greater falsehoods than they. In the excitement nearly all swallowed every word as 'bible truth.' What heroes (asses) those two men must have been in their own estimation. . . . Amidst such excitement no lie was too big to be eagerly swallowed, if it was about Indians. Nothing else was thought of."[66]

Before completing their journeys, many overlanders came to have a healthy skepticism about Indian massacre tales, but it took the wit of one of America's foremost humorists to inform the larger public about the nature of the exaggerations. As a young man in 1861, Mark Twain accompanied his brother, Orion Clemens, to Virginia City, where Orion held the post as secretary to the territorial governor of Nevada. While residing in the mining boomtown, Twain collected stories from the local environs and published his uniquely versed columns in the local newspaper. In 1872, long after he had left the rough-and-tumble frontier, Twain published *Roughing It*, which returned to those earlier tales of half-truth and half-fiction.

Among the most amusing accounts related in the book were the author's anecdotes about his initial stage ride to Virginia City. While traveling west of Fort Laramie, he heard about the 1856 robbery of a

The German artist Leopold Grozelier prepared this lithograph in 1860 and entitled it *On the Prairie*. It portrayed the ubiquitous nineteenth-century view that Indians awaited the arrival of every wagon train so that they could attack, plunder, and drag away luckless captives. Because these scenes were popular with the public, artists frequently borrowed from each other to produce new versions. Grozelier copied this work from a more famous 1856 painting by Carl Wimar entitled *Attack on an Emigrant Train*. Courtesy of Joslyn Art Museum, Omaha, Nebraska.

COMPLETE. **BEADLE'S** NUMBER 45.

DIME NOVELS

THE CHOICEST WORKS OF THE MOST POPULAR AUTHORS

UNITED STATES OF AMERICA
ONE DIME

ESTHER:
A STORY OF THE OREGON TRAIL.

BEADLE AND COMPANY.
NEW YORK: 141 WILLIAM ST. LONDON: 44 PATERNOSTER ROW.
General Dime Book Publishers.

In the mid-nineteenth century, dime novels began to reach a large American and European reading audience. Ann S. Stephens's *Esther: A Story of the Oregon Trail* was typical of the genre, which overstressed the themes of violence and cultural conflict between whites and Indians in order to sell more books. But in this case, Esther, a Dakota woman, warns the white heroine of treachery and impending capture. Thus the dualistic pattern of "noble" Indians and "savage" Indians, popularized in James Fenimore Cooper's earlier novels, continued in the new format. Courtesy of Robert A. Clark and Arthur H. Clark Co.

A mid-nineteenth-century illustration entitled *A Chief Forbidding the Passage of a Train through His Country* frightened eastern audiences who were contemplating a trip across the Great Plains. For many twenty-first-century viewers, the sketch might imply an opposing theme of "noble" Indians standing up for their rights and resisting further exploitation of their resources by overlanders. Courtesy of Robert A. Clark and Arthur H. Clark Co.

George Norton, like other California-bound miners, had this stylized photograph made to show him with all of his grit and determination. In anticipation of Indian threats and other unexpected problems, he carried a Hall carbine, two pepperbox pistols, a bowie knife, and a Colt .44-caliber Walker revolver. One wonders if this heavily armed traveler was not more of a danger to himself than he was to Indians, especially since an accidental discharge from the carbine would have blown off his thumb. Courtesy of Jim Potter (Nebraska State Historical Society) and Western Reserve Historical Society, Cleveland.

Chief Big Elk provided leadership among the Omaha people during a crucial transition period in their tribal life. They resided near the Bellevue (Nebraska) trading post and agency between 1836 and 1854. Long friendly with white fur traders along the Missouri River, the Omahas also aided the Mormon settlement at Winter Quarters in 1846, at least until population pressures destroyed tribal hunting grounds. Big Elk prophetically warned about the "coming flood" of Americans, and in 1854 the Omahas were forced to move sixty-five miles up the Missouri River to Thurston County, Nebraska, where they reside today. From *Twenty-seventh Annual Report of the Bureau of American Ethnology* (1911).

American Indians frequently aided emigrant river crossings by rafting, canoeing, and building bridges. Several important ferry services on the formidable Kansas River were in the vicinity of present-day Topeka, Kansas. None was better known than the ferry operated by mixed-bloods Joseph and Louis Pappan. This September 12, 1856, sketch by Samuel J. Reader shows a portion of James H. Lane's "free soil army" utilizing the ferry during the years of Bleeding Kansas. The crossing was even more important to emigrants departing the Kansas City area for Oregon and California. Courtesy of Kansas State Historical Society.

P. 1. Lane's command crossing at PAPPAN'S FERRY. K. T. Friday morning, Sept. 12ᵗʰ 1856.

This undated painting, *Crossing the South Platte*, was done some years after noted artist and photographer William Henry Jackson made his first trips along the Oregon Trail as a bullwhacker. Yet the scene accurately captured a reality encountered by many overlanders. The presence of Indians trading with the caravans and helping move livestock across the shallow river represented the mutual benefit that occurred for both populations. Courtesy of Scotts Bluff National Monument.

This painting by William Henry Jackson, entitled *Fort Laramie*, shows the older fur-trading post about the time that it was purchased by the U.S. Army in 1849. The two Indian encampments shown here are indeed small compared to the many Lakota villages that existed in this general region during the heyday of the overland trails. Courtesy of Scotts Bluff National Monument.

Sin-Tig-a-leo-ka
Spotted Tail

Spotted Tail (Sinte Galeska), a respected leader among the Brulé Sioux, helped lead the 1854 attack upon Lt. John Grattan's command and upon a mail stage. Yet he subsequently interceded in disputes to help maintain peace along the overland trail. Because many Brulé people set up trading camps between Scotts Bluff and Fort Laramie, they had frequent contacts with white travelers. Unfortunately, the sheer number of emigrants overwhelmed the natural resources in those areas, and epidemics took a heavy toll on the Indians who conducted the trade and offered their services to the wagon trains. Courtesy of the Nebraska State Historical Society.

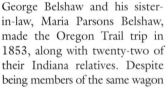

George Belshaw and his sister-in-law, Maria Parsons Belshaw, made the Oregon Trail trip in 1853, along with twenty-two of their Indiana relatives. Despite being members of the same wagon train and experiencing the same daily events, they described the experiences in very different ways. Neither had encountered American Indians prior to their reaching the Missouri River at Council Bluffs, Iowa. But at that first meeting with friendly Omahas or Potawatomies, Maria trembled in fear and placed her trust in God. George did not even record meeting Indians that day. This pattern of opposite reactions continued throughout the trip, with Maria fearing each new group of Indians and George generally stressing their friendliness and desire for trade. The photograph of George Belshaw was taken about the time of the Oregon Trail venture, and Maria Parsons Belshaw's photograph was taken later in life. Both photos in possession of the author and made available originally by Marshall Shore of Spokane, Washington.

One of William Henry Jackson's most famous paintings, *Approaching Chimney Rock* offers a fairly accurate view of the landscape. His attention to detail and representation of a semicircled wagon train are also realistic. As the approaching wagons take their position to complete the circle, the emigrants use the formation to confine the movement of their livestock, not necessarily to protect against anticipated Indian attacks. Courtesy of Scotts Bluff National Monument.

Chief Washakie and his Eastern Shoshone people found themselves in the path of the Oregon, California, and Mormon trails through Wyoming. Although Washakie repeatedly complained to American officials about the increased destruction of animals, grazing lands, and water sources, he maintained a level of peace between the two peoples. In an 1863 treaty signed at Fort Bridger, the Shoshones received a promise of annuities worth $10,000 annually for twenty years if they honored the terms. Five years later, they received from the U.S. government a permanent home on the Wind River Reservation in western Wyoming. Courtesy of the Smithsonian Institution.

Winnemucca, chief of the Paviotso, or Northern Paiutes, often camped among the Bannocks and had frequent contact with emigrants bound for Oregon or California. Although he was not the son of the famous Truckee, as Sarah Winnemucca later recorded, he shared Truckee's sentiment for peace with the whites. He maintained this conciliatory position until his death in 1882, and his acts of kindness were noted in trail journals and government reports. Courtesy of the Smithsonian Institution.

Brigham Young, as he appeared during the 1850s. Young held official positions that strongly shaped Indian and emigrant relations. Appointed as governor of Utah Territory in 1851, he simultaneously held the post of Indian superintendent for the territory (1851–58). Although many emigrants blamed Young and other Mormon leaders for creating Indian problems in Utah and Nevada, Young correctly pointed out that random acts of violence by white travelers were provoking Indian reprisals even against Mormon property. Courtesy of Utah State Historical Society.

William Henry Jackson's painting *White Men Hunting Buffalo* captures the Plains Indians' greatest complaint against the westward movement of Americans. Overlanders could not resist the urge to kill bison both for food and sport, often leaving great numbers of carcasses without any effort to collect meat from them. Loss of the bison not only harmed Plains Indian material culture but also subverted ceremonialism and spiritual values. Courtesy of Scotts Bluff National Monument.

General William S. Harney. The attack he led on September 3, 1855, against the Brulé camp of Little Thunder was regarded as a significant victory by many whites, who wanted revenge against the Sioux for the extermination of Lt. John L. Grattan and his command during the pervious year. But to the Sioux, this military action on Blue Water Creek in western Nebraska constituted an unprovoked massacre of mostly noncombatants. For the mixed-blood Sioux woman Susan Bordeaux Bettelyoun and others, this was the true beginning of troubles between her people and the American army. Overland emigrants would gradually feel the effects of these worsening conditions. Courtesy of Nebraska State Historical Society.

mail coach in which Indians had killed the driver and conductor. In typical Twain fashion, he related that during his stay in Nevada and California, he had interviewed fully 133 people who swore that they had been wounded in that exact same attack. He further explained that "one of these parties told me that he kept coming across arrow-heads in his system for nearly seven years after the massacre; and another of them told me that he was struck so literally full of arrows that after the Indians were gone and he could raise up and examine himself, he could not restrain his tears for his clothes were completely ruined."[67] Tall tales like this, and in the hands of a satirical master such as Twain, poked fun at the ubiquitous massacre stories of the mid-nineteenth century, but they probably did little to alleviate the anxiety of those overlanders whom James Pratt referred to as the "timid men."[68]

Two of the most widely known examples of Indian massacres along the western trails might as well have emanated from the fertile imagination of Mark Twain because they are now recognized as pure fabrications. The infamous 1861 Almo Creek Massacre supposedly occurred in southeastern Idaho when a massive wagon train of sixty wagons and three hundred travelers found themselves under attack by as many as 1,000 Shoshone warriors. Only five whites managed to escape this bloodbath, which local historian Charles S. Walgamott pronounced in 1927 to be "the greatest Indian disaster that ever occurred in the Territory of Idaho, and probably in the entire Northwest."[69]

Although uncritically repeated in a variety of twentieth-century books as if true, the sheer magnitude of the massacre begged authentication. More recent investigations by historian Brigham Madsen revealed no coverage of the monstrous event in contemporary issues of the *Salt Lake City Deseret News* or in the Sacramento or San Francisco newspapers. Nor were there any reports of it in War Department, Bureau of Indian Affairs, or territorial records, or even in other emigrants' accounts. Madsen's further probings led him to a single extended article in a 1938 issue of the *Blackfoot (Idaho) Daily Bulletin*. To whip up enthusiasm for local land sales and historical importance for the area, newspaper editor Byrd Trego had embellished the Walgamott fantasy. So successful had Trego and other promoters been in attracting national attention that they secured an official historical marker in memory of the 295 people who had perished in the horrible event. Despite Madsen's efforts to correct this historical hoax, the erroneous monument was still in place as late as 1999.[70]

Unlike the Almo Creek Massacre, which was primarily a twentieth-century invention, the Doniphan Massacre hoax originated in 1855 during the peak era of the overland migration. The story first appeared in the *Oregon Argus*, published in Oregon City, Oregon, and was supposedly based upon the testimony of John Wiggins, who was one of only nineteen survivors among a total of three hundred emigrants. According to his claims, at least 2,000 Sioux and Cheyenne warriors had attacked his train while it was camped at Devil's Gate. Wiggins witnessed the painful deaths of his wife and three children before he and the other survivors were able to walk the more than two hundred miles to Salt Lake City. One other overlander who was traveling ahead of the Doniphan party also provided an account of the massacre, though his facts did not closely conform to Wiggins's details. Another emigrant who passed through the area two weeks later, however, pronounced the incident to be a hoax, and he further noted that traders in the vicinity of Devil's Gate had not witnessed a single hostile Indian act within a year's time. Despite the lack of evidence associated with the Doniphan Massacre, it was reported as fact in at least five other newspapers as far east as St. Louis and as far west as San Francisco.[71]

Although overlanders certainly died at the hands of Indian warriors throughout the thirty-year height of the Oregon, California, and Mormon trails, the conflicts did not conform to the pulp novel or the Hollywood stereotypes of large, corralled wagon trains besieged by hundreds or thousands of feather-bedecked warriors and with high casualty rates on both sides of the battle. When death did come for either American Indians or whites, it was usually in numbers no greater than one or two. The preponderance of firsthand accounts clearly reveal that most Indian threats were to gain livestock by means of a stampede or to take possessions from a lone hunter or guide who strayed too far from the wagon train. Most western Indians viewed this as part of the reciprocal obligation that emigrants owed to them for traversing their lands and abusing their resources. Only in cases where warriors were strongly motivated by revenge did they premeditatively seek bloodshed, and these occasions remained relatively infrequent.

For the period from 1840 to 1870, only eight well-documented events have been uncovered that somewhat fit the notion of a "massacre" as whites would have defined the term at that time and as most twenty-first-century audiences would define it. The earliest of these occurred in 1851 at Tule Lake, on the California-Oregon border, and it quickly became known as the Bloody Point Massacre. The root cause of the trouble were miners who were pouring into Modoc lands and forcing the inhabitants away from traditional village sites. The massacre was actually a series of attacks during August and September, which began with an assault on a small party of freighters and was followed by an ambush of a civilian militia force. The mutilated bodies of twenty-two emigrants who had the misfortune of crossing the contested area at the wrong time were subsequently discovered. The militia reinforced another emigrant train and drove the Modoc warriors away, after inflicting perhaps twenty casualties on the Indians. In a fit of rage, the militiamen scalped and mutilated their adversaries.[72]

Two years later, approximately thirty Shoshones attacked one section of a wagon train that had split into two groups. Accounts differ as to the cause of this Ward Massacre southeast of Fort Boise, but it possibly stemmed from a lone warrior's attempt to steal a horse. He was killed in the attempt, and this provoked reprisals by his friends. Although reliable Indian casualties were never reported, fully nineteen whites died that day, many of them women and children. When other emigrant parties encountered the bloody scene, they were outraged by the graphic mutilations visited upon almost all of the bodies. Two young sons of Alexander Ward eventually reached Fort Boise to relate the details of the sordid affair.[73] Their story compelled the *Portland Weekly Oregonian* to demand that authorities "either exterminate the race of Indians, or prevent further wholesale butcheries by these worthless races resembling the human form." In its call for revenge, the series of articles made no distinction between guilty and innocent Indians.[74]

Events surrounding the 1857 Holloway Massacre are particularly murky due to conflicting white recollections and because no Indians took credit or blame for the deed. On August 14, while camped near a willow grove at the head of the Humboldt River, ten people were attacked by a small but effective group of unidentified Indians. Only two members of the party survived, including a Mrs. Holloway, who was badly beaten and scalped. Emblematic of the heinous act was the fact that her two-year-old daughter was repeatedly flung against a wagon wheel until she died. Although the raiders looted the three wagons, their original motivation for planning the attack was apparently the theft of livestock. Other travelers who reached the bloody scene later in the day attributed the crime purely to American Indians, but historian John Unruh, Jr., writing in 1979, posed a strong possibility that white robbers actually carried out the atrocity or at least rode with the Indians who perpetrated it.[75]

The probability of participation by white thieves in the Shepherd-Wright Massacre seems even more likely. While traversing the Hudspeth Cutoff of southeastern Idaho during July 1859, several wagonloads of the extended families of Thomas Ferguson Shepherd and James D. Wright came under attack from what was thought to be twenty Shoshones. Trapped in a narrow canyon, the overlanders faced a difficult time defending against marksmen situated on high ground and behind rocks. Four members of the party died in the attack, and another died later from wounds. Survivors of the ordeal petitioned the U.S. government for compensation, but for the moment the main impact of this attack was an increased alarm along the trail and an outpouring of anti-Indian feeling in newspapers. Soldiers under Lt. Ebenezer Gay organized a pursuit some days later from Camp Floyd but did little more than create a larger backlash when they killed several Indians who likely were innocent of the attack. Furthermore, eyewitnesses to the massacre testified that at least three of the attackers had spoken English and appeared to be white men. Considering that the culprits took $725 in gold coins from Annie Shepherd and $50 from the Wrights, white culpability seems highly plausible.[76]

The best known of the eight trail massacres occurred in September 1860, when forty-four persons traveling in an eight-wagon train were attacked by Shoshones approximately fifty miles west of Salmon Falls. Unlike the other seven case studies covered here, this one came closest to paralleling the later dime novel and movie stereotypes. In highly uncharacteristic fashion, the attackers maintained a formal siege of the corralled wagon train for the better part of two days. Eighteen emigrants were killed in the series of attacks, and four children were abducted. Another seventeen survivors were able to escape from the scene, but they endured severe hardship and near starvation before being rescued fully a month and a half after the attack. At the time of their rescue, only twelve remained alive and, according to several statements, they had subsisted on the flesh of the other five who had succumbed to the elements. This famous event, dubbed the Utter–Van Ornum Massacre, was sensationalized by many western newspapers, and it fed the already active rumor mill along the Oregon Trail. Maj. John Owen, who helped free several children, testified that the attack probably was motivated by revenge among some Shoshones and Bannocks who had been mistreated by earlier passing wagon trains.[77]

The Civil War brought new stresses to the overland trails just as Indian-white relations had reached a breaking point on both the Great Plains and the plateau area of Idaho. With fewer regular soldiers available to protect the overland routes, poorly trained militia units found themselves outnumbered and overextended at every point. Delays in authorization of food and other government annuities for the western tribes further strained relations and encouraged the raiding of emigrant livestock. Among the Shoshones, war chiefs such as Pashego seemed to be in ascendancy over traditional peace chiefs such as Washakie. On August 8 and 9, 1862, a series of depredations culminated in bloodshed at Massacre Rocks below the American Falls of the Snake River. Within the two-day period, at least twelve overlanders were killed and fifteen wounded. Estimates placed the number of Shoshone and Bannock attackers as high as two hundred, though the number was probably exaggerated. Sporadic attacks continued along this stretch of the trail through the following month, with additional casualties inflicted on both sides. Various agents warned that raids would continue unless the government accelerated the flow of annuities to the tribes and reopened negotiations with them. Unfortunately, through the remainder of the Civil War, the situation only worsened for emigrants and plateau Indians alike.[78]

As relations deteriorated along the Snake River route, Civil War realities also inflamed the plains tribes located along the Platte River. The Montana-bound wagon train of Josiah Kelly and William Larimer became the innocent victim of Sioux warriors while crossing Wyoming about eighty-five miles west of Fort Laramie. Approximately 250 Lakota warriors (mostly Oglalas) attacked the train the day after they had approached to inquire about trade and an exchange of food. The emigrants were apprehensive, but they had experienced no problems with Indians up to this point. Four men were killed outright, and two women and two children were taken captive. One of these children, Mary, was subsequently killed; Sarah Larimer and her son made their escape during the second day of their captivity and reached the safety of Deer Creek Station. Less fortunate was Fanny Kelly, who remained a captive for five months before being freed by a party of Blackfeet Sioux who took her to Fort Sully, Dakota Territory.[79] Although much discussed among other wagon trains of the era, the Kelly-Larimer Massacre of July 12, 1864, was but a small event compared to the more dramatic incidents of bloodshed that were to follow. Both Plains Indians and whites suffered much between the Third Colorado Volunteers' massacre of Black Kettle's Southern Cheyenne village at Sand Creek, Colorado, in November 1864 and Sioux destruction of William Fetterman's contingent of eighty-one soldiers at Fort Phil Kearny on December 21, 1866.

Amid the widespread raids and reprisals of the Civil War era, western Nebraska became the setting for some of the bloodiest encounters during the summer of 1864. A large party of Cheyennes, joined by some Arapaho and Brulé Sioux allies, swept through the Platte River valley as far east as Plum Creek, or present-day Lexington, Nebraska. Seeking both livestock and revenge for earlier militia attacks against their people, they primarily targeted the road ranches and telegraph stations that had become hated symbols of permanent white habitation between Plum Creek and Julesburg, Colorado. Some wagon trains accepted the advice of army officers not to travel west of Fort Kearny for the time being, but others did not heed the warning. On August 8, as many as one hundred Indians descended upon a small party of travelers, killing eleven men and capturing four women and children. News of the Plum Creek Massacre traveled far, and it continued to receive much national attention because of ongoing efforts to secure release of the captives. The four endured incredible hardships before Maj. Edward W. Wynkoop was finally able to secure the release of the last prisoner a month later.[80]

Instead of the raids dissipating, however, they switched direction and intensified. Throughout the summer and early fall of 1864, this raiding party and others like it roamed through the relatively unprotected western end of the Little Blue River valley. So devastating were the attacks that many settlers fled toward the eastern counties of Nebraska, while others sought refuge at local ranch houses or at Fort Kearny. Two years earlier, no one would have predicted that this settled area of the state could become so imperiled by a new Indian threat.[81]

Even though overland emigrants stood poised on a more dangerous age by the time of the Civil War, the trail experience never reached the level of violence commonly depicted in later literary and cinematic portrayals. Historian John Unruh, Jr.'s statistics confirm the low percentage of attacks and deaths on both sides when compared to the overall numbers of people traversing the western trails. The fact that Unruh found hard evidence of only 362 emigrant deaths and 426 Indian deaths between 1840 and 1860 due to conflict between Indians and whites still testifies to the relatively low level of violence for the extended period. Of course, the average of a mere 18 emigrant mortalities per year probably misses some deaths that went unrecorded in trail journals and military reports. Furthermore, the frequency of attacks and the death rates actually increased in the period after 1857, just about the time that Unruh was ending his study. Other analyses by Glenda Riley, Lillian Schlissel, Robert Munkres, and Christopher Clark parallel Unruh's findings, but they also terminate the focus of their investigations about 1860.[82]

Exact numbers of casualties will always be contested, and assigning the rubric of "massacre" to only eight well-documented cases will spur future debate about definitions.[83] For instance, when one considers the especially dangerous conditions along the Bozeman Trail, running between Fort Laramie and the mining fields of western Montana, the specters of "battle" and "massacre" arose during the American Civil War and the years that immediately followed. The death of Fetterman's troops at Fort Phil Kearny served lethal notice of Lakota military power, but this historical example dealt with combat between soldiers and the Sioux, not with overlanders who, in fact, continued to pass across the region to the south of the Bozeman Trail with far less difficulty.

Yet the pattern that remains most evident throughout the thirty-year cycle is that Indian-white relations along the Oregon, California, and Mormon trails were characterized more by friendship and mutual exchange than they were by contentiousness and bloodshed. Moreover, when acts of violence occurred, they usually did so because of cultural misunderstandings and anxieties, not because of innate or premeditated evil. Distrust was a natural phenomenon between two peoples who were thrust together with so little real knowledge about each other. When combined with two centuries of anti-Indian feelings in American history, it is little wonder that fear of American Indians eventually escalated into dangerous national exaggerations about their threat to the westward migration. Unfortunately, those exaggerations led to increased turmoil during the late 1850s, to total pandemonium during the Civil War, and inevitably toward the far-ranging northern Plains Indian wars of the late 1860s and 1870s.

Captivity Infinitely Worse Than Death

An Exaggerated Tale

A century and a half ago, the cry of "Comanche" generated panic among the thinly settled pioneer families of the southern plains. Texans especially appealed to their state legislature for increased patrolling by ranger companies, and they chided the U.S. government for protecting and abetting these raiders who were residing on reservations above the Red River. Inflammatory newspaper articles, endless citizens' petitions, and heated legislative debates conveyed the venomous feelings that most Anglo and Hispanic residents held for these "Lords of the South Plains," who seemed to move across the frontier counties with impunity. In an emotional entreaty to Governor Hardin R. Runnels in 1858, Capt. John S. "Rip" Ford of the Texas Rangers called for increased expenditures to wage war against the marauders, and he well articulated the sentiments of families throughout the state when he wrote: "Our people have been tortured in the most inconceivable and brutal manner by our savage foes. Women have been violated in the presence of their husbands—daughters have been ravished in the presence of their mothers—children have been carried into captivity infinitely worse than death."[1] The closing refrain—"captivity infinitely worse than death"—resonated with all who believed that death was indeed preferable to a life among the "wild savages."

Captivity narratives, among the oldest and most enduring of American literary forms, originated in Capt. John Smith's fanciful versions of his dealings with Powhatan and in Mary Rowlandson's 1682 account of her abduction during King Philip's War.[2] Puritan society was especially prolific in the creation of this literary genre because it provided a medium through which the group's sacred "errand into the wilderness" could be used to justify wars of extermination against New England tribes. The tales, although viewed as truthful accounts, were actually formula stories illustrating newly discovered religious faith amid extreme privation, and they served as jeremiads to rally true believers and prevent further backsliding that might incur God's wrath.[3]

By the early nineteenth century, these didactic stories of punishment and redemption gave way to a more fanciful series of books and pamphlets written mostly by amateurs who knew little about Indians or frontier life. In turn, celebrated novelists such as James Fenimore Cooper, Charles Brockden Brown, and William Gilmore Simms elevated these captivity narratives to a respectable position within American literature, and they offered the western wilderness as the setting for the contest between savagery and civilization. By the end of the nineteenth century, the captivity stories had been reduced to the penny dreadfuls and pulp thrillers that virtually eliminated the religious and psychological insights of the earlier works and substituted cheap thrills and sexual voyeurism. Not only had the literary quality declined during the nineteenth century, but also the accuracy of the tales and their ethnographical value had fallen to new lows.[4]

Ironically, it was within this period of decline that some of the most important captivity accounts were written by actual survivors of the ordeals, and no region of the vast trans-Mississippi West produced more significant publications than did Texas during the period from 1836 to 1875. Unlike the spiritual autobiographies of Puritan New England, many of these were primarily written as a means to earn money for the financially pressed authors and their sometimes unidentified ghostwriters. Among the earliest published and most influential of all accounts was Sarah Ann Horn's *A Narrative of the Captivity of Mrs. Horn, and Her Two Children, with That of Mrs. Harris, by the Camanche Indians,* issued in cheap format in 1839 to finance the author's return to England. Unfortunately, Horn never made it home before dying from the debilitating effects of her captivity and the continued exploitation by her white rescuer, Benjamin Hill.[5]

A similar fate befell Rachel Plummer, whose fifteen-page pamphlet of 1838 contained all the pathos that a book of this type possibly could. Nevertheless, it was accurate and straightforward in virtually all passages. Unfortunately, later borrowings from the publication embellished the account with contrived examples of Indian fiendish behavior, but sales of the original pamphlet and its later versions did not help Plummer. She died on February 19, 1839, shortly after being reunited with her husband and having never recovered her young son from the Comanches.[6]

Even though publications of this sort rarely achieved the financial success for which they were intended, they were widely read and imitated in fiction. Among eastern and European audiences, far removed from the realities of the frontier, even the most fanciful incidents seemed believable. The sagas thus added to the prevailing anti-Indian biases of the mid-nineteenth century, and doubtless many of the overland emigrants of that era drew their harsh preconceptions about American Indians from the abundant literature of real and fictionalized captivity narratives, especially those with Texas origins. For that reason, many of their letters and diaries were filled with speculations on what it must be like to be forced to live among the "savages." The emphasis upon sexual innuendo in the narratives not only turned the image of the Indian male into a sexual predator, but also his uncontrollable libido became a popular literary metaphor for the threat of savagery against the innocence and purity of America. Many emigrants were therefore conditioned to think that American Indians were predisposed toward abducting or purchasing white women for their lustful harems and also toward acquiring white children for producing additional savages in the future.[7]

While men and women expressed their fears in fairly equal proportions during the early phases of their overland trips, the concern about possible captivity appeared more frequently in the women's accounts. Yet the women's comments were rarely obsessive or detailed, and their captivity concerns frequently constituted only a small element among their larger generic apprehensions about American Indians. Lodisa Frizzell's emotions about the possibilities of both bondage and massacre found their way into her journal, where she admitted that ill-founded rumors had led her to fear the worst from American Indians. Instead of trying to whisk her away at the first opportunity, however, the Indians that she met along the Platte River on her way to California proved to be civil, and their efforts to amuse her with games helped dissipate much of her anxiety.[8]

By way of contrast, Clara Witter did not find the same degree of comfort when she met her first Indians on the banks of the Elkhorn River in northeastern Nebraska. Although only two Pawnees came into her camp, she tossed and turned all night, convinced that they would sneak back in the darkness and either kill or steal her away to their village.[9]

In a similar vein, the youthful indiscretion of Marion W. Battey and her friend Waity presented the perfect opportunity for an Indian abduction of two white women. As they had done on numerous occasions in preceding days, the two friends started walking along the trail and leisurely picking flowers before the wagons had resumed their morning travel. While out of sight of their comrades, they were intercepted by a lone Indian rider who towered above them. Battey noted the "frightful stare from his piercing black eyes" and deduced that he was planning the murder or abduction of this easy prey. Fortunately, according to Battey, the lead two wagons of the train appeared just in time to scare the Indian and his more distant accomplice away from the scene. She further recorded that other members of her party were convinced that the two women would have become unfortunate prisoners had the initial wagons not arrived on the scene at that precise moment.[10] Hollywood movies of the twentieth century could not have better portrayed the stereotypes of a narrowly averted disaster than did this young woman's remembrances—and frequently cinematic directors did utilize this dramatic scenario in their plot lines, which elicited the same fear and loathing among a postfrontier generation.

At the opposite end of the spectrum was the fate of recently arrived Danish emigrant Jenssine Grundvig. While on her way to Salt Lake City with her husband, Frantz Christian, in September 1865, the two fell behind their otherwise heavily defended Mormon train of fifty wagons and were attacked by an unidentified group of Indians, who rapidly descended upon them from dense brush stretched out along a creek. Frantz Christian was badly wounded by five or six arrows, including one that wedged so deeply in his hipbone that it could not be removed until two years later. The last he saw of his wife was her being put on a horse and led away by the attackers. He later recalled that he had remained distraught for many months afterward, until he had a dream that his wife had fallen from her horse and drowned when the Indians tried to carry her back to their camp. The dream had been so vivid that he believed it to be a godly vision sent to relieve his troubled spirit, and he could now take solace in the affirmation that his "beloved wife had not lived to be molested by her captors, and he was comforted."[11]

Virtually all primary accounts of trail life that recorded personal thoughts about Indian captivity fit into one of three models. In the case of Lodisa Frizzell, the preconceived notion proved baseless and resulted in a change of opinion about American Indians. In the examples offered by Clara Witter and Marion Battey, the preconceived notion of Indian malicious intentions remained alive in the minds of the two female travelers. Only in the case of Jenssine Grundvig did the preconception of intrinsic danger prove to be real, and yet this type of event was so seldom recorded along the trail that it was statistically irrelevant. Such was not the case, however, when it came to the persistence of barbaric stereotyping in literature and rumormongering along the trail, where seemingly every Indian male remained a potential abductor.

What place, then, did the taking of captives occupy in American Indian life, and how significant of a threat was it to persons who trudged along the trails to Oregon, California, and Salt Lake City during the mid-nineteenth century? Although generalizations are easy to come by in this regard, differences in individual tribal practices bring the accuracy of all generalizations into question. Ever since the colonial era, many American Indian tribes east of the Mississippi River had routinely taken captives—Indian and white alike—and indeed this frequency helped feed the anti-Indian literature that was generated from Puritan times to the various accounts of Daniel Boone rescuing his daughter, Jemima, from the Shawnees. The Six Nations of the Iroquois League were especially noted for the large numbers of captives who lived within their villages. The motivations for such an extensive practice can be grouped within five categories: to seek revenge on an adversary; to secure prisoners who then could be used to ransom relatives previously captured by that enemy group; to use captives as bargaining chips for opening diplomatic negotiations; to secure prisoners who could be exchanged for trade goods and other forms of wealth; and to enlarge the tribal population by means of formal adoption of enemy captives into the kinship circle.[12]

Taking captives in order to adopt them best explains the behavior of the plains tribes that overland travelers encountered. Even in the era prior to white contact, Pawnees, Cheyennes, Arapahos, Crows, Sioux, and other plains tribes had relied upon this practice to sustain demographic growth. Replacing deceased members, expanding the pool of marriage partners, augmenting the number of warriors for hunting and protection, and widening the circle of relatives upon which one could rely were all necessary goals of tribal societies.[13]

This reality took on greater importance in the early nineteenth century, when regular contact with whites brought intermittent cholera and smallpox epidemics that killed many Great Plains inhabitants. To have relied solely on natural birth rates to replenish the badly depleted populations would have been unrealistic and unwise. Some broadening of kinship lines occurred with the increased frequency of Indian marriages to white fur traders, and these produced several generations of mixed-blood children, who mostly remained with their mother's relatives.[14]

For the most part, however, the cycle of Plains Indian captive taking remained focused on people from other tribes, not from white populations. The rarity of white women and children in the central plains prior to the migrations of the 1840s precluded much chance for Indian men to seize and marry those women, even if they had desired to do so. Instead, they remained content to seek captives from the women and children of competing tribes, persons who could more easily acculturate into the lifeways of their masters. The same pattern held true in the Pacific Northwest, where tribes adopted many Indian but few white captives into their populations. Within the Great Basin and the plateaus of the Snake River Basin, even fewer adoptions of whites occurred.

Since Plains Indians desired the complete absorption of prisoners into their tribes, they gave considerable thought to how prisoners were treated. In the initial days and weeks after being captured, the captive was dealt a series of harsh physical and psychological blows as part of the seasoning process to see how well the individual could adapt to adversity. This initial flurry of cruel treatment was aimed at disorienting individuals, making them feel dependent on their captors, and forcing them to relinquish all hope of returning to their former lives. Those who proved weak were sometimes killed outright, traded to other tribes, or delegated to a lifetime of servile duties with little chance of formal adoption by a family. Those who were too aggressive—especially male adults—were often killed because they represented too much of a threat to their new masters and were not likely to give up resisting even after the passage of time. Others, particularly those who evidenced a physical toughness, a determination to survive, and an accommodationist spirit to their new surroundings, soon found more favorable treatment following their abusive initiation rites. A key element in their successful transition from captive to full-fledged member of the tribe was finding friends and protectors who could blunt the ill treatment and offer advice on adjustment to the unfamiliar culture. These often became the families who formally adopted the individual.[15]

Male children were especially prized as adoptees, because they eventually could replace dead warriors, and their hunting skills could feed elderly couples who were childless. But young girls and mature women were also readily integrated into the families, and many of them, especially the girls who were raised within the tribe most of their lives, ultimately found desirable marriage partners. The adoption ceremony, a formal though not elaborate ritual among most tribes, marked the transition of a person from chattel status to becoming a recognized equal within the group.[16] Ethnohistorian James Axtell discovered the same pattern of capture-adoption during the colonial era among northeastern tribes, whose adoptees often replaced deceased Indian sons and daughters. Although the age and gender may not have always matched, the same social status, honors, obligations, and sometimes even names were extended to the adoptees.[17]

One of the most persistent beliefs in American society since colonial times was that Indian warriors routinely raped captive women and girls. In published captivity narratives and novels, the references to this practice were often obliquely worded because such descriptions offended the delicate sensitivities of Victorian America, and they stigmatized women who allegedly experienced the forcible act. Although these types of moral outrages certainly occurred, they did so at a frequency that fell far below the rumored level. Most Indian warriors pledged abstinence while on the raiding trail to ensure success, and only the most reprehensible of individuals violated sacred taboos that could bring ruin on themselves and their compatriots. Furthermore, the raping of a woman who one day might be adopted into the tribe and marry one of its members endangered the potential kin relationship with the woman and bordered on incest. To force a woman into a sexual relationship violated the sacred concepts of familial adoption and freedom of choice that were essential to the bonding process that most American Indians sought.[18]

The act of taking captives, splitting biological families, using harsh treatment to "break in" the luckless individuals, and imposing a new way of life on them all constituted a disorienting and painful experience that no person willingly chose to undergo. Yet for the captives who ultimately assimilated into the lifeways of their captors, underwent formal adoption ceremonies, married within the new family, and remained in this situation for many years, there was little desire to return to their original families when that chance sometimes came. This reality seemed to be as true among long-term American Indian captives who were held by other tribes as it was among whites who were captured and integrated into tribal societies.

The phenomenon of preferring to remain with one's captors had nothing to do with the Patty Hearst syndrome of being mistreated and brainwashed to the point of total dependency. The transformation had more to do with what Axtell identifies as the attractive features of Indian societies, whose members, after a harsh initiation period, opened their arms and hearts to the adoptee. In Axtell's estimation, the captives "stayed because they found Indian life to possess a strong sense of community, abundant love, and uncommon integrity. . . . But Indian life was attractive for other values—for social equality, mobility, adventure, and as two adult converts acknowledge, 'the most perfect freedom, the ease of living, [and] the absence of those cares and corroding solicitudes which so often prevail with us.'"[19]

Although this reality of extending full rights and honors existed throughout Indian country, the principles remained largely unrecognized by white audiences, who continued to regard captivity as a fate "infinitely worse than death." Cultural differences further obscured this reality, especially among overland emigrants and settlers who consistently misinterpreted the actions of American Indians. On the southern plains, tribes such as the Comanches abducted and, over time, fully integrated many Anglo, Hispanic, and Indian captives into their world.[20] But tribes located along the Platte, Sweetwater, Snake, and Humboldt rivers more often captured white adults not with the intention of forcing their integration into the community but rather to teach the interlopers a lesson about who was in charge of the situation.

In this regard, diarists used the term "captive" frequently, but they used it imprecisely. Typical was the 1847 experience of Thomas Hockett and J. M. Robinson, who, while hunting some distance from their wagon train in southeastern Nebraska, were apprehended by Pawnee warriors. Rather than intending to take the two men back to their camp for the purpose of torture or permanent imprisonment, the Indians were only interested in seizing the men's guns and clothing. When Hockett resisted, the warriors bent him over so that his head rested on his knees, and their leader beat him unmercifully with the back of a bow until his skin was split in long, narrow grooves. In the aftermath of the event, Hockett vowed that he would never lose a chance to kill an Indian—any Indian—when the opportunity availed itself.[21] Similar moments of terror occurred for Nicholas Dawson in 1841, a Mr. Cline in 1852, and Tim Cook in 1854, but in each case the Indians merely relieved the travelers of their valuables and turned them loose. Robbery, not long-term captivity or murder, was clearly the intention behind these actions, as in so many similar cases that dotted the western landscape.[22]

Even when the period of detainment was slightly longer than in these examples, the events still did not conform to the notion of "captivity," nor did the resolution of events represent a narrow escape from torture or death. Near the Grand Island of the Platte River in 1853, Carl Ivins and a friend named Clark went out on the prairie to retrieve some of their cattle that had stampeded during the night. Well beyond sight of the wagons, they were discovered by five heavily armed Indians "whooping and yelling like mad" as they "danced a war dance around their prisoners." The Indians, probably Pawnees, made threatening gestures toward the two men and gave orders at gunpoint for them to follow. The Indians raided Ivins's food supply and insisted upon the use of his bowie knife to cut willow branches to make a temporary shelter. At no time, however, did they attempt to relieve the two white men of their pistols. Ivins played along with the warriors' frequent motions for scalping, and he joined in their laughter as they made further threatening remarks and gestures. Once they were finished with the food and their joke, the Pawnees walked away from their "captives" and continued on their way. Despite evidence to the contrary, Ivins's wife described the event as if Ivins and Clark had been captives of a menacing war party.[23]

One of the most frequently repeated stories of a brief captivity on the trail occurred in 1842 when Asa Lovejoy and Lansford Hastings were surprised by a large group of Indians at Independence Rock. At first the startled Americans commenced shaking hands and greeting the Indians, but when the two men tried to mount their horses, the

Indians grabbed the reins and would not let go. Lovejoy expected that he and Hastings would be killed, especially after the warriors seized their rifles and began touching them with the gunstocks as if counting coups on an enemy. Some were quite menacing, but their leader seemed more interested in impressing upon the white men the supremacy of Indian power, and he kept the situation under control. On the second day of their ordeal, and after being lectured to by the Indian "chief" and physically abused by others, Lovejoy and Hastings were released to convey the object lesson to other members of their party.[24]

Fully four years later, Jessy Quinn Thornton reported that a Sioux man who resided in the camps near Fort Laramie possessed a certificate signed by Hastings, indicating that this was indeed the chief who had "saved" the lives of the two Americans at Independence Rock. Even though different versions of this story were told along the trail and written about during the following years, most renditions stressed the barbarism of Indian captive taking, rather than the probable didactic intentions behind the rough treatment.[25]

This type of profound cultural misunderstanding that overdramatized American Indian enslavement of white male adults was only a small fragment of a larger misperception of Indian practices. Ever since the earliest stages of European contact, the Native inhabitants of North America had been viewed as uncivilized and licentious. During the first half of the nineteenth century, narratives written by western fur traders and explorers expanded this sexually charged stereotype by emphasizing that degraded American Indians responded less to the voice of reason and more to the sirens of primitive passions. Indians were wrongly portrayed as having virtually no sexual taboos, and certainly none that could be compared to rigid Christian ethics.[26]

In this regard, three stereotypes of American Indian women routinely appeared—drudge, prostitute, and beautiful princess. The first two images were closely aligned in the ubiquitous and prejudicial word "squaw," and they represented the extreme opposite of the Pocahontas-type princess who possessed characteristics of nobility. The drudge and prostitute typologies personified white perceptions that many Indian women were ugly, were badly treated by their imperious husbands, worked endlessly to an early death, and were frequently sold and rented out by their husbands and fathers for promiscuous sex that would generate profits for the males.[27]

Emigrant journals are replete with these notions, and most of the descriptions contain unflattering moralistic judgments that condemn all Indian deportment. Many of these lack firsthand observations but are vehemently argued, based only upon rumors that had fueled further rumors. They often share the significant ingredients of Scottish fur trader Alexander Ross's 1849 book, *Adventures of the First Settlers on the Oregon or Columbia River, 1810–1813*, which declared: "Chastity is not considered a virtue by the Chinooke [*sic*] women, and their amorous propensities know no bounds. All classes, from the highest to the lowest, indulge in coarse sensuality and shameless profligacy. Even the chief would boast of obtaining a paltry toy or trifle in return for the prostitution of his virgin daughter."[28]

Despite the multitude of unsubstantiated allegations, demonstrable evidence did exist to give partial credence to charges of illicit sexual practices among some American Indian women. While camped at Council Bluffs in 1850 awaiting ferry service across the Missouri River, Byron McKinstry witnessed an obvious case of prostitution that had a strangely larcenous twist. A succession of white men paid an Indian woman for sex, and when she led them into nearby bushes, the amorous Lotharios naively followed. She would then bolt toward the protection of her own people, money safely in hand, and leave the "greenhorn to be laughed at by both whites and Indians."[29]

Some of the accounts remained disguised in the rhetoric of understatement, while others constituted harsh denunciation of the players. In the former case, Dr. John Wayman described an 1852 sexual rendezvous at Granite Pass, Idaho, when an Indian woman successfully solicited food from several male overlanders without exchanging any trade goods with them. One by one, she led the men into a nearly private area where she "entertained" each of them for a brief time.[30] Lutheran missionary Paul Ferdinand Doederlein was less reserved seven years later in his denunciation of two traders who purchased the services of an Indian woman "to satisfy their satanic lust." He continued with the exclamation, "Oh, what disgraceful conduct on the part of the servants of Satan!" but he left the judgment unclear as to whether he blamed the woman or the traders more for this disgraceful act.[31]

Not all accounts of Indian prostitution were fraudulent, but they often were grossly overstated. Furthermore, many of the credibly reported cases of debauchery were closely associated with Indians' demands for liquor and their willingness to sell or barter anything for even small amounts of it. While alcoholism affected different bands and tribes to differing degrees, the groups that willingly located their villages along the overland trails and near the trading posts were more likely to be adversely affected by alcohol because of their close proximity to the supply. Catherine Adams and William McClellan voiced a commonly held sentiment among overlanders when they independently remarked that Indians were rarely any trouble except when liquor came into play; then their demeanor was moody, unpredictable, and sometimes violent.[32] Alcohol also led to the occasional prostituting of Indian women, and this furthered the stereotype of Indian unbridled promiscuity.

Yet the emigrants' main concern was not the corrupting of white men by Indian women; it instead was the age-old belief that Indian men represented a great sexual threat to white women. John Braly recalled years later the events of his 1847 crossing when Five Crows, a Cayuse man of some importance, tried to purchase Braly's seventeen-year-old sister, Sarah. Not to be denied, the "chief" repeatedly raised his offer of prized ponies, but he was firmly rebuffed on each attempt. When the frightened Sarah crawled into the relative safety of a wagon, he followed her and peered underneath the canvas covering. At that point, one member of the company popped his whip with a loud crack, and Five Crows and his companions left. During the night, Indians drove off seven horses from the wagon train and exacted their revenge for the embarrassing event, according to Braly.[33]

Almost two decades later, Helen Clark described the furious pace of a bartering attempt by some Cheyenne warriors who offered as many as ten fine horses for Clark and a Mrs. Wimple.[34] Clara Witter, always an alarmist when it came to American Indians, wrote about the many Plains Indians who tried to purchase her, and in something of a self-congratulatory tone, she asserted: "I was very fair and they liked white women."[35] The most outlandish tale, however, came from Andrew Chambers, who many years after his 1845 crossing alleged that an unidentified Indian man in the Umatilla Valley of Oregon offered fifty horses and a hundred blankets for his sister, sixteen-year-old Mary Jane. Mary Jane supposedly became so alarmed by the incident that she would never again show her face any time Indians were present. Though the story is a memorable one, it is totally lacking in credibility since no Indian family could or would have offered such a high barter price for a single white or Indian captive of either gender.[36]

Sometimes the purchase stories assumed amusing overtones. George Forman took special delight in poking fun at a forty-five-year-old widow whom he described as "stout and strong smelling of Tobacco being a great smoker, but romantic withal and a great reader of Cooper's Novels and admirer of Indians." She declared that she could understand the Sioux, even though she had no previous experience with them. Furthermore, she alleged that their chief was in love with her and wanted to marry her and carry her off to his camp. Forman doubted not only the veracity of the woman's judgments, but he also had little faith in the nobility of this particular group of Sioux, whom he surmised might be planning a robbery.[37]

Similar cases of possible self-delusion were humorously reported by men and women alike. Forty-niner Elijah Farnham offered generally favorable comments about his initial meetings with the Lakotas, but he paid special attention to one of the Sioux men who evidenced undue interest in a woman of his wagon train. Farnham ended his diary entry about the unsuccessful offer of three ponies for the woman by remarking: "She must of felt herself highly flatterd [*sic*]."[38] Fourteen years later, Harriet Smith encountered several other parties of Sioux while on the way to the Pike's Peak goldfields of Colorado and offered her own ironic twist to the purchase-a-bride story. On the first day of contact, she was approached by a Sioux man who constantly dogged her steps and tried to converse with her. Angered and frightened by the incident, she retreated to the concealment of a wagon, and the man finally went away. Two days later and farther down the trail, another Sioux man dressed in gaudy clothes and sporting six rings on one finger allegedly motioned that he wanted to purchase the twenty-two-year-old Smith. This time she presented a braver front and even recorded self-confidently in her diary: "but I thought I would wait untill [*sic*] some one would give Unc a lot of ponies for me and I would go and stay awhile with them then run away, and then we would have some ponies."[39]

On other occasions, white attempts at joking with Indians about purchases of white servants and brides led to cultural misunderstandings and worse. At age eighty-eight, many years after her 1864 crossing of the plains, Mrs. D. H. Peery recalled the near fate of young Sue Pritchett, beautiful daughter of the captain of their train. When two Sioux men began to admire the young woman, a member of the company named

Oscar Harman dickered with the strangers on how much they would be willing to pay for the object of their affections. A price of two ponies was agreed to, but when they were denied the exchange, the mood of the Indians turned ugly. Peery feared retaliation for the ill-conceived joke, but none came, and she attributed this to the fact that the wagon train was a large and heavily armed one.[40]

Priscilla Merriman Evans recalled her own husband's thoughtless act when he initiated discussions with an Indian man, offering to sell Priscilla for a single pony. Nothing happened until the following day, when the Indian returned with the agreed upon dowry to purchase the white woman. Only the timely intervention of the captain of the wagon train settled the difficulty, but not before frightening Priscilla out of her wits.[41] Similarly, Daniel Bayley began kidding with an Indian at Fort Hall about selling his eighteen-year-old daughter, Caroline. The Indian offered three horses. Bayley demanded six, and the issue was quickly forgotten until the following day, when the man showed up with the asking price of six horses. Upon being rebuffed, he followed the wagon train for several days before finally giving up. Daniel's wife, Betsey, wrote in her diary: "The Indians never joke, and Mr. Bayley took good care ever after not to joke with them."[42]

More serious in tone were the accounts of alleged Indian attacks specifically to secure white women by means of force rather than barter. Mary Jane Hayden later swore that when she was only nineteen or twenty years old and making the Oregon crossing via Fort Hall in 1850, Indians tried to pull her out of the wagon and ride away with her as their captive. Only the quick action of Sumner Barker, who struck the leader of the raiders with a powerful flick of his whip, drove them away.[43] Three years later, two young white women supposedly were saved from certain capture when a man in their group fought back by hitting one of the kidnappers in the ribs with a mighty blow from his gun muzzle. Allegedly, the "beautiful red hair" of one of the women had been the catalyst that drove the libidinous Indians to their desperate act.[44] At a point on the Upper Crossing of the Platte River in 1855, a warrior tried to abduct an eighteen-year-old named Hargraves after she had strayed from camp to milk a cow. She swung the half-full milk pail, hitting the man with force, and in retaliation, he speared her twice and bound a long tether to her wrist. Upon trying to lead the young woman away, the abductor gave up because she either fainted or collapsed from the blood loss of her wounds.[45]

In these three cases of attempted abduction, only the third can be substantiated with corroborating evidence. The pattern found in most of these tales is that they were not recorded at the time of the events in daily diary and journal entries but rather were written many years later in books and articles that were intended to appeal to larger public audiences. Some of the stories were remarkably similar to each other, and some clearly were manufactured to titillate the prospective reading audience. These include celebrated American poet Joaquin Miller, who made the Oregon trip in 1852 and took numerous liberties with the truth in his later "autobiography." Among other apparent fabrications was his story about a beautiful young woman named Wagoner, whose father facetiously offered her to an Indian man for ten spotted horses. Missing the humor of the unfulfilled offer, the angry Indian stormed away "scornfully refusing what presents were offered him for his forbearance," and the young woman threatened to drown herself rather than submit her body to the Indian man.[46]

Equally suspect was the annual address delivered at the 1877 Oregon Pioneer Association by Stephen Staats about one aspect of his overland journey thirty-two years earlier. He told of the relentless efforts of a Sioux warrior to purchase or capture a young woman named Bailey—a "piece of feminine beauty"—and how the Indian was thwarted by Staats's direct intervention to save the young woman from these unwanted advances. Then, as if delivering the punch line to his 1877 audience, Staats informed them that it was he, not the Indian warrior, who ultimately married Bailey—"the much coveted prize."[47]

Although historians have not delved as deeply into the sexual relations between overlanders and Indians as they have into other topics, a clear pattern emerges from their conclusions. In her exhaustive study *Women and Indians on the Frontier, 1825–1915*, Glenda Riley asserts that "there is little support for the idea that American Indians routinely sexually abused their female captives." In contrast to the omnipresent appearance of this theme in popular literature and imagery, the overwhelming number of "women's accounts do not mention or even hint at sexuality, nor do they include fears about impending rape by Indian males." Riley further notes that even if one assumes that women were reticent to discuss such a sensitive issue in autobiographical writings intended for the Victorian public, they certainly would have been more willing to include such matters in the private pages of their diaries or in their petitions entreating the U.S. Congress to pay compensation for

Indian raids and outrages. The fact that they very seldom did either strongly suggested to Riley that the threat of Indian purchase or capture of white women was a rarity, especially in the era of the overland trails along the central route.[48]

John Unruh, Jr., discusses this important issue only in the briefest fashion, but, like Riley, he acknowledges that "in their latter-day reminiscences overlanders were fond of magnifying and even inventing such episodes."[49] Similarly, in connecting the purchase-and-capture issue with the broader stereotype of Indian raider, Robert Munkres concludes: "The threat of Indian attack on the first half of the Oregon Trail during the years of greatest emigrant travel has all too frequently been unduly emphasized by popular writers. Such treatment has tended to romanticize the 'Indian fighting' capabilities of many of the early travelers as well as the 'bloodthirsty' reputation of all plains Indians."[50] The most persuasive of arguments appears in the work of California Trail historian George R. Stewart, who points out that much of this dangerous perception emanated from white preconceptions about American Indians and from the cultural misunderstandings that occurred in these briefest of exchanges. Indians evidenced as much curiosity about white people as whites did about Indians, he states, and Indian inquisitiveness was often misinterpreted as sexually threatening. The truth is that "their warriors were seldom sex-starved, and probably did not lust after paleface maidens, though many an emigrant girl thought that they did."[51]

If the Indian threat to white women seems overwrought in public perceptions about trail life, what about its equally ugly twin—Indian threats to children on the overland trails? During the early weeks of travel across eastern Kansas and Nebraska, when the experience was still new to most people, frequent diary entries warned about paying special attention to the whereabouts of children since they allegedly were the prizes most sought by Indian marauders. Hugo Hoppe recalled a particularly trying moment during his 1851 trip to California with a company of fellow German emigrants. One evening, the young children found several feathered fans that belonged to a woman of the party, and they proceeded to "play Indians" with the feathers. In their amusement, they lost one of the fans and, fearing that they would be severely punished by their fathers, they hid beneath several wagons. Their absence triggered a panic among the adults who immediately concluded that Indians had stolen the children, even though no warriors had been seen in or about the camp. When the incident turned out to be a false alarm, the emigrants hugged their children, and all had a good laugh about the events. Hoppe's tale, which sounds as though it might be apocryphal, summarized in truth or fiction the strong preconceptions about American Indian behavior that many overlanders harbored.[52]

Because the crossing of the Missouri River represented to many people the beginning of the western trip, and because overlanders' anxieties were heightened at that time, some of the best examples of perceived Indian threats to children occurred in those environs. While at Council Bluffs, young Alfred Dyer became the object of much attention among Indians camped nearby, allegedly because they admired the beauty of his long, flowing hair. His disappearance created an alarm, but he was eventually found well cared for in the Indian camp and was returned to his frantic mother. The Indians were acknowledged to be friendly and curious rather than threatening toward the boy.[53]

A similar but less embellished tale was described by Mrs. James Caples at the time of her 1849 encampment along the Little Blue River. When confronted by a group of Indians whom she erroneously identified as Sauks or Iowas, she falsely assumed that their demand for payment of a toll was actually a subterfuge to "kill us all, and take my baby in captivity." Caples further remarked that these were the first Indians she had ever seen, and they "looked ten feet high."[54] Another unidentified woman was thoroughly convinced that the leader of a small group of Indians wanted to steal or trade for her infant. The advice offered by other members of the wagon train that the "chief" intended no harm and the fact that the Indians departed amicably still did not soothe the panicked woman. According to one observer, she remained paranoid for some time thereafter and kept referring to stories she had read in the East about "many mothers losing their babies in the West, and of those babies growing up as Indians in the rough life of the redmen."[55]

Discerning the true intentions of Indians was admittedly difficult for emigrants, in the same way that American Indians had trouble understanding the intentions of whites who often seemed to react with alarm at even the most innocent of gestures. Yet some overlanders did make the distinction between real and imagined threats to their children. John Roger James, who was only a small boy at the time of his 1851 sojourn, later recalled that while camped for the evening, he had followed every step of a motherly-looking Sioux woman who was kind to him. When James's mother saw the woman leading her son, she raced forward and grabbed him from what she thought was a kidnapping attempt. In telling this story many decades later, John remained convinced that no such threat had ever existed and, indeed, that his own actions had precipitated the misunderstanding.[56]

An even more ambiguous case was witnessed by Louise Mueller Rahm in 1862 when an elderly Indian man and his wife, probably from Spotted Tail's Brulé band, came into their camp along the Platte River. The couple took a special interest in sweet baby Jessie, whose hair had just been outfitted with a bright new bow. Jessie's unsuspecting grandmother handed her to the Indian woman, and the woman began to slowly ride away. The baby's grandfather ran after the woman, pointed his gun at her, and demanded the child. According to Rahm, "she came but with a very much injured look and handed the baby to the mother." Had the couple planned to abduct the child or merely give it a brief horseback ride around the camp? No one could be certain.[57]

A seemingly more threatening gesture led to the same kind of divided opinion among another group of white observers. Nancy Campbell Lowell recalled that when she was a child bound for California in 1857, her wagon train was visited by a group of Indian men who, without any warning, made gestures as if they were trying to seize three children, including Nancy, from one of the wagons. Following their less-than-effective maneuver, they quickly galloped away. Lowell expressed the ambiguity of the moment when she later wrote: "Whether the Indians accidentally missed the children, or whether it was their idea of a joke was never known."[58]

The true degree of Indian threats to white children along the Oregon, California, and Mormon trails can never be known with precision, but two examinations of the so-called Goldilocks syndrome have again resurrected the question for modern historians. In 1965, Francis Haines wrote an attention-grabbing article that challenged the prevailing image of Indian savagery to the core. He briefly described the Goldilocks motif as a composite example of the "dimpled darling, three years old" who "had big blue eyes, a fair skin and golden hair with a natural curl."[59] Amid all her beauty and innocence, this fictionalized Goldilocks became the prized catch of Indian warriors of virtually every tribe in the American West. Haines further charged that these types of stories were commonly found in trail literature, especially reminiscences that were written many years after the alleged events. In contrast to the frequency of these tales in later-published accounts, Haines asserted that he could find only two credible cases that were actually entered in diaries or journals at the precise time of the attempted purchases or abductions. Haines then virtually removed the motif from the realm of history and placed it into the realm of folklore.[60]

Thirty-three years later, historian Rosemary G. Palmer returned to this exact question and performed the most precise statistical study of the Goldilocks syndrome. First, she quoted from a cursory interim study by Barre Toelken and a broader array of information compiled by Melvin L. Bashore and Linda L. Haslam at the Historical Department of the Church of Jesus Christ of Latter-day Saints in Salt Lake City. Toelken echoed Haines's findings by arguing that virtually all of the later written accounts incorporated these "legends" to "help socialize people and place them in a cultural value system." Bashore and Haslam furthered the conclusion by demonstrating that only one diary and seventeen reminiscences within "the more than 2,000 first-person accounts that were included within their database search revealed cases of possible attempted purchase or capture of white children."[61]

In the most definitive effort yet attempted, Palmer closely examined twenty-three diaries and letters and 430 reminiscences of children and young adolescents who traversed the Oregon, California, and Mormon trails. Her findings clearly paralleled the conclusions of the other three researchers about the nonreliability of many of the accounts that were written years after the actual events.[62] She spelled out the particular problems of half a dozen reminiscences that had been uncritically reported by other trail historians, including the frequently cited experiences of Catherine Thomas Morris. At age eighty-seven, Morris granted an interview in which she embellished or totally concocted the story of Steven Devenish, a twenty-year-old member of her Oregon-bound wagon train who was "quite a cutup and a great hand at joking." The young man allegedly created a dangerous situation when he began negotiating the sale of ten-year-old Catherine and other girls of the company to an Indian "chief." Upon learning that he was the butt of a white man's joke, the Indian became angry and during the night led a successful livestock raid against the emigrants. After losing half of their animals, the company was forced to abandon fifty of their one hundred wagons and the contents of each. Devenish was banished from the wagon train, but years later Morris's brother found him alive and well in Idaho. The story Morris offered in her old age was a fine one, but it lacked authenticity on many levels.[63]

Despite significant agreement about the overstated Goldilocks motif in trail literature, Palmer criticized the earlier article by Haines because of its anecdotal approach and its failure to identify fully how many diaries and reminiscences were utilized in the sample. Furthermore, she singled out for additional investigation the accounts that she thought possessed enough credibility to be fairly dubbed "history rather than folklore."[64] When the final word is recorded on this subject, it will be clear that not all stories of Indian threats to white children can be dismissed as easily as Haines had indicated. Yet realities of the trail experience demonstrate that exaggerations over time have created a stereotype that does not match historical circumstances.

Although relatively few white captives were taken by Indians during the peak years of the Oregon, California, and Mormon migrations, the fate of one young boy offers insight into the strength of the American Indian assimilation process. Reuben Van Ornum was only ten years old when Shoshones seized him and his three sisters during the Utter–Van Ornum Massacre of October 1860. The girls apparently died during the following several weeks, but the boy survived and apparently was adopted by a Shoshone family. Despite the diligent efforts of his uncle Zachias to find the boy and the alleged expenditure of $5,000 to secure his release, Reuben remained well hidden in the camp of Bear Hunter until Maj. Edward McGarry entered the remote Cache Valley village in November 1862 and confronted the Shoshones. Acting on information about a white captive living among them, McGarry ultimately was able to examine the boy, who was "thoroughly Indian" except for his light-colored hair and blue eyes. Bear Hunter protested that the boy was the son of a French trapper and a Shoshone woman, and residents of the village remained adamantly opposed to surrendering one of their own.[65]

The young boy fought his rescuers in every way possible—fighting, kicking, and scratching—until the soldiers forced him onto a horse and led him away. Reuben's ultimate fate is not entirely clear. He remained with his uncle Zachias for a year or two in Oregon and California and may have been sent east to rejoin relatives in Wisconsin. According to family tradition, however, Zachias was unable to control the boy, and he probably ran away to rejoin his Indian family in the Snake River country.[66] Like so many other tormented souls, from Cynthia Ann Parker to Herman Lehmann, both of whom lived among the Comanches as captives and then as fully adopted members, Reuben Van Ornum's desire to remain with Indians was far stronger than his desire to once again live with whites.

10

From Cooperation to Conflict
A More Dangerous World Begins

Despite the generally favorable fraternization that existed between most overland emigrants and the tribes situated along the Oregon, California, and Mormon trails, the passage of time would ultimately strain these relationships. During the mid-nineteenth century, few white people actively thought of themselves as participants in the herculean task of promoting an American manifest destiny, but some voiced an awareness that continued migrations would have a devastating effect upon the Native inhabitants and would soon turn the vast region into the domain of whites. Jonathan Blanchard, president of Wheaton College, wrote to his wife from Red Buttes near modern-day Casper, Wyoming, in 1864, remarking that gold fever had poisoned cordial feelings between American Indians and whites and "so the poor Indian must fade and disappear before this human avalanche." As a deeply committed representative of the American Home Missionary Society interested in the salvation of lost souls in the Montana mining districts, Blanchard further remarked that if the Indians fully understood where this demographic change was leading, they would unite and stop the migration. He wondered why they had not done so in the face of so many injustices and why the mounting crisis could not overcome the seeming divisiveness within tribal societies.[1]

Emigrants who took the time to record their thoughts about this newly emerging reality remained divided in their opinions about the

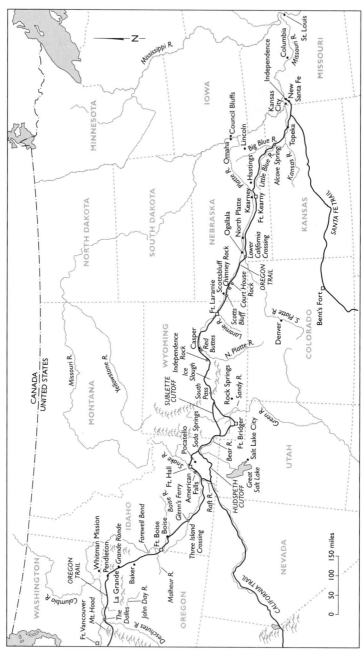

The Great Platte River Road. Adapted with permission from Merrill J. Mattes, *Platte River Road Narratives: A Descriptive Bibliography of Travel over the Great Central Overland Route to Oregon, California, Utah, Colorado, Montana, and Other Western States and Territories, 1812–1866* (Urbana: University of Illinois Press, 1988).

outcome. As early as 1852, John Hawkins Clark had turned John L. O'Sullivan's popularized invocation of manifest destiny from its focus on Mexican and British lands and redirected attention toward the vast domicile of American Indians. Almost with the same cadences presented in O'Sullivan's earlier manifests, Clark wrote in his journal: "Yonder warlike establishment tells them they have masters and must submit to be ruled by a people of another race; and so it is. 'Manifest destiny' is spreading the white race broadcast throughout the fair fields of the great west, shedding the light of science, of civilization, and of religion, covering the dark savage superstition of the native race in the grave of the past."[2]

A year later, while traveling through the eastern half of Nebraska, S. H. Taylor wrote to his hometown Wisconsin newspaper, the *Watertown Chronicle*, about the unlimited agricultural potential of the lands through which he had just passed. He predicted that a city of 10,000 people would soon appear in this region and that it was incumbent upon the federal government to extinguish the Indians' land titles immediately throughout the Platte, Elkhorn, and Loup River valleys.[3] To do otherwise would be a denial of a divine plan to bring civilization and productivity to a land disgraced by slothful nomads. Wellman Packard echoed the expansionist sentiment and self-congratulatory praise for all overlanders when he wrote that Americans "would constitute a mighty host who would wrest an empire from the control of a few indolent Greasers and Digger Indians, and dedicate it to freedom and advancement."[4]

The dogma that underpinned all manifest destiny bombast was based upon racism and cultural insensitivity, and it was furthered even by the writings of people who never directly preached O'Sullivan's vision for the future. American humorist Mark Twain, a curmudgeon who fired his pithy remarks at all divisions of humankind, certainly did not help the public perception of American Indians. His lengthy description of Nevada's Goshutes became a criticism of all western Indians, as far as the general reading audience was concerned. Noting in his popular *Roughing It* that he had always been a devotee of the "Noble Red Man" while under the spell of "the mellow moonshine of romance," he now had changed his mind. Twain described the Goshutes as "treacherous, filthy and repulsive. . . . They deserve pity, poor creatures; and they have mine—at this distance. Nearer by, they never get anybody's."[5]

A man equally important to shaping public views was Francis Parkman, who in 1846 made his legendary excursion along the Oregon Trail as far west as Fort Laramie. By his own admission, Parkman undertook the trip so that he could better observe Indians still living in their "primitive state." This direct contact supposedly would help him understand the motivations and ways of life of Indians who lived in the eastern forests as he tried to write the multivolume history of the colonial wars for empire. Although he commented favorably on some aspects of western Indian life and especially on some individual Indians, this Brahman-bred author never wavered in his opinion that white civilization was superior to Indian savagery. His acerbic words stood for all the literary world to ponder:

> For the most part, a civilized white man can discover very few points of sympathy between his own nature and that of an Indian. . . . Nay, so alien to himself do they appear, that having breathed for a few months the magic air of this region, he begins to look upon them as a troublesome and dangerous species of wild beast, and if expedient, he could shoot them with as little compunction as they themselves would experience after performing the same office upon him.[6]

Writing just a year earlier, while conducting military escorts along the Oregon Trail, Lt. James Henry Carleton expressed more compassion for the Indians, especially those located in eastern Kansas. Even though Carleton was not so naive as to restate the tired clichés associated with the noble Indian image, he unequivocally blamed whites for forcing these people into their current state of impoverishment. He especially sympathized with the Kickapoos and other former Great Lakes tribes that had been repeatedly moved west by a government reluctant to honor its treaty obligations. Hardly had they reached their new homes on the eastern fringes of the Great Plains than they were being forced again to relinquish their lands. The very overlanders whom Carleton was helping escort through this gently rolling farm country were the people causing trouble for the sedentary Indians, and he well recognized the irony of his soldierly duty.[7]

Even so unapologetic an advocate of westward expansion as Horace Greeley expressed some remorse at the failure of government policy toward American Indians. While traveling through the same area of northeastern Kansas that Lt. Carleton had traversed a decade and a half earlier, this outspoken editor of the *New York Tribune* gazed across the farmlands laid out in so neat a fashion near the Sac and Fox mission. He praised the hard work of these "Christianized Indians" and predicted that their lands could produce far more corn than the farms of New York and New England. But Greeley also noted the alleged indolence of many Indians who had not followed the Christian path, and he especially lashed out at those who had become willing victims of alcoholism. Greeley hoped that missionaries and philanthropists could, by their proper example, help these peaceful tribes make the transition into a white lifestyle that emphasized the gospel of hard work. While admitting that the government had failed in its moral and legal commitments to these people, he concluded by saying: "I begin to comprehend, though I do not excuse, the covetous impatience wherewith Indian reservations are regarded by their white neighbors."[8]

As duplicitous as the federal government had been in its dealings with Indians since the 1790s, not all official interaction had been intentionally malicious and punitive. Caught between the mandated provisions of treaties and the ever-increasing public demand for opening new Indian lands, the executive and legislative branches of the federal government waffled in their decision-making—often to the displeasure of Indians and whites alike—but inevitably choosing the will of the voter over the outcry of the ward.

The transcontinental migrations had already reached significant enough levels by 1846 that Superintendent of Indian Affairs Thomas H. Harvey made a direct appeal to Commissioner of Indian Affairs William Medill to purchase the Platte River Trail from as many tribes as might have a reasonable claim to portions of it. Because the full extent of this river valley, as well as its approaches in northeastern Kansas and southeastern Nebraska, belonged exclusively to Indian nations, such an honestly conceived purchase could serve dual purposes. It could not only protect the emigrant passage, but it could also demonstrate government trustworthiness to the tribes, according to Superintendent Harvey.[9] Five years later the new commissioner of Indian Affairs, Luke Lea, could joyfully report that a significant aspect of Harvey's vision had been fulfilled with the purchase of a right-of-way from several Sioux bands through the Platte River valley.[10]

At the heart of this diplomatic endeavor was the Fort Laramie Treaty of 1851 (also known as the Horse Creek Council Treaty), which addressed the concerns of several plains tribes as well as those of the federal government. Signatories to the treaty included representatives from eight tribes but did not include spokesmen for all of the bands and subtribal groupings, since some chose not to attend. Washakie's Wind River band of Shoshones also attended, but since they were not officially invited to the confab, they were not signatories to the treaty. Three of the eight groups—the Teton Sioux, Cheyennes, and Arapahos—had special relevance for the Oregon, California, and Mormon trails, and representatives from each agreed to the provisions laid out in the documents. They acknowledged the government's right to build and maintain the trail and its tributaries; they promised to refrain from depredations against emigrants; and they agreed to make restitution to any whites whose lives or goods might be threatened or damaged in the future.[11] In return, federal officials would present gifts at the conclusion of negotiations, and these would be used to compensate the Indians for the loss of bison, grass, and timber to overlanders during the preceding decade. The treaty also guaranteed an annuity of $50,000 annually, which would be divided among the signatory tribes for a span of fifty years. The yearly payment was later limited to a fifteen-year period, a point that Man Afraid of His Horses (Oglala) and Spotted Tail (Brulé) contended was never explained to them after the Senate's 1852 modification of the treaty terms.[12]

Although Indian spokesmen decried the depletion of wild game along the Platte and Sweetwater rivers and the occasional violent acts precipitated by traders and overlanders, they voiced no significant opposition to the terms in the document. The real difficulty of future enforcement of the 1851 Fort Laramie Treaty lay in its provisions for preventing intertribal warfare.[13] In truth, no amount of diplomatic skill, threats, or bestowing of gifts could end the cycles of combat between tribes. The origins of these conflicts were firmly rooted in past grievances, the need to protect vital resources against enemies, and the perpetuation of a system that allowed young men to become recognized warriors through their heroic exploits on the raiding trail or the war trail. Government representatives failed to fully understand these traditions, and in their haste to foster peace in the West, they hoped to draw official boundaries between the tribes so as to minimize violent conflicts that spilled over to the wagon trains.[14] The fact that Shoshone and Sioux warriors had almost come to blows while assembling for the negotiations vividly indicated that longtime enemies were not about to set aside their feelings for each other merely because the federal government wanted it that way.[15]

Government officials were quick to take credit for the signatures secured at the Horse Creek Council because the treaty seemingly guaranteed peace along the Platte River valley. What the negotiators failed to address, however, was that the treaty signing meant different things to the Indians than it did to whites. American Indians tended to emphasize what was said at councils, not what was written on paper. Indian decision-making had always functioned within a consensus-building framework where all viewpoints could be related openly. Many of their spokesmen had registered their complaints at the 1851 conference, and they did not think that all of these complaints were resolved by government promises. Culturally, they viewed the placing of their identification marks on the treaty as an acknowledgment of their having heard all the words spoken, not as an indication of their acceptance of all that was written in the document. Furthermore, they considered such compacts of peace as transitory, agreements to be nullified by changing conditions or to suit the needs of individual tribal members who wanted to undertake a horse raid for glory or a blood raid for revenge. In making his mark, no Indian "chief" was implying that he could or would control the behavior of all of the members of his village, band, or tribe.[16]

Poor translations of speeches and treaty terms also clouded Indian understanding of events at the Horse Creek Council. Cheyenne elder John Stands In Timber heard from many attendees, especially Wolf Tooth, that the interpreter, John Smith, knew the tribal language well and was married to a Cheyenne woman, but he did not accurately explain matters. Cheyenne tribal leaders were particularly outraged that the Sioux apparently had gained exclusive rights to the Black Hills, even though this area was also considered sacred by the Cheyennes, who especially viewed Bear Butte as the tribe's most revered spot.[17] Other Indian leaders spoke out against the fact that whites had written the treaty even before hearing Indian viewpoints. In their minds, the speeches and their translations were the most important components of the council. They were suspicious of the white delegates' promotion of the paper document above all things, and a few of these refrained from "touching the pen" or marking an *X* after their preprinted name. Again, the cultural vantage point was entirely different, because Indians believed that their marks signified that they were validating all that was said at the council, while whites viewed the signatures only as an acceptance of what was written on paper and translated from it.[18]

Another facet of the 1851 treaty-making process viewed through contrasting cultural prisms was the issue of presents, both those distributed at the council grounds and those promised as annuities to be delivered in the future. Government negotiators regarded the presents primarily as bribes to help secure the immediate goodwill of the tribes, and they viewed the annuities as long-term guarantors of Indian cooperation with the treaty terms. In short, the seeming largess of the government was being extended as a means to an end. The Indians, however, saw the presents as a vital part of the time-honored gift-giving cycle. The Cheyennes referred to the entire range of negotiations as "the Big Issue," and one of the Sioux bison-hide winter counts immortalized 1851 as "the winter of the big distribution."[19] Indian representatives of the various nations had come to Fort Laramie not to sign away their freedoms or territorial claims. They had come for two entirely different purposes: to state publicly their past grievances against the government and their specific desires for the future, and to collect the presents and guaranties of future annuities, both of which confirmed a recognition of their power and completion of the gift-giving cycle.[20] Their marks on the treaty document affirmed that they had accomplished both tasks during the negotiations, but from their perspective, the marks did not limit their future course of action in relating to overland emigrants or other tribes.

Five years later, various Sioux bands met with Gen. William S. Harney at Fort Pierre on the Missouri River to discuss continued thefts along the Platte River Trail. Despite some warnings against creating more "paper chiefs," the government remained adamant that it would recognize only a select group of leaders, would deal exclusively with them, and would hold them personally accountable for the actions of all tribal members who allegedly fell under their rule. Furthermore, a double standard of justice was applied in that Indian warriors suspected of theft or intimidation would have to be surrendered to white authorities for punishment, while under no circumstances would suspected white offenders be turned over to Indians for discipline.[21]

This issue was an especially troublesome one for the Lakotas, who were organized into seven major divisions—Oglala, Brulé, Hunkpapa,

Sans Arc, Minneconjou, Blackfeet, and Two Kettle—and scores of smaller social units within these divisions. The true focus of their identities was found in the smaller *tiospaye*, or bands of extended families united by blood, marriage, or assertion of kinship. These extended families provided a large safety net for all members, and the kinship connectedness created a sense of identity that transcended the atomized individual. Relatives within a tiospaye shared the honor and dishonor of all members, but they could not absolutely control the behavior of each individual.[22] Beyond the basic family units, *itancans*, or band chiefs, could also influence a group's behavior, as could the *akicitas*, or police societies, which provided security for the camps and the group hunts. Lakota society was structured, but within a fluid arrangement that prevented authoritarian rule and assured grassroots governance through consensus-building mechanisms.[23] Although variations existed among the Pawnees, Cheyennes, Shoshones, Paiutes, and other western tribes, the principles of decentralization and nonauthoritarian governance remained constant.[24]

Travelers such as Lt. James Henry Carleton and Francis Parkman, who had some experience among the Lakotas and other tribes along the trail, clearly delineated the grassroots nature of Sioux family relationships and the high degree of independence that this afforded within the larger tribal concept. In discussing the tiospaye allegiance, Carleton accurately remarked that "every band goes to war, or makes peace, when it pleases."[25] Parkman also captured the complex nature of Sioux leadership patterns when he wrote: "Each village has a chief, who is honored and obeyed only so far as his personal qualities may command respect and fear. Sometimes he is a mere nominal chief; sometimes his authority is little short of absolute, and his fame and influence reach beyond his own village, so that the whole band to which he belongs is ready to acknowledge him as their head."[26] Parkman was also quick to point out that any leader who lost the support of his people because of a lack of wisdom, courage, or generosity would quickly see his influence reduced to naught.[27]

Among most overlanders, however, the loose-knit social structure seemed impossible to fathom during their relatively brief contact with each new Indian community. Father Honoré-Timothée Lempfrit voiced one extreme position when he wrote in 1848 that the Sioux "are under the authority of a Great Chief who is absolute lord of the tribe."[28] At the other extreme of misinformed observation, Helen Carpenter contended that no leaders spoke for the Sioux, and negotiations with them were a perfect waste of time.[29]

Rather than trying to understand the dispersed nature of Lakota political authority, plains emigrants mostly recognized the authority of Indian men who carried papers signed by agents, military officers, or other emigrants, attesting to their good behavior and positions as "chiefs." By 1867, Gen. Alfred Sully complained that this false creation of "paper chiefs" was subverting the authority of "proper chiefs" and further factionalizing the bands.[30] Amid the confusion about authority and chains of command, many overlanders adopted the philosophy of the 1856 Fort Pierre Treaty and held all Indians responsible for the actions of a few. Yet those same individuals would have instantaneously rejected any American Indian assertion that all wagon trains should be held accountable for the bad behavior of a few travelers among them.

Although Sioux culture had been well served by its decentralized and quasi-egalitarian nature for a long time, cracks were beginning to widen during the 1840s. This was most readily apparent among the Oglalas, who had experienced continuous contact with white fur traders and overland emigrants via the Fort Laramie trade nexus. At the beginning of the decade, the Oglala communities located nearest the post had split into two factions. Some followed Old Smoke, who had a close relationship with the white traders, and others joined Bull Bear, who was intent upon acquiring a larger share of the trade for his group. Feuding over how gifts were to be distributed, how the liquor exchange would be handled, and whether a barter relationship could be maintained with the notorious John Richard of Pratte, Cabanne and Company led to greater levels of rancor and to Red Cloud's murder of Bull Bear in November 1841. Factionalism and attendant social problems expanded as the Koya and Bad Face factions of the Oglalas remained virtually separated for the next twenty-five years, a crucial period of transition for the Lakota people.[31]

Meanwhile, just as factional disputes worsened among the Lakotas and the number of emigrants increased their pressures on Indian resources, the federal role became more intrusive in American Indian life. The U.S. Army, as the recognized right arm of governing authority, was responsible for protecting the trails and in suppressing warfare among competing tribes. The Fort Kearny military reservation land, which the federal government purchased from the Pawnees in 1848 for $2,000, was vitally important to both goals because it stood on the Platte River in the center of Nebraska and because its reconnaissance patrols overlapped the ranges of three key populations—the Pawnees, Sioux, and Cheyennes. A year later, the federal government purchased Fort Laramie from the American Fur Company, and it became the most visible representation of federal authority along the central route.[32]

The underpaid and understaffed military contingents that operated along the overland trails were not the Indian-hating, vengeance-seeking bands of cutthroats that some people have made them out to be in modern times. Their personal associations with American Indians were as diverse as the relationships between individual Indians and over-landers, but there was one important difference—the army was officially mandated to protect Indian treaty rights and to serve the indigenous people in humane ways. According to fragmentary evidence uncovered by historian John Unruh, Jr., troops arrested up to forty emigrants for desecrating Indian graves and attempting to rape Indian women during the late 1840s. Several of these so-called Pittsburgh emigrants sup-posedly were returned to Leavenworth, Kansas, to face legal action, but given the fact that they had been arrested by military officers and that witnesses to their crimes probably did not travel to the distant court to testify against them, the accused were probably released.[33]

Despite the army's lack of clear authority to arrest and hold civilian lawbreakers, officers made numerous attempts to do just that when they deemed it important to preserving good relations with local Indians. In accordance with terms of the 1851 Fort Laramie Treaty, soldiers briefly detained members of Mary Ringo's wagon train after they fired upon several Sioux in the vicinity of the fort. The Indians then appealed to the commanding officer, who ordered that the guilty persons compensate the aggrieved parties by giving them flour, sugar, coffee, and bacon before being allowed to continue their journey.[34]

More common were army efforts to remove trespassers from Indian land, especially in areas where limited natural resources could not supply Indians and whites alike. As early as 1845, Superintendent of Indian Affairs Thomas Harvey had requested clarification from the Office of the Commissioner of Indian Affairs about his and the army's legal authority to banish violators from Indian domain. Finding nothing in the statutes that was ironclad enough to be enforced in the wide-open spaces of the trans-Missouri West, he demanded tougher federal laws that would allow military officers to take the initiative. As things stood, according to Harvey's interpretation, white trespassers could be removed only upon a specific request filed by legitimate representatives of the Indian nations, and such conditions were clearly impossible to meet in most cases.[35] Just such an incident occurred in 1852 when Elizabeth Holtgreive's family was moved off farmland that they had settled near Oregon's the Dalles. A local Indian leader, whom she identified as Mark, protested to the regional military commander, who then removed the squatters from the land on which they already had made improvements.[36]

A more far-reaching example of army aid to Indians along the Oregon, California, and Mormon trails came in the form of infrequent medical help—especially in dealing with epidemics among the plains tribes. During 1849, perhaps the most virulent period for cholera outbreaks, Capt. Howard Stansbury unpacked the supply of medicine within his exploration party and freely distributed it to every member of a stricken Sioux village located on the North Fork of the Platte River. Stansbury not only helped administer the treatment, but he also talked with many of the 250 residents and gained their trust. One young man who had been stricken three days earlier and was on the verge of death listened intently to Stansbury's reassuring words about the power of the medicine. According to the officer's report, the man's countenance changed immediately, as "the fire came into his eyes, and a radiant smile of confidence and hope, which was beautiful to behold, broke through the previous gloom." Upon departing the village, Stansbury left an additional supply of medicine with the local trader, a Mr. Bissonette, and a full range of instructions on how to administer it in the following days.[37]

At other times, the army's intervention into Indian affairs produced mixed blessings—especially when it intervened in intertribal relations. One of the most frequently repeated examples occurred in the summer of 1849, following a successful Sioux raid on a Pawnee village approximately twenty miles from Fort Kearny. Several wagon trains witnessed the calamitous effects of the attack, and travelers reported seeing Pawnee captives among the more than two hundred Lakota warriors who had participated in the attack. Responding to these accounts, Capt. Robert Chilton dispatched sixty soldiers from the post to track down the raiding party and to secure release of the captives. The dragoons succeeded in their mission and returned the captives to their elated people, though probably not without angering the Sioux, who considered the taking of Pawnee prisoners to be a heroic and justifiable act.[38]

Whatever good intentions the army had in promoting peace between Indians and overlanders, its effectiveness was severely limited by its problems obtaining troops and supplies. When the government purchased Fort Laramie from the American Fur Company, the fort was in such a state of disrepair as to be almost unserviceable. Annie Ruff, wife of a senior officer assigned to the post, wrote to her mother during June 1849 that the fort "is the gloomiest most desolate looking place I ever saw. It looks exactly like a Penitentiary except there are no windows on the outside."[39] The old fur trade buildings gradually gave way to an improved military facility, complete with a large parade ground surrounded by living quarters and administrative buildings made of adobe and brick, but the post did not reach its peak until the 1870s.

Expansion of Forts Laramie and Kearny continued throughout the 1850s, but the never-ending rotation of troops left an inadequate force at both installations. When Andrew McClure reached Fort Laramie in the summer of 1853, he was disappointed at what he found when compared to his expectations. With some sense of exasperation, he wrote in his diary: "The fort here musters about seventy-five soldiers. A mere bite for the Indians in the vicinity."[40] In a similar vein during the following year, William Woodhams described Fort Kearny as "merely a collection of wooden buildings, with a force of 80 men to guard 400 miles of the worst road on the route."[41]

If these two were the premier military installations on the Oregon, California, and Mormon trails, then the westernmost sections of the route were even more poorly served, at least until the Civil War era. Though legendary in folklore, Fort Hall was little more than a few ramshackle traders' buildings. Writing of its dilapidated condition and lack of strategic location in 1849, Maj. Osborne Cross observed in his official report that the army would probably occupy the site only for the briefest of time.[42] Indeed, a brand-new post was soon erected at Cantonment Loring, approximately three miles above the old fur-trading post, but it lasted only a year before being abandoned due to a scarcity of forage and provisions. Not until twenty years later was another namesake post constructed about eight miles south of the present-day town of Blackfoot, Idaho. In all of its three guises, Fort Hall maintained one consistent quality: it was never garrisoned by more than a few score troops and sometimes by as few as a mere company.[43]

Farther south, the vast Great Basin region, which shielded all approaches to the California goldfields, was even less well served by military authority. No post appeared there until Fort Crittenden (originally called Camp Floyd) was established in the Utah desert near the present-day town of Fairfield. Its 1858 inception emerged from the infamous Mormon War between the U.S. government and the Mormon faithful, and its purpose had more to do with manifesting governmental sovereignty over the Church of Jesus Christ of Latter-day Saints than it had to do with protecting wagon trains from the Shoshones, Paiutes, and Goshutes.[44] Not until the Civil War would numerous military posts appear on and near the central route, but most of these were temporary installations that barely survived the 1860s.[45]

Although the frontier army was entrusted to protect the rights of both Indians and whites, American Indians could not ignore the damage done to them by the mid-nineteenth century, and they correctly viewed the army as a facilitator of some of these most destructive changes. The cumulative effects of resource despoliation, epidemics, and occasional acts of violence emanating from wagon trains were partially attributable to the soldiers who guarded the trails, even when they were not directly responsible for these egregious acts. During June 1853, the usually friendly relationship between Fort Laramie soldiers and the nearby Sioux abruptly changed when several Lakota men seized the ferryboat across the Laramie River after they were denied its use. Post commander Lt. Richard B. Garnett sent a small squad of soldiers to arrest the guilty parties, and the confrontation escalated into bloodshed. The troopers killed three Indians, wounded three, and took two prisoners.[46]

Garnett immediately advised emigrants to travel and camp in large groups because Sioux reprisals were expected. Panicked rumors spread quickly, and by the time that Charlotte Stearns Pengra arrived at the post two days later, people swore that 150 or more Indians had participated in the incident, not the 10 or fewer who had actually been there. Overlander William Brown was especially alarmed by the words of a government interpreter who told him that the Lakotas would surely seek revenge on the emigrants if they could not attack the soldiers. Despite the rumormongering, no such Indian threat materialized, and normal trade relations continued between most of the Indians and members of later-arriving wagon trains.[47]

Whatever Sioux ill-feeling might have remained after the ferryboat incident is impossible to discern, but a second event changed sensitivities forever. On August 18, 1854, a lame cow wandered from a Mormon camp near Fort Laramie, and High Forehead slaughtered it for food. Rather than accept Lakota offers of compensation and possible surrender of the alleged offender to military authority, Lt. John L. Grattan and his vindictive interpreter, Auguste Lucien, attempted to arrest the Minneconjou man as a warning to other Sioux for this and other recent cases of Indian pilfering of livestock near the fort. The twenty-nine soldiers found themselves vastly outnumbered in the Sioux encampment, and yet Grattan refused to yield, even ordering a rifle volley, which killed Conquering Bear (Scattering Bear), a primary band chief of the Brulé village. The ultimate result of this unwise confrontation was the extermination of Grattan and his command.[48]

Arriving at Fort Laramie two weeks later, O. A. Nixon, a civilian employee of the quartermaster corps, noted the increased paranoia and combativeness on both sides. Fearing reprisals, the usually cooperative Sioux chief Red Plum feared coming into the post; a Cheyenne party joined some of the Sioux in acts of defiance; and unidentified raiders drove army livestock away from the government corrals.[49] Post commander Lt. Hugh B. Fleming responded by appealing for immediate reinforcements from Fort Leavenworth.[50] Clearly, the anxiety level had been raised higher than at any time in the past, and many on the local scene expected further confrontation.

The army and the eastern press made much of the "Grattan Massacre" and the subsequent Lakota killings of three mail carriers, but the underlying causes of these acts were more important to future developments than were the events themselves. From the perspective of mixed-blood Sioux observer Susan Bordeaux Bettelyoun, revenge was not the resultant demand among the great majority of Sioux and Cheyennes. Rather, many of the Indians grew reluctant to camp near the fort or along the Platte River Road because of an enhanced fear of trigger-happy soldiers and emigrants. For a time, Lt. Fleming even closed the post to all Indian visitors other than those he personally approved.[51]

Revenge came not from the Indians but rather from the highest levels of the army. Gen. William S. Harney, commanding a force of six hundred soldiers, launched a sweep of the region despite opposition from Commissioner of Indian Affairs George Manypenny and Agent Thomas Twiss, both of whom pronounced the operation to be an unnecessary overreaction. On September 3, 1855, Harney reached the large village of Little Thunder on Blue Water Creek, a few miles northwest of Ash Hollow, where Oglala and Brulé bands had hosted mutually beneficial trade with overlanders for the better part of a decade. Little Thunder professed peace and, in the best spirit of Lakota tradition, made offers of compensation for past depredations committed by a relatively small number of Sioux. He also informed Harney that he would not surrender any of his people to the white authorities, whose brand of justice he did not trust. In the subsequent thirty-minute battle, soldiers killed eighty-seven Indians and took seventy women and children as prisoners, with the loss of only four dead and four seriously wounded.[52] When the English adventurer William Chandless traversed the area a short time later, he repeated the unsubstantiated rumor that Harney had directed his troops to avenge Lt. Grattan by killing Sioux.[53]

The Massacre of Blue Water Creek provided the great watershed event in Sioux relations with overlanders on the Platte River Road. Susan Bordeaux Bettelyoun reflected the feelings of many of her people when she later wrote: "The Indians felt uneasy—no matter where they camped they were not safe; it seemed as though the white people wanted to fight them. Many of their relatives were shot down, wounded, or hanged. They were angered by these ruthless injuries. Nearly every day, runners came in from all parts of the country . . . telling of the movements of the armies marching through their country."[54] For Bettelyoun, this was the beginning of the trouble with whites, especially with soldiers whom she dubbed as "scalp hunters."[55] Traveling through the same country two years later, explorer Lt. Gouverneur K. Warren described the changed situation, as the Sioux and their allies manifested little respect toward soldiers and government representatives. Likewise, while they possessed little fear of the military, their anger toward the increasing numbers of emigrants was rising to a dangerous new level.[56]

If events were troublesome for the Sioux and other Plains Indians by the mid-1850s, the results were even more devastating for tribes located along the eastern and western sectors of the overland trails. One by one, reservations were liquidated in northeastern Kansas and eastern Nebraska after passage of the 1854 Kansas-Nebraska Act. By the end of the decade, only the Prairie Band of the Potawatomies, Iowas, Sacs and Foxes, Chippewas, Munsees, and Kickapoos retained lands in Kansas, and the Omahas, Otos, Missouris, and Pawnees were moved to much smaller domains in Nebraska, away from the traffic of the overland trail that wound its way toward Fort Kearny. Other tribes, including the frequently removed peoples of the Great Lakes region such as the Shawnees, Delawares, Iowas, Peorias, Ottawas, Citizen Band Potawatomies, and Wyandots, plus the indigenous Kansas tribes such as the Kansas and Osages, were permanently relocated farther south in Indian Territory.[57]

In California and the Pacific Northwest, violence and harsh treaties further endangered Indian populations and domains. Starting in 1849, the gold rush brought tens of thousands of prospectors into the Sierra Nevada of California, quickly reducing most of the Native inhabitants to servile status and virtually annihilating some of the smaller tribes. Vigilante action by civilians dominated the California scene, more so than did direct Indian confrontations with the U.S. Army. Capt. Edward D. Townsend remarked that the bloodletting against Native tribes had become so horrendous that "if the tale of the poor wretches . . . could be impartially related, it would exhibit a picture of cruelty, injustice and horror scarcely to be surpassed by that of the Peruvians in the time of Pizarro."[58]

Federal officials made some efforts to preserve indigenous land titles, especially during 1851, when three commissions drafted eighteen treaties with California tribes most threatened by the gold rush. Under these terms, approximately 12,000 square miles were set aside as reservations to serve 139 small tribes and bands. The seeming compromise lasted not much beyond the negotiations because of a thunderous outcry by miners to remove all Indians from the gold-mining districts and even from the coastal valleys. The Senate failed to ratify most of these treaties due to public pressure and the tireless work of California's two new senators. Later analysis of the situation by demographer Sherburne Cook demonstrated the devastating effects of the failed treaties, which left the various Indian communities as virtually landless people in their own land. Cook estimated that disease, starvation, and murder reduced the state's indigenous population from 150,000 in 1845, to 100,000 in 1850, to 50,000 in 1855, and to 35,000 in 1860. Unfortunately, this pattern of decline would not end until the early twentieth century.[59]

The situation was equally punitive among the tribes of the Pacific Northwest, even those located far away from the Oregon Trail and the Willamette Valley. Following a brief but brutal war against the Cayuses in 1847–48, during which innocent and guilty Indians alike were punished for the deaths of Marcus and Narcissa Whitman, government representatives embarked on a series of treaties to forcibly remove all tribes from the coastal belt west of the Cascade Mountains. Significant wars broke out along the Oregon-California border and near Fort Colville in northeastern Washington following new mining rushes of the mid-1850s. In the former case, known as the Rogue River War, nine months of operations, primarily by civilian volunteers, culminated in the Battle of Big Meadows. In its wake, the Shastas, Umpquas, Mollallas, and allied groups were uprooted from the borderlands.[60] The so-called Yakama War, waged in the gold-mining area of Fort Colville, was even more devastating to the Yakamas, Klikitats, Chinooks, Walla Wallas, Umatillas, Cayuses, Deschutes, Palouses, Coeur d'Alenes, Nez Percé, Spokanes, and other tribes that found their domains much reduced in a series of punishing treaties.[61]

The Great Basin did not host a nationally heralded Indian war during the mid-1850s, but it continued to be among the most troublesome areas in the long overland trail to California. Diaries were filled with tales of Indian theft of livestock—some authenticated stories and some mere rumors—but relatively few human casualties occurred in these instances. Some of the accounts reflected broader prejudices and suspicions within white society, especially those alleging that the Mormons were encouraging much of the Indian violence against Gentile overlanders.[62]

In response to the deteriorating situation, Brigham Young wrote to the commissioner of Indian Affairs in September 1857 to point out that the greatest fundamental cause of local problems stemmed from the large number of Gentiles who attacked and stole from the local Indians. Young went on to say that the various tribes had come to regard all whites as their enemies and had begun to strike back out of a sense of self-defense and revenge. Hence, the Mormons, not the overlanders, were suffering the most from this turn of events.[63] Frederick W. Lander, superintendent of wagon road construction, partially backed up Young's claim in his official report the following year, alleging that some Gentile traders had openly tried to stir up Shoshone and Bannock bands to steal from the Mormons.[64]

The confused feelings of Shoshone, Bannock, Paiute, and Goshute peoples who inhabited the Great Basin were perhaps best told through the memories of a young Northern Paiute woman named Thocmetony (Sarah Winnemucca). Writing later in life, Thocmetony recalled that

when she was six years old in about 1849 or 1850, she began to perceive a changed relationship between her Paviotso people and the
increasing number of whites who passed through their land. Despite
their leader Truckee's frequent aid to the travelers and his desire to
maintain contacts for trading purposes, Paiute children were taught to
fear the strangers and to keep their distance from the caravans of
wagons. Elders warned about the dangers, and they melded the image
of white men with the Cannibal Owl, a traditional Paiute bogeyman
who killed and devoured disobedient children. At one point in her
young life when she became violently ill, Thocmetony's mother declared
that whites had poisoned her with a gift of food. Yet when a kindly white
woman who had recently lost a daughter nursed her back to health and
gave her many gifts, the young girl's fear somewhat subsided.[65] Clearly
the 1850s was a time of confusion in the Great Basin, as Indians and
whites alike expected the worst behavior from each other and both
witnessed enough violence to heighten their paranoia even more.

While mutual trade, fellowship, and acts of kindness between whites
and Indians did not cease along the overland trails during the late 1850s,
incidents of conflict did significantly increase during the period. Distrust
clouded even the simplest of interactions between Indians and whites,
each of whom regarded the other as the faithless aggressor. As was the
case in earlier years, when individuals from the two groups made efforts
to sit down and communicate directly, both Indians and whites were
able to attain sufficient understanding of and empathy for each other,
and these qualities somewhat ameliorated the paranoia. Unfortunately,
as military relations deteriorated and overlanders and Indians became
less willing to chance the opportunities to get to know each other, the
efforts toward achieving understanding through personal diplomacy
declined proportionately.

In the age of turmoil that followed the Civil War, American Indians
and whites clashed not only over resources and sovereignty but also
over cultural differences regarding what was acceptable and unacceptable
within traditional patterns of violence. Western tribes had long made
distinctions between raiding and warfare. In the case of the former,
young men participated in its rigors to attain property, to gain honors,
and to demonstrate worthiness in the eyes of their people. Warfare,
however, was intended primarily as a method of defending people,
protecting vital resources, driving away enemies, and retaliating against
adversaries for previous acts of violence. In both raiding and warfare,

individual acts of daring, such as the counting of coups against a heavily armed enemy, were much celebrated, but on rarer occasions, young and middle-aged men alike were capable of launching organized and sustained military campaigns that surpassed the emphasis on individual heroics.[66] The Lakotas' success in establishing their domination of the northern plains during the late eighteenth century represented the culmination of this type of planned effort.[67] When they took horses, personal possessions, or other resources from their enemies, they referred in their own languages to the process as "capturing," not as "stealing." No sense of criminality or immorality was inferred unless it involved an act of theft from one's own people.[68]

The principles of warfare that western Indian had once applied only to intertribal relations were by 1860 also applied to whites. Added to this was the traditional practice of "retributive justice," whereby a wrong had to be repaid by an act of revenge. One's friends and relatives were obligated to carry out the act of reprisal, but they were not restricted by a precise timeline or by the need to administer their brand of justice on the exact perpetrator of the original transgression. Thus carrying out retribution on a different emigrant, trapper, trader, or soldier was acceptable within the traditional guidelines, and the act of vengeance might occur many months, or even years, in the future. Retributive justice produced a never-ending cycle of violence that would only increase in frequency as more whites entered the domains of the indigenous tribes.[69] As historian Anthony McGinnis has concluded, many innocent white people suffered directly and indirectly from tribal raiding and warfare, and because much of it seemed nonspecific in its targeting, this only accentuated popular perceptions of Indians as murderers and barbarous nomads.[70]

While few overlanders understood the unique cultural underpinnings of American Indian retributive justice, significant numbers did remark in their diaries, letters, and reminiscences about the efficacy of not seeking revenge on Indians. William Smedley told of a member of his 1862 company who for no apparent reason other than his own maliciousness wanted to kill an unoffending Indian who was merely sitting on a rock observing the passing caravan along the banks of the Columbia River. The would-be assassin did not carry out his threat, but Smedley rightly recorded that these types of hateful individuals were widespread in the West and that their actions often provoked Indian revenge on other innocent wagon trains that later passed through the area.[71] Eight years earlier, Joseph Francl had criticized several members of a company traversing the Humboldt River who "shot and killed every Indian they met on sight, and for that reason the Indians got bad."[72] Likewise, young Henry Ferguson recalled how his father and Rev. J. S. Kirkpatrick, the leader of the wagon train, persuaded other members not to poison a group of Pawnees with strychnine because it would surely lead to reprisals against other emigrants.[73] It was not Indians alone, with their sense of retributive justice, who could perpetuate cycles of revenge; whites could do so as well. In both cases, the catastrophic effects were usually visited upon innocent people.[74]

The outbreak of the Civil War brought three significant military changes to the West that directly affected Indian relations and how the overland trails operated. First, many of the most experienced army officers answered their sectional loyalties and took command of Union or Confederate units in the main theaters of combat east of the Mississippi River. To fill their places, Union officers from various state militias and volunteer regiments in the East were sent to posts in Kansas, Nebraska, Wyoming, Colorado, Utah, and the Dakotas. Like the enlisted men they commanded, these officers possessed little to no experience with Indians. They knew nothing of the cultural differences and little of the tactics utilized in Great Plains combat, and they generally harbored the widespread notions of American Indians as savages.

Equally inexperienced and racially prejudiced were the second type of military force—galvanized Yankee regiments that garrisoned the plains and participated in much of the low-intensity combat. These enlisted men, former soldiers of the Confederacy who had been captured and released from prisoner-of-war status with a pledge to protect the western trails, represented only a thin line of protection. Many of them also chafed under the direction of Union officers to whom they felt little personal attachment or sectional loyalty. Like their prewar predecessors, they suffered immensely from a lack of supplies, proper medical care, and creature comforts at their isolated camps and stage stations.[75]

The third significant change in western military structure was also governed by the need to raise forces for frontier duty quickly and economically. This was accomplished by recruiting directly from the local population of frontiersmen. Unfortunately, these units were often comprised of little more than vengeance-seeking vigilantes who were given official status as soldiers without attaining discipline. Typical of these militia forces was the Third Colorado Volunteers, who were recruited for service under Col. John M. Chivington in late 1864, specifically for Indian service. Allegedly, many of the members were recruited from Denver saloons following impassioned speeches about recent atrocities by Cheyennes and Arapahos in the capital city area. The anti-Indian hysteria was further magnified by the political ambitions of Governor John Evans and Col. Chivington, both of whom saw opportunities in a massive campaign against the Indians—including innocent ones.[76]

Even before open warfare broke out on the Great Plains in 1864, an equally significant set of events had occurred among the Shoshones and Bannocks. This new round of troubles had its origins in the increased pressures brought upon these tribes by passage of overlanders during the 1850s, but the more immediate cause emanated from government neglect, which reached its zenith during the Civil War. The slow arrival of annuities during 1859 and 1860 pushed many of the seminomadic bands to a point of starvation. Their plight was accentuated by the fact that the various Shoshone bands fell under the administrations of different agents and superintendents who fought with each other over jurisdictional powers and thus slowed the flow of rations even more. The situation reached such extremes that the territorial governor and judges of Utah Territory sent a petition to Washington, D.C., in 1860 urging that the government honor its treaty obligations so that the Indians would not have to beg and steal from the wagon trains. The Pyramid Lake War of 1860 and the Owens Valley War of 1862–64 opened much of the Paiute territory to miners and overland travelers.[77]

The outbreak of the Civil War drew national attention away from the plight of various tribes, and the anticipated Indian reprisals increased in Utah and southern Idaho. A public notice that was published by either the War Department or the Indian Bureau was posted at many locations along the overland trails in 1862, warning people to recognize the new level of danger from the Shoshones, Bannocks, and plains tribes along the Platte River.[78] Meanwhile, many Northern Paiutes also suffered during this period of federal neglect. A majority of Northern Paiutes probably shared in the three earlier dream visions of Chief Winnemucca, who warned that his people would soon be overwhelmed by the white advance, complete with its destructive guns, diseases, and frontal assault on the limited desert resources. Winnemucca's dreams were confirmed by a prominent shaman, who painted an even grimmer picture of the future amid the government's unwillingness to listen to Paiute complaints.[79]

The ultimate deluge came not against Winnemucca's Paviotso band but rather against the Shoshones who were more accessible to military reprisals. At daybreak on a cold January 29, 1863, Col. Patrick Connor attacked the large village of Bear Hunter near present-day Franklin, Idaho. In a raging four-hour battle, during which the volunteer troops demonstrated little sympathy for the Indians, casualties mounted on both sides. By the official military reports, fourteen whites were killed and forty-nine wounded. Indian losses were much higher: 224 killed, 160 women and children captured, 175 horses taken, and seventy lodges destroyed. By unofficial accounts, Indian deaths may have reached four hundred.[80] The great loss of lives and property in the Battle of Bear River was only part of the punishment, because a harsh treaty was forced on many of the Shoshone bands. It left them even more destitute by reducing the domains in which they could live and hunt, while simultaneously establishing an increased military presence in their country and opening more trails across its expanse. Especially troublesome to the Shoshones was the fact that the only area reserved for their bison hunting was near the confluence of the Sweetwater and North Platte rivers, too close to the lands of the Arapahos, Cheyennes, and other of their enemies.[81] Although most frontiersmen praised Connor's victory and many pronounced that it would severely reduce the Indian threat in southern Idaho and northern Utah, the bloody incident only exacerbated Indian-white relations within the region. The widespread sexual assaults, mutilations, and murders of women and children foreshadowed the future atrocities that would occur on the Great Plains.

To the east, the situation would prove even more catastrophic because of the much larger Indian populations that would be affected—especially the Cheyennes and Sioux. Indian attacks increased incrementally along the Platte River Trail of western Nebraska and eastern Wyoming throughout the Civil War and reached their peak between 1864 and 1868. Even areas that had been considered relatively safe in earlier years became the center of livestock raids and revenge attacks. Most surprising was the thrust of Sioux and Cheyenne attacks along the Little Blue River of Nebraska during 1864. By one detailed tabulation, fifty-one white settlers, freighters, and mail station operators were killed, nine were wounded, and seven taken captive in western Nebraska Territory within the short period of August 7–16, 1864.[82]

On August 13, telegraphic messages up and down the line reported that due to severe depredations in the Little Blue and Platte River valleys, stagecoach operations would be suspended for a minimum of ten days.[83] Three weeks later, Denver-bound traveler Frank A. Root penned the impassioned words: "We found that nearly all the stations for over three hundred miles were wiped out. Many of the cabins and trading posts of the ranchmen had been pillaged. . . . Knowing what had already occurred, we knew there was nothing in the annals of Indian butcheries too horrible for the infuriated demons to commit."[84] Even though Root's observations exaggerated conditions, real danger did exist all along the trail, and people sought refuge at strongpoints and tried to ride out what they hoped would be a short-term aberration in Indian-white relations.

Winter hope did not give way to spring redemption, however, because one other horrific act poisoned relations for many years to come. On the morning of November 29, 1864, Col. John M. Chivington attacked the peaceful camp of Black Kettle, White Antelope, and Little Raven along the banks of Sand Creek in the plains section of eastern Colorado. Although the Indians had settled on the reservation as instructed and had mostly refrained from acts of violence against whites, they were targeted because of their easy accessibility and their inability to protect themselves. While most of the young warriors were hunting in western Kansas, Chivington and the Third Colorado Volunteers of Denver militiamen attacked the village without warning. Within the space of forty-five minutes, more than two hundred Cheyennes and Arapahos were dead, over two-thirds of them being noncombatant women and children, many of whom were horribly mutilated in the aftermath of the attack.[85]

Upon their return to Denver, the victorious Third Colorado Volunteers received a hero's welcome, and the *Rocky Mountain News* piously declared that the "Colorado soldiers have again covered themselves with glory."[86] Despite further claims that this event would cow the Plains Indians and reduce the pace of their attacks, the Sand Creek Massacre unleashed the full fury of retaliation and soon involved even bands of the Sioux, who had not even been represented at the massacre site. A full-scale war between whites and Indians broke out, and the chances for a negotiated peace disappeared when delays in shipments of annuities and the U.S. Army's inability to protect villages of friendly Indians from white marauders destroyed the last vestiges of confidence in the federal government and its western representatives. In 1865, the Sioux, Cheyenne, and Arapaho destruction of Julesburg, Colorado, in response to the Sand Creek Massacre, plus the burning of many road ranches and telegraph stations along the Platte River Trail, heralded the end of an important era and the beginning of an infinitely more troubled one.[87]

The most widely recognized events in Indian-white relations on the northern plains still lay ahead—Red Cloud's war on the Bozeman Trail, Little Big Horn, and Wounded Knee—but events of the mid-nineteenth century had already set the changes in motion. Ironically, the very Platte River trade that had strengthened these tribes during the 1840s and 1850s simultaneously placed them within a greater dependency cycle for the coming decades. As the Indians sought to make adjustments to meet the new realities, time ultimately ran out on their traditional ways of life. The trickle of whites traveling through their country in 1845 swelled to a flood by the 1850s. Within a decade, the primary issues separating American Indians and whites became ones of land ownership and sovereignty, not the positive forces of mutually beneficial commerce and personal curiosity that had defined their earlier contact years. After that, the diverse Indian populations were destined to be portrayed as either villainous savages or nature's noble men and women in American popular culture. Along the way, the real Native peoples were observed behind a curtain of stereotypes that bore little resemblance to mid-nineteenth-century realities.

Conclusion

L ightweight fantasies and ponderous tomes, replete with their sociological and psychological jargon, have consistently argued that European Americans and American Indians have always lived in such completely different worlds that conflict has been the inevitable result of their relationships. Older interpretations stressed the intrinsic savagery of Indians and repeatedly placed them in an ever-present warlike demeanor arrayed against "civilized society." In more recent times, a dramatic shift in popular and scholarly writing has identified capitalism, racism, sexism, and classism as the interlocking sins of the European and European American worlds. These portrayals stand in stark contrast to the peaceful and noble lifestyles of indigenous peoples throughout the world, including the great numbers of Native peoples who inhabited and continue to inhabit the North American continent. In the most simplistic rendering of this otherwise complex story, American Indians are reduced to little more than passive objects whose lands and lives have been lamentably destroyed by a tidal wave of white invaders at one juncture of history after another.

This theme of "conflict" has also been applied to the United States' most important mass migration story—the epic movement of men, women, and children to Oregon, California, and the Salt Lake Valley between 1840 and 1870. Paintings, novels, movies, documentaries, and books have perpetuated the imagery of relentless Indian attacks upon wagon trains and counterattacks by frightened and sometimes vengeful overlanders whose reprisals merely strengthened the cycle of reciprocal violence. Such a focus presents only part of the story—the ruination of Indian lands and cultures—but it fails to account for the equally compelling reality of cooperation, aid, and mutual benefit that dominated Indian-white relations on the Platte and Sweetwater River routes to the Pacific coast and the Great Basin.

In his 1991 seminal work, historian Richard White explored the complicated mix of Indian tribes and colonial governments in the Great Lakes region between 1650 and 1815. Likening the expansive landscape to a "middle ground," he stressed how Europeans and indigenous people were constantly reinventing new ways to define themselves and to deal with each other. For every act of contentiousness and violence, there were many more compelling acts of accommodation and exchange. Instead of rigid differences separating white and Native worlds, White found in the middle ground "that no sharp distinctions between Indian and white worlds could be drawn."[1] Of course, White was dealing with a region where intercultural contacts took place over a long period of time, during which people's lives intersected on a more continuous basis and frequent intermarriage between Indians and Europeans cemented their alliances and cultural understandings.

The western trail experience did not provide the same kind of permanent relationships that were experienced by fur traders of the early Great Lakes and the later Rocky Mountains, but the middle ground concept is partially applicable to the great overland migration of the mid-nineteenth century. Western Indians and whites progressed quickly from mere curiosity, which marked their first level of association, to a more mutually beneficial relationship based upon exchanges of information, trade items, and personal acts of kindness. As with the Great Lakes tribes of earlier centuries, the Indian nations of the Great Plains and Far West ultimately lost out to the flood of white settlers. The pattern of accommodation that had dominated most of the 1840s and 1850s slowly collapsed amid the increased pressures of white migration and federal efforts to establish sovereignty over Indian lands. From the late 1850s through the end of the 1860s, the transition from middle ground began as the old systems of meaning and exchange weakened along the overland trails. By the following decade, with the arrival of railroads and significantly higher numbers of white settlers, the contest over Indian lands and cultures was well under way.[2]

In keeping with Richard White's analysis of the middle ground concept, it is also necessary to follow the sage advice of ethnohistorian Robert Berkhofer, Jr., who has argued for a more Indian-centered view of historical events.[3] This might seem to be an impossible task for researchers who are interested in understanding the dynamics of Indian-white relations along the overland trails, but such is not the case. It is true that most of the surviving source materials about the mid-nineteenth-century West were generated by white participants and observers, while American Indian oral traditions remain more fragmentary for that long-ago era. Yet when properly interpreted, even records produced by whites can shed considerable light on the specific cultural values that motivated Indian people to act in certain ways during their associations with overland emigrants. Indian people responded as individuals, not as universal types walking in lockstep to an imagined tribal norm. A recognition of their cultural nexus and patterns of social organization, however, can help explain the motivations behind many of these actions. Reading between the lines of sources produced by whites and Indian oral traditions can open new levels of under-standing, but only if tribal social organization, ethics, religion, and kinship obligations are blended into the analysis. Thus a comprehension of American Indian concepts of reciprocity, kinship connections to animals, and obligations to the tiospaye are essential to understanding why they acted as they did and why individuals reacted differently to similar situations.

The conclusion that emerges from this type of ethnohistorical investigation is consistent with Berkhofer's analysis. During the peak years of the central overland trails, Indian people acted according to what they perceived to be in their own best interests. They were not naive romantics who responded in total innocence, nor were they childlike victims of relentless assaults by immoral whites. Often the American Indians who were situated along the trails acted upon their own ethical standards to extend aid without demanding payment of any kind. At other times, they traded items and performed services for whites in order to extract a profit. Like the overlanders, they responded to the realities of the immediate moment. They possessed no collective crystal ball to foresee that the federal government and white settlers would overrun their lands and challenge their sovereignty. Assisting overlanders during the 1840s and 1850s made perfectly good sense within the context of American Indian life, and the material benefits of that exchange seemed, for the moment at least, to strengthen American Indian societies.

The generally favorable fraternization between Indians and whites during the mid-nineteenth century should amplify our notion that this vast region along the trails was more of a "cooperative meeting ground" than a "contested meeting ground." The works of historians John Unruh, Jr., Glenda Riley, Lillian Schlissel, and Robert Munkres demonstrate that Indian attacks upon wagon trains have been greatly exaggerated in popular culture. My close reading of a vast array of diaries, journals, letters, and government documents has confirmed their findings, and these sources have enabled me to present countless examples where cooperation was much more the reality of trail life than previously has been assumed.

The purpose of this study is not to eliminate all cases of conflict from the story, for overlanders and American Indians did at times become involved in acts of violence against each other. Suspicions naturally arose when strangers were constantly on the move and encountering new members of each group every day. An overland family who experienced good relations with Indians during three or four weeks of travel and then encountered a different group of Indians who seemed openly hostile might remain somewhat fearful. Nor could Indians be entirely sure that each passing wagon train would include the same type of friendly individuals who had visited their camps during the previous weeks. The elements of doubt and cultural misunderstanding were always present, even in the best of circumstances, and these could easily trigger conflicts that could escalate into isolated cases of brutality.

Relations between overlanders and American Indians certainly began to deteriorate in most areas of the overland trails by the closing years of the 1850s, but even in the worst of times, cordial relations and acts of mutual benefit never entirely disappeared. Even during the chaos of the Civil War and the years that immediately followed, when most travelers' accounts reflected heightened fear of Indians and a persistent rumor mill fueled speculation about their atrocities, cooperation was still the dominant theme in the travelers' journals.

Indians continued to guide wagon trains through unfamiliar lands; offer advice on water, timber, and foraging sources; provide assistance at river crossings; aid rafting of the Columbia River; and help wagons up steep grades. Likewise, Indians gave, sold, and bartered food, clothing, herbal medicines, and livestock to overlanders, and they rescued lost hunters from possible death. This dominant pattern ended by the early 1870s, but only because the federal government removed all of the Indian people away from the old trails and onto distant reservations. This dramatic change came at about the same time as the 1869 "wedding of the rails," when the Union Pacific and Central Pacific railroads met at Promontory Summit, Utah, to complete the nation's first transcontinental rail service. Because this new mode of travel ran through much of the same territory that had been served earlier by the celebrated central route of the overland trails, these traditional routes of westward migration slowly lost their importance. A new era of Great Plains Indian relations lay ahead, but the particularly chaotic decade of the 1870s was no longer predominately the story of Indian-white relations on the Oregon, California, and Mormon trails.

A singular event that occurred on the Platte River just west of O'Fallon's Bluff in June 1860 represented in an intimate and understated way the essence of many reciprocal acts of kindness between Indians and overlanders during the period from 1840 to 1870. Upon visiting among the residents of a Sioux "trading village," Helen E. Clark encountered an Indian woman who indicated that she had dust in her eyes. The sympathetic Illinois traveler extended a wet cloth to the appreciative Sioux woman, who not only cleaned her face but also washed her baby with it. The endearing words imparted between mother and child led Clark to write in her diary that "it sounded more civilized than anything else we had heard."[4] Emotionally moved by the scene, she subsequently fed a bashful Indian boy who had been reluctant to bother her, even though he was quite hungry. Her dual acts of kindness struck a responsive chord among other Lakotas, and they went out of their way to thank her for the altruistic gestures. Even though this event had no profound impact on Indian-white relations, it demonstrated the social and psychological possibilities when Indians and whites set aside their negative preconceptions and dealt with each other not as strangers but as friends. It serves as eloquent testimony to what might have been in American history rather than what was.

Notes

PREFACE

1. Smith, *Virgin Land*, 99–112; Berkhofer, *White Man's Indian*, 96–104.

2. Tuska, *American West in Film*, 55; Fenin and Everson, *Western*, 131–38, 248–51.

3. Stedman, *Shadows of the Indians*, 217–18.

4. Unruh, *Plains Across*, 184–85; Mattes, *Platte River Road Narratives*, 5.

5. Riley, *Women and Indians*, 155.

6. Schlissel, *Women's Diaries*, 154.

7. Munkres, "Plains Indian Threat," 193–94. Similar conclusions are echoed in Clark, "Myth of Indian Aggression," 26–34.

8. Faragher, *Women and Men*, 31–32; Jennings, *Founders of America*, 366–69.

9. J. D. Willoughby to Agnes Stewart, Jan. 8, 1854, letter attached to Stewart, "Diary."

10. Marshall, *On Behalf of the Wolf*, 77–78.

11. Ibid., 78–79.

12. Ibid., 79–81.

13. Evans, "Missouri Forty-Niner's Trip," 39.

14. Carrington, *My Army Life*, 44–45; Mattes, *Indians, Infants and Infantry*, 54.

15. Harris, *Oyate Iyechinka Woglakapi*.

16. Stands In Timber and Liberty, *Cheyenne Memories*; Hyde, *Life of George Bent*; Bettelyoun and Waggoner, *With My Own Eyes*; Hopkins, *Life Among the Piutes*; Lowry and Scott, *Karnee*.

CHAPTER 1. PREPARING THE WAY

1. Bonney, "Recollections," 37.
2. Holmes, introduction to Sutton, "Travel Diary," 15.
3. "Barnet Simpson," in Lockley, *Conversations with Pioneer Men*, 29–31.
4. Axtell, "Through a Glass Darkly," 17–21.
5. Derounian-Stodola, Zabelle, and Levernier, *Indian Captivity Narrative*, 14; Namias, *White Captives*, 9.
6. Derounian-Stodola, Zabelle, and Levernier, *Indian Captivity Narrative*, 14, 24–25.
7. Berkhofer, *White Man's Indian*, 79–80.
8. Pearce, *Savagism and Civilization*, 200.
9. Ibid., 197–99, 210–11.
10. Berkhofer, *White Man's Indian*, 88–90; Slotkin, *Regeneration through Violence*, 355–61.
11. Barba, "American Indian in German Fiction," 147–65; Ashliman, "American Indian in German Travel Narratives," 836–37.
12. Billington, *Land of Savagery*, 105–108, 133–34.
13. Berkhofer, *White Man's Indian,* 88–89; Dippie, *Vanishing American*, 25–26; Dippie, *Catlin and His Contemporaries*, 17, 55–56, 65–66; Weitenkampf, "How Indians Were Pictured," 217–20.
14. Billington, *Land of Savagery*, 124.
15. Ibid., 125–26.
16. Ruxton, *Life in the Far West*, 38–39.
17. Gregg, *Commerce of the Prairies*, 409–10.
18. Irving, *Tour on the Prairies*, 11; Irving, *Adventures of Captain Bonneville*, 216–17.
19. Gregg, *Commerce of the Prairies*, 420; Bradbury, *Travels in the Interior of America*, 171.
20. Ross, *Adventures of the First Settlers*, 201.
21. Des Montaignes, *Plains*, 37.
22. Parkman, *Oregon Trail*, 89.
23. Kroll, "Books That Enlightened," 106; Andrews, "'Ho! For Oregon and California!'" 50–63; Andrews, "Controversial Hastings Overland Guide," 33–34.
24. Ware, *Emigrants' Guide*, 13, 15, 33.
25. Hastings, *Emigrants' Guide*, 59.
26. Johnson and Winter, *Route Across the Rocky Mountains*, 144–45.
27. Byers and Kellom, *Hand Book*, 31.
28. Andrews, "Satire," 107.
29. Marcy, *Prairie Traveler*, 188.
30. Ibid., 178.
31. Ibid., 188–208.

32. Shively, "Shively Guide," 734–40; Ware, *Emigrants' Guide*, 9.

33. Ebey, "Overland from Missouri," 74.

34. "Western Emigrants Take Notice," *Council Bluffs (Iowa) Frontier Guardian*, May 2, 1849; "Californians! A Word to You," *Council Bluffs (Iowa) Frontier Guardian*, May 16, 1849.

35. *Daily Missouri Republican*, Sept. 9, 1847; June 16, 1850.

36. *Louisville (Ky.) Examiner*, Aug. 20, 1849, quoted in Unruh, *Plains Across*, 175–76.

37. Coward, *Newspaper Indian*, 13.

38. Ibid., 14, 38–39.

39. Hyde, *Pawnee Indians*, 224–25.

40. Derounian-Stodola, Zabelle, and Levernier, *Indian Captivity Narrative*, 26.

41. Jones, *Dime Novel*, 1–3.

42. Ibid., 6.

43. Smith, *Virgin Land*, 100; Jones, *Dime Novel*, 6–7.

44. Everett, "Critical Notices," 303–304.

45. Smith, *Virgin Land*, 101.

46. Elson, *Guardians of Tradition*, 71–73.

47. Ibid., 74–78. Confirmation of these trends continuing in the later period for children's books is found in Berkman, "Vanishing Race," 31–40.

48. Luzena Stanley Wilson, quoted in Levy, *They Saw the Elephant*, 4.

49. Murphy, *Across the Plains*, 7–8.

50. Hill, *Gold Hunter*, 20–21.

51. Hurd, "Letters," 658.

52. Wooten, "Reminiscences," 1–3.

53. Frink, *Journal*, 25–30.

54. Keil, "From Bethel, Missouri to Aurora, Oregon," 26–27.

55. Soule, "Memories," 9–10.

56. Dunham, *Across the Plains*, 4.

57. Minto, "Reminiscences."

CHAPTER 2. ACROSS THE WIDE MISSOURI

1. Prucha, *American Indian Policy*, 2–4, 41–50, 250–73.

2. Reading, "Journal," 149.

3. Rau, *Surviving the Oregon Trail*, 32–33.

4. Harrison, "Recollections," 2.

5. Bagley, "Crossing the Plains," 166.

6. Arms, *Long Road to California*, 3.

7. West, "Calvin B. West," 57.

8. Compton, *Mary Murdock Compton*, 12–13.

9. Kirkpatrick, "Reminiscence," 107.

10. Clark and Clark, *Two Diaries*, 18–19.

11. Byers, "Odyssey," 12n.

12. Other accounts of the Rawhide Creek legend appear in Kellogg, *Notes*, 65–66; Broadwell, "Crossing the Plains," 21; and Dickson, *Covered Wagon Days*, 57–58.

13. Brooks, *Pioneer Mother*, 13.

14. Enos, "Recollections," 1.

15. Stewart, "Diary," 4–7.

16. Haun, "Woman's Trip Across the Plains," 176.

17. Raymond and Howard, *Overland Days*, 63.

18. Jacobs, "Incidents," 79.

19. Williams, *Narrative*, 24.

20. Swingley, "Brief Chronicle," 460.

21. McKinstry, *California Gold Rush*, 97–98, 101.

22. Haines, *Historic Sites*, 38–41.

23. Applegate, *Recollections*, 12–13.

24. Hannon, *Boston-Newton Company Venture*, 85–86; Benbrook, "Pappan's Ferry," 2–21.

25. Williams, *Narrative*, 24.

26. Houghton, *Expedition of the Donner Party*, 15.

27. Johnston, *Overland to California*, 33.

28. Bryant, *What I Saw in California*, 36–37.

29. Pritchard, *Overland Diary*, 57–58.

30. Moorman, *Journal*, 11.

31. Woodhams, "Diary," 51–52.

32. Wooster, *Gold Rush*, 4–5.

33. Searls, *Diary*, 16.

34. Evershed, "Gold Rush Journal," 7.

35. De Smet, *Life, Letters and Travels*, 2:689–91.

36. Hutchings, *Seeking the Elephant*, 94. See also Minto, "Reminiscences," 132.

37. Merrill, *Bound for Idaho*, 31.

38. Berrien, "Overland from St. Louis," 282.

39. Decker, *Diaries*, 61. Similar sentiments were voiced by Wistar, *Autobiography*, 57; and Robinson, "Charles Robinson," 185–86.

40. Kelly, *Excursion to California*, 1:46–47.

41. Clark, "Overland to the Gold Fields," 234–35.

42. Brown, "Over Barren Plains," 18. See also Loomis, "Grandfather Was a Forty-Niner," 36.

43. William P. Richardson to D. D. Mitchell, Oct. 21, 1850, in *Annual Report of the Commissioner of Indian Affairs [ARCIA] for 1850*, 30–31.

44. Frizzell, *Across the Plains*, 10.

45. Kelly, *Excursion to California*, 1:59.

46. Cumming, *Gold Rush*, 38–39.

47. Hammer, *Emigrating Company*, 73–77.

48. Hatton, "Memoirs," 9.

49. Pengra, "Diary," 17.

50. Brown, *Authentic Wagon Train Journal*, 21.

51. Draper, *Autobiography*, 18.

52. Belshaw, "Diary," 9; Williams, "'Diary,'" 191–92.

53. Burrell, "Council Bluffs to California," 229.

54. Draper, *Autobiography*, 18.

55. Kappler, *Indian Affairs*, 608–614.

56. James, "Autobiography," 64.

57. Fletcher and La Flesche, *Omaha Tribe*, 84.

CHAPTER 3. A MUTUAL BARGAIN

1. T. J. Brasser, "Early Indian-European Contacts," in Trigger, *Northeast*, 78–81.

2. Wishart, *Fur Trade and the American West*, 81–83; Jablow, *Cheyenne in Plains Indian Trade Relations*, 44–46, 58–60.

3. Carleton, *Prairie Logbooks*, 60.

4. Ibid., 87–90.

5. Oswalt, *This Land Was Theirs*, 222–24. Demographic tables of Pawnee population decline are presented in Hyde, *Pawnee Indians*, 364–67.

6. Hyde, *Pawnee Indians*, 226–27.

7. Hillyer, "From Waupun to Sacramento," 222.

8. Bagley, "Crossing the Plains," 169. By 1859, a military bridge was erected at the Elkhorn crossing, and the Pawnee were no longer allowed to charge a fee at that spot. See Kellogg, *Notes*, 65; Steele, *Diary*, 62.

9. McAuley, "Iowa," 49.

10. Norton, "My Life and Adventures," 10; Myer, "Journey," 389; Eaton, *Overland Trail*, 79–80.

11. Read, "History of Our Journey," 219–20.

12. Sloan, "Autobiography," 244.

13. Terwilliger, "Diary," 18.

14. Unruh, *Plains Across*, 173.

15. Ferguson, *California Gold Fields*, 20–21.

16. Christensen, "By Handcart to Utah," 339.

17. Clark and Clark, *Two Diaries*, 19.

18. Witter, "Pioneer Life," 166.

19. Hanna, "Diary," 47; Potter, *Trail to California*, 97.

20. Watson, *Journal*, 12.

21. Kelly, *Excursion to California*, 1:95–96.

22. Millington, "Journal," 44.

23. Knight, "Iowa to the Columbia River," 49.

24. Beeson, *Welborn Beeson on the Oregon Trail*, 42; Wayman, *Doctor on the California Trail*, 65; Bender, "Journey Across the Plains," 155.

25. Keller, *Trip Across the Plains*, 4–5.

26. Langley, *To Utah with the Dragoons*, 49.

27. Butterfield, "Michigan to California," 402.

28. Kelly, *Excursion to California*, 1:95.

29. Myer, "Journey," 394.

30. Millington, "Journal," 43.

31. Madsen, *I Walked to Zion*, 44.

32. Barlow, "Reminiscences," 258.

33. Smith, *Journal*, 40.

34. Carpenter, "Trip Across the Plains," 105–106.

35. Bidwell, *Echoes of the Past*, 52.

36. Carpenter, "Trip Across the Plains," 174.

37. Perkins, *Gold Rush Diary*, 101.

38. Woodhams, "Diary," 73; Maynard, "Diary," 57.

39. Scott, "Journal," 105.

40. Buckingham, "Crossing the Plains," 47.

41. Gilfry, "Annual Address," 418.

42. Read, "History of Our Journey," 236–37.

43. Adams and Blank, "Twin Sisters," 304.

44. Maynard, "Diary," 60.

45. De Smet, *Life, Letters and Travels*, 2:557.

46. Burnett, "Recollections," 82.

47. Hixon, *On to Oregon*, 89–90.

48. Johnson and Winter, *Route Across the Rocky Mountains*, 30–31.

49. Bennett, *Overland Journey to California*, 13.

50. Dickenson, *Reminiscences*, 11.

51. Cooke, *Scenes and Adventures*, 336–37.

52. Letter of James M. Maxey, Nov. 10, 1845, in Morgan, *Overland in 1846*, 2:475.

53. Geer, "Diary," 169.

54. Crawford, "Journal," 156.

55. Hastings, "Diary," 21.

56. Broadwell, "Crossing the Plains," 21.

57. Hanna, "Diary," 83. See also Witter, "Pioneer Life," 166; Sutton, "Travel Diary," 71–72.

58. Frink, *Journal*, 45.

59. Glasscock, *Lucky Baldwin*, 53.

60. Hanna, "Diary," 37–38.

61. Bennett, *Overland Journey to California*, 29.

62. Fletcher, *Bride on the Bozeman Trail*, 28–29.

63. Clark and Clark, *Two Diaries*, 37.

64. Chalmers, "Journal," 50. In a similar biased observation, Sarah Davis asserts that Sioux near Chimney Rock had large quantities of horses based upon their robbing of wagon trains. See Davis, "Diary," 180.

65. Dickson, *Covered Wagon Days*, 76–77.

66. Ringo, "1864 Journal," 210.

67. Smith, *Journal*, 34–36. See also Potter, *Trail to California*, 97; Cranston, "Ohio Lady Crosses the Plains," 124.

68. Matthew Small, "Remembrances," in Lockley, *Conversations with Pioneer Men*, 88.

69. Winter, "Traditional Uses of Tobacco," 20–22, 39–40.

70. Chambers, "Brief Account," 27.

71. Bennett, *Overland Journey to California*, 38.

72. Sponsler, "1850 Gold Rush Letter," 135; Frink, *Journal*, 45; Belshaw, "Diary," 14.

73. Delano, *Life on the Plains*, 144.

74. Zeiber, "Diary," 326–27.

75. Millington, "Journal," 160.

76. Numerous studies have analyzed the importance of the horse in transforming plains and plateau tribal economies, trade networks, intertribal warfare patterns, and material cultures. Four of the best include Jablow, *Cheyenne in Plains Indian Trade Relations*; Secoy, *Changing Military Patterns*; Ewers, *Horse in Blackfoot Culture*; and McGinnis, *Counting Coup*.

77. Berrien, "Overland from St. Louis," 302; Potter, *Trail to California*, 97–99; Harmon, *Journals*, 43. Samuel Handsaker noted that among the Sioux, women engaged in all aspects of direct trade with whites except in the exchange or sale of livestock, negotiations reserved exclusively for men. See Handsaker, *Pioneer Life*, 30.

78. Unruh, *Plains Across*, 162.

79. Pleasants, *Twice Across the Plains*, 29; Shepard, "'O Wickedness,'" 10.

80. Matthieu, "Reminiscences," 100; McKinstry, *California Gold Rush*, 193.

81. Carter, "Diary," 104.

82. Ingalls, *Journal*, 47.

83. Further evidence of livestock exchanges that did not fit the "normal pattern" are found in Ruby and Brown, *Indians of the Pacific Northwest*, 97; Watson, *Journal*, 31–32; Belshaw, "Diary," 44; and Ward, *Prairie Schooner Lady*, 78.

84. McDiarmid, *Letters to My Wife*, 42; Kelly, *Excursion to California*, 1:133; McCall, *Great California Trail*, 31.

85. Haun, "Woman's Trip Across the Plains," 177.

86. McBride, "Journal," June 22, 1850, entry.

87. Ross, *Adventures of the First Settlers*, 103.

88. Payne, "Saint Louis to San Francisco," July 2, 1850, entry.

89. Wyeth, *Journals*, 24–25.

90. Stands In Timber and Liberty, *Cheyenne Memories*, 118.

91. Heinrich Lienhard, "The Journal of Heinrich Lienhard," in Korns and Morgan, *West from Fort Bridger*, 163. This portrayal of western Shoshone naïveté and the allegation that they had never seen a pistol may be an apocryphal tale invented or misinterpreted by Lienhard. He gives a slightly different version of the same incident in Lienhard, *From St. Louis to Sutter's Fort*, 119–20.

92. Three examples of overland parties that willingly traded powder and bullets (but not guns) to Indians are Edwin Bryant, "Journal of Edwin Bryant," in Korns and Morgan, *West from Fort Bridger*, 71; Frink, *Journal*, 71; and Harrison, "Recollections," 9–10.

93. Potter, *Trail to California*, 143.

94. Pierce, *Pierce Chronicle*, 20.

95. Hecox, *California Caravan*, 38–39.

96. Lord, *Doctor's Gold Rush Journey*, 69–70.

97. Kellogg, *Notes*, 64–65.

98. Taylor, "Overland to the Gold Fields," 331. Similar warnings about weapons trade to Indians are voiced in Long, *Crossing the Plains*, 10; Bagley, "Crossing the Plains," 176; Variel, "Romance of the Plains," 74; and Roundtree, "Autobiography," 96.

99. Reynolds, *Pioneers of the Sand Plains*, 16.

100. McDiarmid, *Letters to My Wife*, 37.

101. Forman, "Across the Plains," 11.

102. Keller, *Trip Across the Plains*, 4, 20–22.

CHAPTER 4. SEEING THE ELEPHANT

1. Barry, *Beginning of the West*, 920.

2. Mattes, *Great Platte River Road*, 61–62. Civil War soldiers utilized the phrase "seeing the elephant" to refer to their first big battle experience when the realities of combat replaced their romanticized notions of glory. See Frank and Reaves, *"Seeing the Elephant,"* 1–2.

3. Stansbury, *Expedition*, 18–19.

4. Pengra, "Diary," 19.

5. Gibbs, "Diary," 295.

6. Isham, *Guide to California*, 15.

7. Cumming, *Gold Rush*, 40.

8. Ingalls, *Journal*, 41.

9. Wyman, *California Emigrant Letters*, 51–53.

10. Ibid., 112.

11. Ibid., 108; Werner, "Wheelbarrow Emigrant."

12. J. Roderic Korns, quoted in Korns and Morgan, *West from Fort Bridger*, 2.

13. Judson, *Pioneer's Search*, 65.

14. Shaw, *Across the Plains*, 75–77.

15. Wistar, *Autobiography*, 105–106.

16. Bruff, *Gold Rush*, 88–110.

17. Reading, "Journal," 183–84.

18. Bryant, "Journal of Edwin Bryant," 87.

19. Nesmith, "Diary," 354.

20. Farnham, *Travels in the Great Western Prairies*, 74–75. Other examples of the Cayuses acting as guides appear in Crawford, *Scenes of Earlier Days*, 54–55; Chenoweth, "Occasional Address," 34; and Knight, "Iowa to the Columbia River," 66.

21. Burnett, "Recollections," 76–77.

22. Drury, *Where Wagons Could Go*, 87–88, 197–200.

23. Ruby and Brown, *Cayuse Indians*, 103–12.

24. Rose, "Saga," 20–22; Schallenberger, "Overland in 1844," 64–69, 98–99; Kelly and Morgan, *Old Greenwood*, 118–27; Bigler, *Gold Discovery Journal*, 122–23; King, "Crossing the Forty-Mile Desert," 122–37.

25. Hecox, *California Caravan*, 40. Examples of other tribes serving as guides appear in Farnham, *Travels in the Great Western Prairies*, 72–73; Frink, *Journal*, 65; and Crawford, *Journal*, 21–22.

26. Booth, *Forty-Niner*, 14. See also Aram, "Recollections," 628.

27. Young and Young, "Diary," 154; Unruh, *Plains Across*, 157.

28. Thornton, "Oregon and California," 50–62; Stewart, *Ordeal By Hunger*, 114–25.

29. Excellent visual examples and discussion about maps produced by Indians that stretch back to earliest colonial times appear in Warhus, *Another America*; Lewis, *Cartographic Encounters*; Ronda, "'Chart in His Way,'" 43–53; and Lewis, "Indian Maps," 91–108.

30. Ewers, "Making and Uses of Maps," 187–90.

31. McCall, *Great California Trail*, 77.

32. Potter, *Trail to California*, 186.

33. Longmire, "Description of the Trip Across the Plains," 130–31.

34. Barlow, "History of the Barlow Road," 75–80; Palmer, *Journal*, 59. Another shortcut toll road created and improved by the Cayuses through the Blue Mountains is described in Crawford, *Scenes of Earlier Days*, 54.

35. Allyn, "Journal," 418; Pengra, "Diary," 51. A good description of Indians working at the Fort Boise crossing is provided in Gilliam, "Reminiscences," 206–207.

36. Rau, *Surviving the Oregon Trail*, 159.

37. Longsworth, *Diary*, 50–51; Adams and Blank, "Twin Sisters," 309; Nesmith, "Diary," 358; Todd and James, *Ever Westward*, 62.

38. Crawford, *Scenes of Earlier Days*, 56. See also Hastings, "Diary," 23–25.

39. Frémont, *Report*, 187–89; Cross, "Journal," 264.

40. Johnson and Winter, *Route Across the Rocky Mountains*, 35.

41. Jacobs, "Incidents," 81.

42. Braly, *Memory Pictures*, 77. Other details of Indian aid at Cascade Falls are found in Long, *Crossing the Plains*, 12–14; and "Richard Watson Helm," in Lockley, *Conversations with Pioneer Men*, 140.

43. Hammer, *Emigrating Company*, 166.

44. Todd and James, *Ever Westward*, 69.

45. "William A. Colvig," in Lockley, *Conversations with Pioneer Men*, 164.

46. "Andrew Jackson Masters," in Lockley, *Conversations with Pioneer Men*, 334.

47. Newby, "William T. Newby's Diary," 239.

48. Rudd, "Notes," 195–96.

49. Potter, *Trail to California*, 78.

50. Zeiber, "Diary," 311–12.

51. Reid, *Overland to California*, 126.

52. Madsen, *Northern Shoshoni*, 27.

53. Price, *Oglala People*, 30.

54. Boquist, *Crossing the Plains*, 10.

55. Casler, *Journal*, 41–42.

56. Page, *Wagons West*, 184.

57. Kilgore, *Kilgore Journal*, 49.

58. Other examples of Great Basin tribes providing hay, firewood, and water to overlanders appear in Miller, "Journal," 64; Bennett, *Overland Journey*, 43; and Millington, "Journal," 163–67.

59. William Wells, "Letters," typescript, California State Library, Sacramento, letter dated May 15, 1849.

60. McKinstry, "Diary," 210.

61. Bryant, *What I Saw in California*, 37–38, 69–70.

62. Shaw, *Across the Plains*, 32–33.

63. Glasscock, *Lucky Baldwin*, 57–62.

64. Shaw, *Eldorado*, 30–31.

65. Taylor and Taylor, "Letters," 146–47.

66. Staats, "Occasional Address," 50–51.

67. Scroggs, "To the Gold Fields," 149–51.

68. Pringle, *Magic River Deschutes*, 3–5.

69. Sydenham, "Freighting Across the Plains," 174–77.

70. Hebard, *Washakie*, 97–98.

71. "T. L. Jones," in Lockley, *Conversations with Pioneer Men*, 275.

72. Evans, "Missouri Forty-Niner's Trip," 43–44.

73. Hill, "Our Trip to Oregon," 1.

74. Kilgore, *Kilgore Journal*, 31.

75. Hines, "Life and Death," 114–16.

76. Thornton, "Oregon and California," 62–64; Houghton, *Expedition of the Donner Party*, 87–89.

CHAPTER 5. HUMANIZING THE EXPERIENCE

1. Jefferson's instructions are quoted at length in Hawke, *Those Tremendous Mountains*, 26–32.

2. Van Kirk, *Many Tender Ties*, 28–40; Lansing, "Plains Indian Women," 413–33.

3. Washburn, *Indian in America*, 20–21; Grobsmith, "Lakota Giveaway," 123–31.

4. Washburn, *Indian in America*, 22.

5. Hassrick, *Sioux*, 36–38; Price, *Oglala People*, 2–3.

6. Wyeth, *Oregon*, 84.

7. Palmer, *Journal*, 54.

8. Harmon, *Journals*, 54.

9. Ferguson, *California Gold Fields*, 25–26.

10. Sage, *Rocky Mountain Life*, 172.

11. Cross, "Journal," 84–85. See also in the same volume the eyewitness details added by George Gibbs, the civilian naturalist and artist accompanying the expedition, on 313–14.

12. Eaton, *Overland Trail to California*, 201–202.

13. Parsons, "Overland Honeymoon," 240.

14. Keil, "From Bethel, Missouri to Aurora, Oregon," 32–33.

15. McClure, "Diary," 57.

16. Carter, "Diary," 89–90.

17. Ruxton, *Life in the Far West*, 69–72.

18. Hoppe, "Recollections," 41.

19. Warren, *Preliminary Report*, 54.

20. Agent John E. Barrow to Superintendent D. D. Mitchell, Oct. 20, 1850, in *ARCIA for 1850*, 40.

21. Thomas Fitzpatrick to D. D. Mitchell, Sept. 24, 1850, in *ARCIA for 1850*, 24.

22. Annual Report of Commissioner Orlando Brown, Nov. 30, 1849, in *ARCIA for 1849*, 9.

23. Boquist, *Crossing the Plains*, 7.

24. "Lucy Ann Henderson," in Lockley, *Conversations with Pioneer Women*, 56.

25. Hickman, *Overland Journey to California*, 13.

26. Applegate, *Recollections*, 28.

27. Drury, *Where Wagons Could Go*, 56.

28. Drury, *Mountains We Have Crossed*, 78. Others who discussed the high level of Indian curiosity about whites—especially about women and children—include Hadley, "Journal," 67; Johnston, *Overland to California*, 64; and Fletcher, *Bride on the Bozeman Trail*, 33–34.

29. Hillyer, "From Waupun to Sacramento," 229–30.

30. Heiskell, *Forty-Niner from Tennessee*, 55.

31. Goddell and Austin, "Vermillion Wagon Train," 122.

32. Wooster, *Gold Rush*, 5.

33. Crawford, *Journal*, 13.

34. Quoted in Eaton, *Overland Trail to California*, 114–15.

35. Stephens, *Life Sketches*, 11.

36. Schellenberger, "Overland in 1844," 62.

37. Longmire, "First Immigrants," 26.

38. Goddell and Austin, "Vermillion Wagon Train," 96.

39. Chick, "Vicissitudes of Pioneer Life," 211. A colorful description of the "Wild West Show" appearance of a group of Crows and emigrants traveling together in 1852 appears in Brooks, *Pioneer Mother*, 24–25.

40. Bradbury, *Travels*, 178.

41. Lowe, *Five Years a Dragoon*, 51–55.

42. One representative case of Pawnees charging ten-cent fees for their show near the Elkhorn River during the later period of the trails appears in Arnold, "Joseph Warren Arnold's Journal," 472.

43. Aram, "Recollections," 623.

44. Crosby, "History and Journal," 175.

45. Johnson, *Tending the Talking Wire*, 91–92.

46. Burrell, "Council Bluffs to California," 236.

47. Woodhams, "Diary," 85.

48. Slaughter and Landon, *Trail of Hope*, 65.

49. Hastings, "Diary," 18.

50. Johnston, *Overland to California*, 65.

51. Allyn, "Journal," 420.

52. Shaw, *Across the Plains*, 30.

53. Johnson, "Overland Journey," 41.

54. Hines, "Life and Death," 94. Discussion of common food items carried by wagon trains and shared with Native Americans is found in Brooks, "Plains Across," 805.

55. Reading, "Journal," 150; Leach, *Early Day Stories*, 26; Hutchings, *Seeking the Elephant*, 125; Bryant, "Journal," 72, 80–81; Hancock, *Narrative*, 7; Shaw, *Eldorado*, 37; Pritchard, *Overland Diary*, 18.

56. Carpenter, "Trip Across the Plains," 105–106.

57. Tootle, "Diary," 9.

58. Clark, "Overland to the Gold Fields," 252.

59. Luke William Gallup, "Diary," in Larsen and Larsen, *Remembering Winter Quarters*, 151; Wonderley, *Reminiscences of a Pioneer*, 3–4; Farnham, "From Ohio to California," 301.

60. Owen, "My Trip Across the Plains," 6.

61. Barnett, *Long Trip*, 43.

62. Gould, *Oregon and California Trail Diary*, 36. Other descriptions of marksmanship displays and competitions appear in Wooster, *Gold Rush*, 2–3; McClure, "Diary," 57; Smith, *Journal*, 34–35; Soule, "Memories," 12; and Piercy, *Route from Liverpool*, 109–10.

63. Fox, "George W. Fox Diary," 588; Packard, *Early Emigration to California*, 8; Hill, *Dangerous Crossing*, 7.

64. Johnston, *Overland to California*, 62.

65. Langley, *To Utah with the Dragoons*, 40.

66. Slaughter and Landon, *Trail of Hope*, 64–65.

67. Cole, *In the Early Days*, 80.

68. Gibson, *Recollections*, 64.

69. Hoppe, "Recollections," 40–41.

70. Murphy, *Across the Plains*, 11.

71. Stephens, *Life Sketches*, 10–11.

72. Atkin, "Recollections," 382–83.

73. Broadwell, "Crossing the Plains," 22.

74. McDiarmid, *Letters to My Wife*, 91–92.

75. "E. E. Tucker," in Lockley, *Conversations with Pioneer Men*.

76. Neill, "Letters," 2.

77. "Christian L. Christensen," in Madsen, *I Walked to Zion*, 90.

CHAPTER 6. ACCRUING THE BENEFITS

1. Kilgore, *Kilgore Journal*, 23.

2. Washburn, *Indian in America*, 15–16.

3. Stout, *On the Mormon Frontier*, 256–57, 264.

4. Bennett, *Mormons at the Missouri*, 98–104.

5. Fox, "George W. Fox Diary," 588.

6. Pigman, *Journal*, 11.

7. Gilliam, "Reminiscences," 207–208. Further documentation of Stickus's longtime efforts to aid and maintain friendship with Americans is found in Ruby and Brown, *Cayuse Indians*, 98, 108, 133–45.

8. Chambers, "Brief Account," 27.

9. Crawford, *Journal*, 19–20.

10. Geer, "Diary," 159.

11. Smedley, *Across the Plains,* 78–79.

12. Epperson, "Journal," 172–73.

13. Haun, "Woman's Trip Across the Plains," 177. Other examples of this type of alleged Indian duplicity are found in Goodridge, "Mormon Trail," 229–30; Farnham, "From Ohio to California," 300; Keil, "From Bethel, Missouri to Aurora, Oregon," 30; and Williams, "Letter to Mother," 139–40.

14. Keil, "From Bethel, Missouri to Aurora, Oregon," 34.

15. Ibid., 37–38.

16. Ibid., 35. Further evidence of Camaspelo as a peacemaker who was forced into the 1847 Cayuse War appears in Ruby and Brown, *Cayuse Indians,* 106–107, 116–18, 196–97, 218.

17. Hunt, "By Ox-Team to California," 323.

18. Barlow, "Reminiscences," 253–54.

19. Porter, *By Ox-Team to California,* 70, 82.

20. Langley, *To Utah with the Dragoons,* 40.

21. Chandless, *Visit to Salt Lake,* 97.

22. Frush and Frush, *Overland Journals,* 35.

23. Christensen, *Sagwitch,* 19.

24. Bonney, "Recollections," 50.

25. Carpenter, "Trip Across the Plains," 166–69.

26. Wistar, *Autobiography,* 110.

27. Hadley, "Journal," 55.

28. Gibson, *Recollections,* 202–204.

29. Byers, "Odyssey," 24.

30. *ARCIA for 1860,* 111.

31. Bettelyoun and Waggoner, *With My Own Eyes,* 68.

32. Chambers, "'Bad Cheyennes,'" 235.

33. *ARCIA for 1853,* 206–207, 444–46.

34. J. H. Holeman to Brigham Young, Sept. 25, 1852, in *ARCIA for 1852,* 152.

35. Christensen, *Sagwitch,* 19.

36. Quoted in Madsen, "Shoshoni-Bannock Marauders," 12–13.

37. Stewart, "Diary," 14.

38. Cosgrove, "Reminiscences," 263–64.

39. Jacob Holeman to Luke Lea, Sept. 21, 1851, in *ARCIA for 1851,* 444–45. The devastating impact of this trigger-happy mentality on the Pawnees is evaluated in Hyde, *Pawnee Indians,* 224.

40. Schallenberger, "Overland," 65.

41. Swasey, *Early Days,* 32–33. See also the eyewitness account of Bonney, "Recollections," 43–44.

42. Owen, "My Trip Across the Plains."

43. Cole, *Memoirs,* 50–51.

44. Langley, *To Utah with the Dragoons*, 100.

45. Porter, *By Ox-Team to California*, 79–83, 95–96.

46. Cosgrove, "Reminiscences," 259–60.

47. Applegate, *Recollections*, 13. Historian Will Bagley warns that this often-repeated story lacks confirmation from other primary sources.

48. Bonney, "Recollections," 41–43.

49. Stansbury, *Expedition*, 253–54.

50. Slaughter and Landon, *Trail of Hope*, 65.

51. Lowe, *Five Years a Dragoon*, 74.

52. Sage, *Rocky Mountain Life*, 199.

53. White, *Middle Ground*, x.

CHAPTER 7. RESPONDING TO THE ALARM

1. Mattes, *Great Platte River Road*, 178.

2. Wilson, *Fort Kearny*, 57–58.

3. Hafen and Young, *Fort Laramie*, 148.

4. Wyman, *California Emigrant Letters*, 49.

5. *Council Bluffs (Iowa) Frontier Guardian*, July 7, 1850.

6. A helpful chart indicating migration numbers for each year between 1841 and 1866 is printed in Mattes, *Great Platte River Road*, 23. A precise accounting of the 1853 season up to May 20, as recorded on the register at Fort Kearny, was copied by Andrew McClure in his "Diary," 8–9. A good discussion of the varying estimates offered by primary sources appears in Read, "Women and Children," 2–6.

7. De Smet, *Life, Letters and Travels*, 2:671–72.

8. Hebard, *Washakie*, 58.

9. Carleton, *Prairie Logbooks*, 250.

10. Lord, *Doctor's Gold Rush Journey*, 70.

11. Farnham, "From Ohio to California," 308.

12. Nathan Boone to Zachary Taylor, May 27, 1843, in Pelzer, *Marches of the Dragoons*, 197.

13. Frémont, *Report*, 145–46. Similar statistics were provided by American Fur Company representatives at Fort Laramie to Riley Root, in Root, *Journal of Travels*, 9–10.

14. Denig, *Five Indian Tribes*, 81–82; McGinnis, "Intertribal Conflict," 55.

15. De Smet, *Life, Letters and Travels*, 3:948.

16. Franklin, *March to South Pass*, 23.

17. Thomas H. Harvey to T. Hartley Crawford, Sept. 10, 1845, in *ARCIA for 1845*, 535–36.

18. Thomas P. Moore to William Medill, Sept. 21, 1846, in *ARCIA for 1848*, 292–93.

19. Hafen and Young, *Fort Laramie*, 139.

20. Thomas Fitzpatrick to Thomas H. Harvey, Sept. 18, 1847, in *ARCIA for 1850*, 133.

21. Bidwell, *Echoes of the Past*, 13–14.

22. Kelly, *Excursion to California*, 1:55; Farnham, "From Ohio to California," 312.

23. Wyman, *California Emigrant Letters*, 56–57.

24. Minto, "Reminiscences," 150.

25. Holliday, *World Rushed In*, 153.

26. Brown, *Journal of a Journey*, 16; Butterfield, "Michigan to California," 398. See the parallel comments from 1860 in Hambleton, *Gold Hunter's Experience*, 39–40.

27. Barlow, "Reminiscences," 256.

28. Braly, *Memory Pictures*, 54.

29. Clayton, *William Clayton's Journal*, 137.

30. Bidwell, *Echoes of the Past*, 30. Other persons who strongly contrasted Indian and white attitudes toward hunting bison were Hoppe, "Recollections," 43; and "Clifton Wolford," in Lockley, *Conversations with Pioneer Men*, 224.

31. Ruxton, *Life in the Far West*, 63.

32. Cummins, *Autobiography*, 37; Ferguson, *California Gold Fields*, 24.

33. Harlan, "Journal," 37.

34. Mapel, "Experiences"; Tappan, "Gold Rush Diary," 121; Brown, *Journal of a Journey*, 43.

35. Osterhoudt, "Osterhoudt's Ox Train Diary," 2.

36. Kilgore, *Kilgore Journal*, 19.

37. Rhodes, "Joseph Rhodes," 68.

38. Geer, "Occasional Address," 36.

39. Ware, *Indian War of 1864*, 114–15.

40. Linderman, *Pretty Shield*, 250.

41. West, *Way to the West*, 54.

42. Vecsey, "American Indian Environmental Religions," 9; Parkman, *Oregon Trail*, 119.

43. Parkman, *Oregon Trail*, 188.

44. Vecsey, "American Indian Environmental Religions," 21–23. Interesting cultural analysis of the animal-human kinship ties is found in Martin, *Keepers of the Game*. However, Martin's central conclusions are refuted by Sturtevant, "Animals and Disease," 179–88; and Snow, "'Keepers of the Game,'" 61–71.

45. Harrod, *Animals Came Dancing*, 77–78, 105; Vecsey, "American Indian Environmental Religions," 15.

46. Hassrick, *Sioux*, 296–309; Utley, *Lance and the Shield*, 137–38; McLaughlin, *My Friend the Indian*, 97. A good discussion of American Indian spiritual connections to sacred sites as well as to animal spirits is presented in Parks and Wedel, "Pawnee Geography," 143–76.

47. Report of Agent William Hatton, in *ARCIA for 1849*, 1074.

48. Bullock, *Pioneer Camp*, 153.

49. Tootle, "Diary," 10.

50. Boquist, *Crossing the Plains*, 11.

51. Ingalls, *Journal*, 29. By examining the southern plains bison herds, historian Dan Flores sees the 1840s as the beginning decade of decline because of exotic bovine diseases, acceleration of the hide trade, and the increase in Indian populations. Elliott West agrees that the 1840s were the important transition period, and he further argues that "species packing" by domesticated animals such as horses, cattle, and sheep hastened the process. Pekka Hämäläinen challenges this view and pushes the initial date of rapid decline to the late 1700s, when the wide availability of horses to the Plains Indians ended subsistence-level bison hunting and began the era of commercial hunting for hides. See Flores, "Bison Ecology," 465–85; West, *Way to the West*, 51–83; Hämäläinen, "First Phase of Destruction," 101–114.

52. Mayhall, *Kiowas*, 212; Grinnell, *Cheyenne Indians*, 2:164.

53. Powers and Leiker, "Cholera among the Plains Indians," 319.

54. Delano, *Life on the Plains*, 17–18.

55. Hickman, *Overland Journey to California*, 8.

56. Cross, "Journal," 73–74.

57. Cumming, *Gold Rush*, 32–34; Powers and Younger, "Cholera on the Overland Trails," 45.

58. John E. Barrow to D. D. Mitchell, Oct. 4, 1849, in *ARCIA for 1849*, 1077–78.

59. Hyde, *Pawnee Indians*, 229–31; Fulton, "Interview," 1.

60. "Emigration in 1850," 221.

61. Holliday, *World Rushed In*, 114; Page, *Wagons West*, 159; Taylor, "Overland to the Gold Fields," 144–45; Keller, *Trip Across the Plains*, 3.

62. Chenoweth, "Occasional Address," 33.

63. Williams, "Journal," 399.

64. Stansbury, *Expedition*, 43–44.

65. Bettleyoun and Waggoner, *With My Own Eyes*, 44–49.

66. Stands In Timber and Liberty, *Cheyenne Memories*, 121. A different version of this tale as remembered by Cheyenne mixed-blood George Bent is presented in Hyde, *Life of George Bent*, 97n.

67. Hyde, *Life of George Bent*, 96–97.

68. Powers and Leiker, "Cholera among the Plains Indians," 327–32. For a similar effect among the Lakotas, see Bray, "Teton Sioux Population History," 165–88.

69. Loughary, "Travels and Incidents," 122.

70. Case, "Recollections," 274–75.

71. Holt, "Reminiscences," 167–68. Conjecture about a further ruse to scare Indians with the threat of an epidemic is found in Long, *Crossing the Plains*, 4.

72. "William A. Colvig," 163.

73. Berrien, "Overland from St. Louis," 318.

74. McClure, "Diary," 55; Pigman, *Journal*, 19.

75. Hixon, *On to Oregon*, 80.

76. White, *To Oregon in 1852*, 20.

77. Boyd, "Introduction of Infectious Diseases," 112–15, 519–31.

78. Hockett, "Experiences on the Oregon Trail," 13; Ruby and Brown, *Cayuse Indians*, 84–112.

79. Scott, "Journal," 89; Gillette, *Overland to Oregon*, 48–50; Shepard, "'O Wickedness,'" 10.

80. Woodhams, "Diary," 64.

81. Young and Young, "Diary," 156.

82. Frizzell, *Across the Plains*, 23; Taylor, "Overland Trip Across the Plains," 168.

83. Hill, *Dangerous Crossing*, 18–19; Millington, "Journal," 43–44.

84. Potter, *Trail to California*, 77.

85. Buckingham, "Crossing the Plains," 18.

86. Benjamin, *Three Years in America*, 2:263–64.

87. Berrien, "Overland from St. Louis," 309.

88. Stafford, *March of Empire*, 115.

89. Eaton, *Overland Trail to California*, 141–42.

90. Butler, *Journal*, 31–32.

91. Boquist, *Crossing the Plains*, 11.

92. Reynolds, *Pioneers*, 15.

93. Pratt, "Journal," 244.

94. Bratt, *Trails of Yesterday*, 71–72.

95. Barrett and Arno, "Indian Fires," 52–60; Krech, *Ecological Indian*, 101–22; Loscheider, "Use of Fire," 82–92.

96. Brown, "Over Barren Plains," 19.

97. Barnett, *Long Trip*, 43.

98. Ackley, *Crossing the Plains*, 31. Other examples of misplaced conjecture are found in "William A. Colvig," 163; and Wistar, *Autobiography*, 77.

99. Langley, *To Utah with the Dragoons*, 81–82.

100. "C. B. Wiley" in Lockley, *Conversations with Pioneer Men*, 196–97.

101. Glazier and Clark, *Journal*, 16–17.

102. Johnston, *Overland to California*, 44.

103. Stewart, "Overland Trip to California," 177.

104. Christy, *Thomas Christy's Road Across the Plains*, May 13, 1850, entry.

105. Bettelyoun and Waggoner, *With My Own Eyes*, 47. Nineteen-year-old Fanny Kelly, an emigrant who was captured and held by the Oglalas for six months in 1864, wrote in great detail about how a prairie fire moved speedily into the Indian village and was stopped only by the inhabitants pulling up grass by hand

and igniting a backfire to burn off a buffer area. This particular fire was apparently caused by Indian carelessness. See Kelly, *Narrative of My Captivity*, 159–63. Further Indian condemnations of white-initiated prairie fires are found in Hinde, *Journal*, 24; and Howell, *1849 California Trail Diaries*, 22.

CHAPTER 8. MASSACRED BY INDIANS

1. Parker, "Early Recollections," 18–20.
2. Shaw, *Across the Plains*, 33–34.
3. Parsons, "Overland Honeymoon," 280–82; Fox, "George W. Fox Diary," 592.
4. Brown, "Over Barren Plains," 26–27.
5. Harlan, *California*, 46–47. Two further posted signs along the Humboldt River warning about Indian dangers in 1849 and 1850, respectively, are discussed in Decker, *Diaries*, 125; and Langworthy, *Scenery of the Plains*, 113–14.
6. Scroggs, "To the Gold Fields," 160.
7. Stobie, "Crossing the Plains," 207.
8. Lenox, *Overland to Oregon*, 37–38.
9. Brown, "Over Barren Plains," 23. Similar accounts of panics created by the overlanders' own livestock are found in Woodhams, "Diary," 55; Ackley, "Across the Plains," 193–94; Richey, *Trip Across the Plains*, 3–4; and Carpenter, "Trip Across the Plains," 154.
10. Potter, *Trail to California*, 93. See also a similar elk case in Bullock, *Pioneer Camp*, 305–306.
11. Powers, *Woman's Overland Journal*, 56.
12. Merrill, *Bound for Idaho*, 55–56. Even Indians could make mistakes about identifying distant riders on the horizon, as in "Rasmus Neilsen," in Carter, *Our Pioneer Heritage*, 11:155–56; and Bullock, *Pioneer Camp*, 288–89.
13. Haun, "Woman's Trip Across the Plains," 175.
14. Bender, "Journey Across the Plains," 160–61.
15. Chambers, "Reminiscences," 18–19.
16. Schallenberger, "Overland in 1844," 52–53.
17. Butterfield, "Michigan to California," 412–13.
18. Schallenberger, "Overland in 1844," 56–57.
19. Delano, *Life on the Plains*, 65.
20. Gibson, *Recollections*, 31–32.
21. "Mrs. W. C. Kanter," in Lockley, *Conversations with Pioneer Women*, 84–85.
22. Kelley, "Reminiscence," 335.
23. Ringo, "1864 Journal," 230.
24. Hickman, *Overland Journey to California*, 18.
25. Arms, *Long Road*, 31–32.

26. Snyder, "Diary," 231–32.

27. McDiarmid, *Letters to My Wife*, 39–40.

28. Cummins, *Autobiography*, 39–40.

29. Hill, "Our Trip to Oregon," 5–6.

30. Atkin, "Recollections," 382–83.

31. Broadwell, "Crossing the Plains," 22.

32. Madsen, *I Walked to Zion*, 15–17.

33. Cosgrove, "Reminiscences," 259. Other examples where overlanders interpreted Indian actions to be motivated by "saucing" and "jollying," rather than constituting a real threat, are found in Johnson, "Overland Journey," 27; and Hutchings, *Seeking the Elephant*, 101–103.

34. Fox, *Jared Fox's Memmorandom*, 35.

35. Currey, "Occasional Address," 43.

36. Harrison, "Recollections," 5–6.

37. Dickenson, *Reminiscences*, 9; Green, *Diary*, 17; Haun, "Woman's Trip Across the Plains," 182; Henderson, "Young Adventure," 93; "Sammy Burch," in Lockley, *Conversations with Pioneer Men*, 112–13; Spencer, "Mrs. Lucinda Spencer Recollections," 75–76.

38. Tompkins, "Interesting Account of a Trip," 42.

39. Hawk, "Strange Adventures," 163.

40. General discussions of disease, death, taboos, and ghosts among Plains tribes are found in Hassrick, *Sioux*, 246–48, 333–38; Grinnell, *Cheyenne Indians*, 2:99–103; and Lowie, *Crow Indians*, 69–71.

41. Marcy, *Prairie Traveler*, 192–93.

42. Stewart, "Diary," 14–15.

43. Braly, *Memory Pictures*, 52.

44. Stands In Timber and Liberty, *Cheyenne Memories*, 163–67. Slightly different versions of this story are found in Grinnell, *Fighting Cheyennes*, 112–13; and Berthrong, *Southern Cheyennes*, 134–35.

45. Lenox, *Overland to Oregon*, 45; Holeman to Young, Sept. 25, 1852, in *ARCIA for 1852*, 150–51.

46. Keil, "From Bethel, Missouri to Aurora, Oregon," 29; Hulin, "Daybook or Journal," 27.

47. Steck, *Amos Steck*, 40.

48. Garland Hurt to Brigham Young, Sept. 30, 1855, in *ARCIA for 1855*, 199.

49. Hopkins, *Life Among the Piutes*, 22–23.

50. McKinstry, *California Gold Rush*, 223; Casler, *Journal*, 35–41; Wistar, *Autobiography*, 104–105; Brown, *Memoirs*, 21; Hurd, "Letters," 657.

51. "C. B. Wiley," 198. See also the reports of Holeman to Young, Sept. 25, 1852, in *ARCIA for 1852*, 442; and Holeman to Young, Sept. 30, 1853, in *ARCIA for 1853*, 446–47; McClellan, "California Bound."

52. Hill, *Gold Hunter*, 46.

53. *Portland Oregonian*, Dec. 27, 1851, quoted in Unruh, *Plains Across*, 193.

54. Allyn, "Journal," 385–86.

55. Riddle, *History of Early Days*, 8; "Rhoda Quick (Johnson)," in Lockley, *Conversations with Pioneer Women*, 151–52.

56. Root, *Overland Stage to California*, 207.

57. Ringo, "1864 Journal," 8:217; Loughary, "Travels and Incidents," 128, 132.

58. Wyman, *California Emigrant Letters*, 101. Numerous examples of alleged attacks by "white Indians" appear in Unruh, *Plains Across*, 193–97.

59. Smedley, *Across the Plains*, 42–43, 53; Glenn, "Letter from La Grande Ronde," 21. Other cases of white-on-white violence that were blamed on Indians appear in Maxwell, *Crossing the Plains*, 62–72; Allyn, "Journal," 423–24; Eaton, *Overland Trail to California*, 247; Drury, *Mountains We Have Crossed*, 77; and Zanjani, *Sarah Winnemucca*, 55–56.

60. Bonney, "Recollections," 38–39.

61. Waters, "Account of a Trip," 74–75.

62. Keil, "From Bethel, Missouri to Aurora, Oregon," 33.

63. Lord, *Doctor's Gold Rush Journey*, 104.

64. Pengra, "Diary."

65. Cumming, *Gold Rush*, 39.

66. Merrill, *Bound for Idaho*, 63. See also Ferguson, *California Gold Fields*, 25; Stafford, *March of Empire*, 126–27.

67. Twain, *Roughing It*, 43.

68. Cumming, *Gold Rush*, 39.

69. Madsen, "'Almo Massacre' Revisited," 55–56.

70. Ibid., 60–64.

71. Unruh, *Plains Across*, 176.

72. Hunt, "Anatomy of a Massacre," 2–25; Murray, *Modocs and Their War*, 24–27.

73. Frost, "Autobiography," 101–105; Handsaker, "Coming to Oregon," 14–15; Ebey, "Overland from Missouri," 82; Koontz, "Interview," 39–41.

74. Quoted from *Portland Weekly Oregonian*, Sept. 2, 23, and Oct. 21, 1854, in Unruh, *Plains Across*, 190.

75. Maxwell, *Crossing the Plains*, 62–75; Unruh, *Plains Across*, 196–97.

76. Brown, "Attack on the Hudspeth Cutoff," 17–31; Lynn, "Along the Emigrant Trail," 51; Snow, "Diary," 205–207; Norton, "Diary," 53–56.

77. Fuller, *Left by the Indians*, 21–31; Shannon, *Utter Disaster*, 33–140; Unruh, *Plains Across*, 190–92; Madsen, *Bannock of Idaho*, 123–25; Madsen, "Shoshoni-Bannock Marauders," 12–13; Dent, *Military Report*, 57–66.

78. Gould, *Oregon and California Trail Diary*, 58–67; Madsen, "Shoshoni-Bannock Marauders," 17–19. Another event closely associated with the series of Shoshone and Bannock attacks during the summer of 1862 is the Van Zant Massacre, which involved the deaths of six miners returning from Fort Boise to Salt

Lake, along with several members of the Adams wagon train. See Bristol, *Pioneer Preacher*, 266–68. On September 12, 1862, fifteen well-armed men were attacked by approximately forty Shoshones near the Raft River, and six whites were killed. See Madsen, *Shoshoni Frontier*, 162.

79. Kelly, *Narrative of My Captivity*, 19–227; Larimer, *Capture and Escape*; Merrill, *Bound for Idaho*, 65–66; Forman, "Across the Plains," 18–20; Brown, "Attack on the Kelly-Larimer Wagon Train," 16–38.

80. Hill, *Dangerous Crossing*, 25–27; Czaplewski, *Captive of the Cheyenne*, 9–66.

81. Hagerty, "Indian Raids."

82. Unruh, *Plains Across*, 184–85; Riley, *Women and Indians*, 155; Schlissel, *Women's Diaries*, 154; Munkres, "Plains Indian Threat," 193–94; Clark, "Myth of Indian Aggression," 26–34.

83. My conclusion that only eight well-documented cases of full-fledged "massacres" occurred along the California, Oregon, and Mormon trails between 1840 and 1870 is based upon what the surviving record can tell us and upon my somewhat arbitrary notion of what numbers of deaths constituted a "massacre" in that period. First, I do not include in that total the massacres of Indians by white overlanders, even though these particular cases are discussed at length throughout the book. Second, I do not include the Bozeman Trail conflicts of the 1860s because these stories are separate from the California, Oregon, and Mormon trails that I have focused upon throughout this study. Furthermore, the most important single combat along the Bozeman Trail was the 1866 Fetterman debacle at Fort Phil Kearny, which involved soldiers against the Sioux, not civilian overlanders against the Sioux. Third, I have rejected all cases that were clearly falsified, such as the Almo Creek Massacre and the Doniphan Massacre, even though they were widely reported in thirdhand versions. Finally, the killing of one or two whites by an unidentified Indian party does not encompass the full meaning of the word "massacre" as most people would have defined the term in the mid-nineteenth century. Tragic though all individual deaths were, such a random act did not constitute a large and premeditated assault upon a wagon train. If one arbitrarily considers the number of five deaths as the minimal figure for defining a single-event massacre, then only eight such documented cases of full-fledged massacres can be discerned among emigrants utilizing the California, Oregon, and Mormon trails via the Platte and Sweetwater rivers in the period from 1840 to 1870. This conforms to the conclusions drawn by Unruh in *Plains Across*, 189–93.

CHAPTER 9. CAPTIVITY INFINITELY WORSE THAN DEATH

1. John S. Ford to H. R. Runnels, June 2, 1858, in Winfrey and Day, *Indian Papers of Texas and the Southwest*, 240.

2. Arber, *Works of John Smith*; Rowlandson, *Narrative*.

3. Vaughan and Clark, *Puritans among the Indians*, 4–7; Levernier and Cohen, *Indians and Their Captives*, xvii–xviii.

4. Vaughan and Clark, *Puritans among the Indians*, 26–28; Treckel, "Letters to the Editor," 143–44; Kestler, *Indian Captivity Narrative*, xxix–xxx; Myres, *Westering Women*, 49–51.

5. Don Worcester, introduction to Rister, *Comanche Bondage*, 15; House, *Narrative of the Captivity of Mrs. Horn*, 60–66.

6. Plummer, *Rachel Plummer's Narrative*, 4.

7. The theme of sexual innuendo in captivity narratives is best examined in Namias, *White Captives*, 97–112.

8. Frizzell, *Across the Plains*, 10.

9. Witter, "Pioneer Life," 166.

10. Munkres, "Plains Indian Threat," 199.

11. Grundvig, "Recollections," 69–71.

12. Derounian-Stodola, Zabelle, and Levernier, *Indian Captivity Narrative*, 2–5.

13. Stern, "White Indians," 266–81.

14. Lansing, "Plains Indian Women," 413–33.

15. Tate, "Comanche Captives," 239–42.

16. Hassrick, *Sioux*, 111–12; Moore, *Cheyenne Nation*, 186–89, 262–63, 318–19.

17. Axtell, "White Indians," 188–92.

18. Calloway, "Uncertain Destiny," 203; Abler, "Scalping," 13–15; Axtell, "White Indians," 182.

19. Axtell, "White Indians," 206.

20. Tate, "Comanche Captives," 233–36.

21. Hockett, "Experiences on the Oregon Trail," 7–8.

22. Kelsey, "California Heroine," 6; Hawk, "Strange Adventures," 161; Soule, "Memories," 10.

23. Ivins, *Pen Pictures*, 71–75.

24. Lovejoy, "Lovejoy's Pioneer Narrative," 245–48; Hastings, *Emigrants' Guide*, 11–17.

25. Matthieu, "Reminiscences," 81–82; Crawford, *Journal*, 12; Thornton, "Oregon and California," 21; Potter, *Trail to California*, 120.

26. Dippie, *Vanishing American*, 25–30.

27. Klein and Ackerman, *Women and Power*, 5–6.

28. Ross, *Adventures of the First Settlers*, 107.

29. McKinstry, *California Gold Rush*, 90.

30. Wayman, *Doctor on the California Trail*, 70.

31. Doederlein, "Doederlein Diary," 121. Similar examples are found in Reading, "Journal," 175; Delano, *Life on the Plains*, 131; and Hambleton, *Gold Hunter's Experience*, 49–50. Unruh, *Plains Across*, 167, briefly describes another half a dozen cases of Indians allegedly offering to trade female kin to white men.

32. Catherine Adams (Pilling), in Madsen, *I Walked to Zion*, 121–22; McClellan, "California Bound."

33. Braly, *Memory Pictures*, 68–69.

34. Clark and Clark, *Two Diaries*, 38.

35. Witter, "Pioneer Life," 166. See also Matthieu, "Reminiscences," 82–83.

36. Chambers, "Brief Account," 27.

37. Forman, "Across the Plains," 15.

38. Farnham, "From Ohio to California," 307.

39. Smith, "To Pike's Peak," 132–34.

40. Peery, "Mrs. Peery, At Age 88," 267.

41. Evans, "Autobiography," 284.

42. Bayley, "Across the Plains," 36–37. The most unusual and unlikely twist to these stories of trading for white women is John Minto's story of three Sioux women outbidding each other to purchase him as a husband. See Minto, "Reminiscences," 157–58.

43. Hayden, *Pioneer Days*, 19.

44. Ward, *Across the Plains*, 11.

45. Waters, "Account of a Trip," 65; Enos, "Recollections," 2–4.

46. Miller, *Overland in a Covered Wagon*, 77–78.

47. Staats, "Occasional Address," 49–50.

48. Riley, *Women and Indians*, 209–10.

49. Unruh, *Plains Across*, 166.

50. Munkres, "Plains Indian Threat," 221.

51. Stewart, *California Trail*, 89.

52. Hoppe, "Recollections," 44–46.

53. "Alfred Robert Dyer," in Carter, *Our Pioneer Heritage*, 11:53.

54. Caples, "Overland Journey to California," 1–2.

55. McIntosh, *Allen and Rachel*, 82–84.

56. James, "Autobiography," 66.

57. Rahm, "Diary," June 9, 1862, entry. A happier outcome occurred for Mary Variel, who allowed an Indian man to take her baby on a five-minute ride around the camp near Fort Laramie in 1852. See Variel, "Romance of the Plains," 64.

58. Lowell, "Across the Plains," 1–3. Several other cases of real or imagined threats to white children are found in Mattice, "Reminiscences," 464; Hixon, *On to Oregon*, 72–75; Parker, "Early Recollections," 18; and Mattes, *Indians, Infants and Infantry*, 50, 122.

59. Haines, "Goldilocks," 27.

60. Ibid.

61. Palmer, "Goldilocks Revisited," 31–33.

62. Ibid., 31.

63. Ibid., 37; "Catherine Thomas Morris," in Lockley, *Conversations with Pioneer Women*, 92–95.

64. Palmer, "Goldilocks Revisited," 40.

65. Shannon, *Utter Disaster*, 162–74; Madsen, *Shoshoni Frontier*, 172–74.

66. Hart, "Rescue of a Frontier Boy," 52–54; Shannon, *Utter Disaster*, 174.

CHAPTER 10. FROM COOPERATION TO CONFLICT

1. Blanchard, "1864 Overland Trail," 78.

2. Clark, "Overland to the Gold Fields," 242.

3. Taylor and Taylor, "Letters," 133.

4. Packard, *Early Emigration to California*, 12.

5. Twain, *Roughing It*, 98–101.

6. Quoted in Berkhofer, *White Man's Indian*, 95–96. Other overland travelers of less renown than Twain and Parkman also registered their concern that the noble Indian theme had been overplayed in literature and art and that virtually all American Indians were repulsive in their look and manner. See Packard, *Early Emigration to California*, 8; Cook, "Letters," 54; Todd and James, *Ever Westward*, 77; Young, *Dangers of the Trail*, 17; Minto, "Reminiscences," 124; Keller, *Trip Across the Plains*, 5; Woodhams, "Diary," 66–67; Patterson, "Platte River Route," 102; Tootle, "Diary," 9; Herndon, *Days on the Road*, 106, 159.

7. Carleton, *Prairie Logbooks*, 162–63.

8. Greeley, *Overland Journey*, 53, 153–56.

9. Thomas H. Harvey to William Medill, Sept. 5, 1846, in *ARCIA for 1846*, 74.

10. Annual Report of Commissioner Luke Lea, Nov. 27, 1851, in *ARCIA for 1851*, 6.

11. "Treaty of Fort Laramie with Sioux, etc., 1851," in Kappler, *Indian Affairs*, 594; D. D. Mitchell to Luke Lea, Nov. 11, 1851, in *ARCIA for 1851*, 28.

12. "Treaty of Fort Laramie with Sioux," 594–95; Anderson, "Controversial Sioux Amendment," 201–202; De Smet, *Life, Letters and Travels*, 2:675–77, 681–84.

13. "Treaty of Fort Laramie with Sioux," 594–95.

14. McGinnis, "Intertribal Conflict," 56.

15. Lowe, *Five Years a Dragoon*, 61–69; Hebard, *Washakie*, 67–73.

16. Price, *Oglala People*, 33–36; McGinnis, "Intertribal Conflict," 56. Two detailed secondary accounts about the 1851 Fort Laramie negotiations are found in Hafen and Young, *Fort Laramie*, 177–96; and Hafen, *Broken Hand*, 284–301.

17. Stands In Timber and Liberty, *Cheyenne Memories*, 161–62.

18. DeMallie, "Touching the Pen," 40–43.

19. Stands In Timber and Liberty, *Cheyenne Memories*, 161–62; DeMallie, "Touching the Pen," 45–46.

20. DeMallie, "Touching the Pen," 45–46.

21. Munkres, "Indian-White Contact," 450–52, 468–69, for full text of agreement; Adams, *General William S. Harney*, 141–44.

22. Hassrick, *Sioux*, 12–16, 107–109.

23. Price, *Oglala People*, 8–15; Hassrick, *Sioux*, 16–22; Ellis, "Reservation *Akicitas*," 185–210.

24. A unique dualistic system of institutionalized Peace Chiefs (Council of 44) and the heads of the six warrior societies existed among the Cheyennes. See Stands In Timber and Liberty, *Cheyenne Memories*, 36–45. For Paiute decentralized leadership patterns, see Zanjani, *Sarah Winnemucca*, 9. For the Shoshone decentralized system, see Christensen, *Sagwitch*, 8–9.

25. Carleton, *Prairie Logbooks*, 238–39.

26. Parkman, *Oregon Trail*, 118.

27. Ibid., 118.

28. Lempfrit, *Oregon Trail Journal*, 75–76.

29. Carpenter, "Trip Across the Plains," 117–18.

30. Alfred Sully to Nathaniel G. Taylor, June 24, 1867, quoted in Munkres, "Indian-White Contact," 450–51. Humorous descriptions of two "paper chiefs," who became disparagingly known by fellow Sioux as Loafs-Around-Forts, are found in Brown, *Journal of a Journey*, 23; and Steck, *Amos Steck*, 40–41.

31. Paul, *Autobiography of Red Cloud*, 64–70; Olson, *Red Cloud*, 19–22; Larson, *Red Cloud*, 57–61.

32. Cross, "Journal," 55–56; Hyde, *Pawnee Indians*, 227; Hafen and Young, *Fort Laramie*, 137–47.

33. Unruh, *Plains Across*, 231.

34. Ringo, "1864 Journal," 215.

35. Harvey to Crawford, Sept. 10, 1845, in *ARCIA for 1845*, 536.

36. Holtgreive, "Recollections," 195.

37. Stansbury, *Expedition*, 45–46.

38. Wyman, *California Emigrant Letters*, 53; Isham, *Guide to California*, 14; Howell, *1849 California Trail Diaries*, 14; Scamehorn, *Buckeye Rovers*, 12; Searls, *Diary*, 30.

39. Annie Ruff to Mary Dougherty, June 24, 1849, in Ruff and Ruff, "Letters."

40. McClure, "Diary," 27.

41. Woodhams, "Diary," 106–107.

42. Cross, "Journal," 170–72.

43. Frazer, *Forts of the West*, 44–45.

44. Ibid., 166.

45. Brief profiles of each of the forts built during the Civil War era and in the years just after are given in Frazer, *Forts of the West*, 19–35 (California), 84–90 (Nebraska), 90–95 (Nevada), 127–34 (Oregon), 164–67 (Utah), 167–77 (Washington), 177–87 (Wyoming). Further details and photographs of some of these posts are provided in Hart, *Old Forts of the Northwest*, 69–103.

46. Longsworth, *Diary*, 23–24; Allyn, "Journal," 402–403; Belshaw, "Diary," 15. On the day before the ferryboat fight, Henry Allyn had commented on how friendly all the Sioux seemed to be, and, by way of contrast, Andrew McClure remarked on the drunken and obnoxious behavior of the men who operated the ferry. See Allyn, "Journal," 400; McClure, "Diary," 25–26.

47. Pengra, "Diary," 28–30; Brown, *Authentic Wagon Train Journal*, 39; Williams, "'Diary of a Trip Across the Plains,'" 202–203. Three reputable authors agree that significant trouble did emerge from the Fort Laramie ferryboat incident and that the families of the warriors involved demanded revenge raids, but Agent Thomas Fitzpatrick was able to smooth things over. See Hafen and Young, *Fort Laramie*, 210–11; Hyde, *Spotted Tail's Folk*, 56.

48. Bordeaux et al., "Testimony About the Grattan Massacre," 259–61; John W. Whitfield to Alfred Cumming, Sept. 27, and Oct. 2, 1854, in *ARCIA for 1854*, 94–98.

49. Nixon, "Journal," 1.

50. Hafen and Young, *Fort Laramie*, 230.

51. Bettelyoun and Waggoner, *With My Own Eyes*, 53–54, 93.

52. Bandel, *Frontier Life*, 73–98; "Editorials and News Items about General Harney's Sioux Expedition," 273–82; Drum, "Reminiscences," 143–51; Dudley, "Battle of Ash Hollow," 373–99; Todd, "Harney Expedition," 111–14.

53. Chandless, *Visit to Salt Lake*, 74.

54. Bettelyoun and Waggoner, *With My Own Eyes*, 68–69.

55. Ibid., 65.

56. Warren, *Preliminary Report*, 52–53.

57. Full discussions of the various Kansas and Nebraska removals appear in Herring, *Enduring Indians of Kansas*; Wishart, *Unspeakable Sadness*; and Wright, *Guide to the Indian Tribes of Oklahoma*.

58. Townsend, *California Diary*, 55. A particularly colorful letter from a California miner calling for the extermination of all California Indians, published originally in the *New York Herald*, is reprinted in Wyman, *California Emigrant Letters*, 141–42.

59. Utley, *Indian Frontier*, 52. Three excellent and very detailed analyses of the California situation during the 1850s and 1860s are Phillips, *Chiefs and Challengers*; Hurtado, *Indian Survival*; and Rawls, *Indians of California*.

60. Utley, *Frontiersmen in Blue*, 181–87. A more detailed analysis is offered in Beckham, *Requiem for a People*.

61. Utley, *Frontiersmen in Blue*, 187–202; Ruby and Brown, *Indians of the Pacific Northwest*, 145–73.

62. Bender, "Journey Across the Plains," 164; Dunham, *Across the Plains*, 11.

63. Brigham Young to James W. Denver, Sept. 12, 1857, in *ARCIA for 1857*, 310–11. Young's letter to the commissioner highlighting Gentile misdeeds as the cause of Great Basin Indian problems was written one day after the infamous Mountain Meadows Massacre, in which 120 men, women, and children of the Fancher wagon train were disarmed and killed by Mormon and Paiute attackers. See Bagley, *Blood of the Prophets*.

64. F. W. Lander to Alfred Burton Greenwood, n.d., in *ARCIA for 1860*, 171.

65. Hopkins, *Life Among the Piutes*, 7, 11–12, 25, 30–32; Canfield, *Sarah Winnemucca*, 5–7.

66. Hassrick, *Sioux*, 76–80; McGinnis, "Intertribal Conflict," 53.

67. White, "Winning of the West," 319–43.

68. McGinnis, "Intertribal Conflict," 51; Reid, *Patterns of Vengeance*, 25–26; Ewers, "Intertribal Warfare," 402; Hassrick, *Sioux*, 47–48.

69. Washburn, *Indian in America*, 17–19; Reid, *Patterns of Vengeance*, 71–85, 101–117.

70. McGinnis, "Intertribal Conflict," 49–50.

71. Smedley, *Across the Plains*, 67–68.

72. Francl, *Overland Journey*, 47.

73. Ferguson, "Moving of W. W. Ferguson," 3.

74. For other good examples of white warnings not to seek revenge on Indians—especially innocent ones—because to do so frequently would lead to a cycle of counterviolence, see Merrill, "Trip to California," 12; McPherson, "Reminiscences," 253–54; Wood, "Journal," 174; Crawford, *Scenes of Earlier Days*, 44–46; Madsen, *Bannock of Idaho*, 73–74.

75. A good survey of the accomplishments and failures of the various prisoner-of-war units is found in Brown, *Galvanized Yankees*. A more positive assessment of the accomplishments of the First United States Volunteers appears in Butts, *Galvanized Yankees*.

76. Utley, *Indian Frontier*, 87–90.

77. Madsen, "Shoshoni-Bannock Marauders," 10–11; Carling I. Malouf and John M. Findlay, "Euro-American Impact before 1870," in D'Azevedo, *Great Basin*, 514–15.

78. Madsen, "Shoshoni-Bannock Marauders," 16–17.

79. Hopkins, *Life Among the Piutes*, 14–17.

80. Trenholm and Carley, *Shoshonis*, 193–97; Madsen, *Shoshoni Frontier*, 177–99.

81. Stamm, *People of the Wind River*, 38–40.

82. Becher, *Massacre along the Medicine Road*, 453.

83. Miller, *Road to Virginia City*, 5.

84. Root, *Overland Stage to California*, 389.

85. Hoig, *Sand Creek Massacre*, 145–62; Stands In Timber and Liberty, *Cheyenne Memories*, 168–70; Hyde, *Life of George Bent*, 137–63.

86. Utley, *Indian Frontier*, 92.

87. Hafen and Young, *Fort Laramie*, 327–30; Bratt, *Trails of Yesterday*, 59–62; Hodder, "Crossing the Plains," 132–33.

CONCLUSION

1. White, *Middle Ground*, xi.

2. Another incisive study of Indian dynamic accommodation to changing conditions appears in Anderson, *Indian Southwest*, 3–8. Anderson's sophisticated discussion of "ethnogenesis" demonstrates how Texas and southwestern tribes repeatedly reinvented their societies to meet the new realities, without surrendering their value systems in the process.

3. Berkhofer, "Political Context," 357–82; Berkhofer, "Native Americans," 47–49.

4. Clark and Clark, *Two Diaries*, 30.

Bibliography

MANUSCRIPT COLLECTIONS

Ashley, Algeline Jackson. "Diary." Typescript. Henry E. Huntington Library, San Marino, California.

Baldwin, Alfred. "Dictated Recollections of Overland Journey to Oregon, 1845, and on to California, 1846." Typescript. Bancroft Library, University of California, Berkeley.

Bartholomew, Jacob. "Diary." Transcript. Indiana State Library, Indianapolis.

Batchelder, Amos. "Journal." Manuscript. Bancroft Library, University of California, Berkeley.

Beck, Morris H. "Letters." Manuscript. Bancroft Library, University of California, Berkeley.

Belshaw, George. "Diary of George Belshaw." Typescript. Lane County Pioneer-Historical Society, Eugene, Oregon.

Bogart, Nancy M. (Hembree). "Reminiscences of a Journey Across the Plains in 1843." Manuscript. Bancroft Library, University of California, Berkeley.

Briggs, Albert. "Recollections." Manuscript. Bancroft Library, University of California, Berkeley.

Callison, John Joseph. "Diary of Oregon Trail 1852." Typescript. Lane County Pioneer-Historical Society, Eugene, Oregon.

Caples, Mrs. James. "Overland Journey to California." Typescript. Bancroft Library, University of California, Berkeley.

Carpenter, James C. "Recollections: I Crossed the Plains in the 50's." Manuscript. Kansas State Historical Society, Topeka.

Chambers, Margaret White. "Reminiscences." Typescript. Merrill Mattes Collection, National Frontier Trails Center, Independence, Missouri.

Crawford, Peter W. "Recollections." Manuscript. Bancroft Library, University of California, Berkeley.

Dulany, William H. "Letters." Manuscript. Missouri Historical Society, St. Louis.

Ellmaker, Amos. "Recollections." Typescript. Lane County Pioneer-Historical Society, Eugene, Oregon.

Enos, James E. "Recollections of the Plains." Typescript. Merrill Mattes Collection, National Frontier Trails Center, Independence, Missouri.

Farnsworth, John. "From Virginia to California During the Gold Rush." Typescript. Merrill Mattes Collection, National Frontier Trails Center, Independence, Missouri.

Ferguson, Henry O. "The Moving of W. W. Ferguson and Family from Owen County, Indiana to Iowa Territory in 1849." Typescript. Bancroft Library, University of California, Berkeley.

Fish, Juliette G. "Crossing the Plains in 1862." Typescript. Merrill Mattes Collection, National Frontier Trails Center, Independence, Missouri.

Fulton, Thomas. "Interview in *Platte Argus*." *Liberty (Mo.) Weekly Tribune*, December 7, 1849. Copy at Kansas State Historical Society, Topeka.

Furlong, Mary. "When I Crossed the Plains to Oregon." Typescript. California Historical Society, San Francisco.

Garlick, C. P. "Journal." Typescript. Minnesota Historical Society, St. Paul.

Goltra, Elizabeth J. "Journal Kept By Mrs. E. J. Goltra of Her Travels Across the Plains in the Year 1853." Typescript. Lane County Pioneer-Historical Society, Eugene, Oregon.

Haight, Henry W. "Recollections." Manuscript. State Historical Society of Iowa, Iowa City.

Hamilton, Ezra M. "Reminiscences." Typescript. California State Library, Sacramento.

Harrison, J. M. "Recollections." Typescript. Oregon Historical Society, Portland.

Hatton [Kimball], Adelia Almira. "Memoirs." Typescript. Utah State Historical Society, Salt Lake City.

Hentz, Charles. "Letters." Manuscript. Bancroft Library, University of California, Berkeley.

Hill, Sarah. "Our Trip to Oregon." Manuscript. Oregon Historical Society, Portland.

Hockett, W. A. "Experiences on the Oregon Trail." Typescript. Kansas State Historical Society, Topeka.

Holcomb, William Francis. "A Sketch of the Life of William F. Holcomb, a Pioneer of the West." Manuscript. Bancroft Library, University of California, Berkeley.

Hulin, Lester. "Daybook or Journal of Lester Hulin." Typescript. Lane County Pioneer-Historical Society, Eugene, Oregon.

Jewett, George E. "Diary." Photocopy of manuscript. Bancroft Library, University of California, Berkeley.

Johnson, John Lawrence. "Overland Journey of the Rev. Neill Johnson and His Family from Mt. Pleasant, Iowa to Oregon." Manuscript. Beinecke Library, Yale University, New Haven, Connecticut.

Judson, Henry M. "Diary." Transcript. Nebraska State Historical Society, Lincoln.

Lowell, Nancy Campbell. "Across the Plains in '57." Transcript. Merrill Mattes Collection, National Frontier Trails Center, Independence, Missouri.

Lyman, Esther Brakeman. "Diary." Typescript. Lane County Pioneer-Historical Society, Eugene, Oregon.

Mapel, Eli B. "Experiences, 1852–1876, Crossing the Plains." Manuscript. Bancroft Library, University of California, Berkeley.

McBride, W. S. "Journal, 1850." Manuscript. Henry E. Huntington Library, San Marino, California.

McClung, J. S. "Journal." Typescript. Oregon Historical Society, Portland.

McClure, Andrew S. "Diary." Typescript. Lane County Pioneer-Historical Society, Eugene, Oregon.

Merrill, Joseph Henry. "A Trip to California with His Father When He Was About Eighteen Years Old." Manuscript. Merrill Mattes Collection, National Frontier Trails Center, Independence, Missouri.

Miller, Joel. "Journal of Crossing the Plains." Manuscript. Bancroft Library, University of California, Berkeley.

Neill, John H. B. "Letters." Manuscript. University of Missouri Western Historical Manuscript Collection and Missouri State Historical Society Manuscripts, Columbia.

Nixon, Alexander B. "Diary." Manuscript. California State Library, Sacramento.

Nixon, O. A. "Journal." Transcript. Kansas State Historical Society, Topeka.

Norton, Maria J. Elliot. "Diary of a Trip Across the Plains in '59." Typescript. Bancroft Library, University of California, Berkeley.

Owen, Benjamin Franklin. "My Trip Across the Plains, March 31, 1853–October 28, 1853." Typescript. Lane County Pioneer-Historical Society, Eugene, Oregon.

Payne, James A. "Saint Louis to San Francisco: Being an Account of a Journey Across the Plains in 1850." Typescript. Nebraska State Historical Society, Lincoln.

Pengra, Charlotte Emily Stearns. "Diary." Transcript. Lane County Pioneer-Historical Society, Eugene, Oregon.

Rahm, Louise Mueller. "Diary." Photocopy of manuscript. Bancroft Library, University of California, Berkeley.

Reynolds, Edgar. "Diary." Microfilm. Nebraska State Historical Society, Lincoln.

Richardson, Caroline. "Diary." Microfilm. Bancroft Library, University of California, Berkeley.

Rockwood, Albert Perry. "Journal of Albert P. Rockwood." Transcript. Brigham Young University Library, Provo, Utah.

Rodgers, Andrew Fuller. "Recollections." Typescript. California State Library, Sacramento.

Ruff, Charles, and Annie Ruff. "Letters." Typescript. Merrill Mattes Collection, National Frontier Trails Center, Independence, Missouri.

Sharp, Robert Lee. "Life and Diary of Robert Lee Sharp." Typescript. Merrill Mattes Collection, National Frontier Trails Center, Independence, Missouri.

Slater, Nellie. "Journal." Typescript. Western History Collection, Denver Public Library, Denver.

Smith, Elizabeth Drusilla. "Recollections." Typescript. California Historical Society, San Francisco.

Spooner, E. A. "Diary and Letters." Manuscript. Kansas State Historical Society, Topeka.

Stewart, Helen Marnie. "Diary of Helen Marnie Stewart, 1853." Typescript. Lane County Pioneer-Historical Society, Eugene, Oregon.

Thomas, Dr. William L. "Diary." Manuscript. Bancroft Library, University of California, Berkeley.

Tuttle, Charles A. "Letters." Transcript. Bancroft Library, University of California, Berkeley.

Voorhees, Abram H. "Diary." Manuscript. Beinecke Library, Yale University, New Haven, Connecticut.

Warren, Mary Elizabeth. "Recollections." Typescript. Oregon Historical Society, Portland, Oregon.

GOVERNMENT DOCUMENTS

Annual Report of the Commissioner of Indian Affairs, 1840–1860.

Annual Report of the Secretary of War, 1840–1869.

D'Azevedo, Warren, ed. *Great Basin*. Vol. 11 of *Handbook of North American Indians*, William C. Sturtevant, gen. ed. Washington, D.C.: Smithsonian Institution, 1986.

DeMallie, Raymond J., ed. *The Plains*. Vol. 13, parts 1 and 2, of *Handbook of North American Indians*, William C. Sturtevant, gen. ed. Washington, D.C.: Smithsonian Institution, 2001.

Ewers, John C. *The Horse in Blackfoot Culture, with Comparative Material from Other Western Tribes*. Smithsonian Institution, Bureau of American Ethnology, Bulletin 159. Washington, D.C.: Government Printing Office, 1955.

Fletcher, Alice, and Francis La Flesche. *The Omaha Tribe*. 2 vols. *Twenty-seventh Annual Report of the Bureau of American Ethnology*. Washington, D.C.: Government Printing Office, 1911.

Franklin, Lt. William B. *March to South Pass: Lieutenant William B. Franklin's Journal of the Kearny Expedition of 1845*. Ed. Frank N. Schubert. Office of the

Chief of Engineers, Engineer Historical Studies, No. 1. Washington, D.C.: Government Printing Office, 1979.

Frémont, John C. *Report of the Exploring Expedition to the Rocky Mountains in the Year 1842, and to Oregon and California in the Years 1843–44.* Washington, D.C.: Gales and Seaton, 1845.

Heizer, Robert F., ed. *California.* Vol. 8 of *Handbook of North American Indians,* William C. Sturtevant, gen. ed. Washington, D.C.: Smithsonian Institution, 1978.

Kappler, Charles J., comp. and ed. *Indian Affairs: Laws and Treaties.* 5 vols. Washington, D.C.: Government Printing Office, 1903–1941.

Trigger, Bruce G., ed. *Northeast.* Vol. 15 of *Handbook of North American Indians,* William C. Sturtevant, gen. ed. Washington, D.C.: Smithsonian Institution, 1978.

Walker, Deward E., ed. *Plateau.* Vol. 12 of *Handbook of North American Indians,* William C. Sturtevant, gen. ed. Washington, D.C.: Smithsonian Institution, 1998.

Warren, Lt. Gouverneur K. *Preliminary Report of Explorations in Nebraska and Dakota, in the Years 1855–'56–'57.* Washington, D.C.: Government Printing Office, 1875.

Wilcomb E. Washburn, ed. *History of Indian-White Relations.* Vol. 4 of *Handbook of North American Indians,* William C. Sturtevant, gen. ed. Washington, D.C.: Smithsonian Institution, 1989.

PUBLISHED PRIMARY SOURCES

Books and Pamphlets

Ackley, Mary E. *Crossing the Plains and Early Days in California: Memories of Girlhood Days in California's Golden Age.* San Francisco: n.p., 1928.

Alden, Rev. Wyllis. "Overland Journey to Oregon." In *The Ancestors and Descendents of Isaac Alden and Irene Smith, His Wife, 1590–1903,* ed. Harriet C. Fielding. N.p.: n.p., 1903. 45–49.

Anderson, William Marshall. *The Rocky Mountain Journals of William Marshall Anderson: The West in 1834.* Ed. Dale L. Morgan and Eleanor Towles Harris. San Marino, Calif.: Henry E. Huntington Library, 1967.

Applegate, Jesse. *Recollections of My Boyhood.* Roseburg, Ore.: Review, 1914.

Arber, Edward. *Works of John Smith, 1608–1631.* Birmingham, England: n.p., 1884.

Arms, Cephas. *The Long Road to California: The Journal of Cephas Arms, Supplemented with Letters by Traveling Companions on the Overland Trail in 1849.* Intro. John Cumming. Mount Pleasant, Mich.: John M. Cumming, 1985.

Baker, Hozial H. *Overland Journey to Carson Valley and California.* San Francisco: Book Club of California, 1973.

Bandel, Eugene. *Frontier Life in the Army 1854–1861.* Ed. Ralph P. Bieber. Trans. Olga Bandel and Richard Jente. Glendale, Calif.: Arthur H. Clark, 1932.

Barnett, Joel. *A Long Trip in a Prairie Schooner.* Whittier, Calif.: Western Stationery, 1928.

Bean, George Washington. *Autobiography of George Washington Bean—A Utah Pioneer of 1847.* Comp. Flora Diana Bean Horne. Salt Lake City: Utah Printing, 1945.

Beeson, Welborn. *Welborn Beeson on the Oregon Trail in 1853: From the Diary of Welborn Beeson.* Ed. Bert Webber. Medford, Ore.: Smith, Smith and Smith, 1986.

Benjamin, Israel Joseph. *Three Years in America*, vol. 2. Intro. Oscar Handlin. Trans. Charles Reznikoff. Philadelphia: Jewish Publication Society of America, 1956.

Bennett, James. *Overland Journey to California: Journal of James Bennett Whose Party Left New Harmony in 1850 and Crossed the Plains and Mountains until the Golden West Was Reached.* New Harmony, Ind.: Times Print, 1906.

Bettelyoun, Susan Bordeaux, and Josephine Waggoner. *With My Own Eyes: A Lakota Woman Tells Her People's History.* Ed. Emily Levine. Lincoln: University of Nebraska Press, 1998.

Bidwell, John. *Echoes of the Past: An Account of the First Emigrant Train to California.* New York: Citadel Press, 1962.

Bigler, David, ed. *The Gold Discovery Journal of Azariah Smith.* Salt Lake City: University of Utah Press, 1990.

Booth, Edmund. *Forty-Niner: The Life Story of a Deaf Pioneer.* Stockton, Calif.: San Joaquin Pioneer and Historical Society, 1953.

Boquist, Laura Brewster. *Crossing the Plains with Ox Teams in 1862.* N.p.: n.p., 1930.

Bradbury, John. *Travels in the Interior of America, in the Years 1809, 1810, and 1811 . . .,* 2nd ed. London: Sherwood, Neely and Jones, 1819.

Braly, John Hyde. *Memory Pictures: An Autobiography.* Los Angeles: Neuner, 1912.

Bratt, John. *Trails of Yesterday.* Chicago: University Publishing, 1921.

Bristol, Sherlock. *The Pioneer Preacher: An Autobiography.* New York: Fleming H. Revell, 1887.

Brooks, Elisha. *A Pioneer Mother of California.* San Francisco: Henry Wagner, 1922.

Brown, J. Robert. *Journal of a Trip Across the Plains of the United States from Missouri to California in 1856.* Columbus, Ohio: n.p., 1860.

Brown, James Berry. *Journal of a Journey Across the Plains in 1859.* Ed. George R. Stewart. San Francisco: Book Club of California, 1970.

Brown, John E. *Memoirs of a Forty-Niner.* Ed. Katie E. Blood. New Haven, Conn.: Associated Publishers of American Records, 1907.

Brown, John Henry. *Early Days of San Francisco, California.* Ed. Joseph A. Sullivan. Oakland, Calif.: Biobooks, 1949.

Brown, William Richard. *An Authentic Wagon Train Journal of 1853 from Indiana to California.* Mokelumne Hill, Calif.: Horseshoe Printing, 1985.

Bruff, J. Goldsborough. *Gold Rush: The Journals, Drawings, and Other Papers of J. Goldsborough Bruff.* Ed. Georgia Willis Read and Ruth Gaines. New York: Columbia University Press, 1949.

Bryant, Edwin. *What I Saw in California: Being the Journal of a Tour by the Emigrant Route and South Pass.* New York: D. Appleton, 1849.

Bullock, Thomas. *The Pioneer Camp of the Saints: The 1846 and 1847 Mormon Trail Journals of Thomas Bullock.* Ed. Will Bagley. Spokane, Wash.: Arthur H. Clark, 1997.

Butler, J. A. *Journal of Trip to California, April–September, 1856.* LaVerne, Calif.: LaVerne Press, 1993.

Byers, William N., and John H. Kellom, *Hand Book to the Gold Fields of Nebraska and Kansas.* Chicago: D. B. Cooke, 1859.

Carleton, Lt. J. Henry. *The Prairie Logbooks: Dragoon Campaigns to the Pawnee Villages in 1844 and the Rocky Mountains in 1845.* Ed. Louis Pelzer. Chicago: Caxton Club, 1943.

Carrington, Frances C. *My Army Life and the Fort Phil Kearney Massacre.* Philadelphia: J. B. Lippincott, 1910.

Carrington, Margaret Irvin. *Ab-Sa-Ra-Ka, the Home of the Crows: Being the Experience of an Officer's Wife on the Plains.* Philadelphia: J. B. Lippincott, 1868.

Casler, Melyer. *A Journal Giving the Incidents of a Journey to California in the Summer of 1859, by the Overland Route.* Ed. Glen Adams. Fairfield, Wash.: Ye Galleon Press, 1969.

Chandless, William. *A Visit to Salt Lake; Being a Journey Across the Plains and a Residence in the Mormon Settlements at Utah.* London: Smith, Elder, 1857.

Christy, Thomas. *Thomas Christy's Road Across the Plains: A Guide to the Route from Mormon Crossing, Now Omaha, Nebraska, to the City of Sacramento, California.* Ed. Robert H. Becker. Denver: Old West, 1969.

Clark, Helen E., and Calvin P. Clark. *Two Diaries: The Diary of Calvin Perry Clark from Plano, Illinois to Denver and Vicinity over the Santa Fe Trail in 1859, Together with the Diary of Sister Helen E. Clark Who Made a Similar Journey by the Northern Route in 1860.* Ed. John R. Evans and Malcolm Wyer. Denver: Denver Public Library, 1962.

Clayton, William. *The Latter-day Saints' Emigrants' Guide: Being a Table of Distances, Showing All the Springs, Creeks, Rivers, Hills, Mountains, Camping Places, and All the Other Notable Places, from Council Bluffs to the Valley of the Great Salt Lake . . .* St. Louis: Missouri Republican Steam Press–Chambers and Knapp, 1848.

————. *William Clayton's Journal: A Daily Record of the Journey of the Original Company of "Mormon" Pioneers from Nauvoo, Illinois, to the Valley of the Great Salt Lake.* Salt Lake City: Deseret News, 1921.

Clyman, James. *James Clyman, Frontiersman: The Adventures of a Trapper and Covered Wagon Emigrant as Told in His Own Reminiscences and Diaries.* Ed. Charles L. Camp. Portland, Ore.: Champoeg Press, 1960.

Cole, Cornelius. *Memoirs of Cornelius Cole, Ex-Senator of the United States from California.* New York: McLoughlin Brothers, 1908.

Cole, Gilbert L. *In the Early Days Along the Overland Trail in Nebraska Territory, in 1852.* Kansas City, Mo.: Franklin Hudson, 1905.

Collins, John S. *My Experiences in the West.* Ed. Colton Storm. Chicago: R. R. Donnelley and Sons, 1970.

Compton, Mary Murdock. *Mary Murdock Compton.* Ed. Henria Packer Compton. N.p.: n.p., 1953.

Comstock, Loring Samuel. *A Journal of Travels Across the Plains in the Year 1855.* Oskaloosa, Iowa: n.p., n.d.

Cooke, Col. Philip St. George. *Scenes and Adventures in the Army: or, Romance of Military Life.* Philadelphia: Lindsay and Blakiston, 1857.

Coy, Owen Cochran. *The Great Trek of Dr. E. A. Tompkins.* Los Angeles: Powell, 1931.

Coyner, David Holmes. *The Lost Trappers; A Collection of Interesting Scenes and Events in the Rocky Mountains . . .* Ed. David J. Weber. Albuquerque: University of New Mexico Press, 1970.

Crawford, Charles. *Scenes of Earlier Days in Crossing the Plains to Oregon, and Experiences of Western Life.* Petaluma, Calif.: J. T. Studdert, 1898.

Crawford, Lewis F. *The Exploits of Ben Arnold: Indian Fighter, Gold Miner, Cowboy, Hunter, and Army Scout.* Norman: University of Oklahoma Press, 1999.

Crawford, Medorem. *Journal of Medorem Crawford.* Fairfield, Wash.: Ye Galleon Press, 1967.

Cross, Maj. Osborne. "The Journal of Major Osborne Cross." In *The March of the Mounted Riflemen: First United States Military Expedition to Travel the Full Length of the Oregon Trail from Fort Leavenworth to Fort Vancouver, May to October, 1849*, 33–272. Glendale, Calif.: Arthur H. Clark, 1940.

Cumming, John, ed. *The Gold Rush: Letters from the Wolverine Rangers to the Marshall, Michigan, Statesman, 1849–1851.* Mount Pleasant, Mich.: Cumming Press, 1974.

Cummins, Sarah J. *Autobiography and Reminiscences.* Fairfield, Wash.: Ye Galleon Press, 1987.

Curtis, Sam S. "Letters in *Council Bluffs Nonpareil.*" Reprinted in William N. Byers and John H. Kellom, *Hand Book to the Gold Fields of Nebraska and Kansas.* Chicago: D. B. Cooke, 1859.

Dawson, Nicholas. *Narratives of Nicholas "Cheyenne" Dawson.* Ed. Charles L. Camp. San Francisco: Grabhorn Press, 1933.

Decker, Peter. *The Diaries of Peter Decker: Overland to California in 1859 and Life in the Mines, 1850–1851.* Ed. Helen S. Giffen. Georgetown, Calif.: Talisman Press, 1966.

Delano, Alonzo. *Life on the Plains and Among the Diggings; Being Scenes and Adventures of an Overland Journey to California.* Auburn, N.Y.: Miller, Orton and Mulligan, 1854.

Denig, Edwin Thompson. *Five Indian Tribes of the Upper Missouri: Sioux, Arickaras, Assiniboines, Crees, Crows.* Ed. John C. Ewers. Norman: University of Oklahoma Press, 1961.

Dent, Frederick. *Military Report of Frederick Dent, U.S. Army.* Fairfield, Wash.: Ye Galleon Press, 1992.

De Smet, Pierre-Jean. *Life, Letters and Travels of Father Pierre-Jean De Smet.* 4 vols. Ed. Hiram M. Chittenden and Alfred T. Richardson. New York: Francis P. Harper, 1905.

———. *New Indian Sketches.* Fairfield, Wash.: Ye Galleon Press, 1985.

Dickenson, Luella. *Reminiscences of a Trip Across the Plains in 1846 and Early Days in California.* Fairfield, Wash.: Ye Galleon Press, 1977.

Dickson, Albert Jerome. *Covered Wagon Days: A Journey Across the Plains in the Sixties and Pioneer Days in the Northwest.* Ed. Arthur Jerome Dickson. Cleveland: Arthur H. Clark, 1929.

Draper, Elias Johnson. *An Autobiography of Elias Johnson Draper: A Pioneer of California.* Fresno, Calif.: Evening Democrat Print, 1904.

Drury, Clifford Merrill, ed. *The Mountains We Have Crossed: Diaries and Letters of the Oregon Mission, 1838.* Lincoln: University of Nebraska Press, 1999.

———. *Where Wagons Could Go: Narcissa Whitman and Eliza Spalding.* Lincoln: University of Nebraska Press, 1997.

Dunham, E. Allene. *Across the Plains in a Covered Wagon.* N.p.: n.p., n.d.

Enos, A. A. *Across the Plains in 1850.* N.p.: n.p., 1905.

Ewart, Shirley, and Jane and John Anderson. *A Long and Wearisome Journey: The Eakin Family Diaries–1866.* Bend, Ore.: Maverick, 1991.

Fairchild, Lucius. *California Letters of Lucius Fairchild.* Ed. Joseph Schafer. Wisconsin Historical Publications Collections, vol. 31. Madison: State Historical Society of Wisconsin, 1931.

Farnham, Thomas J. *Travels in the Great Western Prairies, The Anahuac and Rocky Mountains, and in the Oregon Territory.* Poughkeepsie, N.Y.: Killey and Lossing, 1843.

Ferguson, Charles D. *California Gold Fields.* Oakland, Calif.: Biobooks, 1948.

Fletcher, Ellen Gordon. *A Bride on the Bozeman Trail: The Letters and Diary of Ellen Gordon Fletcher.* Ed. Francis D. Haines, Jr. Medford, Ore.: Gandee Printing Center, 1970.

Fox, Jared. *Jared Fox's Memmorandom, Kept from Dellton, Sauk County, Wisconsin, toward California and Oregon, 1852–1854.* Ed. Stephen Calvert. Benton, Wis.: Cottonwood Hill, 1990.

Francl, Joseph. *The Overland Journey of Joseph Francl, the First Bohemian to Cross the Plains to the California Gold Fields.* San Francisco: W. P. Wreden, 1968.

Frink, Margaret A. *Journal of the Adventures of a Party of California Gold Seekers.* Fairfield, Wash.: Ye Galleon Press, 1987.

Frizzell, Lodisa. *Across the Plains to California in 1852.* Ed. Victor Hugo Paltsits. New York: New York Public Library, 1915.

Frush, William, and Charles Frush. *The Overland Journals of William and Charles Frush.* Fairfield, Wash.: Ye Galleon Press, 2000.

Fuller, Emeline L. *Left by the Indians.* Fairfield, Wash.: Ye Galleon Press, 1992.

Gardner, Archibald. *The Life of Archibald Gardner: Utah Pioneer of 1847.* Salt Lake City: Alpine, 1939.

Garrard, Lewis H. [Hector Lewis Garrard]. *Wah-To-Yah and the Taos Trail; or, Prairie Travel and Scalp Dances, with a Look at Los Rancheros from Muleback and the Rocky Mountain Campfire.* Western Frontier Library Series. Norman: University of Oklahoma Press, 1955.

Garrison, Rev. Abraham E. *Life and Labour of Rev. A. E. Garrison, Forty Years in Oregon: Seven Months on the Plains.* N.p.: n.p., 1887.

Geer, T. T. *Fifty Years in Oregon.* New York: Neale, 1912.

Gibbs, George. "Diary of George Gibbs." In *The March of the Mounted Riflemen: First United States Military Expedition to Travel the Full Length of the Oregon Trail from Fort Leavenworth to Fort Vancouver, May to October, 1849,* ed. Raymond W. Settle, 275–327. Glendale, Calif.: Arthur H. Clark, 1940.

Gibson, J. Watt. *Recollections of a Pioneer.* St. Joseph, Mo.: Nelson-Hanne, 1912.

Gillette, Martha Hill. *Overland to Oregon and in the Indian Wars of 1853.* Ashland, Ore.: Lewis Osborne, 1971.

Given, Abraham. *Overland to California in 1850.* Frankfort, Ind.: n.p., n.d.

Glasscock, C. B. *Lucky Baldwin: The Story of an Unconventional Success.* Indianapolis: Bobbs-Merrill, 1933.

Glazier, Stewart E., and Robert S. Clark, comps. and eds. *Journal of the Trail,* 2nd ed. Salt Lake City: Church of Jesus Christ of Latter-day Saints, 1997.

Goldsmith, Oliver. *Overland in Forty-Nine: Recollections of a Wolverine Ranger After a Lapse of 47 Years.* Detroit: n.p., 1896.

Gould, Jane A. *The Oregon and California Trail Diary of Jane Gould in 1862.* Intro. Bert Webber. Medford, Ore.: Webb Research Group, 1987.

Goulder, F. A. *Reminiscences: Incidents in the Life of a Pioneer in Oregon and Idaho.* Ed. Joseph Perrault. Boise, Idaho: T. Regan, 1909.

Gray, William H. *William H. Gray: Journal of His Journey East, 1836–1837.* Ed. Donald R. Johnson. Fairfield, Wash.: Ye Galleon Press, 1980.

Greeley, Horace. *An Overland Journey from New York to San Francisco in the Summer of 1859*. New York: C. M. Saxton, Barker, 1860.

Green, Jay. *Diary of Jay Green Covering the Period May 1 to July 27, 1852*. Stockton, Calif.: San Joaquin Pioneer and Historical Society, 1955.

Gregg, Josiah. *Commerce of the Prairies: The Journal of a Santa Fé Trader*. Dallas: Southwest Press, 1933.

Hafen, LeRoy, and Ann W. Hafen, eds. *To the Rockies and Oregon 1839–1842: With Diaries and Accounts by Sidney Smith, Amos Cook, Joseph Holman, E. Willard Smith, Francis Fletcher, Joseph Williams, Obadiah Oakley, Robert Shortess, T. J. Farnham*. Glendale, Calif.: Arthur H. Clark, 1955.

Hambleton, Chalkley J. *A Gold Hunter's Experience*. Chicago: R. R. Donnelley and Sons, 1898.

Hammer, Jacob. *The Emigrating Company: The 1844 Oregon Trail Journal of Jacob Hammer*. Ed. Thomas A. Rumer. Spokane, Wash.: Arthur H. Clark, 1990.

Hancock, Samuel. *The Narrative of Samuel Hancock, 1845–1860*. Intro. Arthur D. Howden Smith. New York: Robert M. McBride, 1927.

Handsaker, Sam. *Pioneer Life*. Eugene, Ore.: n.p., 1908.

Handsaker, Sarah Johnson. "Coming to Oregon." In Sam Handsaker, *Pioneer Life*. Eugene, Ore.: n.p., 1908.

Hanna, Esther Belle McMillan. "Diary." In Eleanor Allen, *Canvas Caravans*. Portland, Ore.: Binfords and Mort, 1946.

Hannon, Jessie Gould. *The Boston-Newton Company Venture: From Massachusetts to California in 1849*. Lincoln: University of Nebraska Press, 1969.

Harlan, Jacob Wright. *California '46–'88*. San Francisco: Bancroft, 1888.

Harmon, Appleton Milo. *The Journals of Appleton Milo Harmon: A Participant in the Mormon Exodus from Illinois and the Early Settlement of Utah, 1846–1877*. Ed. Maybelle Harmon Anderson. Glendale, Calif.: Arthur H. Clark, 1946.

Hastings, Lansford W. *The Emigrants' Guide, to Oregon and California; Containing Scenes and Incidents of a Party of Oregon Emigrants . . . and Incidents of a Party of California Emigrants*. Cincinnati: George Conclin, 1845.

Hayden, Mary Jane. *Pioneer Days*. Fairfield, Wash.: Ye Galleon Press, 1979.

Hays, Lorena L. *To the Land of Gold and Wickedness: The 1848–59 Diary of Lorena L. Hays*. Ed. Jeanne Hamilton Watson. St. Louis: Patrice Press, 1988.

Hecox, Margaret M. *California Caravan: The 1846 Overland Trail Memoir of Margaret M. Hecox*. Ed. Richard Dillon. San Jose, Calif.: Harlan-Young Press, 1966.

Heiskell, Hugh Brown. *A Forty-Niner from Tennessee: The Diary of Hugh Brown Heiskell*. Ed. Edward M. Steel. Knoxville: University of Tennessee Press, 1998.

Herndon, Sarah Raymond. *Days on the Road: Crossing the Plains in 1865*. New York: Burr Printing House, 1902.

Hickman, Richard Owen. *An Overland Journey to California in 1852: The Overland Journal of Richard Owen Hickman.* Ed. M. Catherine White. Sources of Northwest History No. 6. Missoula: State University of Montana, 1929.

Hill, Emma Shepard. *A Dangerous Crossing and What Happened on the Other Side: Seven Lean Years.* Denver: Bradford-Robinson Printing, 1924.

Hill, Jasper Smith. *The Letters of a Young Miner.* Ed. Doyce B. Nunis, Jr. San Francisco: John Howell Books, 1964.

Hill, John Berry. *A Gold Hunter: Memoirs of John Berry Hill.* Ed. Kristin Delaplane. Vacaville, Calif.: Masterpiece Memoirs, 1997.

Hinde, Edmund C. *Journal of Edmund Cavaleer Hinde.* Ed. Jerome Peltier. Fairfield, Wash.: Ye Galleon Press, 1983.

Hixon, Adrietta Applegate. *On to Oregon: A True Story of a Young Girl's Journey into the West.* Fairfield, Wash.: Ye Galleon Press, 1973.

Hopkins, Sarah Winnemucca. *Life Among the Piutes: Their Wrongs and Claims.* Boston: Cupples, Upham, 1883.

Horn, Hosea B. *Horn's Overland Guide, from the U.S. Indian Subagency, Council Bluffs, on the Missouri River, to the City of Sacramento.* New York: J. H. Colton, 1852.

House, E., ed. *A Narrative of the Captivity of Mrs. Horn, and Her Two Children with That of Mrs. Harris by the Camanche Indians.* St. Louis: C. Keemle Printer, 1839.

Howell, Elijah Preston. *The 1849 California Trail Diaries of Elijah Preston Howell.* Ed. Susan Badger Doyle and Donald E. Buck. Independence, Mo.: Oregon-California Trails Association, 1995.

Hutchings, James Mason. *Seeking the Elephant, 1849: James Mason Hutchings Overland Trek to California.* Ed. Shirley Sargent. Glendale, Calif.: Arthur H. Clark, 1980.

Hyde, George E. *Life of George Bent: Written from His Letters.* Ed. Savoie Lottinville. Norman: University of Oklahoma Press, 1968.

Ingalls, Eleazar Stillman. *Journal of a Trip to California by the Overland Route Across the Plains in 1850–51.* Fairfield, Wash.: Ye Galleon Press, 1979.

Ingersoll, Chester. *Overland to California in 1847.* Ed. Douglas C. McMurtrie. Chicago: Black Cat Press, 1937.

Irving, Washington. *The Adventures of Captain Bonneville, U.S.A., in the Rocky Mountains and the Far West.* Ed. Edgeley W. Todd. Norman: University of Oklahoma Press, 1961.

———. *A Tour on the Prairies.* Intro. John Francis McDermott. Norman: University of Oklahoma Press, 1956.

Isham, Giles S. *Guide to California and the Mines, and Return by the Ithsmus* [sic]. Fairfield, Wash.: Ye Galleon Press, 1972.

Ivins, Virginia Wilcox. *Pen Pictures of Early Western Days.* N.p.: n.p., 1905.

Jackson, William Henry. *Time Exposure: The Autobiography of William Henry Jackson.* Albuquerque: University of New Mexico Press, 1986.

James, Edwin. *Account of an Expedition from Pittsburgh to the Rocky Mountains, 1819, 1820 . . . Compiled from Notes by Major Long, Mr. T. Say, etc., by Edwin James.* Ed. Reuben Gold Thwaites. Cleveland: Arthur H. Clark, 1905.

Johnson, Edwin F. *Railroad to the Pacific. Northern Route: Its General Character, Relative Merits, Etc.* New York: Railroad Journal Printing Office, 1854.

Johnson, Hervey. *Tending the Talking Wire: A Buck Soldier's View of Indian Country, 1863–1866.* Ed. William E. Unrau. Salt Lake City: University of Utah Press, 1979.

Johnson, Overton, and William. H. Winter. *Route Across the Rocky Mountains.* Lafayette, Ind.: John B. Semans, 1846.

Johnston, William G. *Overland to California: A Member of the Wagon Train First to Enter California . . . in the Memorable Year of 1849.* Oakland, Calif.: Biobooks, 1948.

Judson, Phoebe Goodell. *A Pioneer's Search for an Ideal Home.* Ed. John M. McClelland, Jr. Bellingham, Wash.: Union Printing and Binding, 1925.

Keller, George. *A Trip Across the Plains and Life in California.* Oakland, Calif.: Biobooks, 1955.

Kellogg, M. G. *Notes Concerning the Kellogg's.* Battle Creek, Mich.: n.p., 1927.

Kelly, Fanny. *Narrative of My Captivity Among the Sioux Indians.* Hartford, Conn.: Mutual Publishing, 1871.

Kelly, William. *An Excursion to California Over the Prairie, Rocky Mountains, and the Great Sierra Nevada.* 2 vols. London: Chapman and Hall, 1852.

Kestler, Frances Roe, comp. *The Indian Captivity Narrative: A Woman's View.* New York: Garland, 1990.

Kilgore, William H. *The Kilgore Journal of an Overland Journey to California in the Year 1850.* Ed. Joyce Rockwood Muench. New York: Hastings House, 1949.

Kimball, Violet. *Stories of Young Pioneers in Their Own Words.* Missoula, Mont.: Mountain Press, 2001.

Korns, J. Roderic, and Dale L. Morgan, eds. *West from Fort Bridger: The Pioneering of the Immigrant Trails Across Utah, 1846–1850.* Rev. and updated by Will Bagley and Harold Schindler. Logan: Utah State University Press, 1994.

Langley, Harold D., ed. *To Utah with the Dragoons, and Glimpses of Life in Arizona and California 1858–1859.* Salt Lake City: University of Utah Press, 1974.

Langworthy, Franklin. *Scenery of the Plains, Mountains and Mines.* Ed. Paul C. Phillips. Princeton, N.J.: Princeton University Press, 1932.

Larimer, Sarah Luse. *The Capture and Escape, or Life Among the Sioux.* Philadelphia: Remsen and Haffelfinger, 1870.

Larsen, Karen M., and Paul D. Larsen, eds. *Remembering Winter Quarters and Council Bluffs: Writings of the Mormon Pioneers at the Missouri River*. Elkhorn, Nebraska: n.p., 1998.

Leach, A. J. *Early Day Stories*. Norfolk, Neb.: Huse, 1916.

Lempfrit, Honoré-Timothée. *Oregon Trail Journal and Letters from the Pacific Northwest, 1848–1853*. Trans. and ed. Patricia Meyer and Catou Lévesque. Fairfield, Wash.: Ye Galleon Press, 1985.

Lenox, Edward Henry. *Overland to Oregon*. Fairfield, Wash.: Ye Galleon Press, 1970.

Leonard, Zenas. *Narrative of the Adventures of Zenas Leonard*. Clearfield, Pa.: D. W. Moore, 1839.

Lienhard, Heinrich. *From St. Louis to Sutter's Fort, 1846*. Trans. and ed. Erwin G. Gudde and Elisabeth K. Gudde. Norman: University of Oklahoma Press, 1961.

Lockley, Fred. *Conversations with Pioneer Men*. Comp. Mike Helm. Eugene, Ore.: Rainy Day Press, 1996.

———. *Conversations with Pioneer Women*. Comp. Mike Helm. Eugene, Ore.: Rainy Day Press, 1993.

Long, Mary Jane. *Crossing the Plains in the Year 1852 with Ox-Teams*. McMinnville, Ore.: n.p., 1915.

Longsworth, Basil N. *The Diary of Basil N. Longsworth, Oregon Pioneer*. Historical Records Survey, Division of Women's and Professional Projects, Works Progress Administration, 1938.

Loomis, Leander V. *A Journal of the Birmingham Emigrating Company*. Ed. Edgar M. Ledyard. Salt Lake City: Legal Printing, 1928.

Lord, Israel Shipman Pelton. *A Doctor's Gold Rush Journey to California*. Ed. Necia Dixon Liles. Lincoln: University of Nebraska Press, 1995.

Lowe, Percival G. *Five Years a Dragoon ('49 to '54) and Other Adventures in the Great Plains*. Ed. Don Russell. Norman: University of Oklahoma Press, 1965.

Lowry, Annie, and Lalla Scott. *Karnee: A Paiute Narrative*. Greenwich, Conn.: Fawcett, 1966.

Marcy, Randolph B. *The Prairie Traveler: A Hand-Book, for Overland Expeditions*. New York: Harper and Brothers, 1859.

Mattes, Merrill J. *Indians, Infants and Infantry: Andrew and Elizabeth Burt on the Frontier*. Denver: Old West, 1960.

Matthews, Leonard. *A Long Life in Review*. St. Louis: n.p., 1928.

Maxwell, William Audley. *Crossing the Plains Days of '57: A Narrative of Early Emigrant Travel to California by the Ox-Team Method*. San Francisco: Sunset Publishing House, 1915.

May, Richard M. *A Sketch of a Migrating Family to California in 1848*. Fairfield, Wash.: Ye Galleon Press, 1991.

McCall, Ansel James. *The Great California Trail in 1849*. Bath, N.Y.: n.p., 1882.

McComas, Evans S. *A Journal of Travel.* Ed. Martin Schmitt. Portland, Ore.: Champoeg Press, 1954.

McDiarmid, Finley. *Letters to My Wife.* Fairfield, Wash.: Ye Galleon Press, 1997.

McIntosh, Walter H. *Allen and Rachel: An Overland Honeymoon in 1853.* Caldwell, Idaho: Caxton, 1938.

McKinstry, Byron N. *The California Gold Rush Overland Diary of Byron N. McKinstry, 1850–1852.* Ed. Bruce L. McKinstry. Glendale, Calif.: Arthur H. Clark, 1975.

McLaughlin, James. *My Friend the Indian.* Lincoln: University of Nebraska Press, 1989.

Meline, James F. *Two Thousand Miles on Horseback: A Summer Tour to the Plains, the Rocky Mountains, and New Mexico.* New York: Catholic Publication Society, 1872.

Merrill, Julius. *Bound for Idaho: The 1864 Trail Journal of Julius Merrill.* Ed. Irving R. Merrill. Moscow: University of Idaho Press, 1988.

Merrill, Marriner Wood. *Utah Pioneer and Apostle Marriner Wood Merrill.* Ed. Melvin Clarence Merrill. N.p.: n.p., 1937.

Miller, James Knox Polk. *The Road to Virginia City: The Diary of James Knox Polk Miller.* Ed. Andrew F. Rolle. Norman: University of Oklahoma Press, 1960.

Miller, Joaquin. *Overland in a Covered Wagon: An Autobiography.* Ed. Sidney G. Firman. New York: D. Appleton, 1930.

Montaignes, Francois des [Isaac Cooper]. *The Plains, Being No Less Than a Collection of Veracious Memoranda Taken During the Expedition of Exploration in the Year 1845, from the Western Settlements of Missouri to the Mexican Border . . .* Ed. Nancy Alpert Mower and Don Russell. Norman: University of Oklahoma Press, 1972.

Moorman, Madison Berryman. *The Journal of Madison Berryman Moorman, 1850–1851.* Ed. Irene D. Paden. San Francisco: California Historical Society, 1948.

Morgan, Dale L. ed. *Overland in 1846: Diaries and Letters of the California-Oregon Trail.* 2 vols. Georgetown, Calif.: Talisman Press, 1963

Mumford, Violet Coe. *The Royal Way West.* Vol. 2, *Crossing the Plains, 1853.* Baltimore: Gateway Press, 1988.

Murphy, Virginia Reed. *Across the Plains in the Donner Party, 1846–47.* Olympic Valley, Calif.: Outbooks, 1977.

Packard, Wellman. *Early Emigration to California, 1849–1850.* Ed. Milo Custer. Bloomington, Ill.: Milo Custer, 1928.

Palmer, Joel. *Journal of Travels Over the Rocky Mountains.* Fairfield, Wash.: Ye Galleon Press, 1983.

Parke, Charles Ross. *Dreams to Dust: A Diary of the California Gold Rush, 1849–1850.* Ed. James E. Davis. Lincoln: University of Nebraska Press, 1989.

Parkman, Francis. *The Oregon Trail.* New York: Washington Square Press, 1963.

Paul, R. Eli, ed. *Autobiography of Red Cloud: War Leader of the Oglalas.* Helena: Montana Historical Society Press, 1997.

Peacock, William. *The Peacock Letters, April 7, 1850–January 4, 1852.* Stockton, Calif.: San Joaquin Pioneer and Historical Society, 1950.

Pelzer, Louis, ed. *Marches of the Dragoons in the Mississippi Valley: An Account of Marches and Activities of the First Regiment United States Dragoons in the Mississippi Valley Between the Years 1833 and 1850.* Iowa City: State Historical Society of Iowa, 1917.

Perkins, Elisha Douglass. *Gold Rush Diary: Being the Journal of Elisha Douglass Perkins on the Overland Trail in the Spring and Summer of 1849.* Ed. Thomas D. Clark. Lexington: University of Kentucky Press, 1967.

Pierce, E. D. *The Pierce Chronicle: Personal Reminiscences of E. D. Pierce.* Ed. J. Gary Williams and Ronald W. Stark. Moscow: Idaho Research Foundation, 1957.

Piercy, Frederick Hawkins. *Route from Liverpool to Great Salt Lake Valley.* With notes by James Linforth. Ed. Fawn M. Brodie. Cambridge, Mass.: Harvard University Press, 1962.

Pigman, Walter Griffith. *The Journal of Walter Griffith Pigman.* Ed. Ulla Staley Fawkes. Mexico, Mo.: Walter G. Staley, 1942.

Pleasants, William J. *Twice Across the Plains, 1849 and 1856.* Fairfield, Wash.: Ye Galleon Press, 1981.

Plummer, Rachel. *Rachel Plummer's Narrative of Twenty-One Months Servitude as a Prisoner Among the Comanche Indians.* Houston: Telegraph Power Press, 1838.

Porter, Lavinia Honeyman. *By Ox-Team to California: Crossing the Plains in 1860.* Oakland, Calif.: Oakland Enquirer, 1910.

Potter, David Morris, ed. *Trail to California: The Overland Journal of Vincent Geiger and Wakeman Bryarly.* New Haven, Conn.: Yale University Press, 1945.

Powers, Mary Rockwood. *A Woman's Overland Journal to California.* Ed. W. B. Thorsen. Fairfield, Wash.: Ye Galleon Press, 1985.

Price, Joseph. *The Road to California: Letters of Joseph Price.* Ed. Thomas M. Marshall. Cedar Rapids, Iowa: Torch Press, 1924.

Pringle, Catherine Sager. *Across the Plains in 1844.* Fairfield, Wash.: Ye Galleon Press, 1989.

Pringle, Octavius M. *Magic River Deschutes: Experience of an Emigrant Boy in 1846.* Fairfield, Wash.: Ye Galleon Press, 1970.

Pritchard, James Avery. *The Overland Diary of James A. Pritchard from Kentucky to California, 1849.* Ed. Dale L. Morgan. Denver: F. S. Rosenstock, Old West, 1959.

Pritchard, William F. *Journal of William Fowler Pritchard.* Ed. Earl H. Pritchard and Phil Pritchard. Fairfield, Wash.: Ye Galleon Press, 1996.

Quindaro; or, The Heroine of Fort Laramie. London: Beadle, 1865.

Rau, Weldon Willis. *Surviving the Oregon Trail, 1852: As Told by Mary and Willis Boatman and Augmented with Accounts by Other Overland Travelers.* Pullman: Washington State University Press, 2001.

Raymond, Sarah, and Dr. Waid Howard. *Overland Days to Montana in 1865: The Diary of Sarah Raymond and Journal of Dr. Waid Howard.* Ed. Raymond W. Settle and Mary Lund Settle. Glendale, Calif.: Arthur H. Clark, 1971.

Reid, Bernard J. *Overland to California with the Pioneer Line: The Gold Rush Diary of Bernard J. Reid.* Ed. Mary McDougall Gordon. Stanford, Calif.: Stanford University Press, 1983.

Reinhart, Herman Francis. *The Golden Frontier: Recollections of Herman Francis Reinhart, 1851–1869.* Ed. Doyce B. Nunis, Jr. Austin: University of Texas Press, 1962.

Richards, Mary Haskin Parker. *Winter Quarters: The 1846–1848 Life Writings of Mary Haskin Parker Richards.* Ed. Maurine Carr Ward. Logan: Utah State University Press, 1996.

Richey, James H. *A Trip Across the Plains in 1854.* Richey, Calif.: n.p., 1908.

Riddle, George W. *History of Early Days in Oregon.* Riddle, Ore.: n.p., 1920.

Roberts, Sidney. *To Emigrants to the Gold Region. A Treatise, Showing the Best Way to California, with Many Serious Objections to Going by Sea.* New Haven, Conn.: n.p., 1849.

Robinson, Zirkle D. *The Robinson-Rosenberger Journey to the Gold Fields of California, 1849–1850: The Diary of Zirkle D. Robinson.* Ed. Francis Coleman Rosenberger. Iowa City, Iowa: Prairie Press, 1966.

Root, Frank Albert. *The Overland Stage to California: Personal Reminiscences and Authentic History of the Great Overland Stage Line and Pony Express from the Missouri River to the Pacific Ocean.* Topeka, Ks.: n.p., 1901.

Root, Riley. *Journal of Travels from St. Josephs to Oregon with Observations of That Country.* Oakland, Calif.: Biobooks, 1955.

Ross, Alexander. *Adventures of the First Settlers on the Oregon or Columbia River, 1810–1813.* Ed. Reuben Gold Thwaites. Early Western Travels Series, 1784–1846, vol. 7. Cleveland: Arthur H. Clark, 1904.

Rowlandson, Mary. *A Narrative of the Captivity and Restauration of Mrs. Mary Rowlandson.* Cambridge, Mass.: Samuel Green, Sr., 1682.

Royce, Sarah. *A Frontier Lady: Recollections of the Gold Rush and Early California.* Ed. Ralph Henry Gabriel. New Haven, Conn.: Yale University Press, 1932.

Ruxton, George Frederick. *Life in the Far West.* Ed. LeRoy R. Hafen. Norman: University of Oklahoma Press, 1951.

Sage, Rufus B. *Rocky Mountain Life or, Startling Scenes and Perilous Adventures in the Far West, During an Expedition of Three Years.* Boston: Wentworth, 1857.

Sanford, Mollie Dorsey. *Mollie: The Journal of Mollie Dorsey Sanford in Nebraska and Colorado Territories, 1857–1866.* Ed. Donald F. Danker. Lincoln: University of Nebraska Press, 1959.

Saunders, Mary. *The Whitman Massacre: A True Story By a Survivor of this Terrible Tragedy Which Took Place in Oregon in 1847.* Fairfield, Wash.: Ye Galleon Press, 1997.

Scamehorn, Howard L., ed. *The Buckeye Rovers in the Gold Rush.* Athens: Ohio University Press, 1965.

Schiel, Jacob H. *Journey Through the Rocky Mountains and the Humboldt Mountains to the Pacific Ocean.* Trans. and ed. Thomas N. Bonner. Norman: University of Oklahoma Press, 1959.

Schlicke, Carl. *Massacre on the Oregon Trail in the Year 1860.* Fairfield, Wash.: Ye Galleon Press, 1992.

Searls, Niles. *The Diary of a Pioneer and Other Papers.* Ed. Robert M. Searls. San Francisco: Pernan-Walsh, 1940.

Shaw, D. A. *Eldorado, or California as Seen by a Pioneer 1850–1900.* Los Angeles: B. R. Baumgardt, 1900.

Shaw, Reuben Cole. *Across the Plains in Forty-Nine.* Farmland, Ind.: W. C. West, 1896.

Shepherd, James S. *Journal of Travel Across the Plains to California, and Guide to the Future Emigrant.* Fairfield, Wash.: Ye Galleon Press, 1978.

Smedley, William. *Across the Plains: An 1862 Journey from Omaha to Oregon.* Boulder, Colo.: Johnson Books, 1994.

Smith, Asa Bowen. *Diaries and Letters of Asa Bowen Smith, Regarding the Nez Perce Mission, 1838–1842.* Ed. Clifford Merrill Drury. Glendale, Calif.: Arthur H. Clark, 1958.

Smith, Charles W. *Journal of a Trip to California—Across the Continent from Weston, Missouri, to Weber Creek, California, in the Summer of 1850.* Ed. R. W. G. Vail. Fairfield, Wash.: Ye Galleon Press, 1974.

Smith, Jesse Nathaniel. *Six Decades in the Early West: The Journal of Jesse Nathaniel Smith.* Ed. Oliver R. Smith. Salt Lake City: Publishers Press, 1970.

Stafford, Mallie. *The March of Empire Through Three Decades.* San Francisco: G. Spaulding, 1884.

Stands In Timber, John, and Margot Liberty. *Cheyenne Memories.* New Haven, Conn.: Yale University Press, 1967.

Stansbury, Capt. Howard. *An Expedition to the Valley of the Great Salt Lake of Utah.* Philadelphia: Lippincott, Grambo, 1852.

Steck, Amos. *Amos Steck (1822–1908), Forty-Niner: His Overland Diary to California.* Ed. Nolie Mumey. Denver: Range Press, 1981.

Steele, Elisha Dunsha. *The Diary of Elisha Dunsha Steele: Crossing the Plains to Boulder, Colorado, in the Year of 1859.* Ed. Nolie Mumey. Boulder, Colo.: Johnson, 1960.

Steele, John. *Across the Plains in 1850.* Ed. Joseph Schafer. Chicago: Caxton Club, 1930.

Stephens, Ann S. *Esther: A Story of the Oregon Trail.* New York: Beadle, 1862.

Stephens, Lorenzo Dow. *Life Sketches of a Jayhawker of '49.* N.p.: n.p., 1916.

Stout, Hosea. *On the Mormon Frontier: The Diary of Hosea Stout, 1844–1861.* Ed. Juanita Brooks. 2 vols. Salt Lake City: University of Utah Press, 1964.

Stuart, Robert. *The Discovery of the Oregon Trail: Robert Stuart's Narrative of His Overland Trip Eastward from Astoria in 1812–1813.* Ed. Philip Ashton Rollins. New York: Charles Scribner's Sons, 1935.

Swasey, William F. *The Early Days and Men of California.* Oakland, Calif.: Pacific Press, 1891.

Thomason, Jackson. *From Mississippi to California: Jackson Thomason's 1849 Overland Journal.* Ed. Michael D. Heaston. Austin, Tex.: Jenkins, 1978.

Thomson, Origen. *Crossing the Plains: Narrative of the Scenes, Incidents and Adventures Attending the Overland Journal.* Fairfield, Wash.: Ye Galleon Press, 1983.

Thornton, J. Quinn. "Oregon and California in 1848." In *"Unfortunate Emigrants": Narratives of the Donner Party,* ed. Kristin Johnson, 14–20. Logan: Utah State University Press, 1996.

Todd, A. C., and David James. *Ever Westward the Land: Samuel James and His Cornish Family on the Trail to Oregon and the Pacific Northwest, 1842–1852.* Exeter, Great Britain: University of Exeter Press, 1986.

Townsend, Edward D. *The California Diary of General E. D. Townsend.* Ed. Malcolm Edwards. Los Angeles: Ward Richie Press, 1970.

Townsend, John Kirk. *Narrative of a Journey Across the Rocky Mountains to the Columbia River.* Philadelphia: H. Perkins, 1839.

Trafzer, Clifford, and Joel R. Hyer, eds. *"Exterminate Them": Written Accounts of Native American Murder, Rape, and Slavery during the California Gold Rush, 1848–1868.* East Lansing: Michigan State University Press, 1999.

True, Charles Frederick. *The Overland Memoir of Charles Frederick True: A Teenager on the California Trail, 1859.* Ed. Sally Ralston True. Independence, Mo.: Oregon-California Trails Association, 1993.

Twain, Mark. *Roughing It.* New York: Holt, Rinehart and Winston, 1965.

Vaughan, Alden T., and Edward W. Clark, eds. *Puritans among the Indians: Accounts of Captivity and Redemption, 1676–1724.* Cambridge, Mass.: Harvard University Press, 1981.

Walker, Mary, and Myra Eells. *On to Oregon: The Diaries of Mary Walker and Myra Eells.* Ed. Clifford M. Drury. Lincoln: University of Nebraska Press, 1998.

Ward, Dillis B. *Across the Plains in 1853.* Wenatchee, Wash.: World, 1945.

Ward, Harriett Sherrill. *Prairie Schooner Lady: The Journal of Harriet Sherrill Ward, 1853.* Ed. Ward G. DeWitt and Florence Stark DeWitt. Los Angeles: Westernlore Press, 1959.

Ware, Eugene. *The Indian War of 1864.* Ed. Clyde C. Walton. Lincoln: University of Nebraska Press, 1960.

Ware, Joseph E. *The Emigrants' Guide to California.* Ed. John Caughey. Princeton, N.J.: Princeton University Press, 1932.

Watson, William J. *Journal of an Overland Journey to Oregon, Made in the Year 1849.* Jacksonville, Ill.: E. R. Roe, Book and Job Printer, 1851.

Wayman, John Hudson. *A Doctor on the California Trail: The Diary of Dr. John Hudson Wayman from Cambridge City, Indiana, to the Gold Fields in 1852.* Ed. Edgeley Woodman Todd. Denver: Old West, 1971.

White, Thomas. *To Oregon in 1852: Letter of Dr. Thomas White, La Grange County, Indiana Emigrant.* Ed. Oscar O. Winther and Gayle Thornbrough. Indianapolis: Indiana Historical Society, 1964.

Wilkins, James F. *Artist on the Overland Trail: The 1849 Diary and Sketches of James F. Wilkins.* Ed. John F. McDermott. San Marino, Calif.: Huntington Library, 1968.

Williams, Joseph. *Narrative of a Tour from the State of Indiana to the Oregon Territory in the Years 1841–1842.* Fairfield, Wash.: Ye Galleon Press, 1977.

Winfrey, Dorman, and James M. Days, eds. *The Indian Papers of Texas and the Southwest, 1825–1916.* 5 vols. Austin, Tex.: Pemberton Press, 1966.

Wistar, Isaac Jones. *Autobiography of Isaac Jones Wistar: Half a Century in War and Peace.* New York: Harper and Brothers, 1937.

Wonderley, Pauline. *Reminiscences of a Pioneer.* Ed. John B. Hassler. Placerville, Calif.: El Dorado County Historical Society, 1965.

Wooster, David. *The Gold Rush: Letters of David Wooster from California to the Adrian, Michigan, Expositor, 1850–1855.* Ed. John Cumming. Mount Pleasant, Mich.: Cumming Press, 1972.

Wyeth, John B. *Oregon; or A Short History of a Long Journey from the Atlantic Ocean to the Region of the Pacific.* Cambridge, Mass.: n.p., 1833.

Wyeth, Nathaniel J. *The Journals of Captain Nathaniel J. Wyeth's Expeditions to the Oregon Country, 1831–1836.* Ed. Don Johnson. Fairfield, Wash.: Ye Galleon Press, 1997.

Wyman, Walker D., ed. *California Emigrant Letters: The Forty-Niners Write Home.* New York: Bookman Associates, 1952.

Young, Charles E. *Dangers of the Trail in 1865.* Geneva, N.Y.: Press of W. F. Humphrey, 1912.

Articles

Ackley, Richard Thomas. "Across the Plains in 1858." *Utah Historical Quarterly* 9 (1941): 190–228.

Adams, Cecelia, and Parthenia Blank. "Twin Sisters on the Oregon Trail." In *Covered Wagon Women: Diaries and Letters from the Western Trails, 1840–1890,* ed. Kenneth L. Holmes, 5:253–312. Glendale, Calif.: Arthur H. Clark, 1986.

Adams, T. M. "Report from Palmyra *Courier,* quoted in *St. Louis Missouri Republican,* Jan. 14, 1845." Reprinted in *Publications of the Nebraska State Historical Society* 20 (1922): 129.

Allred, Reddick N. "Diary of Reddick N. Allred." Ed. Kate B. Carter. *Treasures of Pioneer History* 5 (1956): 307–310.

Allyn, Henry. "Journal of Henry Allyn, 1853." *Transactions of the Oregon Pioneer Association* (1921): 372–435.

Angell, Susan P. "Sketch of Mrs. Susan P. Angell, A Pioneer of 1852." *Transactions of the Oregon Pioneer Association* (1928): 55–56.

Aram, Joseph. "Recollections of a Journey from New York through the Western Wilderness and over the Rocky Mountains to the Pacific in 1846." Ed. James Tompkins Watson. *Journal of American History* 1 (1907): 617–32.

Arnold, Joseph Warren. "Joseph Warren Arnold's Journal of His Trip to and from Montana, 1864–1866." Ed. Charles W. Martin. *Nebraska History* 55 (Winter 1974): 463–552.

Athearn, Prince A. "Log Book of P. A. Athearn." Ed. Lovelia Athearn. *Pacific Historian* 2 (August 1958) 13–16; 2 (November 1958): 9–12; 3 (February 1959): 21–24; 3 (May 1959): 39–42.

Atkin, William. "Recollections." In *Heart Throbs of the West*, ed. Kate B. Carter, 6:380–94. Salt Lake City: Daughters of the Utah Pioneers, 1945.

Babbitt, Almon Whiting. "Biography." In *Our Pioneer Heritage*, ed. Kate B. Carter, 11:513–72. Salt Lake City: Daughters of the Utah Pioneers, 1968.

Bagley, Clarence B. "Crossing the Plains." *Washington Historical Quarterly* 3 (July 1922): 163–80.

Bailey, Mary Stuart. "A Journal of Mary Stuart Bailey, Wife of Dr. Fred Bailey, from Ohio to California, April–October 1852." In *Ho for California! Women's Overland Diaries from the Huntington Library*, ed. Sandra L. Myres, 49–91. San Marino, Calif.: Huntington Library, 1980.

Bailey, Theodore A. "Diary." In *Journeys to the Land of Gold: Emigrant Diaries from the Bozeman Trail, 1863–1866*, ed. Susan Badger Doyle, 2:467–85. Helena: Montana Historical Society Press, 2000.

Baker, Jean Rio. "By Windjammer and Prairie Schooner, London to Salt Lake City." In *Covered Wagon Women: Diaries and Letters from the Western Trails, 1840–1890*, ed. Kenneth L. Holmes, 3:203–281. Glendale, Calif.: Arthur H. Clark, 1984.

Barlow, William. "Reminiscences of Seventy Years." *Oregon Historical Quarterly* 13 (September 1912): 240–86.

Bayley, Betsey. "Across the Plains in 1845." In *Covered Wagon Women: Diaries and Letters from the Western Trails, 1840–1890*, ed. Kenneth L. Holmes, 1:31–38. Glendale, Calif.: Arthur H. Clark, 1983.

Belknap, Dr. Horace. "An Iowan in California, 1850." Ed. Woodrow Westholm. *Annals of Iowa* 36 (1926): 462–65.

Belknap, Keturah. "The Commentaries of Keturah Belknap." In *Covered Wagon Women: Diaries and Letters from the Western Trails, 1840–1890*, ed. Kenneth L. Holmes, 1:189–229. Glendale, Calif.: Arthur H. Clark, 1983.

Belshaw, Maria Parsons. "Crossing the Plains to Oregon in 1853." Ed. Michael L. Tate. *Overland Journal* 14 (Summer 1996): 10–42.

Bender, Flora Isabelle. "A Journey Across the Plains in 1863." *Nevada Historical Society Quarterly* 1 (1958): 145–73.

Berrien, Joseph Waring. "Overland from St. Louis to the California Gold Fields in 1849: The Diary of Joseph Waring Berrien." Ed. Ted Hinckley and Caryl Hinckley. *Indiana Magazine of History* 56 (December 1960): 273–352.

Blanchard, Jonathan. "The 1864 Overland Trail: Five Letters from Jonathan Blanchard." Ed. Robert H. Keller, Jr. *Nebraska History* 63 (Spring 1982): 71–86.

Blythe, Samuel Finley. "Diary." In *Journeys to the Land of Gold: Emigrant Diaries from the Bozeman Trail, 1863–1866*, ed. Susan Badger Doyle, 2:620–44. Helena: Montana Historical Society Press, 2000.

Bonney, Benjamin Franklin. "Recollections of Benjamin Franklin Bonney." Ed. Fred Lockley. *Oregon Historical Quarterly* 24 (March 1923): 36–55.

Booth, Margaret, ed. "Overland from Indiana to Ore.: The Dinwiddie Journal." In *Frontier Omnibus*, ed. John W. Hakola, 181–95. Missoula: Montana State University Press, 1962.

Bordeaux, James, et al. "Testimony About the Grattan Massacre, in the *St. Louis Missouri Republican*, September 5, 13, 1854, January 3, April 15, 1855." Paraphrased in *Publications of the Nebraska State Historical Society* 20 (1922): 259–68.

Broadwell, J. W. "Crossing the Plains with the McMurphy Train." *Lassen County Historical Society* 2 (1966): 17–31.

Brooks, Noah. "The Plains Across." *Century Magazine*, April 1902, 803–820.

Brown, Adam Mercer. "Over Barren Plains and Rock–Bound Mountains: Being the Journal of a Tour by the Overland Route." Ed. David M. Kiefer. *Montana, Magazine of Western History* 22 (Autumn 1972): 16–29.

Buckingham, Harriet Talcott. "Crossing the Plains in 1851." In *Covered Wagon Women: Diaries and Letters from the Western Trails, 1840–1890*, ed. Kenneth L. Holmes, 3:15–22. Glendale, Calif.: Arthur H. Clark, 1984.

Burgess, Perry A. "Diary." In *Journeys to the Land of Gold: Emigrant Diaries from the Bozeman Trail, 1863–1866*, ed. Susan Badger Doyle, 2:547–70. Helena: Montana Historical Society Press, 2000.

Burnett, Peter H. "Recollections and Opinions of an Old Pioneer." *Quarterly of the Oregon Historical Society* 5 (March 1904): 64–99; 5 (December 1904): 370–401.

Burrell, Mary. "Council Bluffs to California, 1854." In *Covered Wagon Women: Diaries and Letters from the Western Trails, 1840–1890*, ed. Kenneth L. Holmes, 6:225–60. Glendale, Calif.: Arthur H. Clark, 1986.

Butterfield, Ira H., Jr. "Michigan to California in 1861." *Michigan History Magazine* 11 (1927): 392–423.

Byers, William N. "The Odyssey of William N. Byers." Ed. Merrill J. Mattes. *Overland Journal* 1 (July 1983): 14–23; 1 (Fall 1983): 12–21; 2 (Winter 1984): 14–23; 2 (Spring 1984): 23–28.

Canfield, Lucy Marie. "Diary." In *Our Pioneer Heritage*, ed. Kate B. Carter, 6:26–30. Salt Lake City: Daughters of the Utah Pioneers, 1963.

Cann, T. H. "From Mississippi to the Valley of the Sacramento: Memories of Fifty Years." *Overland Monthly* 45 (1905): 526–28.

Carpenter, Helen McCowen. "A Trip Across the Plains in an Ox Wagon, 1857." In *Ho For California! Women's Overland Diaries from the Huntington Library*, ed. Sandra L. Myers, 93–188. San Marino, Calif.: Huntington Library, 1980.

Carriger, Nicholas. "Diary of Nicholas Carriger." In *Overland in 1846: Diaries and Letters of the California-Oregon Trail*, ed. Dale Morgan, 1:143–58. Georgetown, Calif.: Talisman Press, 1963.

Carter, William A. "Diary of Judge William A Carter." *Annals of Wyoming* 11 (April 1939): 75–110.

Case, William M. "Recollections of His Trip Across the Plains in 1844." Ed. H. S. Lyman. *Oregon Historical Quarterly* 1 (September 1900): 269–95.

Cason, Mrs. James P. "Saw Massacre from Window." In *Told by the Pioneers*, 1:76–77. Washington Pioneer Project, 1937.

Chalmers, Robert. "The Journal of Robert Chalmers, April 17–September 1, 1850." Ed. Charles Kelly. *Utah Historical Quarterly* 20 (1952): 31–52.

Chambers, A. B. "'Bad Cheyennes,' from *St. Louis Missouri Republican*." Reprinted in *Publications of the Nebraska State Historical Society* 20 (1922): 235.

Chambers, Andrew J. "A Brief Account of a Trip Across the Plains." *Washington Standard*, May 15, 1908, 27; May 22, 1908, 28; May 29, 1908, 29; June 5, 1908, 30.

Chenoweth, F. A. "Occasional Address." *Transactions of the Oregon Pioneer Association* (1882): 28–35.

Chick, Washington H. "The Vicissitudes of Pioneer Life." *Missouri Valley Historical Society Publications* 1 (December 1922): 207–218.

Christensen, Carl C. A. "By Handcart to Utah: The Account of C. C. A. Christensen." Trans. and ed. Richard L. Jensen. *Nebraska History* 66 (Winter 1985): 333–48.

Clark, Bennett C. "Diary of a Journey from Missouri to California in 1849." Ed. Ralph P. Bieber. *Missouri Historical Review* 23 (1928): 3–43.

Clark, John Hawkins. "Overland to the Gold Fields of California in 1852: The Journal of John Hawkins Clark, Expanded and Revised from Notes Made during the Journey." Ed. Louise Barry. *Kansas Historical Quarterly* 11 (August 1942): 227–96.

Colfax, Schuyler. "Hon. Schuyler Colfax's Journey from the Missouri River to California in 1865." *Western Galaxy* 1 (1888): 349–57.

Cone, Anson Sterling. "Reminiscences." Ed. H. S. Lyman. *Oregon Historical Society Quarterly* 4 (September 1903): 251–59.

Cook, Louisa. "Letters from the Oregon Trail, 1862–1863." In *Covered Wagon Women: Diaries and Letters from the Western Trails, 1840–1890*, ed. Kenneth L. Holmes, 8:27–57. Glendale, Calif.: Arthur H. Clark, 1989.

Coon, Polly. "Journal of a Journey Over the Rocky Mountains." In *Covered Wagon Women: Diaries and Letters from the Western Trails, 1840–1890*, ed. Kenneth L. Holmes, 5:173–206. Glendale, Calif.: Arthur H. Clark, 1986.

Cosgrove, Hugh. "Reminiscences of Hugh Cosgrove." Ed. H. S. Lyman. *Oregon Historical Quarterly* 1 (September 1900): 253–69.

Cranston, Susan Amelia. "An Ohio Lady Crosses the Plains." In *Covered Wagon Women: Diaries and Letters from the Western Trails, 1840–1890*, ed. Kenneth L. Holmes, 3:97–126. Glendale, Calif.: Arthur H. Clark, 1984.

Crawford, P. V. "Journal of a Trip Across the Plains, 1851." *Oregon Historical Quarterly* 25 (June 1924): 136–69.

Creigh, Thomas Alfred. "From Nebraska City to Montana, 1866: The Diary of Thomas Alfred Creigh." Ed. James C. Olson. *Nebraska History* 29 (September 1948): 208–237.

Crosby, Jesse W. "The History and Journal of the Life of Jesse W. Crosby." *Annals of Wyoming* 11 (July 1939): 145–81.

Cummings, Mariett Foster. "A Trip Across the Continent." In *Covered Wagon Women: Diaries and Letters from the Western Trails, 1840–1890*, ed. Kenneth L. Holmes, 4:117–68. Glendale, Calif.: Arthur H. Clark, 1985.

Currey, George B. "Occasional Address." *Transactions of the Oregon Pioneer Association* (1887): 32–47.

Davis, Sarah. "Diary from Missouri to California, 1850." In *Covered Wagon Women: Diaries and Letters from the Western Trails, 1840–890*, ed. Kenneth L. Holmes, 4:117–68. Glendale, Calif.: Arthur H. Clark, 1983.

Dodson, John F. "The Diary of John F. Dodson: His Journey from Illinois to His Death at Fort Owen in 1852." Ed. George F. Weisel. *Montana, Magazine of Western History* 3 (Spring 1953): 24–33.

Doederlein, Paul Ferdinand. "The Doederlein Diary, May 1859–February 1860." Ed. Roger Moldenhauer. Trans. William A. Kramer. *Concordia Historical Institute Quarterly* 51 (Fall 1978): 98–135.

Dougherty, Lewis Bissell. "Experiences of Lewis Bissell Dougherty on the Oregon Trail." Ed. Ethel Massie Withers. *Missouri Historical Review* 24 (April 1930): 359–78; 24 (July 1930): 550–67; 25 (October 1930): 102–115; 25 (January 1931): 306–321; 25 (April 1931): 474–89.

Drum, Gen. Richard C. "Reminiscences of the Indian Fight at Ash Hollow, 1855." *Collections of the Nebraska State Historical Society* 16 (1911): 143–51.

Dudley, Nathan Augustus Monroe. "Battle of Ash Hollow: The 1909–1910 Recollections of General N. A. M. Dudley." Ed. R. Eli Paul. *Nebraska History* 62 (Fall 1981): 373–99.

Dutton, Jerome. "Across the Plains in 1850: Journal and Letters of Jerome Dutton, Written during an Overland Journey from Scott County, Iowa to Sacramento County, California in the Year Named." *Annals of Iowa* 9 (1909–1910): 447–83.

Easton, Capt. L. C. "Fort Laramie to Fort Leavenworth via the Republican River in 1849." Ed. Merrill J. Mattes. *Kansas Historical Quarterly* 20 (May 1953): 392–416.

Ebey, Winfield Scott. "Overland from Missouri to Washington Territory in 1854." Ed. Gerald Baydo. *Nebraska History* 52 (Spring 1971): 65–87.

"Editorials and News Items about General Harney's Sioux Expedition in *St. Louis Missouri Republican*, July 13, Sept. 11 and 27, Oct. 25 and 27." Reprinted in *Publications of the Nebraska State Historical Society* 20 (1922): 273–82.

Edmundson, William. "Diary Kept by William Edmundson of Oskaloosa, While Crossing the Western Plains in 1850." *Annals of Iowa* 8 (October 1908): 516–35.

"'Emigration in 1850,' in *St. Louis Missouri Republican* June 1, 1850." Reprinted in *Publications of the Nebraska State Historical Society* 20 (1922): 221.

Epperson, Lucretia Lawson. "A Journal of Our Trip, 1864." In *Covered Wagon Women: Diaries and Letters from the Western Trails, 1840–1890*, ed. Kenneth L. Holmes, 8:163–98. Glendale, Calif.: Arthur H. Clark, 1989.

Evans, James B. "A Missouri Forty-Niner's Trip Across the Plains." *Missouri Historical Review* 43 (October 1948): 38–47.

Evans, Priscilla Merriman. "Autobiography." In *Our Pioneer Heritage*, ed. Kate B. Carter, 14:279–92. Salt Lake City: Daughters of the Utah Pioneers, 1971.

Evershed, Thomas. "The Gold Rush Journal of Thomas Evershed: Engineer, Artist, and Rochesterian." Ed. J. H. Madden and J. W. Barnes. *Rochester History* 39 (January–April 1977): 25–44.

Farnham, Elijah Bryan. "From Ohio to California in 1849: The Gold Rush Journal of Elijah Bryan Farnham." Ed. Merrill J. Mattes and Esley J. Kirk. *Indiana Magazine of History* 46 (September 1950): 297–318; 46 (December 1950): 403–420.

Fenex, Jim. "Little Ada Magill." *Annals of Wyoming* 43 (Fall 1971): 279–81.

Fisher, Rachel. "Letter from a Quaker Woman." In *Covered Wagon Women: Diaries and Letters from the Western Trails, 1840–1890*, ed. Kenneth L. Holmes, 1:97–110. Glendale, Calif.: Arthur H. Clark, 1983.

Flory, Abraham Polk. "Diary." In *Journeys to the Land of Gold: Emigrant Diaries from the Bozeman Trail, 1863–1866*, ed. Susan Badger Doyle, 1:316–30. Helena: Montana Historical Society Press, 2000.

Forman, George. "Across the Plains with George Forman." Ed. T. A. Larson. *Annals of Wyoming* 40 (1968): 5–40, 267–82.

Foster, William C. "Gold Rush Journey: A Letter by William C. Foster, 1850." Ed. Dwayne Bolling. *Nebraska History* 62 (Fall 1981): 400–410.

Fox, George W. "George W. Fox Diary." *Annals of Wyoming* 8 (January 1932): 580–601.

French, C. Adelia. "Reminiscence." In *Journeys to the Land of Gold: Emigrant Diaries from the Bozeman Trail, 1863–1866*, ed. Susan Badger Doyle, 1:233–43. Helena: Montana Historical Society Press, 2000.

Frost, Mary Anna. "Autobiography." In *Told by the Pioneers*, 1:101–105. Washington Pioneer Project, 1937.

Frost, Mary Perry. "Experiences of a Pioneer." *Washington Historical Quarterly* 7 (April 1916): 123–25.

Fuller, Randall. "The Diary of Randall Fuller." Ed. Lois Daniel. *Overland Journal* 6, no. 4 (1988): 2–35.

Gailland, Maurice. "Early Years at St. Mary's Pottawatomie Mission: From the Diary of Father Maurice Gailland, S.J." Ed. Rev. James M. Burke, S.J. *Kansas Historical Quarterly* 20 (August 1953): 501–29.

Geer, Elizabeth Dixon Smith. "Diary of Elizabeth Dixon Smith Geer." Ed. George H. Himes. *Transactions of the Oregon Pioneer Association* (1907): 153–79.

Geer, Ralph C. "Occasional Address for the Year 1847." *Transactions of the Oregon Pioneer Association* (1879): 32–42.

Gentry, Mrs. M. A. "A Child's Experience in '49." With Jennie E. Ross. *Overland Monthly* 63 (January 1914): 300–305; 63 (April 1914): 402–408.

Gilfry, Henry H. "Annual Address." *Transactions of the Oregon Pioneer Association* (1903): 411–23.

Gilliam, Washington Smith. "Reminiscences of Washington Smith Gilliam." *Transactions of the Oregon Pioneer Association* (1904): 202–20.

Gilmore, S. M. "Letter." *Oregon Historical Quarterly* 4 (1903): 280–84.

Glenn, Nancy C. "A Letter from La Grande Ronde, 1862." In *Covered Wagon Women: Diaries and Letters from the Western Trails, 1840–1890*, ed. Kenneth L. Holmes, 8:15–26. Glendale, Calif.: Arthur H. Clark, 1989.

Goddell, Anna Maria, and Elizabeth Austin. "Vermillion Wagon Train Diaries, 1854." In *Covered Wagon Women: Diaries and Letters from the Western Trails, 1840–1890*, ed. Kenneth L. Holmes, 7:79–130. Glendale, Calif.: Arthur H. Clark, 1987.

Goodridge, Sophia Lois. "The Mormon Trail, 1850." In *Covered Wagon Women: Diaries and Letters from the Western Trails, 1840–1890*, ed. Kenneth L. Holmes, 2:207–235. Glendale, Calif.: Arthur H. Clark, 1983.

Graham, Alpheus N. "The Big Circle Back to Kansas." Ed. William E. Koch. *Kansas Magazine* (1966): 52–57.

Griswold, Harriet Booth. "From Ashtabula to Petaluma in 1859." In *Covered Wagon Women: Diaries and Letters from the Western Trails, 1840–1890*, ed. Kenneth L. Holmes, 7:217–42. Glendale, Calif.: Arthur H. Clark, 1987.

Grundvig, Frantz Christian. "Recollections." In *Our Pioneer Heritage*, ed. Kate B. Carter, 9:47–71. Salt Lake City: Daughters of the Utah Pioneers, 1966.

Hackney, John S. "Diary." In *Journeys to the Land of Gold: Emigrant Diaries from the Bozeman Trail, 1863–1866*, ed. Susan Badger Doyle, 1:299–315. Helena: Montana Historical Society Press, 2000.

Hadley, Amelia. "Journal of Travails to Oregon." In *Covered Wagon Women: Diaries and Letters from the Western Trails, 1840–1890*, ed. Kenneth L. Holmes, 3:53–96. Glendale, Calif.: Arthur H. Clark, 1984.

Hadley, C. B. "Plains Indian War in 1865." *Proceedings and Collections of the Nebraska State Historical Society*, 2nd series, 5 (1902): 273–78.

Harlan, Aaron W. "Journal of A. W. Harlan While Crossing the Plains in 1850." *Annals of Iowa* 11 (1913–15): 32–62.

Hastings, Loren B. "Diary of Loren B. Hastings, a Pioneer of 1847." *Transactions of the Oregon Pioneer Association* (1923): 12–26.

Haun, Catherine Margaret. "A Woman's Trip Across the Plains in 1849." In Lillian Schlissel, *Women's Diaries of the Westward Journey*, 165–85. New York: Schocken, 1982.

Hawk, Al R. "Strange Adventures of the Hawk Family in Crossing the Plains in 1852." In *Told by the Pioneers*, 1:158–65. Washington Pioneer Project, 1937.

Henderson, Lucy Ann. "Young Adventure." Ed. and annot. Ronald Thomas Strong. *Nevada Historical Society Quarterly* 16 (1973): 67–100.

Hester, Sallie. "The Diary of a Pioneer Girl." In *Covered Wagon Women: Diaries and Letters from the Western Trails, 1840–1890*, ed. Kenneth L. Holmes, 1:231–46. Glendale, Calif.: Arthur H. Clark, 1983.

Hillyer, Edwin. "From Waupun to Sacramento in 1849." Ed. John O. Holzhueter. *Wisconsin Magazine of History* 49 (Spring 1966): 210–44.

Hines, Celinda. "Life and Death on the Oregon Trail." In *Covered Wagon Women: Diaries and Letters from the Western Trails, 1840–1890*, ed. Kenneth L. Holmes, 6:77–134. Glendale, Calif.: Arthur H. Clark, 1986.

Hodder, Halie Riley. "Crossing the Plains in War Times." *Colorado Magazine* 10 (July 1933): 131–37.

Hoffman, Benjamin. "West Virginia's Forty-Niners." Ed. C. H. Ambler. *West Virginia History* 3 (1941): 59–75.

Holt, James. "The Reminiscences of James Holt: A Narrative of the Emmett Company." Ed. Dale L. Morgan. *Utah Historical Quarterly* 23 (January 1955): 1–33; 23 (April 1955): 152–79.

Holt, Thomas. "The Holt Journal." In *Overland in 1846: Diaries and Letters of the California-Oregon Trail*, ed. Dale L. Morgan, 1:191–98. Georgetown, Calif.: Talisman Press, 1963.

Holtgreive, Elizabeth R. "Recollections of Pioneer Days." *Washington Historical Quarterly* 19 (1928): 193–98.

Hopkins, Rebeka. "Reminiscences." *Oregon Historical Society Quarterly* 4 (September 1903): 251–61.

Hoppe, Hugo. "Recollections." In *Imprints on Pioneer Trails*, ed. Ida McPherren. Boston: Christopher Publishing House, 1950.

Hough, Warren. "The 1850 Overland Diary of Dr. Warren Hough." *Annals of Wyoming* 46 (Fall 1974): 207–216.

Hulbert, Archer Butler, ed. "The First Wagon Train on the Road to Oregon." In *Frontier Omnibus*, ed. John W. Hakola, 43–65. Missoula: Montana State University Press, 1962.

Hunt, Nancy A. "By Ox-Team to California." *Overland Monthly* 67 (1916): 317–26.

Hurd, Cyrus, Jr. "Letters of a Yankee Forty-Niner." Ed. Margaret S. Dart. *Yale Review* 36 (Summer 1947): 643–66.

Iman, Margaret Windsor. "My Arrival in Washington in 1852." *Washington Historical Quarterly* 18 (October 1927): 254–60.

Jacobs, Nancy Osborne. "Incidents of Early Western History." In *Told by the Pioneers*, 1:78–86. Washington Pioneer Project, 1937.

James, John Roger. "Autobiography of John Roger James. In *Told by the Pioneers*, 2:59–77. Washington Pioneer Project, 1938.

Jamison, Samuel M. "Diary of S. M. Jamison, 1850." *Nevada Historical Society Quarterly* 10 (Winter 1967): 3–27.

Jory, James. "Reminiscences of James Jory." Ed. H. S. Lyman. *Oregon Historical Quarterly* 3 (September 1902): 271–86.

Keil, William. "From Bethel, Missouri to Aurora, Oregon: Letters of William Keil, 1855–1870." Trans. William G. Bek. *Missouri Historical Review* 48 (October 1953): 23–41.

Kelley, Mary Foreman. "Reminiscence." In *Journeys to the Land of Gold: Emigrant Diaries from the Bozeman Trail, 1863–1866*, ed. Susan Badger Doyle, 1:331–36. Helena: Montana Historical Society Press, 2000.

Kelsey, Nancy. "A California Heroine." *Grizzly Bear* (February 1915): 6–7.

Kerns, John T. "Journal of Crossing the Plains to Oregon." *Transactions of the Oregon Pioneer Association* (1914): 148–93.

King, Hannah Tapfield. "My Journal." In *Covered Wagon Women: Diaries and Letters from the Western Trails, 1840–1890*, ed. Kenneth L. Holmes, 6:183–222. Glendale, Calif.: Arthur H. Clark, 1986.

Kingman, Romanzo. "Romanzo Kingman's Pike's Peak Journal, 1859." Ed. Kenneth F. Millsap. *Iowa Journal of History* 48 (January 1950): 55–85.

Kirkpatrick, Robert. "Reminiscence." In *Journeys to the Land of Gold: Emigrant Diaries from the Bozeman Trail, 1863–1866*, ed. Susan Badger Doyle, 1:103–121. Helena: Montana Historical Society Press, 2000.

Knight, Amelia. "Iowa to the Columbia River." In *Covered Wagon Women: Diaries and Letters from the Western Trails, 1840–1890*, ed. Kenneth L. Holmes, 6:33–75. Glendale, Calif.: Arthur H. Clark, 1986.

Knight, William H. "An Emigrant's Trip Across the Plains in 1859." *Proceedings of the Historical Society of Southern California* 12, no. 3 (1921): 32–41.

Koontz, Sarah Catherine. "Interview." In *Told by the Pioneers*, 2:39–41. Washington Pioneer Project, 1937.

Lee, Jason. "Diary." *Oregon Historical Quarterly* 17 (June 1916): 116–46; 17 (September 1916): 240–66; 17 (December 1916): 397–430.

Lockey, Richard. "Diary." In *Journeys to the Land of Gold: Emigrant Diaries from the Bozeman Trail, 1863–1866*, ed. Susan Badger Doyle, 2:448–66. Helena: Montana Historical Society Press, 2000.

Longmire, David. "First Immigrants to Cross the Cascades." *Washington Historical Quarterly* 8 (1917): 22–28.

Longmire, James. "A Description of the Trip Across the Plains." In *Told by the Pioneers*, 1:121–46. Washington Pioneer Project, 1937.

Loomis, Thaddeus Levi. "Grandfather Was a Forty-Niner." Ed. Niles Anderson. *Western Pennsylvania Historical Magazine* 50 (January 1967): 33–50.

Loughary, Harriet A. "Travels and Incidents, 1864." In *Covered Wagon Women: Diaries and Letters from the Western Trails, 1840–1890*, ed. Kenneth L. Holmes, 8:115–62. Glendale, Calif.: Arthur H. Clark, 1989.

Lovejoy, Asa. "Lovejoy's Pioneer Narrative, 1842–48." Ed. Henry E. Reed. *Oregon Historical Quarterly* 31 (September 1930): 237–60.

Lynn, Mrs. James. "Along the Emigrant Trail from Tennessee to California, 1847–1859." *Santa Clara Historical and Genealogical Society* 13 (April 1977): 48–51.

Magraw, William F. "Reports in *St. Louis Missouri Republican*, July 15 and 20, August 12 and 21, and October 7, 11, and 21, 1857." Reprinted in *Publications of the Nebraska State Historical Society* 20 (1922): 290–93.

Marvin, George P. "Bull-whacking Days." *Proceedings and Collections of the Nebraska State Historical Society*, 2nd series, 5 (1902): 226–30.

Mason, James. "Diary of James Mason." Ed. James C. Olson. *Nebraska History* 33 (June 1952): 103–121.

Matthieu, Francis Xavier. "Reminiscences." Ed. H. S. Lyman. *Oregon Historical Quarterly* 1 (March 1900): 73–104.

Mattice, Nancy Areta Porter. "Reminiscences." In *Our Pioneer Heritage*, ed. Kate B. Carter, 13:463–67. Salt Lake City: Daughters of the Utah Pioneers, 1970.

Maughan, Mary Ann Weston. "Journal of Mary Ann Weston." In *Our Pioneer Heritage*, ed. Kate B. Carter, 2:373–80. Salt Lake City: Daughters of the Utah Pioneers, 1959.

Maynard, David S. "Diary of Dr. David S. Maynard While Crossing the Plains in 1850." Ed. Thomas W. Prosch. *Washington Historical Quarterly* (October 1906): 50–62.

McAllister, James. "Early Reminiscences of a Nisqually Pioneer." In *Told by the Pioneers*, 1:166–84. Washington Pioneer Project, 1937.

McAuley, Eliza Ann. "Iowa to the 'Land of Gold.'" In *Covered Wagon Women: Diaries and Letters from the Western Trails, 1840–1890*, ed. Kenneth L. Holmes, 4:33–81. Glendale, Calif.: Arthur H. Clark, 1985.

McClellan, William S. "California Bound." *Oakland Tribune*, August 14, 1955.

McKinstry, George. "Diary of George McKinstry." In *Overland in 1846: Diaries and Letters of the California-Oregon Trail*, ed. Dale Morgan, 1:199–215. Georgetown, Calif.: Talisman Press, 1963.

McPherson, Murdoch M. "Reminiscences of Murdoch M. McPherson." *Pacific Northwest Quarterly* 27 (1936): 243–55.

Menefee, Arthur M. "Arthur M. Menefee's Travels Across the Plains, 1857." *Nevada Historical Society Quarterly* 9 (Spring 1966): 5–28.

Millington, Ada. "Journal Kept While Crossing the Plains by Ada Millington." Ed. Charles G. Clarke. *Southern California Quarterly* 59 (1977): 13–48, 139–84, 251–69.

Minto, John. "Reminiscences." *Oregon Historical Quarterly* 2 (June 1901): 119–67.

Morrison, Robert Wilson. "Recollections." Ed. John Minto. *Transactions of the Oregon Pioneer Association* (1894): 53–62.

Mousley, Sarah Maria. "Delaware to Utah, 1857." In *Covered Wagon Women: Diaries and Letters from the Western Trails, 1840–1890*, ed. Kenneth L. Holmes, 7:157–89. Glendale, Calif.: Arthur H. Clark, 1987.

Myer, Nathaniel. "Journey into Southern Ore.: Diary of a Pennsylvania Dutchman." Ed. Edward B. Ham. *Oregon Historical Quarterly* 60 (1959): 375–407.

Myrick, Elizabeth. "Northern Route to California." In *Covered Wagon Women: Diaries and Letters from the Western Trails, 1840–1890*, ed. Kenneth L. Holmes, 6:263–81. Glendale, Calif.: Arthur H. Clark, 1986.

Nesmith, James W. "Diary of the Emigration of 1843." *Oregon Historical Quarterly* 7 (December 1906): 329–59.

Newby, William T. "William T. Newby's Diary of the Emigration of 1843." Ed. Harry N. M. Winton. *Oregon Historical Quarterly* 40 (September 1939): 219–42.

Norton, L. A. "My Life and Adventures." *Pony Express Courier* 1 (1934): 10.

Ogle, Van. "Van Ogle's Memory of Pioneer Days." Ed. Edmond S. Meany. *Washington Historical Quarterly* 13 (1922): 269–81.

Osterhoudt, Solomon S. "Osterhoudt's Ox Train Diary." *Polo (Ill.) Tri-County Press*, March 23, 1961.

Otto, Olive Harriet. "A Mormon Bride in the Great Migration." Ed. Orval F. Baldwin II. *Nebraska History* 58 (Spring 1977): 53–71.

Owen, Isaac. "Isaac Owen—Overland to California." Ed. John R. Purdy, Jr. *Methodist History* 11 (July 1973): 46–54.

Owens, Richard. "Diary." In *Journeys to the Land of Gold: Emigrant Diaries from the Bozeman Trail, 1863–1866*, ed. Susan Badger Doyle, 1:278–98. Helena: Montana Historical Society Press, 2000.

Packwood, William H. "Reminiscences of William H. Packwood." Ed. Fred Lockley. *Oregon Historical Quarterly* 16 (1915): 33–54.

Parker, Inez Eugenia Adams. "Early Recollections of Oregon Pioneer Life." *Transactions of the Oregon Pioneer Association* (1928): 17–35.

Parsons, Lucena. "An Overland Honeymoon." In *Covered Wagon Women: Diaries and Letters from the Western Trails, 1840–1890*, ed. Kenneth L. Holmes, 2:237–94. Glendale, Calif.: Arthur H. Clark, 1983.

Patterson, E. H. N. "The Platte River Route." In *Overland Routes to the Gold Fields, 1859*, ed. LeRoy R. Hafen, 59–197. Glendale, Calif.: Arthur H. Clark, 1942.

Peery, Mrs. D. H. "Mrs. Peery, At Age 88, Recalls Her Pioneer Days." In *Frontier Omnibus*, ed. John W. Hakola, 265–68. Missoula: Montana State University Press, 1962.

Pratt, Louisa Barnes. "Journal of Louisa Barnes Pratt." In *Heart Throbs of the West*, ed. Kate B. Carter, 8:189–256. Salt Lake City: Daughters of the Utah Pioneers, 1947.

Pringle, Virgil K. "Diary of Virgil K. Pringle, 1846." In *Overland in 1846: Diaries and Letters of the California-Oregon Trail*, ed. Dale L. Morgan, 1:159–88. Georgetown, Calif.: Talisman Press, 1963.

Putnam, Nathan, and Charles F. Putnam. "Letters." In *Overland in 1846: Diaries and Letters of the California-Oregon Trail*, ed. Dale L. Morgan, vol. 2. Georgetown, Calif.: Talisman Press, 1963.

Ramsay, Alexander. "Alexander Ramsay's Gold Rush Diary of 1849." Ed. Merrill J. Mattes. *Pacific Historical Review* 18 (November 1949): 437–68.

Read, Martha S. "A History of Our Journey." In *Covered Wagon Women: Diaries and Letters from the Western Trails, 1840–1890*, ed. Kenneth L. Holmes, 5:207–251. Glendale, Calif.: Arthur H. Clark, 1986.

Reading, Pierson Barton. "Journal of Pierson Barton Reading." Ed. Philip B. Bekeart. *Quarterly of the Society of California Pioneers* 7 (September 1930): 148–98.

"Report in *St. Louis Missouri Republican* for June 17, 1854." Reprinted in *Publications of the Nebraska State Historical Society* 20 (1922): 256.

Rhodes, Joseph. "Joseph Rhodes and the California Gold Rush of 1850." Ed. Merrill J. Mattes. *Annals of Wyoming* 23 (January 1951): 52–71.

Ricks, Sarah Beriah Fiske Allen. "Autobiography." In *Our Pioneer Heritage*, ed. Kate B. Carter, 11:135–44. Salt Lake City: Daughters of the Utah Pioneers, 1968.

Ringo, Mary. "The 1864 Journal." In *Covered Wagon Women: Diaries and Letters from the Western Trails, 1840–1890*, ed. Kenneth L. Holmes, 8:199–231. Glendale, Calif.: Arthur H. Clark, 1989.

Robinson, Charles. "Charles Robinson—Yankee Forty-Niner: His Journey to California." Ed. Louise Barry. *Kansas Historical Quarterly* 34 (Summer 1968): 179–88.

Rockafellow, Captain B. F. "Diary of Capt. Rockafellow." In *Powder River Campaigns and the Sawyer Expedition*, ed. LeRoy R. Hafen and Ann W. Hafen, 153–203. Glendale, Calif.: Arthur H. Clark, 1961.

Roundtree, P. H. "Autobiography of P. H. Roundtree." In *Told by the Pioneers*, 2:95–108. Washington Pioneer Project, 1938.

Rudd, Lydia Allen. "Notes by the Wayside En Route to Oregon, 1852." In Lillian Schlissel, *Women's Diaries of the Westward Journey*, 187–98. New York: Schocken, 1982.

Sawyer, Francis H. "Kentucky to California by Carriage and a Feather Bed." In *Covered Wagon Women: Diaries and Letters from the Western Trails, 1840–1890*, ed. Kenneth L. Holmes, 4:83–115. Glendale, Calif.: Arthur H. Clark, 1985.

Schallenberger, Moses. "Overland in 1844." In *The Opening of the California Trail: The Story of the Stevens Party*, ed. George R. Stewart, 46–84. Berkeley: University of California Press, 1953.

Scott, Abigail Jane. "Journal of a Trip to Oregon." In *Covered Wagon Women: Diaries and Letters from the Western Trails, 1840–1890*, ed. Kenneth L. Holmes, 5:21–172. Glendale, Calif.: Arthur H. Clark, 1986.

Scroggs, William Lee. "To the Gold Fields: Personal Recollections." *1955 Denver Westerners Brand Book*, 143–68. Boulder, Colo.: Johnson, 1956.

Sessions, Patty. "A Pioneer Mormon Diary." In *Covered Wagon Women: Diaries and Letters from the Western Trails, 1840–1890*, ed. Kenneth L. Holmes, 1:157–87. Glendale, Calif.: Arthur H. Clark, 1983.

Sharp, Cornelia A. "Diary of Mrs. Cornelia A. Sharp: Crossing the Plains from Missouri to Oregon in 1852." *Transactions of the Oregon Pioneer Association* (1903): 171–88.

Sharp, Joe H. "Crossing the Plains in 1852." *Transactions of the Oregon Pioneer Association* (1895): 91–95.

Shepard, George. "'O Wickedness, Where Is Thy Boundary?' The 1850 California Gold Rush Diary of George Shepard." Ed. David Bigler, Donald Buck, and Merrill Mattes. *Overland Journal* 10 (Winter 1992): 2–33.

Shively, J. M. "The Shively Guide." In *Overland in 1846: Diaries and Letters of the California-Oregon Trail*, ed. Dale L. Morgan, 2:734–42. Georgetown, Calif.: Talisman Press, 1963.

Sloan, William K. "Autobiography of William K. Sloan." *Annals of Wyoming* 4 (July 1926): 235–64.

Smith, Elizabeth Dixon (Geer). "Diary of Elizabeth Dixon Smith." In *Covered Wagon Women: Diaries and Letters from the Western Trails, 1840–1890*, ed. Kenneth L. Holmes, 1:111–55. Glendale, Calif.: Arthur H. Clark, 1983.

Smith, Harriet A. "To Pike's Peak by Ox-Wagon: The Harriet A. Smith Day-Book." Ed. Fleming Fraker, Jr. *Annals of Iowa* 35 (Fall 1959): 113–48.

Snow, Taylor N. "Diary of Taylor N. Snow, Hoosier Fifty-Niner." Ed. Arthur Homer Hays. *Indiana Magazine of History* 28 (1932): 193–208.

Snyder, Jacob R. "The Diary of Jacob R. Snyder, Written while Crossing the Plains to California in 1845." *Quarterly of the Society of California Pioneers* 8 (December 1931): 224–60.

Soule, Andrew. "Memories of the Plains, 1854." *Siskiyou Pioneer* 2 (1954): 8–15.

Speelman, Michael R. "Recollections." *Baker (Ore.) Democrat-Herald*, October 17, 1930.

Spencer, Lucinda. "Mrs. Lucinda Spencer Recollections." *Transactions of the Oregon Pioneer Association* (1887): 74–78.

Sponsler, A. C. "An 1850 Gold Rush Letter from Fort Laramie, by A. C. Sponsler, a Thayer County Pioneer." Ed. David L. Hieb. *Nebraska History* 33 (June 1951): 130–39.

Staats, Stephen. "The Occasional Address." *Transactions of the Oregon Pioneer Association* (1877): 45–59.

Stewart, Agnes. "The Journey to Oregon—A Pioneer Girl's Diary." Ed. Claire Warner Churchill. *Oregon Historical Quarterly* 29 (March 1928): 77–98.

Stewart, J. M. "Overland Trip to California in 1850." *Publications of the Historical Society of Southern California* 5 (1901): 176–85.

Stobie, Charles Stewart. "Crossing the Plains to Colorado in 1865." *Colorado Magazine* 10 (November 1933): 201–212.

Stoughton, J. A. "With Whitman on Way West." In *Told by the Pioneers*, 1:73–74. Washington Pioneer Project, 1937.

Sutton, Sarah. "A Travel Diary in 1854." In *Covered Wagon Women: Diaries and Letters from the Western Trails, 1840–1890*, ed. Kenneth L. Holmes, 7:15–77. Glendale, Calif.: Arthur H. Clark, 1987.

Swingley, Upton. "A Brief Chronicle of My Life." *Journal of the Illinois Historical Society* 42 (December 1949): 457–62.

Sydenham, Moses H. "Freighting Across the Plains in 1856: A Personal Experience." *Proceedings and Collections of the Nebraska State Historical Society*, 2nd series, 1 (1894): 164–84.

Tappan, Henry. "Gold Rush Diary of Henry Tappan." Ed. Everett Walters and George B. Strother. *Annals of Wyoming* 25 (1953): 113–39.

Tate, James A. "One Who Went West." Ed. Hugh P. Williamson. *Missouri Historical Review* 57 (July 1963): 369–78.

Taylor, Calvin. "Overland to the Gold Fields of California in 1850: The Journal of Calvin Taylor." Ed. Burton J. Williams. *Nebraska History* 50 (Summer 1969): 125–50; continued in *Utah Historical Quarterly* 38 (1970): 312–49.

Taylor, Rachel. "Overland Trip Across the Plains." In *Covered Wagon Women: Diaries and Letters from the Western Trails, 1840–1890*, ed. Kenneth L. Holmes, 6:149–83. Glendale, Calif.: Arthur H. Clark, 1986.

Taylor, S. H., and Clarissa Taylor. "Letters of S. H. Taylor to the *Watertown (Wis.) Chronicle*." *Oregon Historical Quarterly* 22 (June 1921): 117–53.

Taylor, William E. "Diary of William E. Taylor." In *Overland in 1846: Diaries and Letters of the California-Oregon Trail*, ed. Dale L. Morgan, 1:118–33. Georgetown, Calif.: Talisman Press, 1963.

Terwilliger, Phoebe Hogebroom. "Diary of Phoebe Hogebroom Terwilliger." *Siskiyou Pioneer* 2 (Fall 1954): 16–25.

Todd, Capt. John B. S. "The Harney Expedition against the Sioux: The Journal of Captain John B. S. Todd." Ed. Ray H. Mattison. *Nebraska History* 43 (June 1962): 89–130.

Tompkins, Mrs. E. O. "Interesting Account of a Trip Across the Plains in 1853." *Grizzly Bear* (January 1908): 42.

Tootle, Mrs. Thomas E. "The Diary of Mrs. Thomas E. Tootle." Ed. Roy C. Coy. St. Joseph Historical Society. *Museum Graphic* 13 (Spring 1961): 3–19.

Tourtillott, Jane Gould. "Touring from Mitchell, Iowa, to California, 1862." In Lillian Schlissel, *Women's Diaries of the Westward Journey*, 217–31. New York: Schocken, 1982.

Trubody, William Alexander. "William Alexander Trubody and the Overland Pioneers of 1847." Ed. Charles L. Camp. *California Historical Quarterly* 17 (1937): 122–43.

Tuller, Miriam A. "Crossing the Plains in 1845." *Transactions of the Oregon Pioneer Association* (1895): 87–90.

Tuttle, Charles M. "California Diary of Charles M. Tuttle, 1859." *Wisconsin Magazine of History* 15 (September 1931): 69–85; 15 (December 1931): 219–33.

Twiss, Thomas S. "Letter of Thomas S. Twiss, Indian Agent at Deer Creek, U.S. Indian Agency on the Upper Platte." *Annals of Wyoming* 17 (July 1945): 148–52.

Variel, Mary Alexander. "A Romance of the Plains." *Grizzly Bear* (July 1907): 30–32; (August 1907): 62–64; (September 1907): 74–76.

Walker, Mary Richardson. "The Diary of Mary Richardson Walker, June 10–December 21, 1838." Ed. Rufus A. Coleman. In *Frontier Omnibus*, ed. John W. Hakola, 74–99. Missoula: Montana State University Press, 1962.

Warner, William. "Overland to California: Letter from an Ohio 'Argonaut.'" *Ohio State Archaeological and Historical Society Publications* 35 (1926): 567–71.

Warren, Daniel Knight. "Reminiscences." *Oregon Historical Quarterly* 3 (December 1902): 296–309.

Waters, Lydia M. "Account of a Trip Across the Plains." *Quarterly of the Society of California Pioneers* 6 (March 1929): 59–79.

Welch, Adonijah Strong. "Three Gold Rush Letters of Adonijah Strong Welch." Ed. William H. Hermann. *Iowa Journal of History* 57 (January 1959): 61–73.

Welch, Nancy Dickerson. "Recollections." *Transactions of the Oregon Pioneer Association* (1897): 97–103.

West, Calvin B. "Calvin B. West of the Umpqua." Ed. Reginald R. Stuart and Grace D. Stuart. *Pacific Historian* 4 (May 1960): 48–57; 4 (August 1960): 87–96, 112.

Williams, John T. "Journal of John T. Williams." *Indiana Magazine of History* 32 (1936): 393–409.

Williams, Lucia Loraine. "A Letter to Mother." In *Covered Wagon Women: Diaries and Letters from the Western Trails, 1840–1890,* ed. Kenneth L. Holmes, 3:127–59. Glendale, Calif.: Arthur H. Clark, 1984.

Williams, Velina A. "'Diary of a Trip Across the Plains in 1853,' with Recollections of O. A. Stearns." *Transactions of the Oregon Pioneer Association* (1919): 178–227.

Willis, Ira J. "The Ira J. Willis Guide to the Gold Mines." Ed. Irene D. Paden. *California Historical Society Quarterly* 32 (September 1953): 193–207.

Willis, James M. "Jasons of 1860." Ed. Bessie L. Lyon. *Palimpsest* 17 (July 1936): 217–34.

Willson, Davis. "Diary." In *Journeys to the Land of Gold: Emigrant Diaries from the Bozeman Trail, 1863–1866,* ed. Susan Badger Doyle, 2:571–619. Helena: Montana Historical Society Press, 2000.

Winne, Peter. "Across the Plains in 1863: The Diary of Peter Winne." Ed. Robert G. Athearn. *Iowa Journal of History* 41 (1951): 221–40.

Winther, Oscar Osburn, ed. "From Tennessee to California in 1849: Letters of the Reeve Family of Medford, New Jersey." *Journal of the Rutgers University Library* 11 (June 1948): 33–82.

Witter, Clara. "Pioneer Life." *Colorado Magazine* 4 (December 1927): 165–74.

Wood, Elizabeth. "Journal of a Trip to Oregon." In *Covered Wagon Women: Diaries and Letters from the Western Trails, 1840–1890,* ed. Kenneth L. Holmes, 3:161–78. Glendale, Calif.: Arthur H. Clark, 1984.

Woodhams, William H. "The Diary of William H. Woodhams, 1852–1854." Ed. Charles M. Martin. *Nebraska History* 61 (Spring 1980): 1–101.

Woodward, Thomas. "Diary of Thomas Woodward While Crossing the Plains of California in 1850." Intro. Mrs. Sidney Woodward Ennor. *Wisconsin Magazine of History* 17 (March 1934): 345–60; 17 (June 1934): 433–46.

Wooten, Martha Ann. "Reminiscences: Coming to California in 1857." *Yolo County Historical Society* 8 (January 1975): 1–5.

Word, Samuel. "Diary." In *Journeys to the Land of Gold: Emigrant Diaries from the Bozeman Trail, 1863–1866,* ed. Susan Badger Doyle, 1:67–102. Helena: Montana Historical Society Press, 2000.

Young, John R. "A Thrilling Experience on the Plains—The Stampede." In *Our Pioneer Heritage,* ed. Kate B. Carter, 7:28–33. Salt Lake City: Daughters of the Utah Pioneers, 1964.

Young, Lorenzo, and Harriett Young. "Diary of Lorenzo Dow Young." *Utah Historical Quarterly* 14 (January–October 1946): 133–70.

Young, Will H. "Journals of Travel of Will H. Young." *Annals of Wyoming* 7 (October 1930): 378–82.

Zeiber, John. "Diary of John Zeiber, 1851." Ed. George H. Himes. *Transactions of the Oregon Pioneer Association* (1920): 301–335.

PUBLISHED SECONDARY SOURCES

Books and Pamphlets

Adams, George Rollie. *General William S. Harney: Prince of Dragoons*. Lincoln: University of Nebraska Press, 2001.

Anderson, Gary Clayton. *The Indian Southwest, 1580–1830: Ethnogenesis and Reinvention*. Norman: University of Oklahoma Press, 1999.

Asher, Brad. *Beyond the Reservation: Indians, Settlers, and the Law in Washington Territory, 1853–1889*. Norman: University of Oklahoma Press, 1999.

Bagley, Will. *Blood of the Prophets: Brigham Young and the Massacre at Mountain Meadows*. Norman: University of Oklahoma Press, 2002.

Barry, Louise. *The Beginning of the West: Annals of the Kansas Gateway to the American West, 1540–1854*. Topeka: Kansas State Historical Society, 1972.

Becher, Ronald. *Massacre along the Medicine Road: A Social History of the Indian War of 1864 in Nebraska Territory*. Caldwell, Idaho: Caxton, 1999.

Beckham, Stephen Dow. *Requiem for a People: The Rogue Indians and the Frontiersmen*. Norman: University of Oklahoma Press, 1971.

Bennett, Richard E. *Mormons at the Missouri, 1846–1852: "And Should We Die . . ."* Norman: University of Oklahoma Press, 1987.

Berkhofer, Robert F., Jr. *The White Man's Indian: Images of the American Indian from Columbus to the Present*. New York: Vintage, 1978.

Berthrong, Donald J. *The Southern Cheyennes*. Norman: University of Oklahoma Press, 1963.

Billington, Ray Allen. *Land of Savagery, Land of Promise: The European Image of the American Frontier in the Nineteenth Century*. New York: W. W. Norton, 1981.

Blaine, Martha Royce. *The Iowa Indians*. Norman: University of Oklahoma Press, 1979,

Boyd, Robert Thomas. "The Introduction of Infectious Diseases among the Indians of the Pacific Northwest, 1774–1874." Ph.D. diss., University of Washington, 1985.

Brown, D. Alexander. *The Galvanized Yankees*. Urbana: University of Illinois Press, 1963.

Butts, Michèle Tucker. *Galvanized Yankees on the Upper Missouri: The Face of Loyalty*. Boulder: University Press of Colorado, 2003.

Canfield, Gae Whitney. *Sarah Winnemucca of the Northern Paiutes*. Norman: University of Oklahoma Press, 1983.

Christensen, Scott R. *Sagwitch: Shoshone Chieftain, Mormon Elder, 1822–1887*. Logan: Utah State University Press, 1999.

Corless, Hank. *The Weiser Indians: Shoshoni Peacemakers*. Salt Lake City: University of Utah Press, 1990.

Coward, John M. *The Newspaper Indian: Native American Identity in the Press, 1820–90.* Urbana: University of Illinois Press, 1999.

Czaplewski, Russ. *Captive of the Cheyenne: The Story of Nancy Jane Morton and the Plum Creek Massacre.* Kearney, Neb.: Morris, 1993.

David, Robert Beebe. *Finn Burnett, Frontiersman.* Glendale, Calif.: Arthur H. Clark, 1937.

Deloria, Philip J. *Playing Indian.* New Haven, Conn.: Yale University Press, 1998.

Derounian-Stodola, Kathryn Zabelle, and James Arthur Levernier. *The Indian Captivity Narrative, 1550–1900.* New York: Twayne, 1993.

De Voto, Bernard. *The Year of Decision, 1846.* New York: Houghton-Mifflin, 1943.

Dippie, Brian W. *Catlin and His Contemporaries: The Politics of Patronage.* Lincoln: University of Nebraska Press, 1990.

———. *The Vanishing American: White Attitudes and U.S. Indian Policy.* Middletown, Conn.: Wesleyan University Press, 1982.

Eaton, Herbert. *The Overland Trail to California in 1852.* New York: G. P. Putnam's Sons, 1974.

Elson, Ruth Miller. *Guardians of Tradition: American Schoolbooks of the Nineteenth Century.* Lincoln: University of Nebraska Press, 1964.

Faragher, John Mack. *Women and Men on the Overland Trail.* New Haven, Conn.: Yale University Press, 1979.

Fenin, George N., and William K. Everson. *The Western: From Silents to the Seventies.* New York: Penguin Books, 1973.

Frank, Joseph Allan, and George A. Reaves. *"Seeing the Elephant": Raw Recruits at the Battle of Shiloh.* New York: Greenwood, 1989.

Frazer, Robert W. *Forts of the West: Military Forts and Presidios and Posts Commonly Called Forts West of the Mississippi River to 1898.* Norman: University of Oklahoma Press, 1965.

Gibbon, Guy. *The Sioux: The Dakota and Lakota Nations.* Malden, Mass.: Blackwell, 2003.

Gibson, Arrell M. *The American Indian: Prehistory to the Present.* Lexington, Mass.: D. C. Heath, 1980.

Gilman, Musetta. *Pump on the Prairie: A Chronicle of a Road Ranch, 1859–1868.* Detroit: Harlo Press, 1975.

Gowans, Fred R. *Discovery and Exploration of the Great Fur Trade Road, 1739–1843.* Salt Lake City: Utah Crossroads Oregon-California Trails Association, 1994.

Gowans, Fred R., and Eugene E. Campbell. *Fort Bridger, Island in the Wilderness.* Provo, Utah: Brigham Young University Press, 1975.

Grinnell, George Bird. *The Cheyenne Indians.* 2 vols. Lincoln: University of Nebraska Press, 1972.

———. *The Fighting Cheyennes.* Norman: University of Oklahoma Press, 1956.

Hafen, LeRoy R. *Broken Hand: The Life of Thomas Fitzpatrick: Mountain Man, Guide and Indian Agent.* Denver: Old West, 1931.

Hafen, LeRoy R., and Ann W. Hafen. *Handcarts to Zion: The Story of a Unique Western Migration, 1856–1860.* Glendale, Calif.: Arthur H. Clark, 1960.

Hafen, LeRoy R., and Francis M. Young. *Fort Laramie and the Pageant of the West, 1834–1890.* Glendale, Calif.: Arthur H. Clark, 1938.

Haines, Aubrey L. *Historic Sites Along the Oregon Trail.* St. Louis: Patrice Press, 1981.

Harris, Ramon I., ed. *Oyate Iyechinka Woglakapi.* 4 vols. American Indian Research Project. Vermillion: University of South Dakota, 1970–72.

Harrod, Howard L. *The Animals Came Dancing: Native American Sacred Ecology and Animal Kinship.* Tucson: University of Arizona Press, 2000.

Hart, Herbert M. *Old Forts of the Northwest.* New York: Bonanza Books, 1963.

Hassrick, Royal B. *The Sioux: Life and Customs of a Warrior Society.* Norman: University of Oklahoma Press, 1964.

Hawke, David Freeman. *Those Tremendous Mountains: The Story of the Lewis and Clark Expedition.* New York: W. W. Norton, 1980.

Hebard, Grace Raymond. *Washakie.* Cleveland: Arthur H. Clark, 1930.

Heckman, Marlin L. *Overland on the California Trail, 1846–1859: A Bibliography of Manuscript and Printed Travel Narratives.* Glendale, Calif.: Arthur H. Clark, 1984.

Herring, Joseph B. *The Enduring Indians of Kansas: A Century and a Half of Acculturation.* Lawrence: University Press of Kansas, 1990.

Hoig, Stan. *The Peace Chiefs of the Cheyennes.* Norman: University of Oklahoma Press, 1980.

———. *The Sand Creek Massacre.* Norman: University of Oklahoma Press, 1961.

Holliday, J. S. *The World Rushed In: The California Gold Rush Experience.* New York: Simon and Schuster, 1981.

Houghton, Eliza P. Donner. *The Expedition of the Donner Party and Its Tragic Fate.* Chicago: A. C. McClurg, 1911.

Hurtado, Albert L. *Indian Survival on the California Frontier.* New Haven, Conn.: Yale University Press, 1988.

Hyde, George E. *The Pawnee Indians.* Norman: University of Oklahoma Press, 1974.

———. *Spotted Tail's Folk: A History of the Brulé Sioux.* Norman: University of Oklahoma Press, 1974.

Isenberg, Andrew C. *The Destruction of the Bison: An Environmental History, 1750–1920.* Cambridge: Cambridge University Press, 2000.

Jablow, Joseph. *The Cheyenne in Plains Indian Trade Relations, 1795–1840.* Monographs of the American Ethnological Society, vol. 19. New York: J. J. Augustin, 1951.

Jeffrey, Julie Roy. *Frontier Women: The Trans-Mississippi West, 1840–1880.* New York: Hill and Wang, 1979.

Jennings, Francis. *The Founders of America: From the Earliest Migrations to the Present.* New York: W. W. Norton, 1993.

Johnson, Dorothy M. *The Bloody Bozeman: The Perilous Trail to Montana's Gold.* New York: McGraw-Hill, 1971.

Jones, Daryl. *The Dime Novel Western.* Bowling Green, Ohio: Bowling Green State University, Popular Press, 1978.

Kelly, Charles, and Dale L. Morgan. *Old Greenwood: The Story of Caleb Greenwood: Trapper, Pathfinder and Early Pioneer.* Georgetown, Calif.: Talisman Press, 1965.

Kimball, Stanley B. *Heber C. Kimball: Mormon Patriarch and Pioneer.* Urbana: University of Illinois Press, 1981.

————. *Historic Sites and Markers along the Mormon and Other Great Western Trails.* Urbana: University of Illinois Press, 1988.

Klein, Laura F., and Lillian A. Ackerman, eds. *Women and Power in Native North America.* Norman: University of Oklahoma Press, 1995.

Krech, Shepard, III. *The Ecological Indian: Myth and History.* New York: W. W. Norton, 1999.

Larson, Robert W. *Red Cloud: Warrior-Stateman of the Lakota Sioux.* Norman: University of Oklahoma Press, 1997.

Lass, William E. *From the Missouri to the Great Salt Lake: An Account of Overland Freighting.* Lincoln: Nebraska State Historical Society, 1972.

Lavender, David. *Westward Vision: The Story of the Oregon Trail.* New York: McGraw-Hill, 1963.

Levernier, James, and Hennig Cohen, eds. *The Indians and Their Captives.* Westport, Conn.: Greenwood, 1977.

Levy, Jo Ann. *They Saw the Elephant: Women in the California Gold Rush.* Norman: University of Oklahoma Press, 1992.

Lewis, G. Malcolm, ed. *Cartographic Encounters: Perspectives on Native American Mapmaking and Map Use.* Chicago: University of Chicago Press, 1998.

Linderman, Frank B. *Pretty Shield, Medicine Woman of the Crows.* Lincoln: University of Nebraska Press, 1972.

Lowie, Robert H. *The Crow Indians.* New York: Holt, Rinehart and Winston, 1935.

Madsen, Brigham D. *The Bannock of Idaho.* Caldwell, Idaho: Caxton, 1958.

————. *Chief Pocatello: The "White Plume."* Salt Lake City: University of Utah Press, 1986.

————. *The Lemhi: Sacajawea's People.* Caldwell, Idaho: Caxton, 1979.

————. *The Northern Shoshoni.* Caldwell, Idaho: Caxton, 2000.

————. *The Shoshoni Frontier and the Bear River Massacre.* Salt Lake City: University of Utah Press, 1985.

Madsen, Susan Arrington. *I Walked to Zion: True Stories of Young Pioneers on the Mormon Trail.* Salt Lake City: Deseret Book, 1994.

Marks, Paula Mitchell. *Precious Dust: The Saga of the Western Gold Rushes*. Lincoln: University of Nebraska Press, 1998.

Marshall, Joseph, III. *On Behalf of the Wolf and the First Peoples*. Santa Fe, N.M.: Red Crane Books, 1995.

Martin, Calvin. *Keepers of the Game: Animal-Indian Relationships and the Fur Trade*. Berkeley: University of California Press, 1978.

Mattes, Merrill J. *The Great Platte River Road*. Publications of the Nebraska State Historical Society, vol. 25. Lincoln: Nebraska State Historical Society, 1969.

————. *Platte River Road Narratives: A Descriptive Bibliography of Travel over the Great Central Overland Route to Oregon, California, Utah, Colorado, Montana, and Other Western States and Territories, 1812–1866*. Urbana: University of Illinois Press, 1988.

Mayhall, Mildred P. *The Kiowas*. Norman: University of Oklahoma Press, 1971.

McGinnis, Anthony. *Counting Coup and Cutting Horses: Intertribal Warfare on the Northern Plains, 1738–1889*. Evergreen, Colo.: Cordillera, 1990.

McHugh, Tom. *The Time of the Buffalo*. New York: Alfred A. Knopf, 1972.

Mintz, Lannon W. *The Trail: A Bibliography of the Travelers on the Overland Trail to California, Oregon, Salt Lake City, and Montana during the Years 1841–1864*. Albuquerque: University of New Mexico Press, 1987.

Moore, John H. *The Cheyenne Nation: A Social and Demographic History*. Lincoln: University of Nebraska Press, 1987.

Moynihan, Ruth Barnes. *Rebel for Rights: Abigail Scott Duniway*. New Haven, Conn.: Yale University Press, 1983.

Murray, Keith A. *The Modocs and Their War*. Norman: University of Oklahoma Press, 1959.

Myres, Sandra L. *Westering Women and the Frontier Experience, 1800–1915*. Albuquerque: University of New Mexico Press, 1982.

Namias, June. *White Captives: Gender and Ethnicity on the American Frontier*. Chapel Hill: University of North Carolina Press, 1993.

Olson, James C. *Red Cloud and the Sioux Problem*. Lincoln: University of Nebraska Press, 1965.

Oswalt, Wendell H. *This Land Was Theirs: A Study of North American Indians*, 3rd ed. New York: John Wiley and Sons, 1978.

Paden, Irene D. *The Wake of the Prairie Schooner*. Gerald, Mo.: Patrice Press, 1985.

Page, Elizabeth. *Wagons West: A Story of the Oregon Trail*. New York: Farrar and Rinehart, 1930.

Palmer, Rosemary G. *Children's Voices from the Trail: Narratives of the Platte River Road*. Spokane, Wash.: Arthur H. Clark, 2002.

Pearce, Roy Harvey. *Savagism and Civilization: A Study of the Indian and the American Mind*. Baltimore: Johns Hopkins University Press, 1953.

Peterson, John Alton. *Utah's Black Hawk War*. Salt Lake City: University of Utah Press, 1998.

Phillips, George Harwood. *Chiefs and Challengers: Indian Resistance and Cooperation in Southern California*. Berkeley: University of California Press, 1975.

Price, Catherine. *The Oglala People, 1841–1879: A Political History*. Lincoln: University of Nebraska Press, 1996.

Propst, Nell Brown. *The South Platte Trail: Story of Colorado's Forgotten People*. Boulder, Colo.: Pruett, 1989.

Prucha, Francis Paul. *American Indian Policy in the Formative Years: The Indian Trade and Intercourse Acts, 1790–1834*. Lincoln: University of Nebraska Press, 1970.

Rawls, James J. *Indians of California: The Changing Image*. Norman: University of Oklahoma Press, 1984.

Reid, John Phillip. *Patterns of Vengeance: Crosscultural Homicide in the North American Fur Trade*. Pasadena, Calif.: Ninth Judicial Circuit Historical Society, 1999.

Reynolds, Henrietta. *Pioneers of the Sand Plains*. N.p.: n.p., 1953.

Riley, Glenda. *Women and Indians on the Frontier, 1825–1915*. Albuquerque: University of New Mexico Press, 1984.

Rister, Carl Coke. *Comanche Bondage*. Lincoln: University of Nebraska Press, 1989.

Ruby, Robert H., and John A. Brown. *The Cayuse Indians: Imperial Tribesmen of Old Oregon*. Norman: University of Oklahoma Press, 1972.

———. *The Chinook Indians: Traders of the Lower Columbia River*. Norman: University of Oklahoma Press, 1976.

———. *Indians of the Pacific Northwest: A History*. Norman: University of Oklahoma Press, 1981.

Rumer, Thomas A. *The Wagon Trains of '44: A Comparative View of the Individual Caravans in the Emigration of 1844 to Oregon*. Spokane, Wash.: Arthur H. Clark, 1990.

Saum, Lewis O. *The Fur Trader and the Indian*. Seattle: University of Washington Press, 1965.

Schlissel, Lillian. *Women's Diaries of the Westward Journey*. New York: Schocken, 1982.

Schlissel, Lillian, Byrd Gibbens, and Elizabeth Hampsten. *Far From Home: Families of the Westward Journey*. New York: Schocken, 1989.

Schwartz, E. A. *The Rogue River Indian War and Its Aftermath, 1850–1980*. Norman: University of Oklahoma Press, 1997.

Secoy, Frank Raymond. *Changing Military Patterns of the Great Plains Indians (17th Century through Early 19th Century)*. Monographs of the American Ethnological Society, vol. 21. Seattle: University of Washington Press, 1953.

Shannon, Donald H. *The Utter Disaster on the Oregon Trail: The Utter and Van Ornum Massacres of 1860*. Caldwell, Idaho: Snake Country, 1993.

Slaughter, William W., and Michael Landon. *Trail of Hope: The Story of the Mormon Trail*. Salt Lake City: Shadow Mountain, 1997.

Slotkin, Richard. *Regeneration through Violence: The Mythology of the American Frontier, 1600–1860*. Middletown, Conn.: Wesleyan University Press, 1973.

Smith, Henry Nash. *Virgin Land: The American West as Symbol and Myth*. New York: Vintage, 1950.

Spring, Agnes Wright. *Caspar Collins: The Life Exploits of an Indian Fighter of the Sixties*. New York: Columbia University Press, 1927.

Stamm, Henry E., IV. *People of the Wind River: The Eastern Shoshones, 1825–1890*. Norman: University of Oklahoma Press, 1999.

Stedman, Raymond William. *Shadows of the Indians: Stereotypes in American Culture*. Norman: University of Oklahoma Press, 1982.

Stegner, Wallace. *The Gathering of Zion: The Story of the Mormon Trail*. New York: McGraw-Hill, 1964.

Stewart, George R. *The California Trail: An Epic with Many Heroes*. New York: McGraw-Hill, 1962.

———. *Ordeal By Hunger: The Story of the Donner Party*. New York: Ace Books, 1960.

Thornton, Russell. *American Indian Holocaust and Survival: A Population History Since 1492*. Norman: University of Oklahoma Press, 1987.

Trenholm, Virginia Cole, and Maurine Carley. *The Shoshonis: Sentinels of the Rockies*. Norman: University of Oklahoma Press, 1964.

Tuska, Jon. *The American West in Film: Critical Approaches to the Western*. Westport, Conn.: Greenwood, 1985.

Unrau, William E. *White Man's Wicked Water: The Alcohol Trade and Prohibition in Indian Country, 1802–1892*. Lawrence: University Press of Kansas, 1996.

Unruh, John D., Jr. *The Plains Across: The Overland Emigrants and the Trans-Mississippi West, 1840–60*. Urbana: University of Illinois Press, 1979.

Utley, Robert M. *Frontiersmen in Blue: The United States Army and the Indian 1848–1865*. New York: McMillan, 1967.

———. *The Indian Frontier of the American West 1846–1890*. Albuquerque: University of New Mexico Press, 1984.

———. *The Lance and the Shield: The Life and Times of Sitting Bull*. New York: Henry Holt, 1993.

Van Kirk, Sylvia. *Many Tender Ties: Women in Fur-Trade Society, 1670–1870*. Norman: University of Oklahoma Press, 1980.

Warhus, Mark. *Another America: Native American Maps and the History of Our Land*. New York: St. Martin's, 1997.

Washburn, Wilcomb E. *The Indian in America*. New York: Harper Colophon, 1975.

West, Elliott. *The Contested Plains: Indians, Goldseekers, and the Rush to Colorado*. Lawrence: University Press of Kansas, 1998.

———. *The Way to the West: Essays on the Central Plains*. Albuquerque: University of New Mexico Press, 1995.

White, Richard. *The Middle Ground: Indians, Empires, and Republics in the Great Lakes Region, 1650–1815.* Cambridge: Cambridge University Press, 1991.

Wilson, D. Ray. *Fort Kearny on the Platte.* Dundee, Ill.: Crossroads Communications, 1980.

Wishart, David J. *The Fur Trade and the American West, 1807–1840: A Geographical Synthesis.* Lincoln: University of Nebraska Press, 1979.

———. *An Unspeakable Sadness: The Dispossession of the Nebraska Indians.* Lincoln: University of Nebraska Press, 1994.

Wright, Muriel H. *A Guide to the Indian Tribes of Oklahoma.* Norman: University of Oklahoma Press, 1951.

Zanjani, Sally. *Sarah Winnemucca.* Lincoln: University of Nebraska Press, 2001.

Articles

Abler, Thomas S. "Scalping, Torture, Cannibalism and Rape: An Ethnohistorical Analysis of Conflicting Cultural Values in War." *Anthropologica* 34, no. 1 (1992): 3–20.

Albers, Patricia, and Jeanne Kay. "Sharing the Land: A Study in American Indian Territoriality." In *A Cultural Geography of North American Indians*, ed. Thomas E. Ross and Tyrel G. Moore, 47–91. Boulder, Colo.: Westview, 1987.

Anderson, Harry H. "The Controversial Sioux Amendment to the Fort Laramie Treaty of 1851." *Nebraska History* 37 (September 1956): 201–220.

Andrews, Thomas F. "The Controversial Hastings Overland Guide: A Reassessment." *Pacific Historical Review* 37 (February 1968): 21–34.

———. "'Ho! For Oregon and California!' An Annotated Bibliography of Published Advice to the Emigrant, 1841–47." *Princeton University Library Chronicle* 33 (Autumn 1971): 41–64.

———. "Satire and the Overland Guide: John B. Hall's Fanciful Advice to Gold Rush Emigrants." *California Historical Society Quarterly* 48 (June 1969): 99–111.

Ashliman, D. L. "The American Indian in German Travel Narratives and Literature." *Journal of Popular Culture* 10 (Spring 1977): 833–839.

Axtell, James. "Through a Glass Darkly: Colonial Attitudes Toward the Native Americans." *American Indian Culture and Research Journal* 1, no. 1 (1974): 17–28.

———. "The White Indians of Colonial America." In *The European and the Indian: Essays in the Ethnohistory of Colonial North America*, 168–206. New York: Oxford University Press, 1981.

Bagley, Will. "Lansford Warren Hastings: Scoundrel or Visionary?" *Overland Journal* 12 (Spring 1994): 12–26.

Barba, Preston A. "The American Indian in German Fiction." *German American Annals* 15 (May–August 1913): 143–74.

Baresel, Karl, and Dorothy Baresel. "Trails and Fords Above the Junction of the North and South Platte." *Overland Journal* 6, no. 2 (1988): 13–24.

Barlow, Mary S. "History of the Barlow Road." *Oregon Historical Quarterly* 3 (March 1902): 71–81.

Barrett, Stephen W., and Stephen F. Arno. "Indian Fires in the Northern Rockies: Ethnohistory and Ecology." In *Indians, Fire and the Land in the Pacific Northwest*, ed. Robert Boyd, 50–64. Corvallis: Oregon State University Press, 1999.

Benbrook, Jimmie G. "Pappan's Ferry and the Oregon-California Trail." *Overland Journal* 19 (Spring 2001): 2–21.

Berkhofer, Robert F., Jr. "Native Americans and United States History." In *The Reinterpretation of American History and Culture*, ed. William Cartwright and Richard L. Watson, Jr., 47–49. Washington, D.C.: National Council for the Social Studies, 1973.

————. "The Political Context of a New Indian History." *Pacific Historical Review* 40 (August 1971): 357–82.

Berkman, Brenda. "The Vanishing Race: Conflicting Images of the American Indian in Children's Literature, 1880–1930." *North Dakota Quarterly* 44 (Spring 1976): 31–40.

Berthrong, Donald J. "Changing Concepts: The Indians Learn About the 'Long Knives' and Settlers (1849–1890s)." In *Red Men and Hat Wearers: Viewpoints in Indian History*, ed. Daniel Tyler, 47–61. Boulder, Colo.: Pruett, 1976.

Boag, Peter. "Idaho's Fort Hall as a Western Crossroads." *Overland Journal* 16 (Spring 1998): 20–26.

————. "'The Indians of This Place Are Snakes in the Grass': The Overlander Perspective on Native Americans in Southern Idaho, 1836–1860." *Idaho Yesterdays* 37 (Fall 1993): 16–26.

Bray, Kingley M. "Teton Sioux Population History, 1655–1881." *Nebraska History* 75 (Summer 1994): 165–88.

Brown, Randy. "Attack on the Hudspeth Cutoff." *Overland Journal* 12 (Summer 1994): 17–31.

————. "Attack on the Kelly-Larimer Wagon Train." *Overland Journal* 5 (Winter 1987): 16–38.

Calloway, Colin G. "An Uncertain Destiny: Indian Captives on the Upper Connecticut River." *Journal of American Studies* 17 (1983): 189–210.

Clark, Christopher G. "The Myth of Indian Aggression in Early Nebraska." *Platte Valley Review* 14 (Spring 1986): 26–34.

Clow, Richmond L. "Mad Bear: William S. Harney and the Sioux Expedition of 1855–1856." *Nebraska History* 61 (Summer 1980): 133–51.

DeMallie, Raymond. "Touching the Pen: Plains Indian-Treaty Councils in Ethnohistorical Perspective." In *Ethnicity on the Great Plains*, ed. Frederick C. Luebke, 38–53. Lincoln: University of Nebraska Press, 1980.

Doyle, Susan Badger. "Indian Perspectives of the Bozeman Trail." *Montana, Magazine of Western History* 40 (Winter 1990): 56–67.

Ellis, Mark R. "Reservation *Akicitas*: The Pine Ridge Police, 1879–1885." *South Dakota History* 29 (Fall 1999): 185–210.

Everett, William. "Critical Notices: Dime Books." *North American Review* 24 (July 1864): 303–309.

Ewers, John C. "Intertribal Warfare as the Precursor of Indian-White Warfare on the Northern Great Plains." *Western Historical Quarterly* 6 (October 1975): 397–410.

———. "The Making and Uses of Maps by Plains Indians." In *Plains Indian History and Culture: Essays on Continuity and Change*, ed. John C. Ewers, 180–90. Norman: University of Oklahoma Press, 1997.

Flores, Dan L. "Bison Ecology and Bison Diplomacy: The Southern Plains from 1800 to 1850." *Journal of American History* 78 (September 1991): 465–85.

Gehling, Richard, and Mary Ann Gehling. "Platte River Itinerary, 1860." *Overland Journal* 5 (Summer 1987): 14–24.

Grobsmith, Elizabeth S. "The Lakota Giveaway: A System of Social Reciprocity." *Plains Anthropologist* 24 (May 1979): 123–31.

Guenther, Todd. "Pioneers Extraordinaire: A Most Unusual Wagon Train." *Overland Journal* 18 (Winter 2000): 2–17.

Hagerty, Leroy W. "Indian Raids Along the Platte and Little Blue Rivers, 1864–1865." *Nebraska History* 28 (July–September 1947): 176–86; 28 (October–December 1947): 239–60.

Haines, Francis. "Goldilocks on the Oregon Trail." *Idaho Yesterdays* 9 (Winter 1965): 26–30.

Hämäläinen, Pekka. "The First Phase of Destruction: Killing the Southern Plains Buffalo, 1790–1840." *Great Plains Quarterly* 21 (Spring 2001): 101–130.

Hart, Newell. "Rescue of a Frontier Boy." *Utah Historical Quarterly* 33 (1965): 51–54.

Holt, Marilyn Irvin. "Joined Forces: Robert Campbell and John Dougherty as Military Entrepreneurs." *Western Historical Quarterly* 30 (Summer 1999): 183–202.

Hunt, Thomas H. "Anatomy of a Massacre: Bloody Point, 1852." *Overland Journal* 7, no. 3 (1989): 2–25.

King, Guy Q. "Crossing the Forty-Mile Desert." *Overland Journal* 21 (Winter 2003): 122–37.

Kroll, Helen B. "The Books That Enlightened the Emigrants." *Oregon Historical Quarterly* 45 (June 1944): 103–123.

Lansing, Michael. "Plains Indian Women and Interracial Marriage in the Upper Missouri Trade, 1804–1868." *Western Historical Quarterly* 31 (Winter 2000): 413–33.

Lewis, G. Malcolm. "Indian Maps: Their Place in the History of Plains Cartography." *Great Plains Quarterly* 4 (Spring 1984): 91–108.

Loscheider, Mavis A. "Use of Fire in Interethnic and Intraethnic Relations on the Northern Plains." *Western Canadian Journal of Anthropology* 7 no. 4 (1977): 82–96.

Madsen, Brigham D. "The 'Almo Massacre' Revisited." *Idaho Yesterdays* 37 (Fall 1993): 54–64.

———. "Shoshoni-Bannock Marauders on the Oregon Trail, 1859–1863." *Utah Historical Quarterly* 35 (Winter 1967): 3–30.

Martin, Charles, and Dorothy Devereux Dustin, "The Omaha-Council Bluffs Area and the Westward Trails." *Overland Journal* 7, no. 4 (1989): 2–11.

Mattes, Merrill J. "The Jumping-Off Places on the Overland Trail." In *The Frontier Re-examined*, ed. John Francis McDermott, 27–39. Urbana: University of Illinois Press, 1967.

———. "Robidoux's Trading Post at 'Scott's Bluffs,' and the California Gold Rush." *Nebraska History* 30 (June 1949): 95–138.

McDermott, John D. "Military Command at Fort Laramie." *Annals of Wyoming* 38 (April 1966): 4–48.

McGinnis, Anthony. "Intertribal Conflict on the Northern Plains and Its Suppression, 1738–1889." *Journal of the West* 18 (April 1979): 49–61.

Metcalf, P. Richard. "Who Should Rule at Home? Native American Politics and Indian-White Relations." *Journal of American History* 61 (December 1974): 651–65.

Munkres, Robert L. "The Arrival of Emigrants and Soldiers: Curiosity, Contempt, Confusion and Conflict." In *Red Men and Hat Wearers: Viewpoints in Indian History*, ed. Daniel Tyler, 63–91. Boulder, Colo.: Pruett, 1976.

———. "Indian-White Contact Before 1870: Cultural Factors in Conflict." *Journal of the West* 10 (July 1971): 439–73.

———. "The Plains Indian Threat on the Oregon Trail Before 1860." *Annals of Wyoming* 40 (October 1968): 193–221.

Ostler, Jeffrey. "'The Last Buffalo Hunt' and Beyond: Plains Sioux Economic Strategies in the Early Reservation Period." *Great Plains Quarterly* 21 (Spring 2001): 115–30.

———. "'They Regard Their Passing as Wakan': Interpreting Western Sioux Explanations for the Bison's Decline." *Western Historical Quarterly* 30 (Winter 1999): 475–97.

Palmer, Rosemary G. "Goldilocks Revisited." *Annals of Wyoming* 70 (Spring 1998): 31–40.

Parks, Douglas R., and Waldo R. Wedel. "Pawnee Geography: Historical and Sacred." *Great Plains Quarterly* 5 (Summer 1985): 143–76.

Pattison, John J. "With the U.S. Army along the Oregon Trail, 1863–1866." *Nebraska History* 15 (April–June 1934): 79–93.

Powers, Ramon, and James N. Leiker. "Cholera among the Plains Indians: Perceptions, Causes, Consequences." *Western Historical Quarterly* 29 (Autumn 1998): 317–40.

Powers, Ramon, and Gene Younger. "Cholera on the Overland Trails, 1832–1869." *Kansas Quarterly* 5 (Spring 1973): 32–49.

Read, Georgia Willis. "Diseases, Drugs, and Doctors on the Oregon-California Trail in the Gold-Rush Years." *Missouri Historical Review* 38 (July 1944): 260–76.

———. "Women and Children on the Oregon-California Trail in the Gold-Rush Years." *Missouri Historical Review* 39 (October 1944): 1–23.

Reid, John Phillip. "Restraints of Vengeance: Retaliation-in-Kind and the Use of Indian Law in the Old Oregon Country." *Oregon Historical Quarterly* 95 (1994): 49–92.

Rieck, Richard L. "A Geography of Death on the Oregon-California Trail, 1840–1860." *Overland Journal* 9, no. 1 (1991): 13–21.

Riley, Glenda. "The Specter of a Savage: Rumors and Alarmism on the Overland Trail." *Western Historical Quarterly* 15 (October 1984): 427–44.

Ronda, James P. "'A Chart in His Way': Indian Cartography and the Lewis and Clark Expedition." *Great Plains Quarterly* 4 (Winter 1984): 43–53.

Rose, James J. "Saga of the Stephens-Townsend-Murphy Party of 1844: First Pioneer Wagons Over the Sierra Nevada." *Nevada County Historical Society Bulletin* 48 (July 1994): 17–26.

Schilz, Thomas F. "Robes, Rum and Rifles: Indian Middlemen in the Northern Plains Fur Trade." *Montana, Magazine of Western History* 40 (Winter 1990): 3–13.

Schindler, Harold. "The Bear River Massacre: New Historical Evidence." *Utah Historical Quarterly* 64 (Fall 1999): 300–308.

Snow, Dean R. "'Keepers of the Game' and the Nature of Explanation." In *Indians, Animals, and the Fur Trade: A Critique of "Keepers of the Game"*, ed. Shephard Krech III, 61–71. Athens: University of Georgia Press, 1981.

Stern, Peter. "The White Indians of the Borderlands." *Journal of the Southwest* 33 (Fall 1991): 262–81.

Sturtevant, William C. "Animals and Disease in Indian Belief." In *Indians, Animals, and the Fur Trade: A Critique of "Keepers of the Game"*, ed. Shephard Krech III, 179–88. Athens: University of Georgia Press, 1981.

Tate, Michael L. "Comanche Captives: People between Two Worlds." *Chronicles of Oklahoma* 72 (Fall 1994): 228–63.

———. "From Cooperation to Conflict: Sioux Relations with the Overland Emigrants, 1845–1865." *Overland Journal* 18 (Winter 2000–2001): 18–31.

Treckel, Paula A. "Letters to the Editor." *William and Mary Quarterly* 33 (January 1976): 143–44.

Trennert, Robert A., Jr. "The Mormons and the Office of Indian Affairs: The Conflict Over Winter Quarters, 1846–1848." *Nebraska History* 53 (Fall 1972): 381–400.

Vecsey, Christopher. "American Indian Environmental Religions." In *American Indian Environments: Ecological Issues in Native American History*, ed.

Christopher Vecsey and Robert W. Venables, 1–37. Syracuse N.Y.: Syracuse University Press, 1980.

Watkins, Albert. "History of Fort Kearny." *Collections of the Nebraska State Historical Society* 16 (1911):227–67.

Weitenkampf, Frank. "How Indians Were Pictured in Earlier Days." *New York Historical Society Quarterly* 33 (October 1949): 213–22.

Werner, Morris W. "Wheelbarrow Emigrant of 1850." http://www.ku.edu/heritage/werner/wheemigr.html.

White, Richard. "The Winning of the West: The Expansion of the Western Sioux in the Eighteenth and Nineteenth Centuries." *Journal of American History* 65 (September 1978): 319–43.

Williams, Carol. "'My First Indian': Interaction Between Women and Indians on the Trail, 1845–1865." *Overland Journal* 4 (Summer 1986): 13–18.

Winter, Joseph C. "Traditional Uses of Tobacco by Native Americans." In *Tobacco Use by Native North Americans: Sacred Smoke and Silent Killer*, ed. Joseph C. Winter, 9–58. Norman: University of Oklahoma Press, 2000.

Index